AF784873

Reforming EU Public Procurement

EUROPEAN PROCUREMENT LAW

Series Editors: Kirsi-Maria Magga, *University of Lapland, Finland* and François Lichère, *University of Jean Moulin Lyon 3, France*

Public procurement is a highly significant and growing area of legal practice. Each book in this series addresses one of the most pressing topics in EU public procurement law and practice, taking a comparative approach and combining cross-cutting thematic chapters with detailed country information. This is both valuable and necessary in understanding how public procurement law is developed and applied – or misapplied – in the EU and in its Member States. In so doing, the series hopes to inspire new approaches and offer guidance in applying the principles and basic (though at times very detailed) rules. The clear descriptions of the practices, regulations, case law and interpretations of public procurement law throughout the EU will assist practitioners both in better understanding the rules as applied in their own jurisdiction and in developing best practices. The books are written by academics and experts from a broad range of Member States who have worked closely together since 2010 in a cross-border research group specialized in public procurement law.

For a full list of Edward Elgar published titles, including the titles in this series, visit our website at www.e-elgar.com.

Reforming EU Public Procurement

Proposals for the Reform of Directive 2014/24/EU

Edited by

Willem Janssen

Utrecht University and University of Groningen, the Netherlands

François Lichère

Université Jean Moulin Lyon 3, France

Kirsi-Maria Magga

Faculty of Law, University of Lapland, Finland

EUROPEAN PROCUREMENT LAW

Edward Elgar PUBLISHING

Cheltenham, UK • Northampton, MA, USA

© The Editors and Contributors severally 2026

Every effort has been made to trace all the copyright holders but if any have been inadvertently overlooked please notify the publisher.

All rights reserved. No part of this publication may be reproduced, stored in a retrieval system or transmitted in any form or by any means, electronic, mechanical or photocopying, recording, or otherwise without the prior permission of the publisher. Without limiting the author's and publisher's exclusive rights, any unauthorised use of this publication to train generative artificial intelligence (AI) technologies is expressly prohibited.

Published by

Edward Elgar Publishing Limited
The Lypiatts
15 Lansdown Road
Cheltenham
Glos GL50 2JA
UK

Edward Elgar Publishing, Inc.
William Pratt House
9 Dewey Court
Northampton
Massachusetts 01060
USA

Authorised representative in the EU for GPSR queries only: Easy Access System Europe – Mustamäe tee 50, 10621 Tallinn, Estonia, gpsr.requests@easproject.com

A catalogue record for this book is available from the British Library

Library of Congress Control Number: 2026931789

This book is available electronically in the **Elgar**online
Law subject collection
https://doi.org/10.4337/9781035368273

MIX
Paper | Supporting responsible forestry
FSC® C014540

ISBN 978 1 0353 6826 6 (cased)
ISBN 978 1 0353 6827 3 (eBook)
ISBN 978 1 0353 9704 4 (ePub)

Printed and bound in the UK by Short Run Press Ltd, Exeter EX2 7LW

Contents

List of contributors vii
Foreword x

1 The reform of Directive 2014/24/EU: A call for a full and not a marginal reform 1
Willem Janssen, François Lichère, and Kirsi-Maria Magga

PART I REFLECTING ON THE SCOPE OF THE DIRECTIVE

2 Expanding the scope of EU public procurement law: Realigning the Classic Directive with its internal market logic while improving its fit with strategic procurement? 12
Albert Sanchez-Graells

3 Fine-tuning the definition of "contracting authority" for increased precision and clarity 26
Miguel Assis Raimundo

4 Reforming the rules on public–public cooperation: Towards legal certainty for Article 12 of Directive 2014/24/EU? 39
Willem Janssen

PART II IMPROVING AND FOSTERING COMPETITION

5 Cooperation between economic operators in tendering 54
Kirsi-Maria Magga and Kris Wauters

6 Strengthening exclusion grounds in EU public procurement for greater fairness and transparency 69
Dacian C. Dragos

7 Simplification by introducing smarter submitting and supplementing rules 84
Martin Burgi and Caroline Schulte Oestrich

8 Framework agreements: How to deal with the CJEU forced contractualization 103
Mario E. Comba

9 Digitalisation and competition: Proposals for upcoming public procurement reform 118
Gabriella M. Racca

10 (Choice of) award procedures: Past, present and future 134
Steven Van Garsse

11 Of many sticks and one mutant carrot: The new external dimension of EU public contracts 150
Roberto Caranta

PART III THE INSTRUMENTAL USE OF PUBLIC PROCUREMENT

12 Environment and public procurement: Proposals for aligning EU law with the European Green Deal 170
Penelope Giosa

13 Public procurement as a stronger leverage for social justice 186
Nicolas Gabayet

14 Access for start-ups and small and medium-sized enterprises and subcontracting 203
François Lichère and Cédric Bernard

15 Innovation and public procurement: The need for the law to match the policy demands 217
Pedro Cerqueira Gomes

16 Reforming procurement for crisis: Proposals for simplified, collaborative and equity responses 233
Annamaria La Chimia

PART IV EXPANDING THE RULES ON CONTRACT PERFORMANCE

17 Modification of directives and contract modifications: Article 72 of Directive 2014/24/EU revisited 253
Piotr Bogdanowicz

18 To terminate or not to terminate 266
Ezgi Uysal

Index 281

List of contributors

Miguel Assis Raimundo is a Professor of Public Procurement Law and Administrative Law at the University of Lisbon School of Law, Portugal, and is an Integrated Research Fellow of the Lisbon Public Law Research Centre.

Cédric Bernard is a researcher at University of Lyon 3, France.

Piotr Bogdanowicz is a Professor at the University of Warsaw Faculty of Law and Administration, Poland.

Martin Burgi is a Professor of Public and European Law at the Ludwig-Maximilians-University Munich, Germany, and Director of the Public and European Law Research Center for Public Procurement Law and Administrative Cooperations.

Roberto Caranta is a Professor of Administrative Law at the University of Turin, Italy.

Pedro Cerqueira Gomes is an Assistant Professor at the Universidade Católica Portuguesa, Porto, Portugal, and a practicing lawyer at Cerqueira Gomes and Associados, who also acts as an arbitrator in public procurement law disputes.

Mario E. Comba is a Professor of Public Comparative Law at the University of Turin, Italy.

Dacian C. Dragos is the Jean Monnet Professor of Administrative and European Law with the Public Administration and Management Department and the Law Doctoral School at the Babes-Bolyai University, Cluj-Napoca, Romania.

Nicolas Gabayet is a Full Professor of Public Law at Jean Monnet University, France.

Penelope Giosa is a Lecturer in EU Law at the University of Reading and Part-time Associate Lecturer at Oxford Brookes University, UK. She is also Member of the Advisory Board of the George Washington University Competition and Innovation Lab and Convenor of the Comparative Law Section in the Society of Legal Scholars.

Willem Janssen is the Endowed Professor of Public Procurement Law holding the chair of the Dutch Association for Public Procurement Law at Groningen University, the Netherlands, and an Associate Professor of European and Dutch Public Procurement Law at the Centre for Public Procurement and the Centre for Regulation and Enforcement in Europe at Utrecht University, the Netherlands.

Annamaria La Chimia is a Professor of Law and Development and Director Public Procurement Research Group, School of Law, University of Nottingham, UK, Research Fellow, African Public Procurement Law Unit, Department of Mercantile Law, Stellenbosch University, South Africa.

François Lichère is a Professor of Public Law at the University of Lyon 3, France.

Kirsi-Maria Magga is a Professor at the University of Lapland, Finland, and holds a Title of Docent at the University of Turku, Finland.

Gabriella M. Racca is a Full Professor of Administrative Law at the Department of Management of the University of Turin, Italy.

Albert Sanchez-Graells is a Professor of Economic Law at the University of Bristol, UK.

Caroline Schulte Oestrich graduated from Ludwig-Maximilians-University Munich, Germany, and works as a research assistant at Professor Martin Burgi's chair and his Research Center for Public Procurement Law and Administrative Cooperations.

Ezgi Uysal is a Post-Doctoral Researcher at the University of Copenhagen Faculty of Law, Centre for Private Governance (CEPRI), Denmark. She is currently part of the Research Project Purchase Power—Sustainable Public Procurement through private Law Enforcement supported by the grant CF21-0317 from the Carlsberg Foundation.

Steven Van Garsse is a Full Professor of Public Law at the University of Hasselt, Belgium.

Kris Wauters is a Professor of Administrative Law and co-director of the public law group at the Faculty of Law of the Université Catholique de Louvain, Belgium, and a lawyer at the Brussels Bar.

Foreword

With great pleasure, we present the 14th volume in the European Procurement Law series, and the seventh volume to be published by Edward Elgar Publishing. In the previous volumes, we have covered various issues relating to public procurement (in-house, remedies, transparency, sustainable public procurement, contracts falling outside the Procurement Directive, qualification and award criteria, the implementation of the 2014 Directives in the Member States, Public–Private Partnerships (PPPs), and concessions, centralized procurement, contract modifications, and buying AI). The 13th volume on public procurement of AI examined both regulation and Member State practices, focusing on how the rules and practical arrangements are designed—or capable of being designed—to meet the requirements for the use of AI in public administration within the procurement process.

In this volume, we focus on the various reform needs of EU public procurement Directive 2014/24/EU. The European Commission has launched the review of the procurement directives, and the Commission's proposal is expected later in 2026.

This edited volume discusses potential future reforms to Directive 2014/24/EU. The editors of this book began the work by reaching out to procurement law scholars with the following message in March 2024:

> Currently, there is little interest in Brussels and among Member States to pursue this [reform of the directive], even though a recent European Court of Auditors report has raised questions about the Directive's overall effectiveness. Therefore, this volume stands out as it starts the conversation on reforms before legislative discussions have begun, indicating that such changes are indeed necessary and, when started, the volume will provide a point of reference for such a reform. Each chapter intends to contribute to the debate on improving Directive 2014/24/EU.

Little did we know that our book project would not only aim to spur academic and policy debate, but that developments within the EU would lead to an actual—yet unexpected—reform.

Each of the relatively short chapters focuses on identifying relevant issues related to a specific part or theme of the Directive, proposing concrete reforms and offering future pathways for addressing these issues in the ongoing reform. Collectively, the contributions issue a clear call for a full reform of Directive

2014/24/EU, rather than a limited revision touching only certain elements. The reform proposals address nearly all aspects of the Directive, indicating that a narrow reform—focused, for example, only on introducing a European preference or making minor procedural adjustments—does not seem justified. The contributions in this book present a variety of reform proposals: some aim to improve provisions of the 2014 Directives, while others introduce entirely new themes not yet covered by the current framework.

The methodology in this volume differs from that applied in earlier books. This is not a comparative law study across multiple jurisdictions, but rather a joint effort by public procurement legal scholars across the EU. Nevertheless, the founding idea of close academic collaboration within the European Procurement Law Group (EPLG) has remained unchanged for nearly two decades since the small group of us first met in Turin in 2008 to discuss in-house providing.

We remain committed to our original vision: EU law needs comparative law and cross-border research collaboration. For us, the comparative approach is both valuable and necessary for understanding how public procurement law is developed and applied—or misapplied—in the EU and in its Member States.

In 2024, Professor Roberto Caranta from Turin, Italy passed the co-leadership of the research group EPLG and the co-editorship of this European Procurement Law book series to Professor François Lichère. Professor Kirsi-Maria Magga (former Halonen) is continuing alongside with François as a co-lead of the research group and co-editor of this book series. This is the first book in the series since François stepped in as series editor.

We want to thank Willem Janssen for co-editing this book with us. Also, the meeting to discuss the drafts of this book in Lyon, France, hosted by François Lichère, was amazing. The next book in the series will cover the issue of enforcement and remedies for public procurement.

Finally we want to thank Roisin Sheridan at Deanta for her invaluable help in the production process.

Kirsi-Maria Magga
Professor, University of Lapland

François Lichère
Professor, University of Jean Moulin Lyon 3

1. The reform of Directive 2014/24/EU

A call for a full and not a marginal reform

Willem Janssen, François Lichère, and Kirsi-Maria Magga

1. INTRODUCTION

EU public procurement law plays an imperative role in regulating the purchasing power of over 250,000 public authorities in the European Union, which totals more than 14–19% of the EU GDP.[1] Effective rules, including Directive 2014/24/EU as its main body of law on public procurement, ensure that the objective of the achievement of an internal market and other societal goals of the Union are met, including those related to climate change and social injustice.

This edited volume discusses and informs potential future reforms of Directive 2014/24/EU. What is clear is that the 2014 reforms brought improvements to public procurement law in the European Union; however, there is a clear need to better the functioning of this Directive, as also shown by the recent evaluation discussed in the following. When we invited scholarship from the European Procurement Law Group and beyond to contribute to this volume, we wrote the following in March 2024 about a future reform:

> Currently, there is little interest in Brussels and among Member States to pursue this, even though a recent European Court of Auditors report has raised questions about the Directive's overall effectiveness. Therefore, this volume stands out as it starts the conversation on reforms before legislative discussions have begun, indicating that such changes are indeed necessary and when started, the volume will provide a point of reference for such a reform. Each chapter intends to contribute to the debate on improving Directive 2014/24/EU.

[1] European Commission, Directorate General for the Environment and ICLEI – Local Governments for Sustainability, *Buying Green! A Handbook on Green Public Procurement*, 3rd edition (Publications Office, 2016) 4, https://data.europa.eu/doi/10.2779/837689, accessed 13 April 2025.

Little did we know that our book project would not only be aimed at spurring academic and policy debate, but that the motions in the EU would lead to an actual yet unexpected reform. Following the publication of the report of the European Court of Auditors (ECA) in 2023, the policy debate based on the Letta and Draghi reports in 2024 (Section 2) and then the reform proposal by the second Von der Leyen Commission put the reform of the 2014 Directives on Public Procurement on the table (Section 3). These events turned this hypothetical academic endeavor intended to spark debate about a future reform into one that actually would inform the current reform in Brussels (Section 4). The point of this introduction is to provide context about how the reform got under way and with what focus and to argue that a full and not a marginal reform is required.

2. FROM ECA TO DRAGHI AND LETTA

Backtracking on how the evaluation and reform process of Directive 2014/24/EU commenced means we need to start at the report of the ECA in 2023.[2] The ECA concluded that, over the past decade, competition for public contracts has declined, and the 2014 reform of the EU procurement directives has not demonstrated a reversal of this trend. This also links with a discussion about the need to tackle the emerging issue of single bids.[3] Overall, the report concluded that competition remains an underemphasized objective in public procurement. Furthermore, the report considers that available data are not systematically used to identify the underlying causes of reduced competition, and efforts to address existing barriers remain fragmented. More harshly said, the ECA concludes more generally that the key aims of the 2014 reform, such as simplifying and accelerating procurement procedures, have not been achieved and, in some cases, may have inadvertently hindered competition. As such, the report recommends a clearer prioritization of public procurement objectives, the closure of data gaps, enhanced monitoring tools for more effective analysis, deeper root cause investigations, and the development of a comprehensive action plan to address the principal barriers to competition in public procurement. Despite the fact that one could discuss the methodology and scope of the report, the latter's focal points appear to have clearly significantly shaped the discussions on Directive 2014/24/EU.

[2] European Court of Auditors, *Special Report: Public Procurement in the EU Less Competition for Contracts Awarded for Works, Goods, and Services in the 10 Years up to 2021*, 2023.

[3] Vitezslav Titl, 'The One and Only: Single-Bidding in Public Procurement', *CESifo Working Paper No. 11697*, 2025.

Moving forward in time, two reports called for a renewed internal market in the subsequent year. Former Commissioner Enrico Letta's report 'Much more than a market' noted that the internal market was 'born in a smaller world', called for 'a fifth freedom' on research, innovation and education, and noted the need to strengthen the EU towards the rest of the world.[4] Former ECB head Mario Draghi's report 'The Future of European Competitiveness' considers that 'the foundations on which we built are now being shaken' and focuses on innovation, decarbonization, security and reducing dependencies.[5] Both the Letta and Draghi reports refer to the role of public procurement in relation to the future of the EU internal market.[6] The public procurement market has become an indispensable tool for the achievement of the EU's objectives. This was already noted by former commissioner Mario Monti in his report that referred to public procurement in 2010 as a 'lever' to instrumentalize public spending, by not just procuring infrastructure, housing, ICT, or healthcare but to simultaneously achieve green and social objectives.[7]

When we zoom in on the Letta report, a diverse picture emerges of what is deemed important for the future of public procurement law. It is somewhat hard to pinpoint the intended course of action, because the report bounces from abstract to concrete proposals, and back again. Overseeing it all, however, it is clear that a legislative reform would be required to implement them. In addition to the discussed potential of joint procurement for healthcare following the COVID-19 crisis and to leverage such collective purchasing power for critical materials, some of the persistently mentioned points of attention, such as improving access for small and medium-sized enterprises (SMEs) and the position of subcontractors and social enterprises, return again to the discussions.

Many of these proposals seem to follow from the European Court of Auditors report of 2023 discussed before and its conclusions on diminishing competition for public tenders. Increasing access to public procurement would, within this line of thought, increase competition. The most fundamental proposal in this report is related to the re-scoping of the objectives of public procurement legislation:

---

4 Enrico Letta, *Much More Than A Market*, April 2024.

5 Mario Draghi, *The Future of European Competitiveness*, September 2024.

6 The following descriptive analysis contains the analysis initially published on European Law Blog. Willem Janssen, 'From Letta, to Draghi, to Reforming the Public Procurement Directives: Has Sustainability Left the Building?', *European Law Blog*, March 2025. https://doi.org/10.21428/9885764c.2d4c8434.

7 Mario Monti, *A New Strategy for the Single Market*, May 2010.

> One of the first steps towards this objective is to streamline and clarify the focus of public procurement goals. By establishing a smaller, more precise set of objectives that are both clear and measurable, the EU can facilitate the efficient realisation of desired outcomes.

This proposal could result in a serious overhaul of the public procurement directives, which are currently focused on market integration. Letta is, however, not specific about what these new or streamlined objectives must be. The content of the public procurement section of the report and its other proposals do shed light on what might have been intended here. A strong focus on innovation and innovation procurement is visible, even with potential minimum quotas, as a means to contribute to the strategic goals of the EU. What's more, Letta notes the importance of 'enhancing the productivity, resilience, and sustainability of the EU economy, as well as ensuring the security of supply'. The latter should, according to Letta, transform the directives even into a regulation to avoid implementation-related differences between the Member States but does not support this change of legislative instrument substantively. Of interest is, finally, that a more European focus is proposed by emphasizing the need to prioritize European suppliers in the defense sector. This focus 'strengthens European demand for domestically produced equipment, fostering the creation of European players that can compete with global defense giants'. This could be part of a review of the Directive on defense and security procurement. This latter review has gained serious traction given the publication of a reform proposal on 17 June 2025. Other mostly policy-oriented proposals refer to the need to drive demand for the circular transition, the need to foster fair wages and conditions and the need to – and perhaps thus use the current legal possibility – to 'uphold social and environmental standards by rejecting unusually low bids for public contracts'.

Whereas Draghi's report echoes competitiveness and innovation in general, it is far less explicit on the role of public procurement, particularly compared to Letta's report. Nonetheless, the references to public procurement do tell a story. Similar to Letta's report, the defense sector is noted to have an ambition to raise the share of joint procurement but mostly also to increase the spending of this sector within the EU given that 78% is currently spent outside of its borders. A joint approach is also proposed in relation to the EU gas strategy and related procurement contracts. Draghi aims to further strengthen Europe's procurement position by proposing to create a dedicated EU Critical Raw Material Platform, thereby joining Letta in his focus on circularity. Finally, the tech sector gains attention as 'multiple different national rules in public procurement generate high ongoing costs for cloud providers', leading to alleged market concentration. It is in this context that an 'explicit minimum quota for the local production of selected products and components in public procurement' is raised as well, which would, as noted in light of Letta's proposals, require legislative action.

3. FROM POLITICAL GUIDELINES TO FUTURE REFORM PROPOSALS

Published between the Letta and Draghi reports, the European Commission presented a similar picture in the Political Guidelines of the second Von der Leyen Commission.[8] Interestingly, the proposals in these guidelines seem to represent a step back in time, where efficiency is emphasized by noting that '1% efficiency gain in public procurement could save EUR 20 billion a year'.[9] In addition to a focus on a single market for defense and the leverage function of procurement to drive innovation, a procurement preference for European products for certain strategic sectors is tabled, thereby following some of Letta's thoughts already back then. None of this is surprising by the way: the dominant theme in public procurement law debates currently revolves around geopolitical developments, among other things, due to the Russian invasion of Ukraine and the need to curb undesirable influence from foreign nations in the EU. This also sparked the introduction of the Foreign Subsidies Regulation and International Procurement Instrument. A more inward-looking European focus does offer some advantages from a sustainability perspective, as shorter supply chains can contribute to the achievement of sustainability goals. Nevertheless, it seems that geopolitical threats are taking precedence over long-term solutions for the planet and the fight against climate change. This mirrors the situation in regular procurement procedures, where sustainability is often sidelined when budgets dominate or in crisis situations where urgent procurement is needed.

This stance by the European Commission is further echoed in its more recent Competitive Compass that coins the reforms of the public procurement directives as one of its flagship initiatives.[10] The Compass solidifies the focus on joint defense procurement but importantly notes that 'the planned review of

[8] Ursula von der Leyen, *Europe's Choice: Political Guidelines 2024–2029*, July 2024.

[9] Note though that competition as such did not make it into the mission letter from Von der Leyen to the responsible commissioner: 'You will revise the Public Procurement Directives to help ensure security of supply for certain vital technologies, products and services, while simplifying the rules and reducing administrative burden. It should enable preference for European products in public procurement for certain strategic sectors and technologies'. Ursula von der Leyen, *Mission letter to Stéfane Séjourné*, 17 September 2024, Brussels.

[10] EU Commission, *Competitive Compass*, January 2026.

the Public Procurement Directives aims at reinforcing technological security and domestic supply chains, as well as simplifying and modernising rules, in particular for start-ups and innovative companies.' Letta's proposals to focus on the productivity, resilience and sustainability of the EU economy, as well as ensuring the security of supply, are clearly represented here. The European preference mentioned before is also solidified in the Compass, which is noted as well in the context of clean production and circularity as a 'mandate or preference in public procurement'. One noted aspect was that sustainability seemed not to be a prime focus for the reforms, noting it had left the building.[11] With some acrobatic skills, one might be able to include sustainability in the phrase 'simplifying and modernising rules', but that seems rather far-fetched. Whether this assumption is true, the reforms will show in due course.

Following the call for evidence that closed in March 2025, the EU Commission is now on its way to prepare proposals to revamp the Public Procurement Directives, including Directive 2014/24/EU. A milestone in this reform process was the publication of the evaluation of the Public Procurement Directives, published in October 2025. The results are – without exaggeration – rather crushing from many perspectives. To name a few. the aims of legal certainty has not been achieved and frequent issues exist related to clarifying the scope of Directive 2014/24/EU, including the concept of a body governed by public law and public contract. Furthermore, procedures have partially become more flexible and open procedures remain in the majority. In this line, administrative burdens have not dropped much and rules did not become simpler. On top of the amount of competition, cross-border activity of procedures remains a point of attention. Even more problematically, when it comes to strategic procurement there was quite some disparity:

> while public authorities tended to believe that the directives encouraged green (56%) and socially responsible (55%) procurement, as well as innovation (45%), economic operators were more sceptical. Only a third recogised increased efforts in environmental standard, and even fewer saw any impact on innovation.

Also relevant for the future reform is 'the extent to which the 2014 Directives improved transparency, prevented corruption and promoted the professionalisation of public buyers remains uneven and difficult to measure in the absence of reliable and comparable data'.[12] In terms of coherence, a point of attention is also that 'the evaluations showed that while coherence was initially improved,

---

[11] Janssen (n 6).

[12] EU Commission, *Commission Staff Document Executive Summary of the Evaluation of the Public Procurement Directives, Staff Working Document Evaluation of Directive 2014/23/EU on Concessions, Directive 2014/24/EU on*

the introduction of procurement provisions in other EU regulatory acts caused legal concerns'.[13]

There is much more to unpack in the evaluation, but the general picture and relevance remains that, according to the EU Commision:

> the evaluation confirms that the 2014 Directives and the objectives they aimed to achieve remain highly relevant today, and in some cases even more so than in 2014. In particular, the need to simplify and modernise public procurement is even more important today, given Europe's compentitiveness challenges and high overall bureaucratic burden. The procurement of sustainable works, products and services remains urgent given accelerated climate change and wider environmental challenges. In the current geopolitical context, the 2014 objective of fostering an integrated internal market is more important than ever for securing Europe's strategic autonomy and economic security.[14]

Furthermore, it seems that there might even be a chance that the Directives will be transformed into Regulations. This is all the more relevant as that regulatory body would then come into effect much faster ('directly applicable'), which seems to be the preferred route for the last two Commissions. This is still very much up in the air, and will only become known once the proposals are published. At this point in time, the projected publication of these proposals is quarters 2 to 4 in 2026, meaning there is time to engage further in the debate on effective regulatory approaches for public procurement in the European Union.

4. THE NEED FOR A FULL REFORM OF DIRECTIVE 2014/24/EU

In this volume, we bring together scholarship that informs and discusses the future reforms of Directive 2014/24/EU. Needless to say, many of the findings will also contribute to the discussions about the other public procurement directives, 2014/23/EU and 2014/25/EU. The focus of each of the relatively short chapters is to detail the relevant issues with a specific part or theme of the Directive, to propose concrete reform proposals and to provide future pathways to solve those in the current reform. If there is one thing that is apparent from all the chapters, it is that there is a clear call for a full reform of Directive 2014/24/EU instead of one that merely touches some elements. The reform proposals included touch upon nearly all aspects of this Directive, meaning

Public Procurement and Directive2014/25/EU on Utilities, SWD(2025) 332 final, 15 October 2025, p. 3–4.

[13] Ibid., p. 5.

[14] Ibid.

that limited reform, by only focusing on adding a European preference or mildly tweaking procedural requirements, does not seem justified.

The contributions of this book propose a variety of reform proposals – some aim to improve the 2014 Directives' provisions and some propose entirely new topics not yet covered by the Directives. First of all, some contributions propose more systematic changes to the logic and scope of the Directives: the chapter by Sanchez-Graells develops a new definition of a public contract to also cover contracts without a direct pecuniary interest.[15] Assis Raimundo, on the other hand, refers to the Court of Justice of the European Union (CJEU) case law and calls for a new definition of bodies governed by public law in his contribution.[16] Furthermore, in Magga's and Wauters' chapter, the need to streamline the rules of horizontal and non-horizontal cooperation between economic operators and the need to address the interlinkages between procurement and competition law are set forward.[17]

The current Directives set a minimum standard for national laws on public procurement. On many aspects, they give flexibility to national legislators as well as to contracting authorities. This combination of flexibility and discretion has, however, increased ambiguities regarding the applicable rules and limited the efficiency of procurement rules to drive changes in society. Thus, many of the contributions in this book suggest removal of discretion for certain matters: according to Dragos all exclusion grounds should be mandatory and self-cleaning must only be made possible regarding minor infringements,[18] whereas Giosa calls for mandatory sustainability criteria and the use of environmental labels in order to use procurement efficiently for sustainability goals.[19] Similarly, in Lichère's and Bernard's chapter, to ensure that the promotion of SME participation is more efficiently underlined, they propose mandatory division into lots and setting a minimum share for contracts to be reserved for SMEs.[20] In a similar vein, Gabayet includes proposals to strengthen the role of women-owned businesses to increase social justice.[21]

Further, due to the need to increase legal certainty and effectiveness of procurement rules, Uysal proposes an obligation (rather than a right) to terminate public contracts that are based on a direct award or suffer from non-permissible contract amendment. Burgi and Schulte Oestrich also suggest in their

15 Chapter 2 in this book.
16 Chapter 3.
17 Chapter 5.
18 Chapter 6.
19 Chapter 12.
20 Chapter 14.
21 Chapter 13.

chapter that the rules should always allow the supplementation of bids instead of subjecting this to the discretion of contracting authorities.[22]

The nature of procurement procedures has changed over the years. Also, more information on innovation partnerships and e-procurement practices has become available, and it appears that they are not working efficiently. Thus, Van Garsse proposes the removal of the innovation partnership procedure and replacing it with precommercial procurement,[23] and Racca calls for a general EU-level framework of rules for e-procurement.[24] Taking into account the decreasing competition in public contracts, the need to ease the methods of proof within the procurement procedure is of particular interest. Burgi and Schulte Oestrich propose that different certifications and documents should be replaced by self-declaration at the bidding stage.[25]

Since the adoption of the 2014 Directives on public procurement, the economic and geopolitical situation has changed profoundly, setting requirements for entirely new fields of regulation. The migration crisis in 2015, COVID-19 and wars in Ukraine and Gaza have challenged the resilience of the EU and set a different reality for public procurement as well. Thus, La Chimia proposes in her chapter the adoption of a particular crisis procurement framework that would ensure professionalism and accountability in times of crisis.[26] Similarly, the need to set European supplier preferences in strategic fields, in particular for SMEs and start-ups, has been called upon by Cerqueira Gomes.[27] Moreover, in his chapter, Caranta calls for rules that resolve the ambiguity raised by the recent CJEU's Kolin decision on the participation of third-country bidders in EU public contract awards.[28]

The efficiency of public procurement rules is connected to their ability to generate competition and consequently to the transparency of the purchasing. Over the years, transparency concerns relating to certain exceptions have become apparent. The 2014 Directives on public procurement introduced codifications of CJEU case law on in-house procurement and horizontal collaboration, contract amendment rules and detailed rules on framework agreements. However, in all of these, there is a need for wider transparency obligations as is stated in this book. Janssen proposes an obligation to publish a notice on the use of in-house procurement or horizontal collaboration in order to allow the

[22] Chapter 7.
[23] Chapter 10.
[24] Chapter 9.
[25] Chapter 7.
[26] Chapter 16.
[27] Chapter 15.
[28] Chapter 11.

market actors to challenge the contracts if the conditions are met.[29] Similarly, Bogdanowicz calls for an obligation also to publish contract amendment notices for amendments based on review clauses and suggests consequences for non-publication.[30] In Comba's chapter, the need to increase transparency within framework agreements is addressed.[31]

Clearly, the noted examples do not do the contents of each individual chapter justice, but they do underline how much work there is to be done in the current reform of Directive 2014/24/EU. The extent of the previously-referred reform proposals and the variety of justifications relating thereto depict how the public procurement sphere has changed within the past 10 years. Taking this into account, it is our understanding as editors of this book that a profound reform of the procurement Directive needs to take place.

29 Chapter 4.
30 Chapter 17.
31 Chapter 8.

PART I

Reflecting on the scope of the directive

2. Expanding the scope of EU public procurement law

Realigning the Classic Directive with its internal market logic while improving its fit with strategic procurement?

Albert Sanchez-Graells

REFORM PROPOSALS

- New definition of 'procurement' to step back from current focus on 'acquisition' and 'choice' by the contracting authority and to include preparatory activities with potential negative impacts on the internal market.
- New definition of 'public contract' to eliminate the requirement of 'pecuniary interest'.

1. INTRODUCTION

EU public procurement law is rooted in the construction of the internal market. To a large extent, its (perceived) contribution to the functioning of the internal market continues to drive discussions on its fitness for purpose, effectiveness and reform. However, through iterative review across several generations of directives and interpretation by the Court of Justice of the European Union (CJEU), the alignment of EU public procurement law with an internal market logic has been eroded, and its fit with other pillars of EU internal market law, such as state aid[1] or the Services Directive,[2] has become increasingly difficult.

The cornerstone of EU public procurement law – what actually constitutes a 'public contract' – is unclear, despite decades of CJEU case law. This creates

[1] Treaty on the Functioning of the European Union [2012] OJ C 326/47, arts 107 to 109.

[2] Directive (EC) 2006/123 on services in the internal market [2006] OJ L 376/36.

uncertainty on the scope of application of EU public procurement law and undermines the coherence and effectiveness of EU internal market law, leaving regulatory gaps. The current review of Directive 2014/24/EU (the 'Classic Directive') should thus prioritise a realignment with its internal market logic and improve, as much as possible, its interaction with other elements of EU internal market law and policy, including emerging approaches.[3] This will be the main motivation for the discussion of the scope of application of the Classic Directive in this chapter.

An underappreciated element in the design of the system of EU public procurement law concerns its scope. By and large, so far, this has replicated the scope of application of international trade agreements to which the EU has acceded – and, in particular, the World Trade Organisation's Government Procurement Agreement (GPA) – to facilitate regulatory compliance across multiple layers of procurement regulation. This is clearly the case in relation to the threshold values that determine subjection to the EU rules (which are in practice pegged to the GPA's) but also largely the case of other elements determining the substantive coverage of a contractual arrangement between the public sector and its suppliers.[4] From a trade liberalisation perspective, a minimalist interpretation of the scope of application of the regime probably makes sense – as an expansive interpretation would also extend the scope of international commitments.

However, the same does not necessarily hold from an internal market logic, as the need to promote the functioning of the internal market for procurement puts pressure against limitations of the scope of application of the relevant rules. This is clear from the (controversial and varying) case law on requirements applicable to procurement 'of a certain cross-border interest' in relation to awards not covered, or not fully covered, by the Classic Directive.[5] Equally, pegging value thresholds to international commitments creates challenges from the perspective of informing internal market policy-making because

[3] This is not to say those approaches are desirable or that the author agrees with them. However, if the goal is to maximise the effectiveness of the next generation of procurement rules, it seems clear that their scope needs to be aligned with intended policy goals and outcomes.

[4] In that regard, the GPA applies to procurement 'by any contractual means, including: purchase; lease; and rental or hire purchase, with or without an option to buy'; Art II:2(b) GPA.

[5] Carina Risvig Hamer (née Hansen), *Contracts Not Covered or Not Fully Covered by the Public Sector Directive* (DJØF Publishing, 2012).

'covered' procurement only represents around 20% of the total of public procurement taking place within the EU internal market.[6]

Moreover, as the objectives pursued through public procurement multiply, the scope of EU public procurement law can become a hindrance or a catalyst for 'procurement-focused' legislative and policy interventions, such as the potential imposition of mandatory sustainability or social requirements, or preferential access for SMEs and start-ups.[7] Similarly, as the EU takes a more protectionist approach to monitoring and enforcing restrictions of access to its procurement markets, the scope of EU public procurement law will delimit the space to be policed under the International Procurement Instrument and the Foreign Subsidies Regulation – as well as areas to be kept *off-limits* for (some) third-country providers, with a view to enshrining a 'European preference' in critical sectors and technologies.[8] A review of the scope of EU public procurement law must consider the intended remit of those legislative and policy instruments.

There is thus a tension between keeping a strict approach to the scope of the Classic Directive to limit the types of public–private contractualised relationships that are covered by its rules, on the one hand, and seeking to expand the policy leverage of procurement, on the other. Altering the scope of application of the Classic Directive would require a review of the relevant elements to either expand or constrain their remits – and could extend to a revision of the relevant value thresholds, though that issue exceeds the possibilities of this chapter.

This chapter submits that the two key defined concepts of 'procurement' and 'public contract', and their judicial interpretation, underpin most of the difficult issues in ascertaining the current scope of application of EU public procurement law. Despite the clarifications intended by the 2014 review of the Classic Directive, the twinned or interrelated concepts of 'procurement' and 'public contract' have remained controversial and problematic and have led to further complications arising from their subsequent interpretation by the CJEU. Adopting a more functional approach to establishing the scope of application of the Classic Directive would improve the future effectiveness of EU public procurement law and associated legislative and policy interventions.

The chapter first reviews developments in the interpretation of the scope of application of the Classic Directive since its 2014 revision (Section 2). It then

---

6 Procurement above EU thresholds has been estimated at 20% of total procurement; European Commission, *Public Procurement: A Data Space to Improve Public Spending, Boost Data-driven Policy-making and Improve Access to Tenders for SMEs* (Communication) [2023] OJ C 98 I/1.

7 See chapters 12–15 in this book.

8 See chapter 11 in this book.

proposes an alternative approach and the associated changes to the Classic Directive (Section 3), and highlights the main advantages that would arise from it (Section 4). The chapter concludes with a brief reflection on the extent to which not implementing a functional approach can reduce the effectiveness of some or many of the broader goals steering the review of the Classic Directive (Section 5).

2. THE EVOLVING SCOPE OF THE CLASSIC DIRECTIVE

The scope of application of the Classic Directive hinges on two related definitions. First, 'procurement', defined as 'the acquisition by means of a public contract of works, supplies or services by one or more contracting authorities from economic operators chosen by those contracting authorities, whether or not the works, supplies or services are intended for a public purpose'.[9] Second, and relatedly, 'public contract', defined as a contract 'for pecuniary interest concluded in writing between one or more economic operators and one or more contracting authorities and having as [its] object the execution of works, the supply of products or the provision of services'.[10] The interpretation of these definitions has focused on two elements: 'choice' and 'acquisition'. The interpretation of these elements has narrowed down the scope of application of the rules compared to expectations after their 2014 review, as described following.

2.1 Focus on 'Contracting Authority Choice'

The definition of procurement, introduced in 2014, requires that the economic operators with which contracting authorities enter into public contracts are 'chosen by those contracting authorities'. The CJEU has interpreted this requirement in a line of case law that progressively increased the importance of 'contracting authority choice'.

In *Falk Pharma*, the CJEU required contracting authorities to specifically choose the relevant economic operator (and its tender) for the award of a public contract to be included in the scope of application of the Classic Directive.[11] This excluded from the Classic Directive's remit schemes 'through which a public entity intends to acquire goods on the market by contracting throughout the period of validity of that scheme with any economic operator who

---

9 Classic Directive, art 1(2).

10 Ibid., art 2(1)(5).

11 Case C-410/14 *Falk Pharma* EU:C:2016:399, para 38.

undertakes to provide the goods concerned in accordance with predetermined conditions, *without choosing between the interested operators*, and allows them to accede to that scheme throughout its validity'.[12]

In *Tirkkonen*, the Court expanded this position to also exclude schemes 'through which a public entity *accepts all the economic operators who meet the suitability requirements* set out in the invitation to tender and who pass the examination referred to in that invitation to tender, even if no new operator can be admitted during the limited validity period of that scheme'.[13]

In *ASADE*, the CJEU stressed that 'procedures, *whereby the contracting authority refrains from comparing and classifying admissible tenders or designating one or more economic operators to whom contractual exclusivity is awarded*, do not fall within the scope of that directive'.[14]

The Court found specific support for this position in the recitals of the Classic Directive, which are ultimately premised on the view that forms of public action keep evolving, but this should not have an impact on the scope of application of the procurement rules because they 'are not intended to cover all forms of disbursement of public funds, but only those aimed at the acquisition of works, supplies or services for consideration by means of a public contract'.[15]

Moreover, the recitals also state that 'situations where all operators fulfilling certain conditions are entitled to perform a given task, without any selectivity, such as customer choice and service voucher systems, should not be understood as being procurement but simple authorisation schemes (for instance licences for medicines or medical services)'[16] and that social services can be organised 'in a way that does not entail the conclusion of public contracts, for example through the mere financing of such services or by granting licences or authorisations to all economic operators meeting the conditions established beforehand by the contracting authority, without any limits or quotas, provided that such a system ensures sufficient advertising and complies with the principles of transparency and non-discrimination'.[17]

This approach by the EU legislator and the CJEU entrenches the importance of the notion of 'public contract' and is not an unavoidable or value-free choice. The evolution of forms of public action can well advocate for an expansive approach to the scope of application of EU public procurement law to boost its effectiveness (through avoiding circumvention) – and, conversely,

---

12 Ibid., para 42, emphasis added.
13 Case C-9/17 *Tirkkonen* EU:C:2018:142, para 41.
14 Case C-436/20 *ASADE* EU:C:2022:559, para 68.
15 Classic Directive, recital 4.
16 Ibid.
17 Ibid., 114.

a reduction in the scope of application of EU public procurement law seeks to preserve areas of Member State domestic regulatory discretion that can undermine the internal market.

In that regard, it should be stressed that the procurement rules have the dual purpose of, on the one hand, regulating permissible restrictions on which economic operators have access to a specific opportunity and, on the other hand, regulating how public buyers choose from among the economic operators to which the opportunity is available. This can be conceptualised as a negative and a positive dimension, with the negative dimension banning impermissible restrictions on the availability of opportunities and the positive dimension imposing procedural and substantive requirements for the exercise of choice. Focusing on choice only and ignoring the *market access* logic and function of the procurement rules leaves regulatory gaps.

The *ASADE* line of case law has narrowed down the scope of application of the Classic Directive in a manner that excludes decisions concerning preparatory acts and the setting up of (quasi)contractual mechanisms that can have the same negative impacts on the functioning of the internal market as 'choice-based' procurement decisions. The key risk of distortion of the internal market not only concerns the relevant authority's choice of one (or a limited number) of economic operators but also, and perhaps more importantly, the exclusion of (potentially very large numbers of economic operators) through the imposition of impermissible restrictions on accessing the opportunity. Ultimately, the design of those schemes and the conditions to access them (whether there is a limit or not on the number of economic operators to be included, or a time limit to request inclusion), as well as the setting of the characteristics of the goods, services or works covered by those schemes, are open to the same risks of distortion of the internal market as (the other) public tenders and contracts covered by the Classic Directive. The exclusion of those schemes from the scope of the Classic Directive makes it more difficult to challenge them, due to the less detailed internal market rules applicable in such cases on the basis of primary EU law only[18] and the absence of access to procurement-specific remedy procedures.[19]

The CJEU's position that 'the risk of favouring national economic operators which [the Classic Directive] seeks to preclude is closely connected to the selection which the contracting authority intends to make from the admissible tenders and to the exclusivity which will result from the award of the contract

[18] See Catherine Barnard, *The Substantive Law of the EU: The Four Freedoms*, 7th ed. (Oxford University Press, 2022), ch 1.

[19] Stephen Weatherill, 'EU Law on Public Procurement: Internal Market Law Made Better' in Sanja Bogojević et al. (eds), *Discretion in EU Public Procurement Law* (Hart Publishing, 2019) 21.

concerned to the operator [or operators] whose tender has been accepted [...] that constituting the objective of a public procurement procedure',[20] is too narrow.

This line of case law also creates inconsistencies in the procurement treatment of different types of 'commercial vehicle' for mass utilisation in public sector activities and in the provision of public services – and, in particular, between 'procurement' framework agreements and dynamic purchasing systems, on the one hand, and 'free choice' or 'customer choice' umbrella contractual mechanisms, on the other. It also raises boundary issues that are common to long-standing discussions on the limits between 'concessions' and 'licences' and, more generally, about the mechanisms for the allocation of 'special or exclusive rights' under EU law.

Moreover, this approach creates a number of boundary or threshold issues of its own, such as the level of detail and prescriptiveness of the conditions of the contracts to be awarded under non-procurement procedures; the threshold point at which a contracting authority would be seen to have exercised 'enough choice' as to influence the exclusivity given to a specific economic operator; or the threshold point at which it should be considered that the systems put in place create *de facto* restrictions or quotas limiting the number of economic operators covered by the scheme (for, at the end of the day, funding for public services will always be limited). It is also notable that setting up 'free choice' schemes would still require compliance with general principles such as transparency or non-discrimination, and this would not reduce but rather displace the regulatory burden arising from compliance with EU internal market requirements. The approach followed thus creates legal uncertainty on the specific requirements applicable to such umbrella contracts or licensing schemes, and the case law in that area (licensing) has notably moved in a direction that tends to converge towards the imposition of requirements that resemble those arising from EU public procurement law (albeit with less detail).[21]

In view of this, there is a need to rethink the scope of a set of rules that primarily seek to prevent arbitrary market distortions and favouritism in the exercise of discretion and to facilitate competitive tension for legal arrangements with the public sector, whether they constitute procurement *stricto sensu*, or not.

---

20 *Falk Pharma* (n 11) para 36; *Tirkkonen* (n 13) para 29.

21 Johan Wolswinkel et al, 'Limited Authorisations Between EU and Domestic Law: Comparative Remarks from Dutch Law' (2019) 25(4) European Public Law 559; Grith Skovgaard Ølykke, 'Is the Granting of Special and Exclusive Rights Subject to the Principles Applicable to the Award of Concessions?' [2014] Public Procurement Law Review 1.

2.2 Focus on 'Direct Economic Benefits'

The requirement for procurement to involve an 'acquisition' through a 'public contract' 'for pecuniary interest' poses related issues. This has led to two interwoven developments concerning whether a given transaction involves sufficient 'direct economic benefits' for *both* the contracting authority and the economic operator.

2.2.1 'Pecuniary interest' as an obligation of the contracting authority

A first issue that creates practical problems is the requirement of 'pecuniary interest', which stems from the assumption that procurement-relevant contracts always involve the transfer of public funds to the economic operator[22] – with the narrow exception of some types of concession contracts. However, increasingly, and especially in the digital context, there are 'for free' transactions whereby the contracting authority acquires goods or services that it would otherwise have had to pay for (and thus procure). This can be problematic from many perspectives, such as in relation to the lock-in effects this can have or the future 'deactivation' of procurement requirements on the basis of the need to enter into follow-on direct awards with the relevant economic operator (e.g., on grounds of interoperability),[23] which is ultimately reflective of 'land and expand' strategies underpinning the initial 'gift' to the contracting authority. There are related issues with *pro bono* contracts where the economic operator does not obtain a clear remuneration or *quid pro quo* but rather derives practical benefits from the 'for free' contract, such as access to datasets, know-how or other immaterial advantages (such as user experience research) that can be difficult to neutralise under the current rules on prior involvement of economic operators.[24] This requires reconsidering the requirement for public contracts to involve *pecuniary* consideration, even if this is interpreted widely.[25]

Indeed, the CJEU has, in principle, interpreted the requirement for 'pecuniary interest' widely. In *NFŠ*, it has confirmed that 'the expression "for pecuniary interest" refers to a contract by which each of the parties undertakes to provide one form of consideration in exchange for another. The synallagmatic nature of the contract is thus an essential characteristic of a public contract, which necessarily results in the creation of legally binding obligations for each of the parties to the contract, the performance of which must be legally

---

22 Case C-451/08 *Helmut Müller* EU:C:2010:168, paras 47 and 48.

23 Case C-578/23 *Ceská republika – Generální financní reditelství* EU:C:2025:4.

24 Classic Directive, art 41.

25 Albert Sanchez-Graells, 'Article 2 – Definitions' in Roberto Caranta and Albert Sanchez-Graells (eds), *European Public Procurement. Commentary on Directive 2014/24/EU* (Edward Elgar, 2021) paras 2.22 ff.

enforceable.'[26] However, the case law to date still requires the pecuniary consideration to be (strictly) monetary, in one way or another.

For example, in *Tax-Fin-Lex*, involving an offer for 0.00 Euro, the Court stated that 'even if that consideration need not necessarily consist of the payment of a sum of money, so that the supply of the service is compensated for by other forms of consideration, such as reimbursement of the expenditure incurred in providing the agreed service [...], the fact remains that the reciprocal nature of a public contract necessarily results in the creation of legally binding obligations on both parties to the contract, the performance of which must be legally enforceable'.[27] Therefore, the Court concluded that 'a contract under which a contracting authority is not legally obliged to provide any consideration in return for that which the other party to the contract has undertaken to provide does not fall within the concept of "contract for pecuniary interest" within the meaning of Article 2(1)(5)' of the Classic Directive.[28]

In *ISE*, the CJEU accepted that undertaking certain obligations in relation to the improvement of software would meet the relevant criteria where it 'results in the financing of supplementary modules which must subsequently be provided to the other partner free of charge'.[29] To the best of the author's knowledge, there have been no cases where a contractual scheme has been considered within the scope of EU public procurement law without the contracting authority having an obligation to disburse funds (at some future point). Whether the existence of other types of obligations would be considered sufficient to class a contractual arrangement as a public contract for the purposes of the Classic Directive remains an open question.

2.2.2 'Acquisition' as 'direct economic benefit'

A second issue concerns the interpretation of 'acquisition', which has also been controversial, especially in relation to contractual arrangements seeking to facilitate access to goods, services or infrastructure by third parties rather than the contracting authority itself. In *SHARENGO*, the CJEU found that

> it follows from Article 1(2) of [the Classic Directive] that a procurement procedure is intended to lead to "the acquisition by means of a public contract of works, supplies or services by one or more contracting authorities". Article 2(1)(8) of that directive

26 Case C-28/23 *NFŠ* EU:C:2024:893, para 44.

27 Case C-367/19 *Tax-Fin-Lex* EU:C:2020:685, para 26.

28 Ibid., para 27.

29 Case C-796/18 *Informatikgesellschaft für Software-Entwicklung (ISE)* EU:C:2020:395, para 50. For discussion, see Miguel Assis Raimundo and Marco Caldeira, 'Relevant EU Procurement Law Requirements' in Christoph Krönke and Patricia Valcárcel Fernández (eds), *Buying AI. The Legal Framework for Public Procurement of Artificial Intelligence in the EU* (Edward Elgar, 2025) 76.

> defines "public supply contracts" as [those] "having as their object the purchase, lease, rental or hire-purchase, with or without an option to buy, of products."[30]

The Court stressed that 'a contracting authority which organises a public supply contract *intends itself to benefit* from the products which it has purchased, leased or rented'.[31] The Court thus considered that the fact that the relevant authority in that case intended to 'entrust an economic operator with the operation of a service enabling third parties to hire vehicles, without seeking to take over it itself or to hire vehicles for its own use' made it impossible 'to characterise the existence of a public supply contract, within the meaning of Article 2(1)(8) of the Classic Directive'.[32]

This compounds the shortcomings in the approach to 'choice' discussed previously, in particular in relation to arrangements seeking to facilitate access to goods, infrastructure or services by third parties, or where the contracting authority outsources an obligation in the public interest. Unless the existence of a permissible advantage has already been assessed under other instruments of EU internal market law (and, notably state aid law), the specific choice of a provider to be granted contractual exclusivity in relation to an activity under the control of the contracting authority should be subjected to the procurement rules because the risks of favouritism and market distortion are present – whichever specific form or legal structure is used in the design of the arrangement. In contrast, this approach to requiring an 'acquisition' to take place further narrows down the scope of the Classic Directive because it is not enough that the contracting authority chooses the specific economic operator with whom to enter into a contract granting exclusivity, but it is *additionally necessary that the contracting authority directly benefits from it.*

This interpretation runs contrary to some understandings of the likely impact of introducing the element of 'acquisition' in the definition of 'public contract' in the Classic Directive in 2014, which expected it to expand the scope of EU public procurement law beyond cases where the contracting authority is the direct beneficiary, and in particular to cases where the procurement is carried out to discharge the contracting authority's public law duties.[33] Although this view was not shared by all commentators,[34] it is arguable that the prior revision

---

30 Case C-486/21 *SHARENGO* EU:C:2022:868, para 66.

31 Ibid., para 67, emphasis added.

32 Ibid., para 69.

33 Roberto Caranta, 'Article 1 – Subject-matter and Scope' in *European Public Procurement* (n 25) paras 1.21 ff.

34 Notably, see Carina Risvig Hamer, 'The Concept of a "Public Contract" Within the Meaning of the Public Procurement Directive' (2016) 3 Upphandlingsraettslig Tidskrift 179, 190–191.

of the Public Procurement Directives may have sought to create flexibility in relation to the award of contracts to facilitate access to goods, infrastructure or services, especially if they are funded by the state. If this remains a regulatory goal, a reconsideration of this approach may be appropriate.

Finally, it is worth stressing that this approach heightens the difficulties in establishing when a contract is to the contracting authority's 'direct economic benefit'. This has resulted in inconsistent case law that seeks to minimise the practical implications of this requirement and muddies the waters. The CJEU has gone as far as recognising, in *NFŠ*, a 'direct economic benefit' in the assumption of commercial risks by a public authority,[35] which makes no sense.[36]

In view of this, there is a need to rethink or reclarify the scope of EU public procurement law in relation to public interventions that can potentially generate favouritism and/or an economic advantage for economic operators, regardless of whether the public sector entity 'acquires' something or not (in the sense of directly benefitting from it), as long as these have not been cleared under state aid law. This would make a positive contribution to future-proofing the revised procurement regime in relation to emerging modes of exchange based on alternative ownership structures, which could soon move from areas not funded by the state (such as micro-mobility of the type involved in *SHARENGO*) to areas funded by the state.

3. AN ALTERNATIVE FUNCTIONAL APPROACH

A potentially helpful approach to avoid the issues discussed prior would require reshaping EU public procurement law around an 'outsourcing or market sourcing' concept, which would also potentially avoid some of the conceptual complexities created by the current approach to excluding in-house and public–public cooperation from the scope of the Classic Directive.[37]

The internal market risks that the Classic Directive seeks to exclude concern (or should concern) favouritism and competitive distortions in market sourcing or outsourcing schemes that are not limited to the explicit and specific choice of an economic operator, or a range of them, but also extend to preparatory activities for such a choice, whether it is ultimately exercised

---

35 *NFŠ* (n 26) para 50. For a full discussion, see Albert Sanchez-Graells, 'A Missed Opportunity to Provide Meaningful Clarification on State Aid Analysis of Procurement Compliance and Some Problematic "Obiter Dicta"' (C-28/23) (*howtocrackanut.com*, 22 October 2024), https://tinyurl.com/u6udpnr6, accessed 22 May 2025.

36 Also against such a misinterpretation of the earlier case law, see Caranta (n 33) para 1.22.

37 See chapter 4 in this book.

by the contracting authority or by a third party (and whether such third party is another contracting authority or not). This is clearly the case, and arguably uncontroversial, in relation to framework agreements and dynamic purchasing systems currently covered in the Classic Directive. There is thus no good reason to exclude functionally equivalent arrangements.

Further, given the evolution of different forms of public action and business models based on exchanges underpinned by alternative ownership structures that reduce the relevance of a focus on the transfers of rights over tangible property in many cases, there is a good reason to introduce flexibility to cover arrangements seeking to support or delegate the discharge of the contracting authority's public law duties, as well as the facilitation on behalf of the contracting authority of access by third parties to goods, services or infrastructure.

Such a functional approach would require a modification of the definitions of procurement and public contract, which could be tentatively drafted as:

> Procurement within the meaning of this Directive is the set of preparatory activities or steps taken towards the conclusion of a public contract of works, supplies or services by one or more contracting authorities with one or more economic operators, whether or not the works, supplies or services are intended for a public purpose, and whether or not they are for the direct use or consumption by the contracting authority or authorities.
>
> Public contract means a legally binding act concluded in writing between one or more economic operators and one or more contracting authorities and having as its object the execution of works, the supply of products or the provision of services.

To avoid an excessive broadening of the scope of application of the Classic Directive, it would be necessary to include a specific exclusion for contracts concerning goods or services procured with a view to commercial sale or resale, or for use in the production or supply of goods or services for commercial sale or resale. It would also be necessary to develop a specific (light-touch) regime for 'for free' contracts where the contracting authority is not under significant legally enforceable obligations as the main purpose would be to check that a competitive procedure is not more adequate, in the long run, to satisfy the contracting authorities' needs.

Given the expanded scope of application of EU public procurement law if such an approach were followed, it would also be necessary to develop additional exclusions for contracts entered into in the context of a state aid measure, as well as an exclusion for purely licensing activities (if necessary to ensure consistency with the Services Directive[38]). Regarding the interaction of procurement and state aid rules, this would create a clearer distinction between transactions susceptible to state aid control and those susceptible to control

[38] Above (n 2).

under the procurement rules, as the current position of parallel obligations generates significant difficulties in some contexts.

There would also be knock-on effects to be explored in relation to other types of contracts, which would, however, depend on how this functional approach fits with other modifications of the Classic Directive.

4. ADVANTAGES

A functional approach more clearly focused on the preparatory steps leading to the award of a contract (or equivalent exclusive right), such as the one sketched out earlier, would have the main advantage of creating a single set of rules for the different types of activities whereby a contracting authority makes decisions that determine which economic operators can (and which cannot) access a specific opportunity to enter into an arrangement with the public sector. A functional approach that moved away from narrow interpretations of consideration or pecuniary interest would have the benefit of creating safeguards for the proper analysis and approval of 'free' or 'unilateral' transactions that can, however, both generate distortions at that point in time, and eschew later procurement decisions.

Such a functional approach would also facilitate a move away from the current narrow focus on transactional exchanges largely premised on a 'sales' model and towards a broader treatment of public–private interactions relating to the functioning of the public sector and the provision of public services.

From the perspective of using procurement as a 'policy delivery platform', revising the scope of application would improve its fit with strategic considerations. It would have the advantage of promoting a potentially broader coverage of 'procurement-focused' mandatory requirements targeted at the public sector, whether they relate to sustainability, social, access, resilience or any other considerations. This would expand the 'area of influence' of procurement as a policy delivery tool and would reduce the risks of inconsistency and ineffectiveness that follow from different approaches being applied to what is currently considered procurement (*stricto sensu*) and to other forms of public activity.

A further advantage of a functional approach is that it would probably facilitate some simplification in relation to the further taxonomy of public contracts (for works, services and supplies, as well as concession contracts – which could all be brought under a single Directive) and that it could be coupled with an alternative approach to creating differential details in the regulation of different types of contracts, not so much based on their object but rather on the balance of obligations between contracting authorities and economic operators.

Requirements to compete for opportunities, in particular, would need to be tiered to ensure proportionality in the application of detailed requirements.

5. SOME FINAL REFLECTIONS

The proposal just sketched may be seen as going too far in expanding the scope of application of EU public procurement law, and it can be difficult to implement given the change in approach it would imply for specific (contentious) areas of procurement and internal market law that can clearly impinge on Member States' interests in different ways.

However, not implementing a (similar) functional approach can reduce the effectiveness of some or many of the broader goals steering the review of the Classic Directive if its scope of application is further narrowed down due to the inclusion of other types of clarifications, or new elements susceptible to a narrow interpretation by the CJEU in the future.

It seems clear that one of the main goals of the current review of the Classic Directive is to increase its effectiveness as a policy delivery tool. From that perspective, a reconsideration of its scope of application should be a priority.

3. Fine-tuning the definition of "contracting authority" for increased precision and clarity

Miguel Assis Raimundo

REFORM PROPOSALS

This chapter identifies reform proposals to the central notion of contracting authorities in the public procurement Directive. These proposals – which are aimed at finding better solutions, adding legal certainty, or a combination of both – can be summed up as follows:

- The category of "associations of contracting authorities" should be clarified (as detailed in Section 2). We suggest that the rules should: (i) specify if this category is limited to entities wholly composed of other contracting authorities, and (ii) if they are limited to entities with or without legal personality. Also, it is suggested that (iii) it should be clarified that the same conditions applicable to bodies governed by public law (control by another contracting authority and meeting needs in the general interest without commercial or industrial nature) are required for being considered a contracting authority under that heading.
- We also suggest some clarifications to the notion of "body governed by public law" (Section 3). Namely: (i) clarifying, as per existing caselaw, that the entity does not need to have been specifically created to undertake needs in the general interest; (ii) clarifying the nature and contents of the act which charges an entity with meeting those needs; (iii) admitting that entities which undertake only marginal public missions should not be considered bodies governed by public law, or contracting authorities at all; (iv) codification and clarification of some aspects of the "majority funding"

requirement; (v) codification and clarification of the "management supervision" requirement, namely in collective control situations.[1]

1. INTRODUCTION

If we consider the foundational texts of EU public procurement law, the definition of a contracting authority is one of the points that has suffered a more obvious evolution.[2] The first Directives applied essentially to the state, regional and local authorities and a handful of other authorities specifically mentioned. A lot has changed since then, which is demonstrated by the very wide scope of covered entities we have today (see art. 2(1), 1 to 4, of Directive 2014/24/EU). The expansion of the entity coverage of the Directives was a reaction to the growing diversity of legal arrangements used to carry out public missions.[3] Ultimately, it aimed to include those entities that, despite possessing a private legal form and applying private law, substantially act as instruments of other contracting authorities.[4]

In addition to the evolution of the legal texts (and sometimes at the origin of it), the Court of Justice of the European Union (CJEU) has played a major role in this field, devoting a significant part of its caselaw to explaining and developing the entity coverage of EU public procurement law,[5] with the vast

---

1 A broader point will not be addressed here but should be kept in mind: whether the entity coverage of the 2014 Directives could be simplified in the event of the (desirable) consolidation of all the public procurement Directives (Concessions, Classical Sectors, Utilities and Defence Procurement), as others have suggested with good arguments – see, before the 2014 Directives, S. Arrowsmith, "Modernizing the European Union's Public Procurement Regime: A Blueprint for Real Simplicity and Flexibility", *Public Procurement Law Review*, 3 (2012), pp. 71 ff. (77–78), which remains pertinent.

2 For a detailed account of the entity coverage – which is beyond the purpose of this chapter – see, for example, A. Sánchez-Graells, "Article 2 - Definitions", in Roberto Caranta and Albert Sánchez-Graells (Eds.), *European Public Procurement - Commentary on Directive 2014/24* (Northampton/Cheltenham: Edward Elgar, 2021), pp. 17–30 (20 ff.); M. Steinicke and P. L. Vesterdorf (Eds.), *EU Public Procurement Law – Brussels Commentary* (Baden-Baden/München/Oxford: Nomos/C.H.Beck/Hart, 2018), pp. 137 ff.; S. Arrowsmith, *The Law of Public and Utilities Procurement. Regulation in the EU and UK* (Vol. 1, London: Sweet and Maxwell, 2014), pp. 339 ff.

3 Steinicke and Vesterdorf, *EU Public Procurement Law*, p. 138.

4 A. Sánchez-Graells, *Public Procurement and the EU Competition Rules* (2nd ed., Oxford-Portland, Oregon: Hart Publishing, 2015), p. 265.

5 Ibid., p. 264.

majority of those decisions covering the concept of “bodies governed by public law”.[6].

In recent years, the topic of entity coverage seems to have stabilized. The 2014 Directives explicitly stated that they did not intend to change the subjective scope of EU public procurement law (see Recital 10 of Directive 2014/24). The caselaw of the CJEU regarding this topic has also clearly diminished since the last Directives, which arguably means that the legal actors incorporated, or at least acknowledged, the main principles of the caselaw on these matters.

In light of this, the entity coverage of EU public procurement law is probably not the most likely topic for major changes in the next reform of the legal framework – unless there is a big surprise, which of course can happen in the less predictable world we live in today. However, this does not mean that no open questions remain or that there is no room for improvement. For this chapter, we selected a group of issues in which an intervention by the legislator seems important.

2. CLARIFYING THE CATEGORY OF “ASSOCIATIONS OF CONTRACTING AUTHORITIES”

2.1 Doubts Under the Current Law

The notion that associations of contracting authorities should also be considered contracting authorities is present from the very origins of EU public procurement law, in Directive 71/305/EEC – a discrete reference, included in an annex of the Directive. Nowadays, art. 2(1)(1) *in fine* of Directive 2014/24, after mentioning the two basic categories of contracting authorities (the *state, regional and local authorities*, and the category of *bodies governed by public law*), mentions this third category: “associations formed by one or more such authorities or one or more such bodies governed by public law”. The rationale

6 On this topic, see, especially, the following decisions of the CJEU: *FIGC e Consorzio Ge.Se.Av.*, 03.02.2021, C-155/19 and C-156/19; *‘LitSpecMet’ UAB*, 05.10.2017, C-567/15; *IVD*, 12.09.2013, C-526/11; *Wall*, 13.04.2010, C-91/08; *Hans and Christophorus Oymanns*, 11.06.2009, C-300/07; *Bayerische Rundfunk*, 13.12.2007, C-337/06; *Commission v. Germany*, 18.11.2004, C-126/03, *Commission v. Spain*, 16.10.2003, C-283/00; *Korhonen*, 22.05.2003, C-18/01; *Adolf Truley*, 27.02.2003, C-373/00; *Universale-Bau*, 12.12.2002, C-470/99; *Agorà*, 10.05.2001, C-223/99 and C-260/99; *Commission v. France*, 01.01.2001, C-237/99; *University of Cambridge*, 03.10.2000, C-380/98; *BFI Holding*, 10.11.1998, C-360/96; *Mannesmann*, 15.01.1998, C-44/96.

behind this category seems straightforward: it is a "category of accumulation,"[7] an "expression of the intent on the part of Community legislators" to "cover cooperation with public-sector participation" which is not covered by any of the other two categories.[8]

The simplicity of this category is only apparent. Its scope has raised significant doubt in the literature and, perhaps even more visibly, also among EU Member State legislators. Arguably, it can be seen as an example of how the harmonization goals of the directives have not been totally achieved.

The shortcomings of the current legal text on this matter are at least bifold.

First of all, the Directive does not indicate the legal nature of these "associations" in terms of having *legal personality* or not. This is in contrast with the definition of bodies governed by public law: in this latter case, the Directive explicitly indicates they have legal personality (article 2(4)(b)).

Second, and a more serious problem, the Directive does not indicate what kind of relationship should exist between the "association" and the contracting authority (or authorities) for it to be qualified as a contracting authority. The Directive does not, for example, contain any indication of what kind of *control* over the "association" must exist (if any), for it to be qualified as a contracting authority.

2.2 Legal Personality or Lack Thereof

In light of this ambiguous situation, some authors take the view that only associations of contracting authorities with *no autonomous legal personality of their own* belong to the concept (such as *consortia* in most legal systems), with all other "associations" (i.e. leading to the creation of actual legal persons) being qualified as bodies governed by public law if they fulfill the respective criteria, or not covered at all.[9] It is controversial if this understanding has been indirectly accepted by the Court of Justice regarding previous Directives, by way of Advocate General La Pergola's Opinion on *BFI Holding*.[10] Other voices accept the possibility that this category may also cover associations with an

7 Steinicke and Vesterdorf, *EU Public Procurement Law*, p. 158.

8 Ibid.

9 This is the position of Steinicke and Vesterdorf, *EU Public Procurement Law*, p. 158.

10 In fact, the Advocate General's Opinion in case C-360/96 (*BFI Holding*) defends this understanding, and the Court of Justice seems to accept the Opinion. The point is controversial, though – see Arrowsmith, *The Law of Public and Utilities Procurement*, *1*, p. 369.

autonomous legal personality.[11] This difference of understanding seems to have its consequences also at the national level: in French law, for example, this category is defined as having legal personality,[12] whereas in Italian law, the definition refers to "associations, unions or consortia,"[13] which assumes the possibility of entities without legal personality to be covered (with the reference to consortia[14]). Other EU jurisdictions exist where the issue is debated.[15]

It is undesirable that this ambiguity exists in such a far-reaching topic as the concept of contracting authority, and it should be solved in the next version of Article 2 of the Directive. It is suggested that the notion should cover both entities/bodies with legal personality and without it, in any case subject to additional conditions, as mentioned following.

2.3 The Need for Additional Conditions to be Qualified as a Contracting Authority

Notwithstanding the relevance of the point we just mentioned, the most important point to be addressed is the definition of the relationship between the association and the contracting authorities that compose it.

The current wording has been used to suggest that an association where one contracting authority is *present* is automatically qualified as a contracting authority, regardless of the fact that such a contracting authority actually

[11] This seems to be the final position of Arrowsmith, *The Law of Public and Utilities Procurement, 1*, p. 369.

[12] Article L.1211–1 of the French *Code de la commande publique* defines the third category of contracting authorities as "the private law bodies with legal personality formed by contracting authorities with a view to carrying out certain activities in common" (author's translation).

[13] Cf. the "Allegato I.1, q)" of the 2023 *Codice dei contratti pubblici*, pursuant to its article 13(6). This was also the case during the 2016 Code [article 3(1)(a)].

[14] Under Italian law, some "consorzi" of public entities form a different legal personality (the ones gathering local entities), but the general rule is that consortia are a simple form of contractual cooperation not giving rise to a separate legal entity.

[15] It is the case in Portugal – see M. A. Raimundo, *Direito dos Contratos Públicos* (Vol. 1, Lisboa. AAFDL, 2022), pp. 141 ff., J. Pacheco de Amorim and R. Mesquita Guimarães, "O enquadramento das «associações-empresas» no leque de entidades adjudicantes: Uma oportunidade a não perder na revisão do Código dos Contratos Públicos", in P. Costa Gonçalves/L. Torgal (Eds.), *Estudos em Homenagem a Mário Esteves de Oliveira* (Coimbra: Almedina, 2017), pp. 419–448.

controls the association.[16] This is a consequence of the fact that the conditions for being a body governed by public law – fulfilling needs in the general interest not having an industrial and commercial character and subject to control by a contracting authority – are not explicitly stated in this case, as they should be.

It is suggested that even under current law, this position is not correct. It would be contrary to the general conditions for being a contracting authority as provided for in the Directive and to the purposes of the subjective scope of public procurement (namely, to the conditions for being a body governed by public law) that, for example, a private association formed by 500 private individuals in which one contracting authority simply participates as a member would be qualified as a contracting authority.

The suggested solution is to make explicit, in the wording of the Directive, what seems to be the correct interpretation of the current (ambiguous) provision: that an association of contracting authorities should be considered a contracting authority only when it fulfills needs in the general interest not having an industrial and commercial nature, *and* is controlled by other contracting authorities (in the same way as a body governed by public law), which will be the case when the association is wholly composed of contracting authorities.

One might ask if this clarification would make the concept of "associations of contracting authorities" redundant and therefore unnecessary, given the existence of the concept of bodies governed by public law. However, associations of contracting authorities should include bodies with no legal personality, setting a difference with bodies governed by public law, which require legal personality. Additionally, it would be welcomed if the Directive clearly stated that an association exclusively composed of contracting authorities and tasked with meeting needs in the general interest with no industrial or commercial character will always be considered a contracting authority (with no need to assess specific control).

3. CLARIFICATIONS TO THE NOTION OF "BODIES GOVERNED BY PUBLIC LAW"

3.1 The Test of "Meeting Needs in the General Interest, Not Having an Industrial or Commercial Character"

The current definition of bodies governed by public law depends on three well-known cumulative conditions: the existence of legal personality, that "they are established for the specific purpose of meeting needs in the general interest,

[16] This seems to be the opinion of Arrowsmith, *The Law of Public and Utilities Procurement*, *1*, p. 368.

not having an industrial or commercial character"; and what is commonly referred to as the condition of being subject to a dominant influence by another contracting authority, which can be revealed by three alternative criteria: that "they are financed, for the most part, by the State, regional or local authorities, or by other bodies governed by public law [i.e. *majority funding* criterion]; or subject to management supervision by those authorities or bodies [*management supervision*]; or have an administrative, managerial or supervisory board, more than half of whose members are appointed by another contracting authority [so-called *appointment criterion*]."

The existence of legal personality is usually easy to assess, so the doubts and caselaw focus on the other two conditions. The practice of the application of these conditions and their development by the CJEU shows a very case-dependent appreciation, apparently making it difficult to advance much further in terms of codification. The test of meeting needs in the general interest is understood to be general and to rest mainly in the *second* part of that condition – the lack of commercial or industrial character of the activity actually carried out, in the specific case.[17]

The condition of activities in the general interest with no commercial or industrial nature is based on a number of indicators that the CJEU has identified (such as offering goods and services in the market, bearing the costs of activity, the goal of turning a profit) but which do not all need to be present and may have different weights in each case.[18] Therefore, it is particularly difficult to codify it.[19] In addition to that, the Recitals of the current Directive 2014/24/EU already point to some aspects of the caselaw (Recital 10). A precision made in the Recital, drawn from caselaw, is that the entity does not need to have been initially created for meeting the needs in the general interest, since it refers to the needs "that it has been set up to meet or been given the task of meeting."[20]

[17] As Steinicke and Vesterdorf, *EU Public Procurement Law*, p. 142, mention regarding several important cases on the topic, the Court seemed to be "less concerned with the nature of the activity undertaken, and focussed more on whether the entity operated on a commercial basis".

[18] Ibid., pp. 144–147.

[19] As Steinicke and Vesterdorf, *EU Public Procurement Law*, p. 145, put it: public needs in the general interest not of an industrial or commercial character "cannot form the basis of general delimitations according to which a specific type of activity in all cases – i.e. regardless of the specific conditions applicable to the individual entity – relates to such needs".

[20] As the Court restated in *FIGC*: "since its establishment or afterwards" (par. 37).

Despite the limitations created by the nature of such a test, some improvements can indeed be made in the future reform of the Directive. One of the points that should be inserted in the provisions (not just the recitals) is the precision we mentioned last. In fact, the current wording of article 2(1)(4)(a), which refers to the entity being "*established* for the specific purpose" of meeting needs in the general interest, leaves unwanted doubt and has been overcome by caselaw.[21] Another point that could be clarified regards the "specific creation" of the entity to meet needs in the general interest. The Court has recently restated that "the entity concerned must actually meet needs in the general interest, *and the assumption of responsibility for meeting those needs must be capable of being objectively determined*."[22] However, the caselaw does not clarify what is necessary for this assumption of responsibility. The future wording of the Directive should clarify that there needs to be a *legally binding commitment* for the entity to do so (not simply the fact that the entity *does carry out* these needs), and the *form* of such a commitment: if there needs to be a law or regulation or if a mere contract, administrative decision or corporate statute are enough.

Considering now more than simple adjustments, a background issue regarding the definition of the commercial or industrial nature of the activity could be considered. The CJEU has always held that "it is immaterial whether, in addition to its duty to meet needs in the general interest, an entity carries out other activities, and the fact that meeting needs in the general interest constitutes only a relatively small proportion of the activities actually pursued by that entity is also irrelevant."[23] However, this has been criticized as well,[24] and should be further discussed and possibly changed.

It is submitted here that it is fundamentally unconvincing to claim that an entity that is tasked with meeting *some* needs in the general interest will *always* be under the risk of adopting non-economic criteria in *all* its procurement options, especially if separate accounting is kept in relation to the "public service" part of its activity. If a certain company performs the vast majority of its business to commercial clients, in an environment where it needs to compete with other players to get that business, it seems unconvincing to say that

---

21 Also remarking this point and therefore offering a "purposive interpretation (…) regardless of the wording (…)", Steinicke and Vesterdorf, *EU Public Procurement Law*, p. 150.

22 CJEU 03.02.2021, *FIGC*, C-155/19 and C-156/19, par. 37 (emphasis added).

23 See, for example, CJEU 03.02.2021, *FIGC*, C-155/19 and C-156/19, par. 43.

24 Arrowsmith, *The Law of Public and Utilities Procurement, 1*, p. 366: "Applying the directives to procurement that relates purely to the commercial activities of 'mixed' entities is inappropriate".

it will adopt non-economic criteria in all its purchases, because if it were the case, that revenue would probably stop and the entity would become stifled.

This position by the CJEU is particularly difficult to accept when we consider that other areas of EU law are sensitive to the distinction between commercial and non-commercial activities.[25] Cross-subsidies are also a concern, but as Arrowsmith has argued, the entity can always demonstrate that such subsidies do not exist.[26] Also, the scope of the EU public procurement directives themselves is sensitive to the *degree of commercial activities* as relevant to defining if an entity should be considered an "instrument" of public tasks or not.[27] Concerns regarding the "non-industrial or commercial tasks" can be addressed by imposing procurement rules solely on the contracts concerned with those tasks (similar to what already happens with subsidized contracts).

It is therefore suggested that the Directive should have a more balanced approach, by providing relevance to the fact that an entity receives the majority of its revenue from truly commercial business or activity, and accepting that in such cases the entity should not be qualified as a body governed by public law, even if it carries out some other activities in the general interest without an industrial or commercial nature, with a marginal relevance in the overall revenue of the entity. Only entities that are clearly outside the realm of competition should be contracting authorities, and this probably should lead to abandoning the strict and no-exception rule according to which the commercial revenue and activities are irrelevant. All in all, this probably means making the assessment of this condition closer to the logic of articles 34 and 35 of the current Utilities Directive.[28]

3.2 Codification and Clarification of the "Majority Funding" Test

As mentioned prior, the third condition for being considered a body governed by public law is being subject to a specific type of control by another contracting authority, revealed through one of three alternative criteria: majority funding, management supervision and the majority appointment condition. The latter criterion (appointment of the majority of members) is relatively

[25] Arrowsmith, *The Law of Public and Utilities Procurement, 1*, p. 366.

[26] Ibid.

[27] This is the case, for example, with the funding subcriterion for the purpose of being qualified as a body governed by public law, which depends on the *majority* of revenue coming from such sources (as mentioned in Recital 10 of the Directive 2014/24). Therefore, an entity that receives as much as 48% or 49% public funding is *not* under the control of public entities. *Mutatis mutandis*, the same reasoning could apply here.

[28] As suggested by Sánchez-Graells, "Article 2 - Definitions", p. 23.

straightforward in its application. The majority funding and especially management supervision criteria are more complex and very case-dependent. Having that in mind, some clarifications would be welcome, namely in what concerns funding.

After the *University of Cambridge*[29] ruling of the Court of Justice, it has become undisputed that only funding provided "without any specific consideration" is relevant for this purpose.[30] However, it is submitted that at least three topics are worth discussing (and possibly changing) here.

The first concerns the evolution of how public authorities provide public funding. Nowadays, it is very difficult, if not impossible, to find an example of a payment made by a public entity that does not give rise to some kind of specific consideration or duty from the entity receiving it, which creates doubt, at least, as to the existence of public funding. This is true of traditional grants and subsidies given to private entities but also funding between public entities. For example, it has become commonplace that entities such as public hospitals are no longer provided with a general sum in the public budget; rather, their budgets are dependent on the number of patients treated, the pathologies for which they were treated and other quantitative aspects, which are measured and form the basis of the funds allocated to them. The common practice today is that even "awards or grants paid for the support of research work" (which were at stake in *University of Cambridge*) are dependent on strict conditions, foreseen in contracts or other arrangements entered into by the recipient entities, making it more and more difficult to distinguish subsidies from commercial consideration.[31] It would be a welcome input for legal certainty for the next Directive to include more detail on the notion of relevant public funding, having in mind the evolution of the way in which grants and other public funding are awarded today.

The second point concerns the doubts created by the caselaw of the Court of Justice, most notably in the *IVD*[32] ruling, concerning indirect public funding in contexts where the entity has some autonomy in determining the value of the contributions of third parties for these to count as public funding. The previous decisions in *Bayerische Rundfunk*[33] and *Hans & Christophorus Oymanns*[34]

---

29 CJEU 03.10.2000, *University of Cambridge*, C-380/98.

30 Steinicke and Vesterdorf, *EU Public Procurement Law*, pp. 152–153; Arrowsmith, *The Law of Public and Utilities Procurement, 1*, p. 349.

31 Steinicke and Vesterdorf, *EU Public Procurement Law*, p. 153, point out that "In practice, the line between public-sector financing (support) and contractual remuneration is blurred".

32 CJEU 12.09.2013, *IVD GmbH & Co. KG*, C-526/11.

33 CJEU 13.12.2007, *Bayerischer Rundfunk and Others*, C-337/06.

34 CJEU 11.06.2009, *Hans & Christophorus Oymanns*, C-300/07.

had established that indirect funding can be relevant. In the former, the fee that energy users would pay was defined by public regulations; and in the latter, reference was made to the "very limited discretion" of the entities in question (the health insurance funds) to define the contributions of members, because those contributions would have to be in line with the social character of the health insurance scheme and they were approved by a supervisory body, and therefore the value of contributions could be said to be "laid down by law" (pars. 54 and 55).

In *IVD*, however, the Court found that the entity in question – the *Ärztekammer Westfalen-Lipperztekammer*, a German State Medical Bar – could not be considered as receiving public funding in the form of contributions by its members because it had a significant degree of autonomy in determining the value of those contributions. One might wonder if this is completely well-founded and coherent with the previous caselaw, the legal texts and the purposes of the public funding test. If one considers the very striking facts that all medical doctors acting in the geographical area of the Medical Bar in question are members of the bar, and these are obliged to pay the fees the entity establishes, it seems clear that, whatever the specific value determined and the means to determine it, there is always a public law duty upon doctors to pay that value and thus, to finance the entity, which undertakes clear public interest missions (including regulating the medical profession). The difference between the situation of the health insurance funds in *Hans & Christophorus Oymanns* and the *Ärztekammer* in *IVD* is not easy to see.[35]

It is suggested that an intervention by the legislator on this point would be positive, at least for legal certainty. It would codify into law the possibility of indirect funding, the main characteristics of that funding according to the caselaw, and also – if the legislator wishes to maintain the IVD caselaw, which this author does not endorse – a reference to the element of *autonomy in the self-definition of the amount of contributions* as an *excluding* factor of indirect public funding.

The third issue to mention relates to the reference period of one budgetary year which is commonly used since the *University of Cambridge* ruling[36] and the possible relevance of changes during the period which would alter the status of the entity (in the sense that it would receive more public funding than expected and fall under the scope of majority funding). As some have noted,

35 For a different view on the *IVD* decision, see Sánchez-Graells, "Article 2 - Definitions", p. 25.

36 There is consensus about this point in the caselaw and in the literature – see Sánchez-Graells, "Article 2 - Definitions", p. 25; Steinicke and Vesterdorf, *EU Public Procurement Law*, pp. 154–155; Arrowsmith, *The Law of Public and Utilities Procurement, 1*, pp. 349–350.

this is a doubt left unsolved by caselaw.[37] The new version of the Directive should clarify that if the entity receives more public funding than anticipated, it should not change its legal status in the year in question but only in the following year – or more precisely, in the procurements to be launched in the following year – provided that the initial estimate was realistic. For the same reasons of legal certainty, it would also be positive to articulate this topic with the topic of *contract modifications* (current article 72 of the Directive) to clarify if and in what way the entity is bound to apply the regime on contract modifications to contracts it may have awarded in a period when it was *not* considered a contracting authority (or vice versa).

3.3 Codification and Clarification of the "Management Supervision" Test

The criterion for management supervision is one of those in which the CJEU has intervened more often, and it has developed several important guidelines.[38] Again, these guidelines seem difficult to put into provisions, since those provisions would do nothing more than mention the *possibility* of a certain aspect being relevant. To give an example, the Court has considered that *ex ante* powers of control are more relevant to management supervision than *ex post* powers because the former provide an opportunity to effectively influence decisions of resource allocation before they happen, which is not the case for the latter.[39] However, it seems that developments such as these should not be codified since the Court always presents them "in principle":[40] in a different case, with a different context, the solution could be different.

One point, however, that probably could benefit from codification regards the issue of management supervision in cases of complex management structures. It is submitted that the recent *FIGC* ruling of the CJEU has demonstrated yet again the shortcomings of the existing provisions of the Directives to adequately ascertain management supervision (and also the "appointment criterion") in contexts of complex institutional arrangements, characterized

37 Steinicke and Vesterdorf, *EU Public Procurement Law*, p. 155.

38 For a detailed analysis, see Steinicke and Vesterdorf, *EU Public Procurement Law*, pp. 156–158; Arrowsmith, *The Law of Public and Utilities Procurement, 1*, pp. 352–356.

39 CJEU 03.02.2021, *FIGC*, C-155/19 and C-156/19, par. 51; CJEU 02.09.2013, *IVD*, C-526/11, par. 29.

40 For example, the abovementioned par. 51 of the *FIGC* ruling reads as follows: "Consequently, *in principle*, a review *ex post facto* does not satisfy that criterion, in that it does not enable the public authorities to influence the decisions of the body in question with regard to public contracts" (emphasis added).

by a distribution of control/influence powers between different entities. In the same way that *joint control* was codified in the context of the in-house exception (see article 12(3), 2nd par., of Directive 2014/24), it would be positive to define and codify it for joint management supervision (and joint appointment of the members of management, supervisory and administration boards) using essentially the same principles used for in-house.

4. CLOSING REMARKS

Together with the notion of public contracts, the definition of contracting authorities is at the heart of EU public procurement law. And EU public procurement law, we believe, is crucial to competition, sustainability, integrity and accountability across the Member States.

The definition of contracting authorities is a topic in which no drastic changes to existing law seem necessary, but some incremental improvements are possible. This chapter suggests some improvements having in mind two main goals: precision and legal certainty.

The definition of contracting authorities must encompass *all* the entities which, according to the underlying principles and values of this field of the law – and EU law altogether – should be made to comply with these rules, but *no more*. This entails a need for *precision* in the design of the conditions for being a contracting authority, guaranteeing that only entities clearly outside competition are covered (as seen especially in Sections 2 and 3(a)).

As for legal certainty, it is crucial in matters pertaining to the scope of the rules. Lack of clarity and too much reliance on caselaw may have terrible consequences here: any misinterpretation of the rules can lead to a covered entity not complying at all with procurement – with great damage to competition. For this reason, we suggest clarifying, in particular, some of the conditions for being qualified as a body governed by public law, where the need for clarity is more acute.

4. Reforming the rules on public–public cooperation

Towards legal certainty for Article 12 of Directive 2014/24/EU?

Willem Janssen

REFORM PROPOSALS

- Explicitly exclude reversed awards and horizontal awards in joint control scenarios in the institutionalised exemption.
- Add a limitation for third-party participation and private capital participation for the institutionalised and non-institutionalised exemptions.
- Streamline the scope of the institutionalised and non-institutionalised exemptions by expanding them to all types of public tasks.
- For the calculation of the activities criteria for the institutionalised and non-institutionalised exemptions, a functional approach should be taken instead of a grammatical approach.
- Publish the use of Article 12 Directive 2014/24/EU to increase enforcement.

1. INTRODUCTION

The performance of public tasks in modern-day society continues to lead to heated debates about the desired role of the state, market and everything in between and beyond. This is further stressed by societal transitions in relation to climate change and social injustice, and the subsequent question of who should be in charge of providing an answer to them. Even though EU public procurement law takes a distant stance towards impeding on the 'make, buy or ally' decision,[1] it is clear that these rules also apply when public authori-

[1] See, for instance, Rubén Medina Serrano, María Reyes González Ramírez and José Luis Gascó Gascó, 'Should We Make or Buy? An Update and Review' (2018) 24 *European Research on Management and Business Economics* 137; Alvin

ties wish to cooperate for the provision of such tasks, either in a non-institutional setting, meaning contractual cooperation among public authorities, or an institutional setting, meaning cooperation with a separate legal entity. Both exemptions stem from the starting point that a contracting authority can always provide a service with its own department (so-called in-house performance or self-supply). A clear and legally certain inclusion of any rules related to these two types of cooperation is of importance as a manifestation of the right to self-organisation[2] because it affects the proper functioning of public tasks, ranging from back-office services to supporting the performance of public tasks relating to, for instance, health care, education and waste services.

Despite the improvements made by the EU legislator in 2014 when it codified a long line of jurisprudence by the Court of Justice of the European Union (CJEU) and further clarified these exemptions in Article 12 Directive 2014/24/EU,[3] it is clear that – also exemplified by the various cases before the CJEU and the national courts in recent years – there is much room for improvement for a future provision on this topic. In this chapter, the aim is to discuss the above-mentioned context by highlighting the status quo but mostly to provide food for thought when it comes to the reform of this Directive on several issues that still hinder an effective functioning of these exemptions.[4]

This contribution is structured as follows: Firstly, both exemptions, which are referred to in this chapter as the institutionalised exemption (also referred to as the vertical exemption or the Teckal exemption) and the non-institutionalised exemption (also referred to as the Commission/Hamburg exemption or the horizontal exemption) and their legal requirements are introduced (Section 2). Secondly, a number of reform proposals are tabled that generally stem from legal uncertainty in applying these exemptions, without having the ambition to be exhaustive in any way (Section 3). In doing so, the discussion focuses on

---

J Silk and Marta M Stiglin, 'Build It, Buy It, or Both? Rethinking the Sourcing of Advertising Services' (2016) 8 *International Journal of Marketing Studies* 1.

2 Willem Janssen, *EU Public Procurement Law & Self-Organisation: A Nexus of Tensions & Reconciliations* (Eleven International Publishing 2018) chapters 1 and 2.

3 The provision is similarly included in Article 28 of Directive 2014/25/EU.

4 See Case C-51/15 *Remondis* [2016] EU:C:2016:985; Case C-328/19 *Porin Kaupunki* [2020] EU:C:2020:483. This chapter does not address the transfer of competences and responsibilities, even though there is also work to be done in that remit. For instance, it is unclear what a genuine transfer entails given the CJEU's unclear decision in *Porin Kaupunki*, when it accepted involvement of the transferring parties in the control of the in-house entity. The question here is how the transfer of competences and responsibilities relates to an institutionalised cooperative scenario.

the following issues: the question of whether reversed and horizontal awards can be exempted in joint control scenarios, (Section 4), the question of whether third-party participation or private capital participation should be allowed in relation to these exemptions (Section 5), the question of for which tasks these exemptions can be used (Section 6) and, finally, the question of how the related turnover requirements must be interpreted for both exemptions (Section 7).

2. THE INSTITUTIONALISED AND NON-INSTITUTIONALISED EXEMPTIONS

As interpreted for the first time by the CJEU in the milestone cases *Teckal* and *Commission/Germany*,[5] Article 12 Directive 2014/24/EU codified the subsequent lines of the CJEU's jurisprudence and changed its contents as well.[6] For both these exemptions, the discussions in academia and practice have predominantly focused on their scope, whereby public authorities have often aimed at a broad interpretation to allow for their cooperative plans and whereby, contrarily, economic operators have challenged such interpretation to ensure that related contracts are in fact tendered on the market. This state–market dynamic is likely to continue to influence the legislative debate as well. This is even more relevant in light of the discussion following the report of the European Court of Auditors on competitive concerns, as it could be argued that a limited scope for exemptions in fact increases the amount of competition as more contracts would need to be competitively tendered.

[5] Case C-107/98 *Teckal* EU:C:1999:562, [1999] ECR I-08121; Case C-480/06 *Commission v. Germany* EU:C:2009:357, [2009] ECR I-04747.

[6] See, for instance, J Wiggen, 'Public Procurement Rules and Cooperation Between Public Sector Entities: The Limits of the In-house Doctrine under EU Procurement Law' (2011) *Public Procurement Law Review* 157; J Wiggen, 'Public Procurement Law and Public-public Co-operation: Reduced Flexibility but Greater Legal Certainty Ahead? The Commission's Staff Working Paper on the Application of EU Public Procurement Law to Relations Between Contracting Authorities and the 2011 Proposal for a New Directive' (2012) *Public Procurement Law Review* 225; Kris Wauters, *Cooperative Agreements between Public Authorities: The Influence of CJEU Case Law on National Legal Systems* (Intersentia 2015); Janssen (n 2); Mario Comba and Steen Treumer (eds), *The In-House Providing in European Law* (DJØF 2010); Elisabetta Manunza, *EG-aanbestedingsrechtelijke problemen: bij privatiseringen en bij de bestrijding van corruptie en georganiseerde criminaliteit* [*EU public procurement problems related to privatisations and the fight against corruption and organised crime*] (Kluwer 2001); Willem Janssen, 'The Institutionalised and Non-Institutionalised Exemptions from EU Public Procurement Law: Towards a More Coherent Approach?' (2014) 10 *Utrecht Law Review* 168.

As included in Article 12(1–3) Directive 2014/24/EU, the institutionalised exemption notes that a public contract awarded to a legal person governed by private or public law can be exempted if three cumulative conditions are fulfilled.[7] Accordingly, the control criterion means that ‘the contracting authority exercises over the legal person concerned a control which is similar to that which it exercises over its own departments’ (a), the activities criterion means that ‘more than 80 % of the activities of the controlled legal person are carried out in the performance of tasks entrusted to it by the controlling contracting authority or by other legal persons controlled by that contracting authority’ (b), and the private participation criterion means that ‘there is no direct private capital participation in the controlled legal person with the exception of non-controlling and non-blocking forms of private capital participation required by national legislative provisions, in conformity with the Treaties, which do not exert a decisive influence on the controlled legal person’ (c). Additionally, joint control, as was interpreted by the CJEU in the *Coditel* case,[8] is further defined by noting the need for the fact that: a) ‘the decision-making bodies of the controlled legal person are composed of representatives of all participating contracting authorities’, which includes the possibility to have individual representatives represent several or all of the participating contracting authorities, b) ‘those contracting authorities are able to jointly exert decisive influence over the strategic objectives and significant decisions of the controlled legal person’, which is similar to that of singular control, and that c) ‘the controlled legal person does not pursue any interests which are contrary to those of the controlling contracting authorities’. It was further clarified by the EU legislature that control can also exist in a holding structure and that horizontal awards and reversed awards, which use existing institutionalised exemptions, are also allowed.[9]

Furthermore, the non-institutionalised exemption as vested in Article 12(4) Directive 2014/24/EU, which was codified after much less case-law from the CJEU when compared to the institutionalised exemption,[10] notes that a contract concluded ‘exclusively between two or more contracting authorities’ falls outside the scope of Directive 2014/24/EU if ‘the contract establishes or implements a cooperation between the participating contracting authorities with the aim of ensuring that public services they have to perform are provided with a

---

7 Wojciech Hartung, ‘Commentary on Article 12(1–3) Directive 2014/24/EU’ in Roberto Caranta and Albert Sanchez-Graells (eds.), *EU Public Procurement* (Edward Elgar 2021).

8 Case C-324/07 *Coditel* EU:C:2008:621, [2008] ECR I-08457.

9 Article 12(2) Directive 2014/24/EU.

10 Most prominently, Case C-159/11 *ASL di Lecce* [2012] EU:C:2012:817; Case C-386/11 *Piepenbrock* [2013] EU:C:2013:385; *Commission v. Germany* (n 5).

view to achieving objectives they have in common' (a), if 'the implementation of that cooperation is governed solely by considerations relating to the public interest' (b) and 'the participating contracting authorities perform on the open market less than 20 % of the activities concerned by the cooperation' (c).

3. JOINT CONTROL AND REVERSED/HORIZONTAL AWARDS FOR INSTITUTIONALISED EXEMPTION

At present, it is unclear if reversed and horizontal awards in cases of joint control in an institutionalised setting can benefit from the exemption of Article 12(2). It is argued here that this is not possible based on current case-law of the CJEU, and that such an approach should be included in the reform of this provision.

In this light, it is noteworthy that the EU legislature has refrained from expressly including reversed and horizontal awards within the scope of exemptions applicable to jointly controlled legal entities in the legal text of Article 12.[11] Although a reading of Article 12 Directive 2014/24/EU that would emphasise the Directive's approach of allowing more scope for exemptions, and thus, applying a teleological approach, might suggest that it can indeed be extended to joint control scenarios, such an interpretation remains unconvincing. One could argue, for instance, that both paragraphs 2 and 3 of Article 12 explicitly refer to paragraph 1. In addition, unclarity exists rightly so due to the reference in the activities criterion ('other legal persons controlled by the same contracting authorities'), which should be taken out in the next revision of this provision to avoid such discussions.

Contrarily, and more convincingly, the most compelling counterargument lies in the absence of an explicit provision within Article 12 extending this exemption to jointly controlled entities. In contrast, exemptions for scenarios involving individual control are expressly included. Whereas this interpretation is supported by the legislative history of Article 12 in which it was proposed but not included in the final text and the need to interpret exemptions in a narrow manner,[12] the current case-law of the CJEU appears to answer this question already. In *Sambre/Biesme*,[13] the Court noted in reference to a cooperation in Belgium in which a holding structure was applied that:

> However, it should be pointed out that, unlike paragraphs 1 and 2 of that article, that provision does not provide that the conditions relating to control of the contracting

---

11 Janssen (n 2) 196.

12 *Teckal* (n 5).

13 Joined Cases C-383/21 and C-384/21 *Sambre/Biesme* [2022] EU:C:2022:1022.

> authority over the legal person to whom the contract is awarded may be satisfied indirectly.

As noted before, the possibility to control entities via a holding structure is also included in Article 12(2), next to that of reversed and horizontal awards. As such, this conclusion can be easily translated to joint control scenarios as well. In addition, it is still clear that joint control also limits the possibility of reversed and horizontal awards should the Member States have chosen to implement a more limited version of Article 12(2), such as was done in the Netherlands in which articles 2.24a (singular control) contain this possibility, and 2.24b (joint control) does not include it. This approach would rest on the case-law of *Irgita*, in which the CJEU confirmed the legality of such implementations, as it would ultimately benefit the coming about of the internal market.[14] Accordingly, it is recommended to codify this case-law and settle this debate in practice. It also means that awards to other entities further removed than those controlling the entity in a corporate holding structure should also not be included in its scope.

4. THE ROLE OF THIRD PARTIES AND PRIVATE CAPITAL

A particular concern related to the institutionalised and non-institutionalised exemptions is that their application would affect competition in the internal market by favouring one entity over another without following a public procurement procedure. In relation to the institutionalised exemption, this comes to the fore through the private capital criterion, and in relation to the non-institutionalised exemption, through the involvement of private entities in the cooperation, not being contracting authorities. In both scenarios, it is necessary to take a strict approach to avoid such anti-competitive effects.

This approach is rooted in the case-law of the CJEU. When it comes to the non-institutionalised exemption, the CJEU confirmed in *Commission v. Germany* that private undertakings must not be placed in a position of competitive advantage over their market counterparts.[15] This was again emphasised in *Asl di Lecce*; the Court found that the agreement contained provisions allowing the involved university to rely on third parties in performing its contractual obligations, which was deemed unlawful. A similar concern was addressed

[14] Case C 285/18 *Irgita* [2019] EU:C:2019:829. See Willem Janssen and Erik Olsson, 'On Competition, Free Movement and Procurement' (2020) 15 *European Procurement & Public Private Partnership Law Review* 2; Willem Janssen, 'Swimming Against the Tide' (2019) 14 *European Procurement & Public Private Partnership Law Review* 145.

[15] *Commission v. Germany* (n 5) para 47.

in *Stadt Köln*,[16] which again brought into focus the implications of involving third parties in cooperative arrangements between contracting authorities. The Court even went as far as noting the need to ensure that the source code of the involved IT services would be made available to bidders in future public procurement procedures.[17] Accordingly, it would be useful to include this limitation in the text of a future Article 12(4) Directive 2014/24/EU. Furthermore, it would be odd not to extend this limitation to private capital participation in bodies governed by public law, as was also suggested by the Commission in its initial proposal for a Directive in 2011, which noted the criterion '(e) there is no private participation in any of the contracting authorities involved'.[18] This latter comment also brings us to the question of private participation in an institutionalised cooperation.

In this context, similar questions arise when it comes to allowing private capital in institutionalised cooperations. The CJEU has rightly taken the approach in the case of *Stadt Halle* of banning such participation as it provides a competitive advantage to a selected entity benefiting from direct awards via private capital participation. Whilst there is a need to define 'private capital', the EU legislative has, contrarily, allowed for specific participation in Article 12(1)(c) Directive 2014/24/EU. This provision seems to have a rather limited effect in practice though, given that it is bound by strict conditions, including that private capital participation needs to be 'required by national legislative provisions'. The latter is also in need of clarification; in particular, the question is what type of legislation is meant here (i.e. national or also local) and to what extent this can be used (i.e. unlimited possibility or if there is actually a limit in light of competitive concerns). Taking into account that there is a clear way to construct such capital positions via the *Acoset* route,[19] the future reforms should clarify that such participation does not fit within a consistent application of the principle of equality in the broader internal market context. The fact that it concerns capital, and not a contract, should not provide for an inconsistent regulatory approach.

---

16 Case C-796/18 *Stadt Köln* [2020] EU:C:2020:395.

17 Ibid., para 75.

18 European Commission, 'Proposal for a Directive of the European Parliament and of the Council on Public Procurement' (2011) COM(2011) 896 final 2011/0438 (COD), article 11(4) sub e.

19 Case C-196/08 *Acoset* EU:C:2009:628, [2009] ECR I-09913.

5. THE QUESTION OF SCOPE: WHAT TYPE OF TASKS?

For a long time, a major distinguishing factor between the institutionalised and the non-institutionalised exemption was the scope of these exemptions, and more specifically the type of tasks for which they could be used.[20] Through the case-law of the CJEU, these exemptions seem to have grown closer together as noted following.

Generally speaking, the scope of the institutionalised exemption was perceived as broader given that all types of services could be included, ranging from waste collection to back office services, leaving difficult discussions about whether they constituted formal public tasks vested in the law aside. Contrarily, the CJEU was stricter on the type of tasks for which a non-institutionalised exemption could be used. In *Commission/Germany*, the Court referred to 'ensuring that a public task that they all have to perform, namely waste disposal, is carried out'.[21] In this case, it meant that the involved regional governments could benefit from this exemption, as all of them had to fulfil their tasks in light of the applicable Directive 75/442/EEC.[22] Similarly, the Court noted in *ASL di Lecce* that this exemption concerns those contracts 'which establish cooperation between public entities with the aim of ensuring that a public task that they all have to perform is carried out'.[23] In the latter case, it meant that the cooperation between the involved university and the local health authority could not fall under its scope as they were not responsible for the same public tasks. In practice, it was since then assumed that the public task vested in the law applicable to all of the involved entities would be the safest option to apply this exemption. However, Article 12(4) Directive 2014/24/EU significantly expanded the scope of this provision by referring to 'a cooperation between the participating contracting authorities with the aim of ensuring that public services they have to perform are provided with a view to achieving objectives they have in common'. This has also led to much debate, including the question of whether 'public services they have to perform' is the same as 'a public task that they all have to perform' and if 'with a view to achieving the objectives they have in common' loosens this provision even more. Most importantly, the preamble notes now that:

20 Willem Janssen, 'Commentary on Article 12(4–5) Directive 2014/24/EU', in Roberto Caranta and Albert Sanchez-Graells (eds.), *EU Public Procurement* (Edward Elgar 2021) 143.

21 *Commission v. Germany* (n 5) para 37.

22 Council Directive 75/442/EC of 15 July 1975 on waste, OJ L 194/39.

23 *ASL di Lecce* (n 10) para 34.

> Such cooperation might cover all types of activities related to the performance of services and responsibilities assigned to or assumed by the participating authorities, such as mandatory or voluntary tasks of local or regional authorities or services conferred upon specific bodies by public law.

This confirms a broad scope compared to the CJEU's case-law, including 'voluntary' tasks, and even those 'assumed' by the authorities themselves. Building on this recital, the CJEU's case of *Stadt Köln* complicated matters further by introducing the concept of 'ancillary activity', as suggested by the opinion of Advocate-General Campos Sánchez-Bordona in this case. The Court notes that '"all types of activities" can potentially cover an activity ancillary to a public service as long as that ancillary activity contributes to the effective performance of the public service task to which the cooperation between the participating contracting authorities relates'.[24] Given that there is no definition for 'ancillary activities', the scope discussion has become more problematic. What's more, the Court in the *Stadt Köln* case, whilst referring to recital 33, even noted that the software for the functioning of the fire department might even constitute the performance of a public task itself and not a back office service that is merely ancillary by concluding that: 'In addition, it is not certain that software for tracking fire service operations in firefighting, technical assistance, emergency rescue and disaster control, like that at issue in the main proceedings, which would seem to be essential to the performance of those tasks, can be reduced to the status of a purely ancillary activity'.[25]

As a consequence, it would be useful to clarify the concept of 'ancillary activity' in the next reforms, or even more boldly, streamline the scope of the type of tasks between the institutionalised and non-institutionalised exemptions. The latter would mean, for instance, that the non-institutionalised exemption could also be used for back-office services instead of limiting it to public tasks and those that are ancillary to it. This is particularly the case as there seems to be no normative backing to limit the scope of one of the exemptions more strongly than the other, particularly when the EU legislator has already broadened the scope of the non-institutionalised exemption quite extensively. It seems odd to limit the scope in this sense in light of *how* tasks are organised instead of *what* tasks are being organised.

---

24 *Stadt Köln* (n 16) para 60.

25 Ibid., para 61.

6. TURNOVER IN RELATION TO THE ACTIVITIES CRITERIA – WHAT TURNOVER?

The institutionalised and the non-institutionalised exemption both rely on a version of the activities criterion, requiring, respectively, a calculation of 80% of the turnover to be carried out for the entity or entities that control the related legal person and that the contracting authorities perform on the open market less than 20% of the activities concerned by the cooperation.[26] Even though the granted clarity in this provision from moving away from 'essential part' and a variety of percentages in the case-law,[27] the textual inconsistency of referring to 80% or 20% is still unnecessary and can be easily fixed by referring to either one of them in both instances.

As noted in Article 12(5) Directive 2014/24/EU, the measurement method of the turnover is stipulated by the Directive as well, which notes that 'the average total turnover, or an appropriate alternative activity-based measure such as costs incurred by the relevant legal person or contracting authority with respect to services, supplies and works for the three years preceding the contract award shall be taken into consideration'. Should this not be possible due to the commencement of activities or a reorganisation, then 'it shall be sufficient to show that the measurement of activity is credible, particularly by means of business projections'.

More importantly, however, is the outstanding question of *what* turnover is intended in relation to both the exemptions discussed. For the institutionalised exemption, this question revolves around the debate of whether grammatical interpretation or a more functional interpretation should be taken when considering the scope of the activities criterion. This pertinent question is the subject of the currently pending case before the CJEU in the *Irado* case.[28] In this Dutch case, the BAR-municipalities, a cooperation of three municipalities, concluded a contract for processing of residual household waste with

---

[26] Article 12(3)(b) and 12(4)(c) Directive 2014/24/EU.

[27] *Teckal* (n 5); Case C-295/05 *Tragsa* EU:C:2007:227, [2007] ECR I-02999; Case C-231/03 *Coname* EU:C:2005:487, [2005] ECR I-7287.

[28] Case C-692/23 *Irado* [2025] EU:C:2025:310, Opinion of AG Rantos. During the finalisation of this chapter, the CJEU published its final decision in this case. The Court concludes briefly said that the turnover of the holding should indeed be used to calculte the activities criterion and that there is no reason to not assume this was always the correct interpretation. Interestingly, the Court did not apply the two step approach as noted by the Advocate-General. The Court simply referred to the joint annual accounts as a means of proof and did not link the discussion to the definition of 'undertaking'. Case 692/23 *Irado* [2026] ECLI:EU:C:2026:4.

Irado in 2019.[29] Furthermore, Afvalsturing Friesland (AF) heads a group of subsidiaries processing waste and operates a landfill in the Friesland province, receiving industrial waste and waste from local municipalities.[30] AF was contracted by Irado to process household waste. Both awards relied on Article 12(3) Directive 2014/24/EU to be exempted from a duty to tender.

Competitor AVR-Afvalverwerking brought an action to the District Court in The Hague, arguing that the conditions for an in-house award were not satisfied and seeking annulment of both the BAR-Irado and Irado-AF contracts.[31] The District Court dismissed the action and argued that the conditions for an in-house award were indeed satisfied.[32] On appeal, the Court of Appeal in The Hague submitted preliminary questions to the CJEU regarding the interpretation of Article 12(3) point b Directive 2014/24/EU read in conjunction with Article 12(5) of that Directive.

The first preliminary question is particularly relevant for this discussion as it questions whether for the application of the 80% rule only the turnover from the legal person should be taken into account or also the turnover of subsidiaries if the legal person is the head of a group of undertakings. At the time of writing, Advocate-General Rantos' Opinion has been published, whilst the judgement is expected in the autumn of 2025. While noting some critical preliminary observations outside the scope of the preliminary questions,[33] the AG dismissed a grammatical interpretation of Article 12 Directive 2014/24/EU, as it would mean that for the purposes of calculating the total turnover solely, the turnover of the legal person concerned should be relevant, in this case AF, and not its subsidiaries.[34] This interpretation builds upon the idea that the institutionalised exemption considers the relationship between a contracting authority or authorities and a separate legal entity, which would mean that this contractual relationship forms the basis of the calculation of the activities criterion and, thus, the calculation of the turnover. Based on this approach, it

[29] Ibid., para 18.

[30] Ibid., paras 11–12.

[31] Ibid., para 20.

[32] Ibid., para 21.

[33] Ibid., para 38–40. According to A-G Rantos, the indirect control from the three municipalities through BAR, Irado and AF leads to a dilution of the initial control, raising questions about departing from the *ratio legis* of the in-house exception, which is based on the idea that contracting authorities perform public tasks using their own resources. Secondly, the timeline of the conclusion of the contracts is notable, and it is unclear when the conditions for the in-house exception were met.

[34] Ibid., para 49.

would, consequently, make sense not to include the turnover of subsidiaries within a holding structure.

Coined as a too 'formalistic approach', the Advocate-General argues that this would allegedly run counter to the case-law of the CJEU, which has consistently invited national courts to take account of 'all the facts of the case, both qualitative and quantitative'.[35] However, even though a more functional approach can indeed be argued for, it seems that the latter would not provide sufficient argumentation. Given that EU law must be given independent and uniform interpretation, the Advocate-General then still concludes that the provision should be interpreted in line with the definition of 'consolidated financial statements' from Articles 22 and 24 of Directive 2013/34/EU on obligations regarding financial statements and, if the entities involved fall outside the scope of this Directive, that the interpretation should align with the definition of 'undertaking' in EU competition law and its related single entity doctrine.[36]

Advocate-General Rantos argues that the choice to include the subsidiaries' turnover should also count towards the 80% rule and should be 'made in relation to the capacity of the [unconsolidated turnover] to disclose whether the controlled legal person carries out a significant part of its economic activity under the controlling contracting authorities'.[37] The choice of using consolidated turnover as the starting point is then grounded in number of arguments. According to the A-G, the consolidated turnover provides a more accurate picture of the real and effective size of that controlled legal person, and thus the possibility to assess the likelihood of the legal person or its subsidiaries entering into competition with other undertakings.[38] Such a market test, however, seems far apart from the current interpretation of the institutionalised exemption and the related activities criterion. Furthermore, if it is a parent undertaking benefits from an in-house award, subsidiaries can benefit from this materially and gain a position of advantage versus their competitors, leading to unfair competition.[39] Most convincingly, choosing consolidated turnover would prevent the option for contracting authorities to divide the formal structure of controlled entities as is commonly done in many Member States, which could in turn lead to circumventing the principle of open competition.[40]

---

[35] Ibid., para 50; Case C-553/15 *Undis Servizi* [2016] EU:C:2016:935, paras 31–32.

[36] *Irado*, Opinion AG Rantos (n 28) paras 59–67.

[37] Ibid., para 53; Case C-340/04 *Carbotermo* EU:C:2006:308, [2006] ECR I-4166, para 63.

[38] *Irado*, Opinion AG Rantos (n 28) para 55.

[39] Ibid., para 56.

[40] Ibid., para 57.

Accordingly, 'average total turnover' would thus need to be interpreted as the 'consolidated turnover' based on the Advocate-Generals's opinion.[41]

Furthermore, if this Directive is not applicable, the criteria derived from the concept of 'undertaking' should be used.[42] This approach leads to the same outcome, but instead applies the approach taken in competition law. In this context, 'undertaking' is an 'autonomous term which designates the perpetrator of an infringement of competition law' and covers 'any entity consisting of personal, tangible and intangible elements which is engaged in an economic activity, irrespective of its legal status and the way in which it is financed'.[43] Based on a functional interpretation, formal separation is not decisive, whereas the deciding factor is the existence of unity of conduct on the market. This is relevant to avoid the application of article 101 and article 102 within holding structures and to ensure that the holding company can be held liable for the anti-competitive conduct of a subsidiary.[44] The approach of the Advocate-General in the *Irado* case is rather convincing as it leads to consistency across EU law concepts by aligning the concept of economic operator and undertaking,[45] but mostly also avoids circumvention of the rules by establishing separate entities to ensure that they can operate outside their scope. Accordingly, it would be useful to include this in the reform of Article 12 Directive 2014/24/EU.

Similarly, the question of what type of turnover also arises in light of the non-institutionalised exemption. The 80–20 percentage rule again leads to questions about what the 100% constitutes. As noted elsewhere,[46] the question arises of whether it relates to the individual activities of each contracting authority involved in the cooperation, to the aggregate volume of their joint activities or if it must be measured against the totality of all activities conducted by the participating authorities, including those carried out on the open market. The third interpretation appears particularly burdensome, if not

---

41 Ibid., para 58.

42 Ibid., para 68.

43 Case C-41/90 *Höfner* EU:C:1991:161, [1991] ECR I-01979; Case C-152/19 *Deutsche Telekom v. Commission* [2021] EU:C:2021:238, para 72.

44 Okeoghene Odudu and David Bailey, 'The Single Economic Entity Doctrine in EU Competition Law' (2014) 51 *Common Market Law Review* 1721; Vassilis Hatzopoulos, 'The Economic Constitution of the EU Treaty and the Limits between Economic and Non-Economic Activities' (2012) 23 *European Business Law Review* 973.

45 Berend Jan Drijber and Hélène Stergiou, 'Public Procurement Law and Internal Market Law' (2009) 46 *Common Market Law Review* 805.

46 Willem Janssen, 'Commentary on Article 12(4–5) Directive 2014/24/EU' in Roberto Caranta and Albert Sanchez-Graells (eds.), *EU Public Procurement* (Edward Elgar 2021).

unworkable in practice, given the inherently unstable and fluctuating nature of third-party market activity. The more persuasive reading is that the 20% threshold relates to the cumulative volume of activities arising from the cooperation itself, from which up to 20% may be conducted on the open market. This interpretation is reinforced by the Directive's explicit reference to activities 'concerned by the cooperation' and its use of the plural form 'contracting authorities', indicating a collective rather than individual assessment. In addition, it would appear contrary to the structure of the provision for contracting authorities to manipulate financial figures – either by artificially inflating the costs attributed to the 80% internal turnover or by suppressing those activities linked to the 20% external turnover – in an attempt to expand the permissible scope of market activities. In the next reform of Article 12(5), it is pertinent that this clarification is included in the workings of this provision.

7. PUBLISH THE USE OF ARTICLE 12 DIRECTIVE 2014/24/EU TO INCREASE ENFORCEMENT

Overseeing the noted recommendations, we close with putting the enforcement deficit of Article 12 Directive 2014/24/EU on the agenda. At this point in time, there is no obligation to publish the use of the institutionalised and non-institutionalised exemptions. How does an economic operator know if the 80–20 rule is met? How does that operator know if illegal private capital is involved or if there is in fact sufficient control? The answer is that these operators do not know in many cases. As a consequence, it means that it is likely that many cooperations that do not meet the requirements of Article 12 remain unchallenged. An exemption to this standpoint is when an operator has been contracted out initially, and subsequently a public–public cooperation is preferred meaning that the next contract is not put up for tender. The de-throned operator can of course challenge such decisions before the courts, but this is the exemption given that other operators would be unaware of such a decision. It is argued here that including an obligation for contracting authorities to publish their reliance on these exemptions should be considered in the next reform because it would aid enforcement and compliance without overburdening contracting authorities.[47] In fact, it is a personification of transparency in light of good governance.

[47] For a brief first introduction to this proposal, see Janssen (n 2) 7. This proposal is further fleshed out in Willem A. Janssen, 'Make-or-Buy Decisions and EU Public Procurement Law: A Stronger Role for Transparency?' (forthcoming 2026) *Public Procurement Law Review*.

PART II

Improving and fostering competition

5. Cooperation between economic operators in tendering

Kirsi-Maria Magga and Kris Wauters

REFORM PROPOSALS

- Streamlining the rules on horizontal and vertical cooperation and applying the same rules to all forms of cooperation.
- Separating the rules applicable during the award stage and contractual stage.
- Introducing exemptions or limitations on joint bidding on the basis of strategic goals such as sustainability, security, or a European preference.
- Addressing competition law related requirements of necessity and efficiency also within the Public Procurement Directives and clarifying the interlinkage of competition and public procurement law.

1. INTRODUCTION

The level of competition within public procurement procedures has caused concern over the years, and recently the Special Report by the European Court of Auditors[1] raised the issue of competition both at the level of competitive procedures – fewer bids for contract awards, as well as the increased amount of non-competitive procedures – and more direct awards as one of the major challenges the public procurement regime is facing. This issue is likely also to be addressed during the ongoing public procurement reform. While contracting authorities may set conditions and requirements that limit the pool of potential bidders, the rules aim to enable companies of all sizes and resources to participate by allowing cooperation with other companies through different methods. This chapter discusses the legal framework that surrounds cooperation between economic operators when they wish to participate in the tender procedure of a public contract.

1 https://www.eca.europa.eu/en/publications?ref=sr-2023–28.

First, the chapter briefly reviews the reasons why such cooperation is pertinent and analyzes the legal framework governing the aforementioned cooperation (Section 2). Thereafter, it views the cooperation from the perspective of competition (Section 3) and makes a number of proposals for the forthcoming public procurement directive (Section 4).

2. THE LEGISLATIVE FRAMEWORK FOR COOPERATION AND THE POTENTIAL FLAWS

2.1 Why Cooperation?

2.1.1 Reasons for economic operators to engage in cooperation

There can be several reasons why economic operators cooperate. Often it is a consequence of the design of procurement documents and the requirements set thereto. The subject of the contract may be too complex for one economic operator to perform alone – meaning that the contract requires different areas of expertise or higher standards or resources than one economic operator can provide solo.[2] A concrete example of this is public–private partnerships for the realization of infrastructure works, where the future contractor usually has to design and build the infrastructure and either finance or maintain or manage the infrastructure. On the other hand, there are also other economic explanations for the presence of such cooperation, namely reducing operating costs for the economic operators.

The cooperation can also be necessary and not just practical in order to participate in a tender procedure. All bids must meet the criteria set out in procurement documents, and should a single economic operator not meet the criteria, cooperation is necessary in order to submit a bid. This kind of cooperation also has been addressed and approved in CJEU case law, where the Court has held that an economic operator has a right to use resources belonging to one or more other entities, in addition to its own resources, in order to carry out a contract.[3] A prohibition thereto could be considered an obstacle to the opening-up of public contracts to competition.[4] Cooperation can, thus,

---

[2] See also S. Arrowsmith, *The Law of Public and Utilities Procurement*, Vol. I, London, Sweet and Maxwell, 2014, p. 1321.

[3] C-94/12, *Swm Costruzioni 2* and *Mannocchi Luigino*, ECLI:EU:C:2013:64, para 32.

[4] Compare C-94/12, *Swm Costruzioni 2* and *Mannocchi Luigino*, ECLI:EU:C:2013:64, para 34.

have a pro-competitive effect if it increases competition for a particular public contract.[5]

2.1.2 Reasons for allowing cooperation

Originally, the EU procurement directives had two objectives: the free movement of services and free competition in this sector. Economic operators should be able to move and supply services without any restriction.[6] One of these objectives also has been recalled by the CJEU in two recent public procurement cases: 'that the principal objective of the EU rules on public procurement is the opening-up of public procurement to undistorted competition in all the Member States'.[7] Cooperation between economic operators that bid for public contracts should be viewed from this background.

There are several reasons that justify the presence of cooperation. These reasons are well reflected by the CJEU in CoNISMa where the Court stated that: '[o]ne of the primary objectives of Community rules on public procurement is to attain the widest possible opening-up to competition [...] and that it is the concern of Community law to ensure the widest possible participation by tenderers in a call for tenders [...] It should be added that the widest possible opening-up to competition is contemplated not only from the point of view of the Community interest in the free movement of goods and services but also the interest of the contracting authority concerned itself, which will thus have greater choice as to the most advantageous tender which is most suitable for the needs of the public authority in question.'[8]

All of this is an expression of a neutrality idea, whereby European Union law does not distinguish between (legal) persons and their capacities in order to gain access to a market in another Member State. The implication of the aforementioned objectives is that a public authority has an interest in ensuring that as many economic operators as possible compete in as many ways as possible in a tender procedure and that economic operators have the right to participate in it in different capacities.[9] This access criterion seems also to explain the wider acceptance of cooperation between economic operators when they

[5] A. Sanchez-Graells, *Public Procurement and the EU Competition Rules*, Hart Publishing, 2015, 339.

[6] Opinion Advocate General Leger, C-176/98, *Holst Italia SpA*, ECLI:EU:C:1999:447, para 14.

[7] C-927/19, *Klaipėdos regiono atliekų tvarkymo centras*, EU:C:2021:700, p. 115. See also C-652/22, *Kolin Inşaat Turizm Sanayi ve Ticaret*, ECLI:EU:C:2024:910 para 46.

[8] C-305/08, *CoNISMa*, ECLI:EU:C:2009:807, para 37.

[9] Opinion Advocate General Leger, C-176/98, *Holst Italia SpA*, ECLI:EU:C:1999:447, para 28.

want to participate in a public procurement procedure. This is reflected also in C-389/92, *Ballast Nedam Groep*, on the possibility for companies to cooperate in order to gain access to the award procedure of a public contract.[10] Moreover, the presence of the possibility of cooperation promotes the access of small and medium-sized enterprises (SMEs) to a public contract, which is confirmed in recital 124 of the 2014/24 Directive. The idea of cooperation as a way to promote SME access is also further supported by CJEU case law.[11]

2.1.3 Forms of cooperation

An economic operator can participate in a tender process in various forms. In doing so, the operator may have recourse to a third party's resources. This relationship to that third party can take mainly two forms. In a vertical relationship, the entity called upon by the tenderer has no direct contractual link with the contracting authority, whereas this is the case in a horizontal relationship. It has been submitted in legal literature that the 'reliance on the capacities of other entities' constitutes a third category of 'collaboration',[12] but in our view, it is rather one demonstration of a vertical relationship and is thus comparable to subcontracting. The concepts of 'vertical' and 'horizontal' cooperation are rarely found in academic work related to public procurement law. One does, however, find the concepts of 'consortium' or 'subcontracting'.[13] In our view, the first term then refers to a horizontal cooperation, while the second term refers to a vertical cooperation.

From a perspective regulating the cooperation between economic operators, another distinction should also be made between, on the one hand, the period prior to the conclusion of the contract and, on the other hand, the period after the conclusion of the contract. Regarding the first period, it follows from the case law of the Court of Justice that there does not necessarily have to be a specific contract yet: 'that the tenderer is free to choose, on the other hand, the legal nature of the links it intends to establish with the other entities on whose

---

10 C-389/92, *Ballast Nedam Groep v Belgische Staat*, ECLI:EU:C:1994:133, p. 6. See also Opinion Advocate General Leger, C-176/98, *Holst Italia SpA*, ECLI:EU:C:1999:447, para 44.

11 C-94/12, *Swm Costruzioni 2 SpA and Mannocchi Luigino DI v Provincia di Fermo*, EU:C:2013:646, para 34; C324/14, *Partner Apelski Dariusz v Zarząd Oczyszczania Miasta*, EU:C:2016:214, para 34.

12 See K. Søs Jacobsen Cesko, *Collaboration Between Economic Operators in the Competition for Public Contracts: A Legal and Economic Analysis of Grey Zones between EU Public Procurement Law and EU Competition Law*, PhD thesis, Copenhagen Business School, 2022, https://research.cbs.dk/files/75603513/kathrine_s_s_jacobsen_cesko_phd_series_27_2022.pdf, pp. 31–33.

13 See, for example, Arrowsmith 2014, p. 1196, 1321 et seq.

capacities it relies in order to perform a particular contract'.[14] In that sense, the qualification of the relationship between the members, which are part of the cooperation, is not yet relevant at the tendering stage. In the event that the tenderer calls on a third party to satisfy some selection criterion, it is sufficient that 'the candidate or tenderer relying on the capacities of one or more other entities proves to that authority that it will actually have at its disposal the resources of those entities necessary for the execution of the contract'.[15] After the conclusion of the contract, the tenderer will choose a specific form of cooperation according to its national law.

2.2 Possibility to Cooperate

The applicable public procurement directives themselves provide in several provisions, in particular Articles 19(2), 63, and 71, the possibility for a tenderer to cooperate with other economic operators. Under these provisions, the CJEU has confirmed this as a general rule. In the *Ballast Nedam* cases, the CJEU made it clear that an economic operator can cooperate with or call upon other economic operators in order to participate in a tender procedure and to submit a tender.[16] In *Holst Italia*, the Court mentioned the possibility of subcontracting part of the contract to third parties and of the submission of tenders by groups of service providers without their being required to assume a specific legal form in order to do so.[17] Furthermore, it follows from the CJEU's case law that cooperation with a third party can take any legal form at the tender stage[18] and that the group of economic operators refers both to temporary and permanent associations.[19] Even when an economic operator relies on a third party to meet certain selection criteria, it may do so through many forms: 'a company relies on the resources of entities or undertakings with which it is directly or indirectly linked, whatever the legal nature of those links may be.'[20]

---

14 C-234/14, *Ostas celtnieks*, ECLI:EU:C:2016:6, para 28.

15 C-94/12, *Swm Costruzioni 2 and Mannocchi Luigino*, ECLI:EU:C:2013:64, para 33.

16 C-389/92, *Ballast Nedam Groep v Belgische Staat*, ECLI:EU:C:1994:133; C-5/97, *Ballast Nedam Groep v Belgische Staat*, ECLI:EU:C:1997:636.

17 C-176/98, *Holst Italia SpA*, ECLI:EU:C:1999:593, para 23–24.

18 C-357/06, *Frigerio Luigi & C.*, ECLI:EU:C:2007:818, para 25.

19 C-631/21, *Taxi Horn Tours BV*, ECLI:EU:C:2022:869, para 47.

20 C-234/14, *Ostas celtnieks*, ECLI:EU:C:2016:6, para 25.

2.3 Access Conditions

The internal market law in principle prohibits contracting authorities from restricting economic operators' access to a tender procedure, which means that an economic operator can participate in such procedure in any form that it chooses. It follows from the case law of the CJEU that any condition that a contracting authority attaches to the possibility for an economic operator to cooperate constitutes a restriction on free movement and, as such, is, in principle, prohibited.[21] In accordance with the case law of the Court, a prohibition on restrictions on freedom of movement is not absolute: 'such a restriction may be justified in so far as it pursues a legitimate objective in the public interest, and to the extent that it complies with the principle of proportionality in that it is suitable for securing the attainment of that objective and does not go beyond what is necessary in order to attain.'[22]

The possibility for a contracting authority to restrict vertical cooperation is also included in Directive 2014/24/EU. Article 63(2) allows contracting authorities to require that certain critical tasks are performed by the main contractor(s), but the European legislator did not further define the concept of critical tasks.

In earlier case law, the CJEU used the notion of 'exceptional circumstances' to justify a restriction to the possibility of cooperation and defined the concept of 'exceptional circumstances': 'the provisions of Directive 2004/18 do not preclude the exercise of the right[23] established in Articles 47(2) and 48(3) thereof from being limited in exceptional circumstances [...] It is conceivable that there may be works with special requirements necessitating a certain capacity which cannot be obtained by combining the capacities of more than one operator, which, individually, would be inadequate'.[24] Like any exception, it must be interpreted and applied restrictively.

2.4 Differences and the Principle of Equality

For an economic operator who wants to participate in a public procurement procedure, the choice for either horizontal or vertical cooperation is not limited by law. In this sense, both forms of cooperation are on an equal footing viewed from the neutrality principle. Thus, one would also expect both forms of cooperation to be subject to the same legal rules. However, when analyzing

---

21 Compare C-298/15, *Borta*, ECLI:EU:C:2017:266, para 49–50.

22 Ibid., para 51.

23 The right to rely on a third person.

24 C-324/14, *Partner Apelski Dariusz v Zarząd Oczyszczania Miasta*, EU:C:2016:214, para 39–40.

the case law and applicable legislation on the award of public contracts, one nevertheless discovers some legal distinctions between these two types of cooperation.

According to Article 57(4)(d), contracting authorities may exclude or may be required by Member States to exclude from participation in a public procurement procedure any economic operator where the contracting authority has sufficiently plausible indications to conclude that the economic operator has entered into agreements with other economic operators aimed at distorting competition. In legal literature, it has been submitted that this applies also to consortium bidding, but not to subcontracting.[25] We submit, however, that the same principles should apply to both horizontal and vertical cooperation and thus subcontracting can also be considered as an 'agreement' within the meaning of Article 57(4)(d).

In a two-stage tender procedure, a bid may only be submitted by an economic operator selected as tenderer in the first stage. The economic operator submitting the bid shall, in principle, be the same person as the one that has been pre-selected.[26] However, the CJEU held in *MT Højgaard and Züblin* that if a pre-selected consortium is dissolved, the remaining consortium may continue with the procedure. This substitution may take place without infringing the principle of equality, provided that it is established that the remaining consortium or its single member alone satisfies the requirements initially defined by the contracting authority and that its continued participation in the procedure does not lead to a deterioration in the competitive situation of the other tenderers. Hence a contracting authority cannot exclude the consortium from the contract award procedure.[27] Although there are no rules regarding vertical cooperation on this aspect, we submit that the same rule should apply to vertical cooperation in a corresponding manner.[28]

The same rules, however, do not apply to replacing an economic operator after bids are submitted. A change in the composition of a consortium after bids are submitted can be considered a significant change requiring a new award procedure and necessitates an amendment of the award decision, which may be regarded as substantial if, in the light of the particular features of the award procedure in question, it alters one of the essential elements that

---

25 P. Friton and J. Zöll, 'Article 57 – Exclusion Grounds' in R. Caranta and A. Sanchez-Graells (eds), *European Public Procurement*, Cheltenham, Edward Elgar Publishing, 2021, p. 614, no. 57.85. Ibid., pp. 614–615, no. 57.87.

26 Case C-697/17, *Telecom Italia*, pts. 27 and 29.

27 Ibid., pt. 35; C-396/14, *MT Højgaard and Züblin*, EU:C:2016:347, para 48 and C-403/23 and C-404/23, *Luxone*, ECLI:EU:C:2024:805, para 67.

28 Compare Jacobsen Cesko 2022, 212.

were decisive in the award decision.[29] This also applies to vertical cooperation in the event where the participation of a subcontractor or a 'capacity entity' is necessary to meet the requirements of the procurement in question or has been evaluated as a part of the tender evaluation.[30] Thus, the approach adopted for horizontal cooperation appears to apply also to vertical cooperation if the cooperation was necessary for meeting the requirements or being the best bid in the tender evaluation.[31]

Although it is submitted that the same rules should apply to both horizontal and vertical cooperation, there is a limitation relating to the issue of liability, mainly due to reasons of national contract law and differences in the contractual link. Under horizontal cooperation, all members of a consortium are contracting parties to the contracting authority. In vertical cooperation, only the main contractor is a contracting party and subcontractors are linked to the contracting authority through their contract with the main contractor. The question then arises whether, with regard to this public interest, it would not be logical for the contracting authority also to be able to take contractual action directly against the aforementioned third party. Conversely, Article 71(2) allows Member States to provide a system whereby a contracting authority can directly pay a subcontractor. A question possibly arises regarding liability of whether the contractual relationship is pertinent as a criterion to distinguish between a horizontal or vertical cooperation. Could one not reach a different solution if one tries to answer the question from the objective of serving the public interest?

3. COMPETITION LIMITATIONS OF COOPERATION

3.1 Competition Law Limiting the Cooperation

Directive 2014/24/EU addresses competition concerns throughout different articles. In these provisions, the perspective is mostly to prevent distortions of competition by the design of award procedures by contracting authorities. Competition concerns, however, also relate to the collaboration between

---

29 See C-161/13, *Idrodinamica Spurgo Velox and Others*, para 39.

30 See C-91/08, *Wall*, EU:C:2010:182, para 39. In C-223/16, *Casertana Costruzioni*, the Court stated between the lines that the form of cooperation is not relevant, but rather it is important whether the bidder has lost the ability to meet the requirements set in the contract award. If that is the case, allowing a replacement would amount to a substantial change of the tender, see paras 29–30, 38–42. The Court refers to the articles governing reliance on the capacity of other entities in particular when analyzing the matter (see 29–30 and 42).

31 Compare Jacobsen Cesko 2022, 212.

economic operators participating or potentially participating in public contract awards. Public procurement law has adopted an approach where it does not set any limitation for the organization of tenderers and in fact considers that requiring a certain operational form or relationship is harmful to competition, equal treatment, and SMEs' access to public contracts.

Competition law applies to all horizontal and vertical cooperation between economic operators and thus procurement is not immune to it either, regardless of the approach adopted in public procurement law. Article 101 of the Treaty on the Functioning of the European Union (TFEU) prohibits agreements and collaboration between independent market operators, which restrict competition. This agreement or collaboration can be of any form or nature. Hence collaboration between undertakings within a public procurement procedure is prohibited provided that these are independent (not belonging to the same business group)[32] and the cooperation has a negative competition effect, for example by decreasing the competition (amount of independent bids) in a particular public contract award.[33]

From a competition law perspective, cooperation within a contract award procedure can in some cases be permissible. This includes cooperation that has a *de minimis* effect on competition or that meets the requirements under Article 101(3) of the TFEU.[34] This would require that a list of conditions is met: the undertakings can submit a more competitive bid than the one they would have been able to submit individually, it benefits consumers, the collaboration does not go further than necessary to achieve that objective, and the undertakings do not get the possibility of eliminating competition for the concerned contract.[35] Collaboration can be considered efficient if it increases the competition for a particular public contract. If an undertaking could not bid independently or be accepted as a bidder due to the capacity requirements

---

32 Under EU Competition Rules, companies belonging to the same business group are not considered as separate undertakings, see e.g. C-73/95 P, *Viho*, where the ECJ states that 'Parker and its subsidiaries thus form a single economic unit within which the subsidiaries do not enjoy real autonomy in determining their course of action in the market, but carry out the instructions issued to them by the parent company controlling them' (para 16).

33 A. Sanchez-Graells, *Public Procurement and the EU Competition Rules*, 2nd ed., Hart Publishing, 2017, pp. 338–339.

34 See further Communication from the Commission, Guidelines on the applicability of Article 101 of the Treaty on the Functioning of the European Union to horizontal cooperation agreements [2011] OJ C11/1.

35 See Danish Competition Authority, *Joint Bidding under Competition Law*, Guidelines, 2018, available at https://en.kfst.dk/media/50765/050718_joint-bidding-guidelines.pdf (visited 15 Jan 2025), p. 29.

or the extent of the contract in question, collaboration increases and intensifies competition.[36] However, the interpretation is left to Member States on a case-by-case basis, and it varies across Member States what is considered to be a necessity for joint bidding (temporary lack of resources) all the way to the inability to submit a solo bid even if expanding resources beyond the original resources of the undertaking in question (permanent necessity).[37]

During the recent year, discussion on the relationship between sustainability and competition has intensified. New commission guidelines on horizontal cooperation agreements create new permissible forms of cooperation where the purpose of cooperation is to promote sustainability objectives.[38] In some cases – and in particular where the design of public procurement sets high sustainability requirements or objectives – this new exemption could provide a justified reason for cooperation.

3.2 Public Procurement Law Allowing the Cooperation

In Directive 2014/24/EU, the actual competition restrictions through collaboration are not explicitly mentioned elsewhere than in Article 57(4)(d) on non-mandatory exclusion grounds relating to contracts with anticompetitive effect. But a reference to competition restriction through collaboration can be read between the lines of Article 63 (reliance on others' capacities), which entails a notion of 'when appropriate and for a particular contract' and thus sets a limitation to collaboration. For some reason, similar limitations are not mentioned in the rules applicable to subcontracting (Article 71) or consortium bidding (Article 19 (2) and (3)). From the perspective of competition restrictions, the

36 OECD 2007, *Public Procurement: The Role of Competition Authorities in Promoting Competition*, DAF/COMP(2007)34, available at: https://www.oecd.org/en/publications/public-procurement-the-role-of-competition-authorities-in-promoting-competition_8ed0c7ba-en.html, p. 34 and Sanchez-Graells 2017, pp. 338–339.

37 See cases from Däckia and Euromaster, consortia tender on car tires (Stockholm tingsrätt, Sweden, T-18896–10); Dansk Vejmarkerings Konsortium, road works consortia (Competition Appeals Tribunal, Denmark, 11.4.2016); Samarbejdsaftale mellem Ove Juel Catering A/S og T.H. Schultz A/S (Decision of the Competition Council of 26 November 2003, Denmark); Ski Taxi and Follo Taxi, transport service consortia (Høyesterett HR-2017-1229-A, Norway). Cr. recent Italian Competition Authority, case 10 Dec 2018, Baxter Manufacturing S.p.A. e Baxalta Italy S.r.l and Danish Competition Authority, Joint bidding under competition law, Guidelines 2018, p. 11.

38 Communication from the Commission, Guidelines on the applicability of Article 101 of the Treaty on the Functioning of the European Union to horizontal cooperation agreements (2023/C 259/01), part 9.

technical form of collaboration between the companies is not relevant. Thus, the same approach 'when appropriate' should apply to all forms of collaboration equally, as information exchange between competitors or lowering the amount of bids in a contract award procedure due to unnecessary cooperation may follow from any type of collaboration.

From competition law's perspective, cooperation is permissible only when it is efficient and/or necessary (not possible to fulfill the qualifications and submit a bid without collaboration). Procurement rules do not refer to these limitations but leave the issue solely to be resolved through EU competition law rules and national law of Member States. However, public procurement law also recognizes certain limitations to the organizational neutrality approach. First, the Public Procurement Directive allows contracting authorities to require that a consortium shall, after being awarded a contract, organize themselves in a form of a single operational unit. Second, it has been accepted in the CJEU case law that a contracting authority sets limits on the use of subcontracting or reliance on others' capacities for critical parts of the contracts when proportionate, but the analysis of the possibility needs to be done case-by-case.[39] A general prohibition or limitation on using subcontracting is not in accordance with the public procurement rules.[40]

As mentioned prior, competition rules do not apply to companies belonging to the same business group. Thus, competition rules do not set any limitations for simultaneous entry and bidding for such companies. Public procurement rules differ in this regard as they view the situation within a particular contract award. Multiple bids from the same undertaking or bids from companies belonging to the same business group are not independent. In the cases of *Specializuotas transportas* and *Lloyd's of London*, the Court submitted that all bids need to be autonomous and independent from each other, and if this is not the case, they should be excluded.[41]

---

[39] See case C-94/12, *Swm Costruzioni* (para 35).

[40] See case C-63/18, *Vitali SpA*, ECLI:EU:C:2019:787 where the Court considered a limitation of 30 percent for subcontracting set by the national law not to be in accordance with the Procurement Directive (paras 40–42).

[41] See cases C-531/16, *Specializuotas transportas*, EU:C:2018:324 and C-144/17 *Lloyd's of London*, EU:C:2018:78. This is shortly addressed also in European Commission, Notice on tools to fight collusion in public procurement and on guidance on how to apply the related exclusion ground (2021/C 91/01), p 17. In Belgium, the Council of State accepts that a company may, in interlocutory proceedings, challenge the legality of an award decision on the grounds that two affiliated companies have submitted a tender that may constitute collusion: Council of State 29 July 2019, nr. 245.246, Dutry Power; Council of State 11 September 2023, nr. 257.273, Cerbul.

Sustainability objectives are likely one of the most researched and discussed topics within public procurement law at the moment. Nonetheless, and unlike in the competition law context, sustainability aspects have not, at least not yet, created any particular exemptions from the obligations set by the procurement rules.

4. POTENTIAL REFORM PROPOSALS AND TOPICS OF DISCUSSION

4.1 Structural Proposals

Currently, the legal rules, which deal with the (horizontal and vertical) cooperation between economic operators, are scattered among several provisions in Directive 2014/24/EU. In order to simplify the application of these rules, it is submitted that all rules governing cooperation should be gathered together. Moreover, the rules should be streamlined and obey similar logic (unless there are clear justifications for them to differ in certain cases) as from a competitive perspective, both horizontal and vertical cooperation can be equally harmful to the fairness and amount of competition. The CJEU case law guiding the change of composition of tenderers during the award stage should be incorporated within these new rules and be considered applicable to both horizontal and vertical cooperation. Similarly, these articles should also consider potential permissible limitations to cooperation, such as extending the 'critical tasks' exception also to all forms of cooperation equally.

Moreover the rules on cooperation should distinguish between the pre-contractual and contractual phases, as the situations for change of composition during the tendering stage and contract term differ. The focus in the Public Procurement Directive is on the award stage, leaving the contract execution stage to be regulated mostly under the significant contract modification rules. We submit that the Procurement Directive should have a more comprehensive section dedicated to the execution of public contracts. That section could then address, among others, the changes within the consortium or in subcontractors during the contract term. In that section, the new directive could also address the issue of the contractual liability of the members of the consortium and of the subcontractor in a harmonized manner.

4.2 Impact of Sustainability Objectives

This chapter has established that the ability of an economic operator to cooperate vertically or horizontally and any restrictions related thereto rests mainly on economic and budgetary objectives. These objectives have underpinned public procurement legislation for a very long time. The current Procurement

Directive 2014/24/EU also sets other, parallel sustainability objectives that contracting authorities and Member States are required to take into account. This is the case in particular in relation to Article 57(4) on exclusion due to violation of environmental, social, and labor law as well as Article 71(5) requiring tenderers to share information on their subcontractors in fraud-sensitive fields. Thus, it is worth considering whether sustainability objectives should also be taken into account when dealing with the vertical and horizontal cooperation of economic operators.

So far, the rules governing cooperation between economic operators have not been impacted by sustainability rules. However, the CJEU in *Tim* considered that to comply with the principle of equal treatment, a contracting authority has to verify whether there is any failure to comply with those obligations relating to environmental, social, and labor law in respect not only of all the economic operators who have submitted a tender, but also in respect of all the subcontractors indicated by those operators in their respective tenders.[42] But taking into account the likely focus on sustainability and security of supply in the upcoming procurement directive reform, it is worth opening up discussion on whether, for example, the cooperation between economic operators could be more broadly allowed in the context of procurement if the purpose of cooperation is – at least in part – related to sustainability. Could we apply similar argumentation as in competition law where there are exemptions for sustainability contracts, although here in the public procurement context the ultimate aim for joint bidding is not meeting sustainable objectives but rather is of a commercial nature? Moreover, perhaps there should be more discretion to contracting authorities to set collaboration limitations for contracts that are considered particularly important or vulnerable from security or resilience perspectives, that is, following the line of argumentation presented by the CJEU in *Swm Costruzioni* concerning 'critical works'.

4.3 Reliance on a Third Person

As discussed earlier, the possibility of cooperation between economic operators within European procurement law relies mainly on the principles of free movement and effective competition, which connects to ideas of free trade and lack of protectionism also outside EU borders. The internal market benefits from allowing as many economic operators as possible to participate in a public procurement award procedure. In addition, this is also in the interest of the contracting authority. The internal market principle naturally applies especially to economic operators who have their registered office in the European

42 See case C-395/18, *Tim*, ECLI:EU:C:2020:58, 46.

Union. However, from the perspective of competition and the contracting authorities, there are also benefits if the award procedure also attracts companies that are not based in the European Union. The access to the EU market for companies outside the EU is based on Article 25, which requires similar treatment for companies from Agreement on Government Procurement (GPA) countries. Nonetheless, the practice has also been such that many contracting authorities also allow access to third-country bidders outside GPA.

Recently, in *Kolin*, the Court of Justice decided that these third-country bidders (outside GPA) do not enjoy the same rights as EU and GPA tenderers. According to the Court, they cannot rely on the procurement directive to ensure their tender is treated equally to those submitted by tenderers from Member States and by the tenderers from third countries referred to in Article 43 (GPA).[43] This statement can be framed within a paradigm shift that takes place within the European Union regarding its industrial policy: a model of open strategic autonomy where access and rights are based on mutually beneficial bilateral relations in order to protect us from future crises.[44]

It appears that this new industrial policy combined with the *Kolin* decision justifies that the next directives could limit the participation and cooperation between economic operators in the event where the collaborator or the capacities relied upon are an economic operator from a third country which has not concluded an international agreement with the European Union.

4.4 Relationship Between Competition Law and Procurement Rules

Interlinkages between competition and public procurement law regarding cooperation between economic operators have not been addressed in the 2014 Directives. Certain issues relating to collusion and joint and parallel bidding have been discussed by the European Commission in the 2021 notice and by local competition monitoring authorities' soft law. This is causing ambiguity from the perspective of contracting authorities and economic operators alike on the actual limits of permissible cooperation. Allowing, and at times even encouraging, cooperation through public procurement rules is creating risks for competition law infringements. Thus, it is submitted that the competition law related requirements of necessity and efficiency should also be addressed

43 C-652/22, *Kolin Inşaat Turizm Sanayi ve Ticaret*, ECLI:EU:C:2024:910, pt. 45.

44 Europe's moment: Repair and Prepare for the Next Generation, COM(2020) 456 final, 5.1.,https://eur-lex.europa.eu/legal-content/EN/TXT/HTML/?uri=CELEX:52020DC0456. European Commission, 'A Renewed Trade Policy for a Stronger Europe. Consultation Note' 16 June 2020, 8, www.astrid-online.it/static/upload/comm/0000/commue_trade-policy-review_consultation-note.pdf.

within the procurement directives in the rules governing cooperation – not necessarily at the level of legal provisions, but at least in recitals concerning the rules on cooperation. Moreover, addressing these linkages between competition and procurement law likely will result in an increase in the need to seek and receive advice from national competition authorities regarding the detection and resolution of potentially illicit cooperation between economic operators.

5. CONCLUSION

Cooperation in general is important in order to achieve public interest objectives and to maximize competition within a public contract award procedure. From the perspective of these objectives, EU procurement directives should promote cooperation as much as possible all while creating a link to the limitations set out by competition law. The rules governing cooperation between economic operators are ambiguous in their current form, and these should be clarified within the next reform both in terms of concentrating and systemizing different forms of cooperation as well as creating interlinkages between public procurement and competition law. The procurement directive reform also provides an avenue for setting some limitations for cooperation for strategic purposes, such as security, sustainability, security of supply, or European preference.

6. Strengthening exclusion grounds in EU public procurement for greater fairness and transparency

Dacian C. Dragos

REFORM PROPOSALS

The chapter conducts a critical analysis of the current exclusion mechanisms, identifying the case law that could be codified as well as gaps and limitations that undermine the efficacy of exclusion grounds. Also, several reform proposals are advanced to address these challenges:

- A first proposal arises from the mandatory-discretionary grounds dichotomy. Discretionary grounds are not really discretionary, as accepting a bidder that can be excluded on the basis of a discretionary ground while excluding others on other discretionary grounds might be considered a breach of equal treatment. In that context, maybe uniformizing the categories and having only mandatory exclusion grounds would be beneficial for the "sanity" of the process. The question here is also whether there should be a limit on the exclusion grounds at the EU member states level. The same proposal is relevant when considering the exclusion grounds provided by EU sectoral legislation (deforestation directive, and others, referred to briefly following).
- A central list of approved economic operators or of exclusion grounds would ease the workload of contracting authorities and would contribute to transparency and to the effectiveness of the exclusion grounds system.
- The self-cleaning mechanism should be limited to minor offenses and should not be applicable to the whole spectrum of exclusion grounds, as it kind of defeats the purpose of such grounds—ensuring the reliability of tenderers. A self-cleaning mechanism complicates the life of contracting authorities and increases the risk of litigation in the awarding phase.

1. INTRODUCTION

Beyond the economic justification, a predictable regulation of the public procurement system at the European level is crucial for achieving the free movement of goods and services, the right of establishment, and the prohibition of discrimination based on nationality.[1] On the other hand, integrity and reliability are of the essence in public procurement, so the track record of tenderers should be assessed in order to determine their fitness for carrying out the contracts.

A lot of time was spent until 2014 by contracting authorities on the exclusion grounds. This has changed with the new Directives from 2014. One of the major improvements of Directives from 2014 as opposed to the previous Directives from 2004 in what impacts the exclusion grounds has been the introduction of the Electronic Single Procurement Document (ESPD),[2] a document in which tenderers must provide data on whether they fall into one of the exclusion situations referred to in Article 57 of Directive 2014/24/EU. The actual proof that no exclusion ground applies will be asked only from the winner. A failure to declare in the ESPD the incidence of exclusion grounds may represent false declarations and will entail the incidence of the exclusion ground provided for in Article 57, paragraph (4)(h) of Directive 2014/24/EU (the provision of false declarations to verify the absence of the grounds for exclusion).

Currently, Article 57 of Directive 2014/24/EU delineates the grounds for exclusion from public procurement procedures, which can be categorized mainly into mandatory/discretionary.[3] However, some member states, such as Romania and France, have transposed the Directive 2014/24/EU in such a way that all exclusion grounds are mandatory.[4] This complicates the life of contracting authorities, especially when administrative capacity is low.

---

[1] Christopher Bovis, "Public Procurement in the EU: Jurisprudence and Conceptual Directions" (2012) 49 *Common Market Law Review*, Issue 1, pp. 247–289.

[2] Article 59 of Directive 2014/24/EU.

[3] Pascal Friton and Janis Zoll, "Article 57 Exclusion Grounds" in Roberto Caranta and Albert Sanchez-Graells (eds), *European Public Procurement, Commentary on Directive 2024/24/EU* (Edward Elgar 2021), p. 592.

[4] François Lichère, "Transposition of the Public Procurement Directive in France: Between over implementation and questionable implementation" and Dacian Dragos and Bogdana Neamtu, "Transposition of the EU Procurement Directives in Romania: Complex Issues of Implementation and Control" in Steen Treumer and Mario Comba (eds), *Modernising Public Procurement – The Approach of EU Member States, European Procurement Law Series* (Edward Elgar 2018), at pp. 93–112 and 173–201, respectively.

The exclusion significantly affects the procurement participants.[5] The contracting authority must meticulously evaluate whether its decision to exclude an operator from the public procurement procedure adheres to the criterion of proportionality. This concept, among others, stipulates that contracting authorities must refrain from implementing measures that exceed what is essential to fulfill the law's objectives. The principle is likewise pertinent to the reasons for exclusion.[6]

In the following sections, we will go through the mandatory and discretionary grounds and show the case law that could be considered for codification in the next directives and proposals for streamlining and digitalizing their application.

2. MANDATORY EXCLUSION GROUNDS

2.1 Criminal Activities

Criminal activities includes participation in a criminal organization, corruption, fraud, terrorist offences or offences linked to terrorist activities, money laundering or terrorist financing, child labour and other forms of trafficking in human beings. The purpose of legislating the ground for exclusion for final conviction is to prevent the award of public procurement contracts to operators who are not trustworthy. The principle of proportionality limits the scope of the ground for exclusion so that "offenses without any connection to the professional activities should not be sufficient for mandatory exclusion."[7] However, there is no support in the actual text of the Directive 2014/24/EU for such an interpretation, so this could be one of the issues to be clarified by the next Directives. Also, these exclusion grounds should be exhaustive, as member states have sometimes added to them through national legislation.[8] Directive 2014/24/EU provides in Article 57(3) for the possibility for member states to establish derogating rules, namely the possibility for the contracting authority not to exclude the convicted operator, in exceptional cases, for overriding reasons of general interest, such as public health or environmental protection (exemplified in recital 100).

---

5 OECD, "Use of Official Automatic Exclusion Lists in Public Procurement" *SIGMA Public Procurement Briefs*, No. 24, OECD Publishing, Paris, 2013, https://doi.org/10.1787/5js4vmn2zwls-en.

6 Jolien Grandia and Leentje Volker, *Public Procurement: Theory, Practices and Tools* (Palgrave Macmillan 2023), p. 46.

7 Pascal Friton and Janis Zoll (n 3), p. 598.

8 François Lichère (n 4), pp. 93–112.

When verifying the exclusion ground, the contracting authority is not limited to the ESPD submitted by the tenderer; it may also conduct its own investigations. For this reason, a central list at the EU level with these convictions might be a very good idea. Though it might be difficult to include all persons that pertain to a certain company, at least it can be operationalized for legal entities convicted of listed offenses.

2.2 Breach of Tax Obligations

The current Article 57, paragraph (2) of Directive 2014/24/EU, delineates two scenarios:[9] the first scenario (mandatory exclusion) is based on a definitive court ruling confirming that the bidding operator has breached its obligations concerning tax, fee, and contribution payments to the general consolidated budget. The determination by the relevant authority to disqualify a tenderer may also stem from a ruling by the state's competent authority indicating that the operator failed to meet its obligations concerning the payment of taxes, duties, and contributions to the public budget, which has become definitive due to a lack of challenge. The second scenario (in principle discretionary exclusion, but which can be made mandatory by the member states) pertains to instances where no definitive court ruling exists, yet the contracting authority can ascertain, through any means, that the bidding operator has violated these obligations. In the second scenario, the contracting authority assumes a pivotal role, functioning as a genuine investigative entity that substantiates, through appropriate means, the bidding operator's breach of obligations pertaining to tax, fee, and social security contributions. The initial reference may be the data submitted by the tenderer in the ESPD; however, the methods by which the contracting authority may acknowledge the tendering operator's non-compliance with its responsibilities are not restricted.

Although it must be used only as a source of information, it might be helpful in the upcoming directives to establish central lists (at the national or even EU level) that offer data on court decisions verifying which economic operators violated their duties with regard to tax, fee, and contribution payments to the general consolidated budget. When making decisions about a specific procurement process, a contracting authority may refer to the central list, but it cannot utilize it as a de facto automatic exclusion list. In the *La Cascina* case,[10] the CJEU opined on the failure to pay taxes or social security contributions and

[9] Pascal Friton and Janis Zoll (n 3), p. 601.

[10] Joined cases *La Cascina Soc. coop. arl* and *Zilch Srl v Ministero della Difesa and Others* (C-226/04) and *Consorzio G. f. M. v Ministero della Difesa and La Cascina Soc. coop. arl* (C-228/04), ECLI:EU:C:2006:94.

how self-cleaning can be used as redress (although by that time self-cleaning was not expressly regulated in the directives).

3. DISCRETIONARY EXCLUSION GROUNDS

Recital 101 of Directive 2014/24/EU provides the rationale for discretionary exclusions: it is imperative that contracting authorities possess a legal foundation to exclude from public procurement procedures those operators who have demonstrated unreliability in the execution of prior contracts or whose conduct during the public procurement procedure or in the pre-procedure period contravenes the principles of public procurement.[11] Member states possess the authority to mandate contracting authorities to implement optional grounds for exclusion by converting them into mandatory grounds for exclusion; however, they cannot prevent contracting authorities from applying these grounds for exclusion if they choose to do so. The principle of equal treatment applies to exclusions.[12] This approach should be continued but made simpler and more straightforward in the next directives.

Directive 2014/24/EU set nine situations as grounds for optional exclusion. Certain grounds for exclusion outlined in Article 57, paragraph (4) of the Directive 2014/24/EU pertain to the operator's behavior in prior contracts, while others relate to the conduct of the bidding operator during the current public procurement procedure. Additionally, some grounds, such as conflicts of interest or the economic operator's involvement in the public procurement procedure's preparation, are intended to prevent irregularities from arising during the award process that would result in the violation of the principles provided in Directive 2014/24/EU. Currently, it is inconsequential whether member states implemented these nine circumstances as optional or required exclusion grounds, as all states have adopted the self-cleaning mechanism, which effectively transforms any mandatory exclusion ground into an optional one.

As to the violation of applicable obligations, the obligations are those referred to in Article 18(2), pertaining to environmental, social, and labor relations. According to the CJEU in case *Tim*,[13] due to the fact that the exclusion ground is "drafted impersonally, without specifying the author of the breach of the obligations provided for in Article 18(2) of that directive" (para 35), the

[11] Directive 2014/24/EU, Recital 101.

[12] Pascal Friton and Janis Zoll (n 3), p. 607; Carina Rigsvig Hamer, "Article 57 Exclusion Grounds" in Michael Steineke and Peter Vesterdorf (eds), *EU Public Procurement – Brussels Commentary* (Nomus 2018), p. 617.

[13] C-395/18, *Tim SpA – Direzione e coordinamento Vivendi SA v Consip SpA and Ministero dell'Economia e delle Finanze*, ECLI:EU:C:2020:58.

exclusion can be applied also when the perpetrators are the subcontractors. The next directive should codify this case law taking into account how it correlates with the current Article 71 of the Directive 2014/24/EU on subcontracting.

The main issue with the third exclusion ground—grave professional misconduct—Article 57(4)(c) read in conjunction with recital 39 and 101 is that it is defined quite broadly and often leads to inconsistencies in its interpretation by different contracting authorities. The current Directive 2014/24/EU does not codify the case law of the CJEU in Forposta,[14] which has made the point that "the concept of 'professional misconduct' covers any 'unlawful conduct which has an impact on the professional credibility of the operator in question and not only breaches of the rules of professional conduct in the strict sense of the profession to which that operator belongs, which would be found by the disciplinary body provided for in that profession or by a judicial decision with the authority of *res judicata*'." The Court even went on and linked the grave misconduct to "culpable intent or negligence of a certain gravity."

In all cases, the contracting authority is sovereign in assessing the reasons for grave professional misconduct.[15] The CJEU has made clear in *Meca*[16] that member states cannot restrict such an assessment motivated by the fact that there is a legal challenge of the alleged misconduct. The new directive could add this condition, for legal certainty. Also, since the finding of such misconduct does not require a final judgment, a decision by a national competition authority establishing that an operator has infringed the competition rules may certainly constitute an indication of the existence of grave professional misconduct by that operator.[17] Finally, in *Connexxion Taxi Services BV*, the CJEU established that the contracting authorities could bind themselves through procurement documents to reject without any assessment of proportionality those tenderers who are guilty of professional misconduct.[18]

Whether the assessment of the exclusion ground is exclusively the competence of the contracting authority or not was a matter of discussion in the case law of the CJEU. In *Consorzio Nazionale Servizi*,[19] the Court stated that EU law is precluding a national provision restricting the freedom of the contracting authorities to assess a competition law infringement independently when such infringement has already been established and penalized by the national competition authority by a decision upheld by the courts. In the same vein, in

---

[14] C-465/11, *Forposta SA, ABC Direct Contact sp. z o.o.*, ECLI:EU:C:2012:801, para 27, 30

[15] C-552/18, *Indaco Service*, EU:C:2019:997.

[16] C-41/18, *MECA*, ECLI:EU:C:2019:507.

[17] C-465/11, *Forposta and ABC Direct Contact*, EU:C:2012:801, para. 28.

[18] C-171/15, *Connexxion Taxi Services BV*, ECLI:EU:C:2016:948, Conclusions.

[19] C-425/18, Consorzio Nazionale Servizi, ECLI:EU:C:2019:476, para 32.

Indaco Service, the CJEU held that willful violation of competition laws is considered serious professional misconduct, and the operator that the national competition authority has determined through a decision has violated these rules is not eligible to participate in the public procurement procedures.[20] On the other hand, the CJEU established in *Phrenos and Others v. Commission* the need to have sufficient proof in order to demonstrate grave professional misconduct committed by the tenderer.[21]

The proposed reform could refer to a more explicit and comprehensive definition of "grave professional misconduct" within the Directive, and the competence of assessment, integrating insights from CJEU jurisprudence.

Bankruptcy or insolvency provided in Article 57(4)(b) relates to the ability of an insolvent economic operator to fulfill the contract awarded after the public procurement process which must be substantiated by compelling evidence that assures the authority of the tenderer's reliability beyond any doubt. Consequently, the assumption is that this operator is incapable of fulfilling the contract. Although, apparently, the legislator chose to provide for the mandatory nature of the exclusion in the event that the tenderer is insolvent, by allowing self-cleaning it established a relative, and not an absolute, presumption of impossibility of execution. There is no case law on the situation where a company enters insolvency during the public procurement procedure or the execution of a contract already awarded. The exclusion might be reconsidered in the next directive, as most national legislation (for instance in Romanian Law no. 85/2014 on insolvency, Book VI of the French Commercial Code, in the Polish Restructuring Law of 15 May 2015, etc.) provides for the possibility of insolvent companies carrying out awarded contracts under certain conditions.

The exclusion provided in Article 57(4)(g) of the Directive 2014/24/EU—significant deficiencies in performance of prior public contracts—is based exclusively on the evaluation of the economic operator's reliability by the contracting authority commencing the public procurement procedure, a rationale upheld by the jurisprudence of the CJEU in Meca.[22] Also, in *Delta Antrepriză*,[23] the Court stated that Article 57(4)(g) of Directive 2014/24/EU must be interpreted as meaning that the subcontracting, by an economic operator, of part of the works under a prior public contract, decided upon without the contracting authority's authorization and which lead to the early termination of that contract, constitutes a significant or persistent deficiency shown in the performance of a substantive requirement under that public contract, within the

20 C-552/18, *Indaco Service*, EU:C:2019:997.

21 T-715/18, *Phrenos et al v. Commission*, EU:T:2019:370.

22 C-41/18 *Meca*, ECLI:EU:C:2019:507, paras 28, 29, 32 and 34.

23 C-267/18, *Delta Antrepriză de Construcţii şi Montaj 93 SA v Compania Naţională de Administrare an Infrastructurii Rutiere SA*, ECLI:EU:C:2019:826.

meaning of that provision; it is therefore capable of justifying that economic operator being excluded from participation in a subsequent public procurement procedure if, after conducting its own evaluation of the integrity and reliability of the economic operator concerned by the early termination of the prior public contract, the contracting authority that organizes that subsequent public procurement procedure considers that such subcontracting entails breaking the relationship of trust with the economic operator in question.

Again, a central list of companies that have been assessed with "poor performance" in previous contracts would be a useful source of information for contracting authorities. Contracting authorities could check for each public procurement procedure that they conduct whether an economic operator applying to participate is listed on the poor performance list and assess its reliability based on self-cleaning remedies. For instance, in Romania, the Public Procurement Electronic System (SEAP) provides for the obligation to publish poor performance notices, but they are not aggregated together in a list of companies but rather scattered within each individual contract where they occurred, which makes them difficult to identify even by diligent contracting authorities.

The conflict-of-interest exclusion ground has benefited from quite a number of cases from the CJEU. The Court has contributed to the understanding of the concept by stating that the conflict of interest must be real and not hypothetical and that the mere possibility of a conflict of interest cannot be sufficient for that purpose (*Vakakis kai Synergates v Commission*).[24]

The doctrine[25] has observed that the ground for exclusion provided by Article 57(4)(d) and (f)—conflict of interest and distortion of competition—only sanctions the conclusion of agreements aimed at distorting competition, although Article 101 of the TFEU prescribes that decisions and any other concerted practices which may affect trade between member states and which have as their object or effect the prevention, restriction, or distortion of competition within the common market are incompatible with the internal market and prohibited. Two opinions have surfaced: one which considers that the ground for exclusion regulated by Article 57 paragraph (4) cannot be extended to other aspects not expressly provided for by the Directive 2014/24/EU, and such violations may possibly represent grave professional misconduct,[26] and a

---

[24] T-292/15, *Vakakis kai Synergates/Commission*, ECLI:EU:T:2018:103.

[25] Albert Sanchez-Graells, *Public Procurement and the EU Competition Rules*, 2nd ed. (Hart Publishing 2015), p. 298; Sue Arrowsmith, *The Law of Public and Utilities Procurement*, vol. 1, 3rd ed. (Sweet & Maxwell 2014), paras 12–115 at p. 1268.

[26] H J Priess, *The Rules on Exclusion and Self-cleaning under the 2014 Public Procurement Directive*, in "Public Procurement Law Review" 3/2014, p. 119.

second one,[27] which argues that Article 101 of the TFEU cannot be rendered ineffective, and exclusion is possible for all categories of infringements provided for in Article 101 of the TFEU, even if Article 57(4)(d) only refers to the conclusion of agreements aimed at distorting competition. The issue was settled by the CJEU in its judgment in *Kilpailu- ja kuluttajavirasto*,[28] in favor of the full application of Article 101 of the TFEU including concerted practices.

Finally, in *Infraestruturas de Portugal*,[29] the Court held that national legislation cannot limit the possibility of excluding a tenderer when significant evidence proves distortion of competition and that the power to decide to exclude economic operators from public procurement procedures, on the grounds of a breach of competition rules, cannot be entrusted solely to the national competition authority.

The distortion of competition can also result from the prior involvement of the tenderer—the instance provided in Article 57(4)(f)—"where a distortion of competition from the prior involvement of the economic operators in the preparation of the procurement procedure, as referred to in Article 41, cannot be remedied by other, less intrusive measures." Before the contracting authority excludes a tenderer in this situation from the procedure, it must give that tenderer the opportunity to demonstrate that its involvement in the preparation of the public procurement procedure does not effectively distort competition.

The exclusion ground was examined by the CJEU, which, by its judgment in *European Dynamics Luxembourg SA and Others v EUIPO*,[30] held that a person could, even unintentionally, influence the terms of the public procurement contract in a way that would strengthen its competitive position vis-à-vis the other tenderers. However, the conclusion should come after a case-by-case analysis. This conclusion is also found in *Vakakis kai Synergates – Symvouloi gia Agrotiki Anaptixi AE Meleton*:[31] "the contracting authority must assess and verify the existence of a real risk of practices that could threaten transparency and distort competition between tenderers and must allow the tenderer who risks being excluded from the procedure the opportunity to demonstrate that, in his case, there is no real risk of such a conflict of interest."

In terms of misrepresentation, Article 57(4)(h) has been analyzed in several judgments of the CJEU. In *Flying Holding NV, Flying Group Lux SA,*

---

27 Albert Sanchez-Graells (n 25), p. 298; Sue Arrowsmith (n 25), p. 1268.

28 C-450/19, *Kilpailu- ja kuluttajavirasto*, ECLI:EU:C:2021:10.

29 C-66/22, *Infraestruturas de Portugal and Futrifer Indústrias Ferroviárias*, ECLI:EU:C:2023:1016.

30 T-556/11, *European Dynamics Luxembourg SA and Others v EUIPO*, EU:T:2016:248.

31 T-292/15, *Vakakis kai Synergates – Symvouloi gia Agrotiki Anaptixi AE Meleton*, ECLI:EU:T:2018:103, para 100, 148.

Flying Service NV v Commission,[32] *Rad Service*,[33] and *Esaprojekt sp*.z.o.o,[34] the CJEU delineated the parameters of the term "false declarations" that automatic exclusions are forbidden and that negligence is sufficient and there is no need to prove intentional misconduct. This provision does not need to be revised. As to the issue of undue influence, under Article 57(4)(i), there is no EU case law on it, and at a closer look, it might be rewritten in order to incorporate the exclusion stemming from the prior involvement of tenderers.

4. SECTORAL EXCLUSION GROUNDS

There are several sectoral legislations that provide for extra exclusion grounds. They must be coordinated with the next Public Procurement (PP) directives and operationalized through an EU-wide mechanism of enforcement and verification (by using registries of companies debarred or sanctioned based on each of these regulations). The new directives in public procurement should address the sectoral legislation, and the EU legislator should solve these overlapping provisions on that occasion.

For instance, the Foreign Subsidies Regulation,[35] meant to counteract the competitive imbalances resulting from subsidies received by companies from non-EU countries confers a reason for exclusion of economic operators from the public procurement procedure (Recital 53). The Deforestation Regulation[36] provides for an exclusion of a maximum of 12 months for non-compliance with the Regulation, while, based on the Shipments of Waste Regulation, contracting authorities may exclude for a limited period of time economic operators that violate its provisions.[37] The Ecodesign Regulation empowers member

---

[32] Joined causes T-91/12 and T-280/12, *Flying Holding NV, Flying Group Lux SA, Flying Service NV/Commission*, ECLI:EU:T:2014:832, para 75.

[33] C-210/20, *Rad Service and others*, ECLI:EU:C:2021:445, Conclusions.

[34] C-387/14, *Esaprojekt sp.z.o.o,* ECLI:EU:C:2017:338, recitals 71 and 72.

[35] Regulation (EU) 2022/2560 of the European Parliament and of the Council of 14 December 2022 on foreign subsidies distorting the internal market, OJ L 330, 23.12.2022.

[36] Regulation (EU) 2023/1115 of 31 May 2023 on the making available on the Union market and the export from the Union of certain commodities and products associated with deforestation and forest degradation and repealing Regulation (EU) No 995/2010 [2023] OJ L 150/206.

[37] Regulation (EU) 2024/1157 of the European Parliament and of the Council of 11 April 2024 on shipments of waste, amending Regulations (EU) No 1257/2013 and (EU) 2020/1056 and repealing Regulation (EC) No 1013/2006.

states to establish penalties that should include fines and time-limited exclusion from public procurement procedures.[38]

5. OVERARCHING REFORM PROPOSALS

A first proposal arises from the mandatory-discretionary grounds dichotomy. Discretionary grounds are not truly discretionary because it may be deemed a violation of equitable treatment to accept a bidder who may be rejected on that basis while rejecting others on other discretionary grounds. In that context, maybe uniformizing the categories and having only mandatory exclusion grounds would be beneficial for the "sanity" of the process. Another proposal stems from the fact that some member states have profited from the fact that there is no limit to the number of exclusion grounds and added multiple other exclusion grounds.[39] The question here is whether there should be a limit on the exclusion grounds at the EU level. The same proposal is relevant when considering the exclusion grounds provided by EU sectoral legislation (the deforestation regulation and others, discussed briefly here). Also, there is a need to establish clear time limits for how long exclusion grounds (such as previous contract deficiencies or criminal convictions) can be used against economic operators, ensuring a balance between deterrence and fairness.

5.1 A Central List of Approved Economic Operators

Directive 2014/24/EU allows member states to create official lists of approved economic operators that have provided satisfactory evidence of their capability to fulfill public sector contracts. The SIGMA Procurement Brief 24[40] shows that an official list system enables economic operators to apply for registration at any time by providing evidence to the relevant public authority overseeing the list. Economic operators must submit evidence as required by the Directive

[38] Regulation (EU) 2024/1781 of the European Parliament and of the Council of 13 June 2024 establishing a framework for the setting of ecodesign requirements for sustainable products, amending Directive (EU) 2020/1828 and Regulation (EU) 2023/1542 and repealing Directive 2009/125/EC, at Recital 114 and art. 74.

[39] For instance, in France, respectively article L2141-7–2 of the Code de la commande publique introduced by Act no. 2023–973 of 23 October 2023 (art. 29) and article L2141-7–1 of the Code de la commande publique introduced by the Act no. 2021–1104 22 August 2021 (art. 35).

[40] SIGMA, Brief 24 Public Procurement. Use of Official Automatic Exclusion Lists in Public Procurement, 2016, available at https://www.sigmaweb.org/en/publications/use-of-official-automatic-exclusion-lists-in-public-procurement_9018a003-en.html last accessed 28.05.2025.

2014/24/EU and the implementation legislation of the member state to demonstrate their suitability for selection. This evidence may relate to the criteria for mandatory or discretionary exclusion, as well as economic and financial standing and technical and professional capability. An economic operator registered on an official list may submit a certificate of registration, issued by the competent authority managing the official list, to the contracting authority during a specific public procurement procedure. The contracting authority may utilize that certificate as proof of suitability concerning the specified grounds. Registration on the official lists of other member states is required to be accepted. According to current EU procurement law principles, contracting authorities cannot require registration on an official list of approved economic operators as a condition for participation in the tender process or contract award. They must also accept other equivalent means of demonstrating suitability for participation in public procurement procedures.

Another option would be to restrict the prior-discussed list only to exclusion grounds. Telles[41] has put forward the proposal to "move the compliance and enforcement outside the procurement process altogether." In that scenario, each member state should conduct those checks centrally as they frequently possess the requisite information to proceed with the verification. Frequently, economic operators must gather statements from various public entities and thereafter submit them to the contractual body, so this will be done centrally. The exception will remain the economic operators from third countries, which may necessitate a classical approach. All conflicts, complaints, and timelines associated with exclusions would be removed from the jurisdiction of the individual procurement officer and managed centrally. Economic operators would not be required to submit new documentation each time they tender or, at a minimum, upon each successful bid.

A similar approach was provided by SIGMA–OECD:[42] an EU-level central registry/list of economic operators should be established, containing documented information supplied by contracting authorities that may justify the exclusion of these operators (similar to the official lists of approved economic operators in the public sector that are permitted under Directive 2014/24/EU). Contracting authorities undertaking a public procurement process would be obligated to verify the central registry/list. If an economic operator interested in a public procurement procedure or having submitted a tender is registered

41 https://www.telles.eu/rethinking-the-procurement-directives-moving-exclusions-out-of-the-procurement-process-2/ last accessed 18.06.2025.

42 SIGMA, Brief 24 Public Procurement. Use of Official Automatic Exclusion Lists in Public Procurement, 2016, available at https://www.sigmaweb.org/en/publications/use-of-official-automatic-exclusion-lists-in-public-procurement_9018a003-en.html last accessed 28.05.2025.

in the central list, the contracting authority must conduct further inquiries by acquiring any requisite information and evidence from the economic operator, subsequently determining whether, under the specific circumstances and in compliance with EU law, the economic operator should be excluded from the public procurement procedure. Contracting authorities would be prohibited, however, from utilizing the central registry as an unofficial automatic exclusion list, without evaluating mitigating circumstances or pertinent information on an individual basis.

An example of a centralized list of excluded operators is to be found already in the Deforestation Regulation, although it is not yet operational. The Regulation has created an "EU-wide debarment (...) system,"[43] in the form of a centralized database of excluded economic operators. The system would be construed on two levels—a national database and an EU database. The system is yet to be tested in practice, but it may be the starting point for a more expanded exclusion database system for all mandatory grounds.

These mechanisms could be developed starting from the eForms system,[44] meant to standardize the collection of data in EU-wide public procurement.[45]

5.2 The Removal or Restriction of the Elusive Concept of "Self-Cleaning"

"Self-cleaning" (Article 57(6) and Recital 102 of the Directive 2014/24/EU) can be defined as the possibility granted for the tenderer, who would otherwise have been excluded, to be maintained in the public procurement procedure

---

[43] C Falvo and F Muscaritoli, "Towards Deforestation-Free Public Procurement?" (2024) 19 *European Procurement & Public Private Partnership Law Review* 91.

[44] Commission Implementing Regulation (EU) 2019/1780 of 23 September 2019 establishing standard forms for the publication of notices in the field of public procurement and repealing Implementing Regulation 2015/1986 (eForms) [2019] OJ L272/7; Commission Implementing Regulation (EU) 2022/2303 of 24 November 2022 Amending Implementing Regulation (EU) 2019/1780 Establishing Standard Forms for the Publication of Notices in the Field of Public Procurement [2022] OJ L305/12.

[45] Albert Sanchez-Graells, *Digital Technologies and Public Procurement: Gatekeeping and Experimentation in Digital Public Governance* (Oxford University Press 2023) 176 and next; Nadia-Ariadna Sava, "The eForms Regulation and Sustainable Public Procurement Data Collection" (2023) 18 *European Procurement & Public Private Partnership Law Review* 178.

due to the fact that it has adopted all the necessary measures to prevent future infringements.[46]

According to another doctrinal opinion, the self-cleaning mechanism does not apply to all the grounds for exclusion provided for in Articles 57, since some grounds are relevant only for the ongoing public procurement procedure, such as the situations provided for in Articles 57(4)e, 57(4)f, and 57(4)i of Directive 2014/24/EU.[47] This matter should be addressed by the next directives.

There is just one case law of the CJEU referring to self-cleaning, Case C-387/19, *RTS infra and Aanemingsbedrijf Noree-Behaegel*, where the CJEU held (para 33) that proof of corrective measures can be provided by the economic operator concerned on its own initiative or at the express request of the contracting authority at the time of submission of the request to participate or the tender or at a later stage of the public procurement procedure. Other case law is only tangentially referencing the obligation of assessing the situation of each tenderer before exclusion. For instance, in *Connexxion*,[48] the Court has underscored the importance of allowing economic operators to demonstrate their reliability through effective remedial measures. In other cases, the Court has determined that each contracting authority must ascertain, based on its own judgment, whether an economic operator facing exclusion or having committed an irregularity may be retained in the award process. According to scholarly opinion,[49] the principle of proportionality, likely the foundation for the legislation governing the self-cleaning mechanism, is infringed when an economic operator is excluded from the public procurement procedure due to small breaches.

While self-cleaning promotes rehabilitation,[50] there are arguments for removing this possibility altogether. The self-cleaning mechanism in itself defeats the legitimacy of the exclusion grounds—it allows contractors to

---

46 Pascal Friton and Janis Zoll (n 3), p. 621. G M Racca and C Yukins, "Debarment in Public Procurement: Rationales and Realization" in G M Racca and C Yukins (eds), *Integrity and Efficiency in Sustainable Public Contracts* (Bruylant 2014), p. 253.

47 Pascal Friton and Janis Zoll (n 3), p. 622.

48 C-171/15, *Connexxion Taxi Services BV v Staat der Nederlanden (Ministerie van Volksgezondheid, Welzijn en Sport) and Others*, ECLI:EU:C:2016:948, conclusions; C-41/18, *MECA*, ECLI:EU:C:2019:507, para. 41; C-552/18, *Indaco Service*, ECLI:EU:C:2019:997, para. 27; C-395/18, *Tim SpA – Direzione e coordinamento Vivendi SA v Consip SpA and Ministero dell'Economia e delle Finanze*, ECLI:EU:C:2020:58, para 49; C-472/19, *Vert Marine*, ECLI:EU:C:2020:468, para. 20.

49 G M Racca and C Yukins (n 46), p. 253.

50 Carina Rigsvig Hamer (n 12), p. 567.

demonstrate reliability and obliges contracting authorities to assess each case individually and not apply the exclusions automatically. Allowing self-cleaning reduces the fear of exclusion, weakening the deterrent effect of procurement penalties. Without lasting consequences, repeat offenders may continue unethical practices, knowing they can "self-clean" again. Also, they might implement cosmetic compliance measures (e.g., temporary reforms) just to qualify for contracts, without genuine cultural change, and contracting authorities lack the resources to verify whether self-cleaning is substantive. Not to mention that assessing self-cleaning claims requires additional scrutiny from contracting authorities, leading to delays and higher costs, and subjective evaluations could lead to inconsistent decisions, risking legal challenges.

Moreover, companies that have always complied with rules face competition from previously non-compliant firms that exploited self-cleaning. This distorts market fairness and rewards bad behavior if penalties are not sufficiently stringent. Another argument is that taxpayers may lose confidence in public procurement if entities with past violations (e.g., fraud or corruption) continue winning contracts. The perception of leniency could damage the EU's reputation for upholding integrity in public spending.

The first solution would be to create an entity in charge of assessing national self-cleaning. This approach would ignore the recent ECJ case law for non-mandatory exclusion grounds (*Infraestruturas*)[51] and entrust national authorities with this assessment; also, from other case law it seems that the CJEU is in favor of member states trusting courts for self-cleaning appraisals (*Vert Marine*[52]).

A second solution is the zero-tolerance approach (e.g., mandatory temporary bans), which could prove more effective in preventing repeated misconduct. Instead of self-cleaning, stricter but proportionate exclusions (with clear time limits) could be applied, ensuring punishment while allowing eventual rehabilitation.

In conclusion, removing self-cleaning would reinforce accountability, ensure a level playing field, and strengthen public trust in procurement processes. If retained, it should at least be stricter, available only for discretionary exclusion grounds, with higher evidentiary burdens and longer mandatory exclusions before relief is granted.

---

51 C-66/22, *Infraestruturas de Portugal and Futrifer Indústrias Ferroviárias*, ECLI:EU:C:2023:1016.

52 C 472/19, *Vert Marine*, ECLI:EU:C:2020:468.

7. Simplification by introducing smarter submitting and supplementing rules

Martin Burgi and Caroline Schulte Oestrich

REFORM PROPOSALS

- The rules on means of proof for the selection criteria, the absence of exclusion grounds, and the award criteria under Article 58–61 of Directive 2014/24/EU should be both more flexible and more precise. This could be achieved, in particular, by making the use of self-declarations mandatory. Furthermore, the requirements for certain references should be clarified.
- The possibility to supplement tenders under Article 56(3) of Directive 2014/24/EU must be made mandatory in national legislation and must not be left to the discretion of the contracting authorities. In addition, Article 56(3) should establish a clear time limit for such supplementation and define the specific circumstances under which it is applicable.
- Article 18 of Directive 2014/24/EU should serve as a normative anchor of simplification. It should emphasise the significance of proportionality within the public procurement process and encourage contracting authorities to make use of smarter submitting and supplementing rules that align with this well-established principle.

1. INTRODUCTION

In the general debate, the provisions on submitting and supplementing tenders in public procurement procedures are often not given enough attention. Yet they have the potential to significantly enhance public procurement practices. By introducing targeted changes to them, it is possible to unlock significant benefits, including increased competition and improved procurement outcomes. Furthermore, a more flexible approach to these provisions can facilitate the achievement of broader policy objectives, such as sustainability and innovation. The objective of this chapter is to investigate the potential advantages of revising the submitting and supplementing rules. It will demonstrate how reforms in these areas can lead to more effective and efficient public procurement procedures, which will ultimately benefit both public authorities and tenderers.

2. DEFINITION AND CURRENT LEGAL FRAMEWORK

The submitting rules pertain to the process by which economic operators[1] present their tenders. The modalities of submitting tenders exhibit slight variations contingent on the specific procedure. Nevertheless, there are specific criteria that must be met in order for tenderers to be deemed eligible or to obtain a public contract. Firstly, tenderers are required to meet the stipulated selection criteria and not fulfil any of the exclusion grounds in order to participate in a public procurement procedure. Secondly, tenders are evaluated according to the established criteria for contract award. These criteria must be substantiated when applying for a public contract.

Supplementing rules address the possibility of including additional information in the original tender during the subsequent public procurement process. This pertains to instances wherein the tender itself is inadequate to satisfy the criteria set forth by the contracting authority.

The current legal framework for submitting rules is particularly rigorous. With regard to supplementary rules, there is a further narrowing of scope. In general, the contracting authority should utilise contract notices to call for competition in respect of all procedures.[2] In accordance with Article 49 of Directive 2014/24/EU, calls for competition should contain the information set out in Annex V part C. This encompasses the selection criteria, as well as the contract award criteria. It is crucial that contracting authorities verify whether 'the tender complies with the requirements, conditions and criteria set out in the contract notice'.[3] Furthermore, it is imperative that they determine whether

---

1 In accordance with Art. 2(1)(10) of Directive 2014/24/EU, economic operators are defined as 'any natural or legal person or public entity or group of such persons and/or entities, including any temporary association of undertakings, which offers the execution of works and/or a work, the supply of products or the provision of services on the market'. This definition is also reflected in Art. 5(2) of Directive 2014/23/EU and Art. 2(6) of Directive 2014/25/EU.

2 Exceptions are the restricted procedure and the competitive procedure with negotiation in the case of prior information notice pursuant to Art. 48(2) of Directive 2014/24/EU. Another exception is the negotiated procedure without prior publication (Art. 32). Art. 49 sets out these requirements.

3 Art. 56(1)(1)(a) of Directive 2014/24/EU.

the tenderer is not excluded and meets the established selection criteria.[4] Still, in the event that an economic operator submits information or documents that are or appear to be incomplete, erroneous or where specific documents are missing, contracting authorities may request the operator to 'submit, supplement, clarify or complete the relevant information or documentation within an appropriate time limit'.[5] This possibility is contingent upon the absence of disparate implementation of the directive at the national level. Secondly, the request must be made 'in full compliance with the principles of equal treatment and transparency'. This rule is noteworthy for its unique status as the sole provision within the directive that addresses formal errors pertaining to the tender process.

A comparable set of rules is set forth in Directive 2014/25/EU. Once more, Article 76(4) empowers the contracting authority to request additional information or documentation. The stipulations are analogous to those set forth in Article 56(3) of Directive 2014/24/EU. It is notable that Directive 2014/23/EU does not include a similar rule. In general, the corpus of written provisions concerning the procedure is relatively limited. Article 30(1) explicitly guarantees 'the freedom to organise the procedure leading to the choice of concessionaire'. Nevertheless, there are requirements concerning the concession notice (Article 31), selection and qualitative assessment of candidates (Article 38), and award criteria (Article 41).

3. CONTEXT AND DEBATE

3.1 Political Impulses

The present legal framework on public procurement necessitates a considerable administrative burden for both economic operators and contracting authorities. Accordingly, a reduction in excessively bureaucratic directives would be advantageous for all parties involved. As indicated in Ursula von der Leyen's Political Guidelines, an efficiency gain of 1% in public procurement could result in savings of EUR 20 billion.[6] On May 24, 2024, the Council adopted the European Court of Auditors' (ECA) conclusions on public procurement,[7] emphasising the significance of competition to achieve the stated goal. As Pierre-Yves Dermagne, Belgian Deputy Prime Minister and Minister for the Economy and Employment, commented, it is crucial to 'obtain the maximum value for every euro spent on public purchases, ensuring that the rules are

4 Art. 56(1)(1)(b) of Directive 2014/24/EU.
5 Art. 56(3) of Directive 2014/24/EU.
6 See Ursula von der Leyen, 'Europe's Choice' (2024), 11.
7 Laid down in ECA, 'Public Procurement in the EU' (Special report, 2023).

clear, that information is easily available and that there is real competition among all participants'.[8]

The current form of public procurement legislation is unduly complex. Accordingly, any reform of the Public Procurement Directives should seek to 'reduce any unnecessary administrative burden'.[9] Simplifying the rules plays an instrumental role in making better use of public procurement.[10]

Public procurement represents a substantial economic factor within the European Union, accounting for 14% of gross domestic product (GDP).[11] Its strategic application can facilitate a substantial contribution to the development of a more sustainable economy. This is referred to as 'strategic procurement'. In essence, contracting authorities are empowered to deviate from the lowest price criterion, instead pursuing the 'most economically advantageous tender' (MEAT) among the tenders received. Such considerations encompass social, ecological, and innovative attributes. As criteria for the award of contracts, they must be set forth in the contract notice.

In general, public procurement has a significant impact on the single market. This is demonstrated in the 'Council Conclusions on a Single Market for the Benefit of All'. In the paragraph entitled 'Enhancing the Single Market's potential benefits',[12] the Council requests that the Commission analyse 'the existing public procurement legislative framework towards resilient and sustainable public procurement and effective competition'.[13] In his report 'Much More Than a Market', Enrico Letta emphasised the potential of strategic procurement to 'harness market power to encourage wider economic shifts towards innovation and sustainability'.[14] In Letta's view, public procurement should serve as a 'key instrument for promoting social value, enhancing social capital, and aligning with the EU's ambitions for green and digital transformations'.[15] As a pioneer, the public sector can provide an impetus for a work environment that increasingly reflects social and green values.

---

8 Quoted from the Council of the EU's press release from May 24, 2024 www.consilium.europa.eu/en/press/press-releases/2024/05/24/council-adopts-conclusions-on-the-court-of-auditors-report-on-public-procurement/, accessed June 11, 2025.

9 See ECA, 'Public Procurement in the EU' (Special report, 2023), 51.

10 See Ursula von der Leyen, 'Europe's Choice' (2024), 11–12.

11 See Ursula von der Leyen, 'Europe's Choice' (2024), 11.

12 Council of the EU, 'Council Conclusions on a Single Market for the Benefit of All' Council Conclusion 10298/24 (2024), 8–10.

13 Council of the EU, 'Council Conclusions on a Single Market for the Benefit of All' Council Conclusion 10298/24 (2024), 8.

14 Enrico Letta, 'Much More Than a Market' (2024), 42.

15 Enrico Letta, 'Much More Than a Market' (2024), 45.

Nevertheless, the ECA's special report on public procurement shows that in all Member States the majority of contracts were awarded on the basis of the lowest price.[16] A major factor contributing to this situation is the legal uncertainty experienced by public purchasers. At regional and local level in particular, there is less expertise in implementing strategic public procurement policies.[17] In view of this, the Fit for Future Platform proposes to clarify the definitions and criteria in question and to provide guidance on the MEAT criteria, possibly in the form of a handbook.[18]

On the other hand, it should be borne in mind that any requirement in the public procurement process represents an additional administrative burden for interested economic operators. Businesses already face numerous obligations. Duties such as reporting add to the bureaucratic expenses. Overall, this can burden economic operators with numerous tasks that are unrelated to their core business activities.

This is particularly problematic in a global comparison. Excessive administrative burdens on businesses can potentially compromise the EU's competitiveness.[19] Therefore, doing business in Europe must be made easier and faster.[20] The Commission's 2024 work programme sought to ensure the EU's competitiveness and economic stability, 'while balancing the requirements this puts on businesses and administrations with cuts in red tape for our businesses and administrations'.[21] In 2025, the Commission aspires to achieve a 'simpler and leaner European Union'.[22] The European Council's Strategic Agenda for 2024–2029 also addresses this issue. According to this agenda, the Council will 'reduce the bureaucratic and regulatory burden at all levels, and simplify, accelerate and digitise administrative procedures, including

---

16 See ECA, 'Public Procurement in the EU' (Special report, 2023), 30–32.

17 See Fit For Future Platform Opinion, 'Public Procurement A WP 2023' (2023), 6–7.

18 See Fit For Future Platform Opinion, 'Public Procurement A WP 2023' (2023), 8–11.

19 See European Commission, 'Commission Work Programme 2024' COM (2023) 638 final, 4.

20 See Ursula von der Leyen, 'Europe's Choice' (2024), 7.

21 Ursula von der Leyen quoted from Commission's press release from October 17, 2023 https://ec.europa.eu/commission/presscorner/detail/en/ip_23_4965, accessed June 11, 2025.

22 Ursula von der Leyen quoted from Commission's press release from February 12, 2025 https://ec.europa.eu/commission/presscorner/detail/en/ip_25_466, accessed June 11, 2025.

permitting, to meet the needs of a modern, dynamic and consumer-friendly investment environment'.[23]

It is evident that the two objectives of simplifying the public procurement rules and reducing the administrative burdens, on the one hand, and enhancing strategic public procurement, on the other, can be in direct conflict. In a context where price is no longer the sole award criterion, the public procurement principles gain strength, and clear and precise rules become even more vital. It is imperative that reforms address this challenge in order to ensure an optimal outcome from public procurement.

3.2 The Bigger Picture

The recently enacted Net-Zero Industry Act (NZIA) exemplifies efforts outside public procurement law to reduce regulatory burdens by accelerating permitting procedures and allowing more flexibility in the supplementation of documents. While the ensuing analysis will concentrate on these aspects, it is imperative to acknowledge that the NZIA incorporates provisions concerning public procurement. In line with the objectives of the EU's Green Deal Industrial Plan, the initiative aims to promote a more sustainable energy system and enhance the EU's global competitiveness. As Ursula von der Leyen outlined, the NZIA creates 'a regulatory environment that allows us to scale up the clean energy transition quickly'.[24]

The NZIA introduces measures to streamline and expedite approval processes for net-zero technology projects. These include maximum time limits for the permit-granting process[25] and the standardisation of procedures.[26] Furthermore, in accordance with Article 6, single points of contact have been established to facilitate and coordinate the permit-granting process and serve as the sole point of contact for project holders as outlined in Article 6(3). In accordance with Article 9(10), the single point of contact also requests that the applicant provide any missing information in the event that the submitted application is incomplete.

This is merely one illustration of the EU's endeavours to diminish the administrative burden. The EU maintains its focus on regulatory streamlining to expedite the green transition and safeguard Europe's industrial

---

[23] European Council, 'Strategic Agenda 2024–2029' (2024), 7.

[24] Ursula von der Leyen quoted from Commission's press release from March 16, 2023, https://ec.europa.eu/commission/presscorner/detail/en/IP_23_1665, accessed June 11, 2025.

[25] Art. 9 of Regulation EU 2024/1735.

[26] Among other things, through access to procedural information, as set forth in Art. 7 of Regulation EU 2024/1735.

competitiveness. In light of these developments, a revision of the provisions governing submission procedures and the supplementation of documents in public procurement appears to be a logical subsequent step.

3.3 Relevant Principles

In the process of revising the submitting and supplementing rules, it is important to take into account the underlying principles that underpin said provisions. In regard to the submitting and supplementing rules, the fundamental objectives are transparency, equal treatment and competition. Transparency is a critical factor that determines the extent to which economic operators can engage in public procurement. This ensures that the fundamental principle of equal treatment is upheld.[27] The principle of equal treatment is rooted in the Treaty on the Functioning of the European Union(TFEU) and is derived from the prohibition of discrimination.[28] The absence of discrimination is of paramount importance in ensuring competition.[29] These principles are set forth in the Public Procurement Directives, among other places, in Article 18(1) or Article 56(3) of Directive 2014/24/EU. Furthermore, Article 18(1) states that the design of procurement shall not be made with the intention of 'artificially narrowing competition'. Although there is no clear consensus on whether competition can be considered a principle,[30] the Court has consistently underscored

[27] See Kirsi-Maria Halonen, 'Many Faces of Transparency in Public Procurement' in Kirsi-Maria Halonen, Roberto Caranta, Albert Sanchez-Graells (eds), *Transparency in EU-Procurements* (Edward Elgar 2019), 9.

[28] See Michael Steinicke, 'Art. 18 of Directive 2014/24/EU' in Michael Steinicke, Peter L. Vesterdorf (eds), *EU Public Procurement Law* (Nomos, C. H. Beck, Hart 2018), para 10–13.

[29] See Michael Steinicke, 'Art. 18 of Directive 2014/24/EU' in Michael Steinicke, Peter L. Vesterdorf (eds), *EU Public Procurement Law* (Nomos, C. H. Beck, Hart 2018), para 15; Carina Risvig Hamer, Marta Andhov, 'Art. 18 of Directive 2014/24/EU' in Roberto Caranta, Albert Sanchez-Graells (eds), *European Public Procurement* (Edward Elgar 2021), para 18.29.

[30] On this debate, Michael Steinicke, 'Art. 18 of Directive 2014/24/EU' in Michael Steinicke, Peter L. Vesterdorf (eds), *EU Public Procurement Law* (Nomos, C. H. Beck, Hart 2018), para 171–173 with reference to Sue Arrowsmith, 'The Purpose of the EU Procurement Directives: Ends, Means and the Implications for National Regulatory Space for Commercial and Horizontal Procurement Policies' (2011–12) 14 Cambridge Yearbook of European Legal Studies 1, 34; for an overview on different positions, Robert Molden, 'The New Competition Principle in the New EU Public Procurement Directives — from a Swedish Perspective' (2019) ErT 591.

its vital role within the framework of public procurement.[31] Generally speaking, competition in public procurement has the potential to yield optimal outcomes in terms of cost, quality, and contractual terms.[32] The submitting and supplementing rules of Directive 2014/24/EU—along with those set forth in the other two directives—place considerable emphasis on maintaining a transparent and equal process for all economic operators.

First, this becomes relevant when contracting authorities call for competition. Both principles stipulate that all the conditions and rules pertaining to the award procedure are explicitly delineated in a clear, precise, and unequivocal manner.[33] Subsequently, they play an important role when economic operators submit their tenders. Tenderers usually use a self-declaration to prove that they are not in a situation where they shall or may be excluded from the procedure and that they meet the selection criteria. In order to facilitate the submission of self-declarations, the EU legislator established a standard form, the European Single Procurement Document (ESPD).[34] The wording of Directive 2014/24/EU does not imply an obligation for the contracting authorities to request the ESPD.[35] However, it serves as preliminary evidence. In accordance with Article 59(4) of Directive 2014/24/EU, the contracting authority can ask tenderers 'at any moment during the procedure to submit all or part of the supporting documents where this is necessary to ensure the proper con-

---

[31] For example, C-243/89 *Commission v Denmark* [1993] ECR I-33533, para 33; C-286/99 *Lombardini* [2001] ECR I-9233, para 35; C-336/12 *Manova* [2013] ECLI:EU:C:2013:647, para 28.

[32] See Steven L. Schooner, 'Desiderata: Objectives for a System of Government Contract Law' (2002) 11 Public Procurement Law Review 103, 104.

[33] See Wojciech Hartung, Katarzyna Kuzma, 'Art. 49 of Directive 2014/24/EU' in Roberto Caranta, Albert Sanchez-Graells (eds), *European Public Procurement* (Edward Elgar 2021), para 49.14.

[34] On the contents of the ESPD self-declaration, see Art. 59(1) of Directive 2014/24/EU. Where applicable, the economic operator can also prove that it fulfils rules and criteria that have been set out pursuant to Art. 65.

[35] See the wording in Art. 59(1), also Gabriella M. Racca, 'Electronic Qualitative Selection of Economic Operator: The Challenge of the European Single Procurement Document (ESPD)' in Martin Burgi, Martin Trybus, Steen Treumer (eds), *Qualification, Selection and Exclusion in EU Procurement* (Djøf 2016), 307. Others understand the use of the ESPD as mandatory; see for example, Carina Risvig Hamer, 'Art. 59 of Directive 2014/24/EU' in Michael Steinicke, Peter L. Vesterdorf (eds), *EU Public Procurement Law* (Nomos, C. H. Beck, Hart 2018), para 1. Nevertheless, in certain countries, there is a degree of discretion with regard to the decision of whether or not to request self-declarations and the ESPD. For example, in Germany, this is addressed in § 48(2) and (3) Procurement Ordinance.

duct of the procedure'. Only the tenderer to whom the contracting authority has decided to award the contract is required to submit up-to-date supporting documents prior to contract award.[36] The means of proof are further regulated in Article 60 and Article 62. It should be noted that some documents may not be issued by Member States and that 'equivalents' may be accepted in lieu of such documents.

Eventually, the principles of equal treatment and transparency are essential in the case of Article 56(3). In the event that tenderers are requested to submit, supplement, clarify, or complete information pertaining to their tender, such requests must be made 'in full compliance with the principles of equal treatment and transparency'. However, the point at which this requirement is satisfied remains ambiguous. Thus far, only case law has permitted the assumption that this condition has been met. Both principles are deemed to be violated when the request will 'in reality lead to the submission of a new tender'.[37] This shall be the case when the document in question has not existed prior to the tender deadline.[38] Moreover, the principle of equal treatment requires that 'comparable situations must not be treated differently and that situations must not be treated in the same way unless such treatment is objectively justified'.[39] This comparison is largely contingent upon the specific circumstances of the situation in question.[40]

It is important to note that there is no obligation for contracting authorities to request rectification. Member States can even exclude such possibility. However, some argue that exceptions must be made in regard to the principle

[36] An exception is made for contracts based on framework agreements where such contracts are concluded in accordance with Article 33(3) or Article 33(4)(a) of Directive 2014/24/EU.

[37] C-599/10 *SAG ELV Slovenso and Others* [2012] ECR I-10873, para 40. Later *inter alia* referred to by C-336/12 *Manova* [2013] ECLI:EU:C:2013:647, para 36; C-324/14 *Partner Apelsi Dariusz* [2016] ECLI:EU:C:2016:214, para 64; C-131/16 *Archus and Gama* [2017] ECLI:EU:C:2017:358, para 31.

[38] See C-336/12 *Manova* [2013] ECLI:EU:C:2013:647, para 39; also Carina Risvig Harmer, 'Art. 56 of Directive 2014/24/EU' in Michael Steinicke, Peter L. Vesterdorf (eds), *EU Public Procurement Law* (Nomos, C. H. Beck, Hart 2018), para 24.

[39] For example C-21/03 and C-34/03 *Fabricom SA v Belgian State* [2005] ECR I-1559, para 27; in general C-434/02 *Arnold André* [2004] ECR I-11825, para 68; C-304/01 *Spain v Commission* [2004] ECR I-7655, para 31.

[40] Further information from Pascal Friton, Janis Zöll, 'Art. 56 of Directive 2014/24/EU' in Roberto Caranta, Albert Sanchez-Graells (eds), *European Public Procurement* (Edward Elgar 2021), para 56.60–62.

of proportionality where errors in the tender are obvious.[41] Nevertheless, Article 56(3) does not reflect this.

In Germany, for instance, contracting authorities are afforded the discretion to require rectification.[42] They are similarly at liberty to exclude this possibility. In practice, it can be unclear whether the contracting authorities are permitted to request further documents. Once more, the question of whether the supplementation is permissible is governed by case law.[43] Similarly, the legal framework in Spain is comparable. Only in instances of self-declarations and documentation pertaining to selection criteria is there a legal obligation to request rectification.[44] In all other cases, authorities have discretionary power, which is expanded upon by the judicial system.[45] In France, the contracting authority also has discretion as to whether or not to require rectification. In general, this is the case in every type of procedure.[46] Depending on the

---

[41] For further information and the exact requirements, Sue Arrowsmith, *The Law of Public and Utilities Procurement: Regulation in the EU and UK* (3rd edn, Sweet & Maxwell 2014), para 7.278–282 and 7.293; Carina Risvig Harmer, 'The Principle of Proportionality' (2022) 3 EPPPL 190, 200; Pascal Friton, Janis Zöll, 'Art. 56 of Directive 2014/24/EU' in Roberto Caranta, Albert Sanchez-Graells (eds), *European Public Procurement* (Edward Elgar 2021), para 56.74 and 56.83 with further relation to European case law.

[42] See § 56(2) Procurement Ordinance.

[43] In accordance with the ruling of the OLG München Verg 02/18, a request for rectification may be made in the event that a criminal record fails to meet the requisite period of validity. Conversely, certifications contingent upon individual agreements shall not be permitted. This includes, for example, insurance certificates that do not meet the required coverage amount; see OLG Karlsruhe 15 Verg 10/19. Furthermore, it is generally assumed that only missing documents can be submitted at a later stage and that errors, apart from those that are clearly obvious, such as spelling mistakes, cannot be corrected; see OLG Düsseldorf VII-Verg 42/17. This can result in instances where minor inaccuracies in the initial data lead to the rejection of tenders, while missing information can be supplemented. In Germany, it is not evident whether this conclusion must be derived from Art. 56(3); in favour see, OLG Düsseldorf VII-Verg 42/17; in opposition see, Elke Tegeler, Matthias Einmahl, 'Flexiblerer Umgang mit dem Nachfordern bei fehlerhaften Unterlagen?' (2020) VergabeR 549, 550.

[44] See Art. 141(2) Ley 9/2017, de 8 de noviembre, de Contratos del Sector Público.

[45] For further information see Juan Carlos Gris González, 'Aclaración y subsanación de las ofertas en los contratos del sector público' (2022) Cuadernos de Derecho Local 160, 160–179.

[46] See R. 2152–2 du Code de la commande publique.

applicable public procurement procedure, the scope for exercising this option varies.[47]

The consequence of these rules is that economic operators are required to adhere to a multitude of formal requirements. This is particularly challenging given the varying national implementations.[48] In its special report on public procurement in the EU, the ECA asserts that public procurement procedures 'generate costs for potential bidders that exceed those incurred when they compete for private sector procurement contracts'.[49] Consequently, a considerable number of potential bidders are dissuaded from engaging in the bidding process.

In contrast with the intention of fostering competition, the complex provisions can, in fact, have the opposite effect.[50] This is not only contrary to the significant role of competition in European public procurement, it also hinders the achievement of the best possible results through competition. Instead, qualitatively inferior bidders who have submitted to administrative requirements are awarded contracts.

3.4 A New Balance Between Certainty and Risk

Eventually, reducing the bureaucratic burdens for submitting and supplementing tenders will also result in alterations to the prevailing balance between certainty and risk in public procurement. Such modifications affect the degree of clarity and predictability within the process. It is reasonable to conclude that strict submitting and supplementing rules help ensure that tenders comply with the requirements stipulated in the tender documents. Less rigorous procedures—for instance, the increasing use of self-declarations or the more flexible acceptance of missing documents—may elevate the risk of admitting bidders who do not genuinely align with the criteria for qualitative selection. For example, if the technical capacity of bidders is not verified, contracting authorities may award contracts to unqualified entities. Conversely, the current multitude of requirements prevents more effective tenders. Thus, it is imperative to implement smarter submitting and supplementing rules. However, it is crucial to recognise that this request necessitates a novel equilibrium between risk and certainty.

47 For further explanation, see Philippe Guellier, Laurent Bonnard, 'Qualification et régime des offres irrégulières, inacceptables et inappropriées' (2022) *Contrats Publics* 26, 30.

48 Addressing the issue of legal discrepancies Fit For Future Platform Opinion 'Public Procurement A WP 2023' (2023), 6.

49 ECA, 'Public Procurement in the EU' (Special report, 2023), 44.

50 See ECA, 'Public Procurement in the EU' (Special report, 2023), 44.

Furthermore, the introduction of additional flexibility in the submission and supplementation guidelines reinforces the principle of proportionality as the fundamental basis for decision-making. As indicated in Article 18(1) of Directive 2014/24/EU, proportionality is an overarching principle in the context of public procurement. It aims to ensure that only essential requirements are established and that overly burdensome administrative procedures are not introduced.[51] In addition, it is a mechanism to ensure that there is equal treatment and competition among tenderers.[52] This objective can be achieved if each competitor is treated in a proportionate way. Therefore, the less formalised the procedure is, the more important it is for the contracting authority in question to act proportionately. In instances where discretion is present, the principle of proportionality is a primary determinant in the decision-making process.

Simplification of the submitting and supplementing rules under Directive 2014/24/EU is essential to achieve better public procurement outcomes and to maintain overall competitiveness within the EU. This can facilitate more efficient public procurement processes, thereby encouraging broader participation and potentially leading to better quality tenders. However, it is crucial to ensure that such simplifications do not undermine other important objectives and principles of public procurement practice, such as strategic procurement goals, transparency, and equal treatment. With this in mind, any changes need to be carefully integrated into the broader context of public procurement law. This integration should ensure that these key principles are upheld, thereby ensuring the effectiveness and integrity of the public procurement system. Ultimately, the enhanced effectiveness and integrity of this process will benefit all stakeholders.

4. REFORM PROPOSALS

A reform would have to be based on Articles 18, 56, 58–61 (including Annex XII of Directive 2014/24/EU). In Directive 2014/25/EU, this only pertains to Article 36. Given that Article 80(2) and (3) already refer to the provisions set forth in Directive 2014/24/EU, no additional amendment is required at this stage. With regard to Directive 2014/23/EU, only Article 3 can be compared to Directive 2014/23/EU. The absence of equivalent provisions, such as Articles

51 See Carina Risvig Hamer, Marta Andhov, 'Art. 18 of Directive 2014/24/EU' in Roberto Caranta, Albert Sanchez-Graells (eds), *European Public Procurement* (Edward Elgar 2021), para 18.20–23.

52 See Carina Risvig Hamer, Marta Andhov, 'Art. 18 of Directive 2014/24/EU' in Roberto Caranta, Albert Sanchez-Graells (eds), *European Public Procurement* (Edward Elgar 2021), para 18.26.

56 and 58–61, is a result of concession procurement being less formalised than public contracts. This is due to the intention to make this type of public procurement more flexible.[53] This objective is explicitly stated in recital 68.

4.1 More Flexible and Precise Rules on Means of Proof for the Selection Criteria, Absence of Exclusion Grounds, and Contract Award Criteria

Thus far, numerous prerequisites must be fulfilled by a tenderer in order to become eligible for the further procedure or to be awarded a contract. In certain instances, it is not evident which measures should be employed to demonstrate the suitability of the proof provided. In the process of revising the rules on means of proof, it is essential to consider their impact on public procurement. The implementation of flexible yet precise rules has the potential to foster competition and enhance transparency, as it would clarify what contracting authorities expect. It is, however, essential to guarantee equal treatment when tenders in different situations are subjected to the same provisions. In this context, the principle of proportionality assumes greater significance. Accordingly, the objective of more flexible and precise rules should be to facilitate the submission of means of proof while still accounting for the differences among tenderers.

It should be noted that Article 60 already accounts for the possibility that documents may not be issued in all EU Member States. This allows for greater flexibility in referencing for the tenderer. Nevertheless, there is potential for further flexibility in the tender submission process. Firstly, it would facilitate the submission of tenders for bidders if the preferred acceptance of self-declarations was made mandatory for Member States. At present, this is not the case. In Germany, for instance, the decision of whether to request self-declarations is left to the discretion of the contracting authority.[54] Submitting self-declarations is typically less onerous for bidders than providing proof issued by third parties. Thus, the implementation of self-declarations as a mandatory means of proof could potentially result in an increase in the number of prospective

[53] With further information also in regard to the German implementation Martin Burgi, Daniel Wolff, '§ 12 KonzVgV' in Martin Burgi, Meinrad Dreher (eds), *Vergaberecht*, vol 2 (4th edn, C. H. Beck 2025), para 3–8; more general, Christopher Bovis, Charles Clarke, 'Art. 30 of Directive 2014/23/EU' in Michael Steinicke, Peter L. Vesterdorf (eds), *EU Public Procurement Law* (Nomos, C. H. Beck, Hart 2018), para 2–3.

[54] See § 48(2) of Procurement Ordinance for Germany.

bidders, leading to a more robust competitive process.[55] Additionally, the use of similar forms of evidence could facilitate a more comparable assessment of tenders, thereby expediting the decision-making process within the contracting authority. E-certis could serve as an accessible supplement to these self-declarations.[56]

Moreover, the revised submitting rules could provide greater clarity on the expectations regarding the sufficiency of 'references'. For instance, Article 58(4) refers to 'suitable references from contracts performed in the past' as a means of proving that the requisite level of experience has been attained. Consequently, contracting authorities are presented with a vast array of options they may request. Conversely, this may result in a significant administrative burden for all parties involved. Despite the fact that Article 60 and Annex XII establish a variety of potential means of proof, the precise requirements for each are not always evident. For instance, with respect to lists of contracts for the purpose of demonstrating technical ability, the directive does not stipulate whether these lists must encompass all previous work performed and all goods and services provided.[57]

Ultimately, the objective of providing greater guidance to contracting authorities while avoiding the introduction of an additional layer of complexity can be achieved through the formulation of more flexible and precise rules governing the means of proof.

4.2 Expansion and Specification of Article 56(3) of Directive 2014/24/EU

The introduction of Article 56(3) represented a notable advancement in the legislative landscape of EU public procurement law. It marks the first instance of a rule explicitly authorising requests for additional information or documentation in all cases where tenders appear to be incomplete or erroneous.[58]

---

55 Describing the German § 48(2) Stefan Mager, '§ 48 VgV' in Martin Burgi, Meinrad Dreher (eds), *Vergaberecht*, vol 2 (4th edn, C. H. Beck 2025), para 28.

56 In relation to the ESPD system see Pedro Telles, 'Art. 61 of Directive 2014/24/EU' in Roberto Caranta, Albert Sanchez-Graells (eds), *European Public Procurement* (Edward Elgar 2021), para 61.02.

57 According to Pedro Telles, 'Art. 60 of Directive 2014/24/EU' in Roberto Caranta, Albert Sanchez-Graells (eds), *European Public Procurement* (Edward Elgar 2021), para 60.17.

58 See Carina Risvig Harmer, 'Art. 56 of Directive 2014/24/EU' in Michael Steinicke, Peter L. Vesterdorf (eds), *EU Public Procurement Law* (Nomos, C. H. Beck, Hart 2018), para 20. Previously, Art. 51 of Directive 2004/18/EC only permitted 'to supplement or clarify the certificates and documents submitted'

Supplementing tenders can assist in the prevention of the hasty exclusion of potential contract award winners. This can not only lead to better public procurement outcomes in a specific instance but the knowledge that one is not immediately excluded from the procedure for minor errors might encourage a greater number of bidders to participate in public procurement procedures. This can result in a more diverse range of competitors and more effective public procurement in general.

Therefore, this opportunity must be seized in all cases. Thus far, this has not been the case. Firstly, Member States are at liberty to determine whether they wish to implement the option of supplementing tenders. Secondly, contracting authorities have discretion whether to ask for rectification or not. As a result, Member States and contracting authorities have the option of formalising public procurement procedures at the cost of more effective public procurement processes. Therefore, neither the Member States nor the contracting authorities should be permitted to refrain from requesting that tenderers submit, supplement, clarify, or complete the relevant information or documentation.

Furthermore, Article 56(3) stipulates that rectification must be completed 'within an appropriate time limit'. The appropriate time limit is contingent upon the circumstances of the case at hand.[59] Consequently, the ease with which information or documentation can be obtained determines the length of the prescribed time limit. The easier an information or document is to acquire, the shorter the time limit. This can be seen as a consequence of the request for rectification being voluntary for the contracting authority.[60] In addition to the lack of clarity surrounding the definition of 'appropriate time limits', this provides a reason to introduce a maximum time limit. In the event that the request for rectification is mandatory, rectification requests cannot be considered a mere gesture that allows contracting authorities to set time limits in their favour.

Moreover, the term of rectification 'in full compliance with the principle of equal treatment and transparency' requests further clarification. As already

---

in relation to the selection criteria, see Matthias Mantler, 'Zur (zweifelhaften) Europarechtskonformität der Nachforderungsregelungen in VOB/A, VOL/A, VOF und SektVO' (2013) VergR 166, 169–170.

[59] See Carina Risvig Harmer, 'Art. 56 of Directive 2014/24/EU' in Michael Steinicke, Peter L. Vesterdorf (eds), *EU Public Procurement Law* (Nomos, C. H. Beck, Hart 2018), para 29; Pascal Friton, Janis Zöll, 'Art. 56 of Directive 2014/24/EU' in Roberto Caranta, Albert Sanchez-Graells (eds), *European Public Procurement* (Edward Elgar 2021), para 56.86.

[60] Seen this way by Carina Risvig Harmer, 'Art. 56 of Directive 2014/24/EU' in Michael Steinicke, Peter L. Vesterdorf (eds), *EU Public Procurement Law* (Nomos, C. H. Beck, Hart 2018), para 29.

mentioned, only case law defines whether this requirement is met. Article 56(3) itself is too vague to clearly define when contracting authorities are in full compliance with these principles, leaving significant room for interpretation. To ensure legal clarity for both contracting authorities and tenderers, it is imperative to establish clearer supplementing rules. These rules should provide a comprehensive and transparent overview of the circumstances under which a rectification must be demanded. This should also encompass instances where a correction does not result in the introduction of new offers. For instance, considerations should include the extent to which modifications to the initial tender's substantive content, as presented by the bidder, are permissible post-submission. It is imperative that these rules guarantee that requests for supplementary information or documentation are addressed in a manner that does not contravene the principles of equal treatment or transparency. In the absence of such clarity, contracting authorities may be disinclined to request rectifications, apprehending that doing so might confer an unfair advantage upon certain tenderers. This reluctance could impede the efficacy of public procurement processes, ultimately constraining opportunities for enhanced competition and outcomes. Establishing clear rules would therefore assist in fostering more competitive and efficient public procurement practices across Member States.

4.3 Consolidation and Clarification of the Principle of Proportionality (Article 18(1) of Directive 2014/24/EU)

As previously stated, the proposed alterations necessitate a revised equilibrium between the risk and certainty inherent to EU public procurement law. The implementation of less bureaucratic procedures for the submission and supplementation of tenders could facilitate the participation of a larger number of potential bidders in the public procurement process. Such measures serve to enhance competition and may ultimately result in more optimal public procurement practices. Concurrently, it is imperative not to overlook the other two pivotal principles that underpin the submission and supplementation process. It is of the utmost importance that an adequate level of transparency and equal treatment be ensured at all times.

At this juncture, the principle of proportionality assumes significant importance. The objective is to interpret the Public Procurement Directives in a manner that strikes a balance between the procedural burdens on the one hand and the public procurement objectives on the other.[61] This entails a responsibility

---

[61] See Sue Arrowsmith, *The Law of Public and Utilities Procurement: Regulation in the EU and UK* (3rd edn, Sweet & Maxwell 2014), para 7.24–25;

on the part of the contracting authorities to assess the necessity of bureaucratic requirements. The less rigorous the submitting and supplementing rules, the greater the potential for the administration to request (supplementary) information and establish further requirements. In some instances, this can give rise to additional challenges and result in disparate outcomes within the EU. To illustrate, Article 58 leaves it to the contracting authority to determine which selection criteria to establish. Nevertheless, the criteria must be 'proportionate to the subject-matter of the contract'.[62] This results in a significant degree of variation across Member States. While some Member States limit the discretion of contracting authorities by providing comprehensive guidance on proportionate selection criteria, others do not. In addition to the discrepancies that exist within the EU public procurement system, the limited discretion available to contracting authorities could also impede their ability to innovate.[63] In light of these considerations, it is evident that the principle of proportionality plays a pivotal role in the context of public procurement rules and should be given a central role in any deliberations on this matter.

Furthermore, the principle of proportionality itself requires supplementing rules. As previously discussed, some argue that in the event of evident errors in tenders, the contracting authority may be obliged to request rectification in accordance with Article 56(3) in order to act proportionately. It bears noting once more that this obligation is not explicitly stated in Article 56(3). Nevertheless, this should be the case.

In comparison to the other public procurement principles, the principle of proportionality is particularly fluid. While transparency and equal treatment are unambiguous objectives, proportionality serves to provide a counterbalance to a variety of aims.[64] The principle of proportionality has consistently held a significant position in the context of public procurement.[65] As a general public procurement principle, it helps to fill gaps in public procurement rules. While the discretion afforded to contracting authorities in filling these gaps may result in more flexible public procurement procedures, it can

Martin Burgi, *Vergaberecht* (3rd edn, C. H. Beck 2021), § 6 para 24–26.

62 Art. 58(1)(2).

63 See Roxana Vornicu, 'Art. 58 of Directive 2014/24/EU' in Roberto Caranta, Albert Sanchez-Graells (eds), *European Public Procurement* (Edward Elgar 2021), para 58.06.

64 See Carina Risvig Harmer, 'The Principle of Proportionality' (2022) 3 EPPPL 190, 200.

65 See Michael Steinicke, 'Art. 18 of Directive 2014/24/EU' in Michael Steinicke, Peter L. Vesterdorf (eds), *EU Public Procurement Law* (Nomos, C. H. Beck, Hart 2018), para 155–157.

simultaneously give rise to legal uncertainties.[66] Ultimately, this ambiguity can impede the implementation of innovative and flexible public procurement strategies. It is therefore recommended that the public procurement rules aim to remove this concern from the minds of contracting authorities.

This objective can be achieved through the consolidation and clarification of the principle of proportionality as set forth in Article 18(1). In essence, this principle has significant implications not only in the context of EU public procurement law but also in the context of any action undertaken by public authorities.[67] Therefore, public authorities are well-versed in the application of these rules. Consequently, contracting authorities should be encouraged to exercise their discretion in accordance with the principle of proportionality. As this becomes especially important with smarter submitting and supplementing rules, the principle's importance in relation to these rules should already be clarified in the general rule of Article 18(1). A precise reference to the submitting and supplementing rules can highlight the importance of proportionate decision-making and offer assistance for those who feel uncertain towards more flexible and innovative approaches.

5. CONCLUSION

It can thus be surmised that smarter submitting and supplementing rules would diminish the administrative burden for both contracting authorities and bidders. One of the principal objectives of the Public Procurement Directives is to foster competition. As long as the participation of potential tenderers in the public procurement process is unduly encumbered by excessive bureaucratic effort, many potential tenderers are deterred from taking part in the process. Accordingly, the competitive process can be enhanced through the deregulation of relevant provisions.

A more instrumental approach to submitting and supplementing rules also allows contracting authorities greater discretion. This enables them to achieve superior public procurement outcomes. By affording contracting authorities greater discretion, it is hoped that they will be encouraged to take into account factors beyond mere cost, such as green, social, and innovative procurement.

66 See Carina Risvig Hamer, Marta Andhov, 'Art. 18 of Directive 2014/24/EU' in Roberto Caranta, Albert Sánchez-Graells (eds), *European Public Procurement* (Edward Elgar 2021), para 18.03.

67 See Carina Risvig Harmer, 'The Principle of Proportionality' (2022) 3 EPPPL 190, 193; with special reference to the rule of law Oliver Dörr, '§ 97 GWB' in Martin Burgi, Meinrad Dreher (eds), *Vergaberecht*, vol 1 (4th edn, C. H. Beck 2022), para 55–57.

Clarification and supplementary explanations can also help preserve administrative resources.

In conclusion, the proposed modifications can enable contracting authorities to allocate resources more efficiently. A revision of the submitting and supplementing rules should concentrate on areas where clarification and further explanations are required, as well as areas where unnecessary and overly formal bureaucratic obstacles can be removed. This affords public authorities the opportunity to utilise their discretion and resources to address deficiencies in crucial areas for improving public procurement outcomes. Consequently, they are not required to concern themselves with the complexities of interpreting vague specifications.

However, these considerations are primarily relevant to Directives 2014/24/EU and 2014/25/EU. Directive 2014/23/EU contains only a minimal number of formal requirements, reflecting an effort to make concessions more flexible. This also indicates that the public procurement process could be made more responsive to the needs of all parties involved by reducing the number of strict rules in the other two directives.

8. Framework agreements

How to deal with the CJEU forced contractualization

Mario E. Comba

REFORM PROPOSALS

- To restore the non-contractual nature of Framework Agreements (FAs), by removing the obligation of a maximum amount introduced by the Court of Justice of the European Union (CJEU) in *Autorità* and *Simonsen*), possibly introducing transparency and competition protection measures, such as forbidding FAs in cases of a single economic operator (expanding CJEU in *EPIC*), or mandatory exclusivity clauses for contracting authorities using Framework Agreements[1] or even imposing the obligation to establish a *minimum* guaranteed amount for each economic operator admitted to the FA, in order to encourage participation and remunerate their availability, OR
- To follow CJEU's approach to the ends and regulate the legal consequences of exceeding the maximum amount, in the case of FAs managed by Central Purchase Bodies with more than one contracting authority, by allocating the risk and consequent liability between the contracting authority who carried out the FA and the contracting authority that concluded the contract exceeding the overall limit and by protecting the *bona fide* economic operator's reliance.

1 Perhaps in the milder version that exclusivity is presumed, unless stated otherwise, with due motivation.

1. OUTLINE OF THE CONTEXT AND MOST PRESSING ISSUES[2]

1.1 Introduction: ECA Report, Gramework Agreements and Competition

The Report of the European Court of Auditors (ECA)[3] mentions Framework Agreements only in the considerations regarding the Data Analysis Methodology and indicates that "only data in relation to second stage awards are included." In fact, it is not possible to obtain official data on the use of Framework Agreements from the Tenders Electronic Daily (TED) because the search key relating to "techniques of procurement" is not provided and therefore, as the Court of Auditors points out, only second stage awards are included, without, however, being able to trace them back to the original Framework Agreement.

For official data on the number and value of Framework Agreements, it is therefore necessary to resort to national procurement authorities or to use other sources from which it appears that, in general, the use of Framework Agreements in the European Union has grown steadily.[4]

---

[2] For an analysis of legislation, case law and doctrine on Framework Agreements in European law, please refer to the Ph.D. Thesis by Magdalena Socha, *Parallel Framework Agreements*, submitted on 31 August 2024, chapter 3 of which provides a complete and up-to-date reconstruction, also enriched by numerous and interesting observations on the legislation and case law of the Member States. For a general overview, with comparative considerations also outside the EU, see S. Filipon, *Framework Agreements, Supplier Lists, and Other Public Procurement Tools: Purchasing Uncertain or Indefinite Requirements*, Hart Publishing, Oxford, 2023. For aspects relating to the economic analysis of Framework Agreements and, in particular, for the main conformations of mini-competitions, see G.L. Albano – C. Nicolas, *The Law and Economics of Framework Agreements: Designing Flexible Solutions for Public Procurements*, CUP, 2016.

[3] European Court of Auditors, *Public Procurement in the EU. Less Competition for Contracts Awarded for Works, Goods and Services in the 10 Years up to 2021*, Brussels, 2023.

[4] M. Socha, cit., p. 61 and 65 where, citing the World Bank 2021, "Guidebook for Setting up and Operating Framework Agreements," it is stated that: "The 2019 data from TED shows that 5 years later 13 EU Member States were using Framework Agreements for at least a quarter of their public procurement." See also: European Commission, *Annual Public Procurement Implementation Review 2012 (Brussels, 9.10.2012, SWD(2012)342 final) 26*, referring to year 2010, according to which 14% of public procurement was carried out through Framework Agreements.

Nor does the ECA Report address the topic of procurement aggregation techniques in general – in the context of which Directive 2014/24/EU places Framework Agreements – despite the fact that the centralization of procurement is a topic that significantly affects the development of competition.[5] In particular,[6] the ECA Report identifies three elements symptomatic of the reduced competition that has developed since the 2014 directives: a significant increase in single bidding overall, a high level of direct contract awards, and a limited level of cross-border procurements between Member States. Framework Agreements constitute an award technique that can effectively counteract precisely these phenomena as, by aggregating the needs of the contracting authorities, they make the contract more economically attractive and thus tend to reduce the cases of single bidding and direct contracting. And this happens especially when Framework Agreements are carried out by Central Purchasing Bodies (double level of centralization), with the involvement of several economic operators and several contracting authorities. As far as cross-border procurements are concerned, although there is a lack of official data, it appears from some sectoral sources[7] that they are mainly carried out by means of Framework Agreements, which actually constitute a particularly suitable procurement technique for cross-border procurements.[8]

In the UK, Framework Agreements for large contracts increased from 20% of contracts by value in 2018–19 to 68% in 2021–22, as reported in: House of Commons Committee for Public Accounts, *Competition in* Public Procurement, 7 December 2023, p. 6.

5 A different approach is followed by the House of Commons Committee for Public Accounts, *Competition in* Public Procurement, 7 December 2023, which addresses the relation between Framework Agreements and competition in Recommendation no. 3 (p. 6) and in paras 20–26 (pp. 13–14), under the title: *Guidance on using Framework Agreements.* For an economic analysis of the pro-competitive effects of Framework Agreements see Albano – Nicolas, cit., ch. 7.

6 ECA Report, cit., p. 5.

7 IprocrementNet, *Joint Cross-border Public Procurement in Europe*, 2021, which shows that out of 10 cross-border procurements in the field of security and defense, six were carried out with Framework Agreements.

8 M.E. Comba, *Framework Agreements for Cross-border Procurements: A Critical Assessment and Some Proposals*, paper presented at the 2024 EPCO Public Procurement Conference, Luxembourg, 17 October 2024, unpublished. In a nutshell, the use of the Framework Agreement allows, at least at the contract execution stage, to differentiate the applicable legislation and the language used in the contract documents, as well as the e-platform, which are among the main practical problems in the implementation of cross-border procurements, as highlighted in: R. Lombardi – S. Rossa, *Theoretical Models and Implementation Practices:*

Obviously, the potential anti-competitive effects of the use of Framework Agreements are not ignored; indeed, it was precisely this latter aspect that prompted the CJEU to issue the *Autorità* and *Simonsen* rulings. These issues will be examined in the following paragraphs, but the consideration raised by the analysis of the ECA Report indicates that there is a lack of an in-depth and up-to-date study on the actual effects of Framework Agreements on competition[9] and on the advantages of this award technique for cross-border procurements. In order to carry out such a study in a serious and well-documented manner, it will be necessary to have complete data on the actual use of Framework Agreements, which confirms the importance pointed out by the ECA Report that the TED allows for this type of data mining.

1.2 The "Contractualization" Process of Framework Agreements (CJEU *Autorità* and *Simonsen* Judgments)

It is first of all necessary to understand, from a comparative perspective, the purpose for which the procurement technique consisting of Framework Agreements was introduced.[10] The operational need, in the main legal systems that have introduced techniques similar to Framework Agreements, is to find a legal instrument that allows the contracting authority to deal with unforeseeable, uncertain purchase requirements, in object and quantity, and that, in the face of this specific characteristic, allows it to ensure "security and flexibility of supply over a period of time at short notice,"[11] while secondary objectives, common to all forms of procurement aggregation, may be to obtain efficiency, better terms, and administrative convenience. This requires great flexibility, both in terms of technical characteristics and quantities. On the contrary, the simple repetitiveness of purchases, with certain or at least foreseeable quality and quantity, is not essential since, if it is a matter of repetitiveness of certain purchases, normal procurement techniques are sufficient,

Critical Legal Analysis of Joint Cross-Border Procurement, in "CERIDAP," 2024, pp. 91–92.

[9] With the exception of Albano – Nicolas, cit., which was published in 2016 and therefore refers to a situation prior to the implementation of the 2014 directives. Some reflections on this issue are made by Filipon, cit., p. 6–7, who mainly refers to the two hypotheses of: a) impossibility for other operators to access the Framework Agreement for its duration and b) shortcomings in the regulation and control of the second stage.

[10] The considerations made here are taken from S. Filipon, cit., pp. 1–6, where the elements characterizing PUIRs (Purchase of Uncertain or Indefinite Requirements) are listed.

[11] Filipon, cit., p. 6.

which can be improved by the use of lots or a specific scheduling of deliveries, as well as the introduction of purchasing options. This is an important aspect, but it is not explicitly stated in the Public Procurement Directives. Recitals 60 to 62 of Directive 2014/24/EU do not indicate what the specific function of Framework Agreements is, as they merely note that Framework Agreements are widespread in the Member States and therefore need uniform regulation, compatible with the Treaties. One must probably derive from the recitals the presumption that, if Framework Agreements are already present in the Member States' legislation, they will be useful and the European legislator's only concern is to make them compatible with the Treaties. Then, as we have seen, the Directive places Framework Agreements among the "techniques (...) for (...) aggregated procurements," but does not distinguish with respect to centralized procurements nor with respect to occasional joint procurements, nor to Dynamic Purchasing Systems.[12]

In fact, Directive 2014/24/EU allows contracting authorities to make use of Framework Agreements without any limitation and thus recognizes that they can also be used outside the cases outlined prior (uncertainty in the quantity and quality of supplies required), even when the same need could be satisfied through the use of normal contracts, possibly accompanied by option or periodic procurement clauses.[13]

It is in this context that the *Autorità*[14] and *Simonsen*[15] judgments should be placed, which represent the only relevant intervention of the CJEU in the field of Framework Agreements to date (in addition to *Epic*,[16] which will be discussed following). It will not be possible to analyze these two judgments here, for which we refer to the numerous doctrines,[17] but we will simply point out that they have been much criticized in that they imposed an anti-literal inter-

[12] The distinction between Framework Agreements and DPS is even more blurred than with centralized or joint occasional procurements, since DPS can be considered "as a variant of Framework Agreements," where the main difference is that FA are closed while DPS are open to new economic operators (F. Lichère – S. Richetto, *Framework Agreements, Dynamic Purchasing Systems and Public E-procurements*, in F. Lichère – R. Caranta – S. Treumer, *Modernising Public Procurement. The New Directive*, Djoef Publishing, Copenhagen, 2014, p. 220.

[13] Lichère – Richetto, cit., pp. 185–186, highlights the misleading effect of the definition "Techniques for aggregated procurements."

[14] CJEU, Case C-216/17, *Autorità Garante della concorrenza e del mercato-Antitrust v. Coopservice*, ECLI:EU:C:2018:1034.

[15] CJEU, Case C-23/20, *Simonsen and Weel*, ECLI:EU:C:2021:490.

[16] CJEU, Joined Cases C-274/21 and 275/21, *EPIC Financial*, ECLI:EU:C:2022:565.

[17] Socha, cit., pp. 59–60 and 67–80, with interesting references to the case law of other Member States.

pretation, going beyond the clear text of the directive to impose an obligation on contracting authorities to indicate the maximum amount of the Framework Agreement, establishing that any purchases above that ceiling must be considered ineffective.

In a nutshell, *Autorità* and *Simonsen* state that under the principles of transparency and competition, immanent in the European legal system, a Framework Agreement must necessarily indicate the maximum amount within which it is valid, because otherwise there would be an excessive restriction of competition. In essence, the Court carried out a balancing of interests between the contracting authority's need to use the Framework Agreement as an instrument of flexibility and the need to protect competition and transparency, letting the latter prevail over the former, unlike the choice made by the European legislator who instead considered it sufficient, for the purpose of respecting competition, that the Framework Agreement be limited to four years, and that the list of participating contracting authorities and the identity of the economic operators be predefined.

It is not the intention here to discuss the merits of the balancing act, merely pointing out that it involves a political appreciation that should be up to the legislator and not the judiciary.

However, some considerations can be made on the probable consequences produced by the CJEU rulings insofar as they have set in motion a process that seems to lead to the distortion of the Framework Agreement, in order to transform it into a true and proper Contract Agreement.[18] In essence, we are witnessing a contractualization of the Framework Agreement, moreover already foreshadowed by the CJEU with the *EPIC* judgment in which it was stated, with reference to the Remedies Directive, that if the contractual terms are already all defined, as in the case where there is only one economic operator, then one must speak of a Framework Contract and not of a Framework Agreement. It cannot be ruled out that the process of contractualization of the Framework Agreement, initiated with the *Autorità* and *Simonsen*,

[18] The difference between Framework Agreements and Contracts is the subject of discussion in the doctrine: Socha, cit., p. 135 et seq. For Filipon, cit., p. 121, the difference would not be relevant to the extent that, for example, in France the Framework Agreement is defined as a contract without any difference, which means that if it has no binding conditions it cannot exist (pp. 123–124). The issue is very complex as the definition of a contract may be different in different national laws, which makes the borderline between Framework Agreement and Procurement Contract mobile: M.E. Comba, *Modification of a Framework Agreement: Interpretation of EU Law and Hints for a Comparative Law Analysis*, in Risvig Hamer – Halonen – Socha, *Public Procurement – Centralisation and New Trends*, Djof Forlag, Copenhagen, 2024, pp. 283–288.

systematically framed by *EPIC* and confirmed by some national courts,[19] will sooner or later be completed by the CJEU, with the consequences explained in the following paragraph.

1.3 The Main Consequences of the "Contractualization" of Framework Agreements

The imposition of the maximum amount introduced by the CJEU and the consequent process of contractualization of the Framework Agreement raised some pressing issues, stemming from this distortion of the original scheme. The main ones will be briefly analysed following.

The first: What happens to the implementing agreement that exceeds the maximum amount, in the case of multiple buyers, who are not reciprocally informed of the purchases made by other buyers? According to the CJEU, "Once that limit has been reached, the agreement will no longer have any effect,[20] with the consequence that the implementing contracts concluded should be regarded as direct awards in violation of the procurement procedure,[21] but the reality is not so simple. In procurement contracts, exceeding the maximum amount is easily identifiable and is normally qualified as a modification of the contract, which may or may not be considered permissible under Article 72 of Directive 2014/24/EU. In the case of the Framework Agreement, the two-tier structure makes even the mere ascertainment of the exceeding of the maximum amount more problematic: think of the case of a Framework Agreement concluded by a Central Purchasing Body (CPB) on behalf of several contracting authorities, each of which may operate independently for the conclusion of implementing contracts. It is not necessarily the case that the CPB has the tools to monitor the purchases made under the implementation contracts as a whole and thus can know when the maximum amount is exceeded, nor can the

---

19 For example, in Finland, KHO 2019:84, 26.6.2019, available in English at https://eplgroup.eu/judgment/1272/, where it is stated that, precisely as a result of *Authority*, it is necessary for the Framework Agreement to provide economic operators with a minimum amount on which they can rely. The CJEU also seems to move in this direction, albeit indirectly: C-285/18 _*Irgita* which seems to establish the obligation of a minimum amount for each contract, commented in Socha, p. 258, according to which: "the CJEU suggested that the lack of the minimum value in a public contract can be considered a failure to define the buyer's requirements sufficiently clearly" and "Although *Irgita* did not concern a framework agreement, this same conclusion can be applied by analogy to parallel framework agreements" (p. 259).

20 *Authority*, cit., para. 61; *Simonsens*, cit., para. 64,

21 Socha, cit., p. 79.

individual contracting authorities, which operate separately. Under the original scheme of the Framework Agreement without a maximum amount, this problem did not arise, but now it is urgent. Furthermore, the solution of considering contracts concluded in excess of the maximum amount as ineffective does not take into account certain operational problems: Which agreements are ineffective, if some exceed the maximum amount at the same time? What about the third economic operator who, in good faith,[22] concluded the contract protected? Is liability for any damages to be attributed to the party that concluded the Framework Agreement, or to the contracting authority that concluded the implementing contract in excess of the maximum?[23] It can therefore be said that the trend towards the contractualization of the Framework Agreements, initiated by the CJEU with the above-mentioned judgments, creates considerable legal problems of an operational nature, which must be solved systematically if this approach is to be maintained. It will probably be the case law of the national courts that will provide the first legal solutions, and it will be the task of comparative law scholars to collect and systematize them.[24]

The second concerns the relationship between the Framework Agreement and the implementing contracts, which may have very different structures depending on the combination of three pairs of factors: one or more contracting authorities; automatic award or mini-competition; and one or more economic operators. Mini-competition is excluded in the case of a Framework Agreement with only one economic operator; in all other cases, it is necessary to identify a selection criterion among the economic operators awarded the Framework Agreement, which can be modulated according to the objective to be pursued.[25] Among the automatic criteria, the most common are the

[22] In the case of a Framework Agreement with more than one economic operator, the individual economic operator cannot know when the overall maximum amount of the Framework Agreement is exceeded.

[23] Chaire de droit des contrats publics, *Modification des contrats de la commande publique*, Report of June 2023, where the issue of exceeding the maximum amount of a Framework Agreement is dealt with, from a comparative perspective, on pp. 127–132. In general, on the modification of the Framework Agreement (and not only on the exceeding of the maximum amount), see Comba, *Modifications of a Framework Agreement* ..., cit.

[24] The website of European Procurement Law Group – www.eplgroup.eu – offers a growing database with National Court decisions classified in relation to articles of the Directive 2014/24/EU which constitutes an original and precious source for comparative analysis and for the creation of European *ius commune* in the field of public procurements.

[25] See the economic analysis by Albano – Nicolas, cit, ch. 4 and, for mini-competitions, ch. 11.

cascade and quota criteria,[26] whereas in the case of mini-competitions in the strict sense, additional award criteria will have to be identified in addition to those of the Framework Agreement. It is then necessary to define the relationship between the first selection (Framework Agreement) and the second (mini-competition): the question was raised as to whether they constitute the same procedure or whether they constitute two autonomous procedures and thus whether the criteria of the second selection can be autonomous – and possibly even conflicting – with those of the first.[27] If, however, these problems are examined from the point of view of the tendency to contractualize a Framework Agreement, they lose their relevance and fade away, as the Framework Agreement will have to contain all the elements of the contract and therefore also the selection criteria, so that at the mini-selection stage the contracting authority will have very limited, if not non-existent, discretion and will therefore be able to resort only to automatic criteria. Of course, this is not yet the current state of the case law, but this paper argues that the trend towards transforming the Framework Agreement into a contract could lead to such consequences. This trend is even more dangerous when one considers the use of Framework Agreements for the purchase of rapidly obsolete goods: in such a case, it will be necessary for the Framework Agreements to provide maximum flexibility for the mini-competition criteria, in order to allow the purchase of technologically up-to-date goods.

Then there are other pressing issues that are linked to the main one outlined earlier on the contractualization of Framework Agreements.

---

[26] According to the European Commission, *Explanatory note on Framework Agreements*, Ref. Ares(2016)810203 – 16/02/2016, in the cascade model, the Contracting Authority first contacts the economic operator whose tender for the award of a Framework Agreement establishing all the terms (Framework Contract) was considered the best and turns to the second one where the first one is not capable of or interested in providing the goods, services or works in question. In the quota model, on the contrary, each economic operator admitted to the Framework Agreement is entitled to a share of the contract, usually in proportion to his ranking (ex: 50% to the first, 30% to the second, 20% to the third).

[27] Andhov – Soloveicik, *The Relationship Between Initial Tender and Mini-Competition: EU and Lithuanian Perspectives on Framework Agreements*, Vilnius University Press, 2021, pp. 45–61 analyzes a Lithuanian judgment that considers the inconsistency between the criteria of the Framework Agreement and those of the implementation contract to be admissible. For Filipon, cit., p. 129, inconsistency between the two phases is not permissible, but becomes inevitable if the subject matter of the Framework Agreement is too broad, and the mini competitions are specific, or if the Framework Agreement is awarded only with the lowest price and then the mini-competitions with MEAT (p. 130).

An important issue is the obligation to identify contracting authorities, which is in fact the first concern highlighted by recital 60 of Directive 2014/24/EU: "the contracting authorities that are parties to a specific Framework Agreement from the outset should be clearly indicated, either by name or by other means, such as a reference to a given category of contracting authorities within a clearly delimited geographical area, so that the contracting authorities concerned can be easily and unequivocally identified."[28] As it has been pointed out,[29] this is a generic obligation, without the need for a binding legal commitment on the part of each participating contracting authority. The problem is precisely that the mere indication of the contracting authorities that may use the Framework Agreement does not necessarily entail an obligation to purchase at least a certain amount, which reverberates on the issue addressed in the previous point. In fact, in the case of Framework Agreements carried out by CPBs, it will not be possible for the CPB to indicate with reasonable precision the maximum and minimum amount of the Framework Agreement, and therefore there will tend to be an over-evaluation, which could mislead economic operators. However, it appears that in practice many CPBs, before launching a Framework Agreement, carry out an analysis with the contracting authorities concerned in order to define the presumed maximum amount of the Framework Agreement and sometimes also require a legally binding purchase commitment from the contracting authorities.[30] Moreover, in cases where CPB operates as a wholesaler and not as an agent, the purchase commitment is always required for obvious reasons of financial sustainability of the transaction.[31]

Although it is not necessary for contracting authorities to be mentioned by name in the Framework Agreement, they have to be identifiable *a priori* on the basis of categories or territorial areas, and therefore the expression "contracting authorities established in the Member State in question" cannot be used.[32]

---

[28] In general, Directive 2014/24/EU prohibits generic Framework Agreements because it requires the prior definition of contracting authorities and economic operators, but Filipon (cit., p. 134) notes that they have always been used in the UK.

[29] Socha, cit., p. 82 ff.

[30] Socha, cit., pp. 358–360.

[31] This is how the French UGAP (Union des groupements d'achat public) operates, in a manner illustrated by O. Giannoni, legal director of UGAP, during an interview with the author of this paper.

[32] A special case occurs in Italy, where the law (Legislative Decree 36/23, Art. 62–63) requires contracting authorities to be pre-qualified for contracts exceeding €140,000 (services and supplies) and €500,000 (public works). In Italy there is therefore an official list of contracting authorities authorized to carry out

This requirement is not only for the protection of competition but also for the need of economic operators, who in this way can know with whom they will have to conclude contracts and could decide not to participate if there are contracting authorities that could pose risks in the regularity of payments.

Another problematic topic is that of modifications to Framework Agreements and executive contracts in the course of execution,[33] which has already been examined under Section 1.3 but limited to the exceeding of the maximum amount of the Framework Agreement, whereas it will be addressed here, albeit briefly, in more general terms.

Article 72 of Directive 2014/24/EU explicitly foresees, except for in some minor cases, its application also to Framework Agreements, whereas for implementing contracts no extension rule is necessary, as Article 72 applies directly to them, being procurement contracts to all intents and purposes. The problem lies mainly in the coordination between the amendments of the Framework Agreement and those of the implementing contracts: if an implementing agreement is amended, for example due to unforeseeable circumstances under Article 72, para. 1(c) of Directive 2014/24/EU, this amendment is also reflected in the Framework Agreement, the total amount of which will have to be adjusted to the new amount of the implementing contract. It should be noted here that, in the context of the process of contractualization of the Framework Agreements, the relevance of this coordination issue is reduced, as the level of detail of the Framework Agreement will become such that the room for maneuver for the implementing contracts will become very limited, with the consequence that a change in the latter will automatically be reflected in the former.

Finally, it seems interesting to point out the very topical and stimulating subject of Parallel Framework Agreements, which is also of undoubted operational relevance and which is at the crossroads of numerous legal (administrative law, contract law, and competition law) and economic issues. On this point, it is possible to refer to the Ph.D. Thesis by Magdalena Socha,[34] whose conclusions can be shared. With a view to the tendency to contractualize

---

procurement procedures (currently just under 5,000) and therefore, strictly speaking, a Framework Agreement referring to all Italian contracting authorities could be compatible with the requirements of the directive as it would still allow all of them to be identified in advance.

33 Comba, *Modifications of a Framework Agreement* ..., cit., Filipon, cit., pp. 128–129; A. Gouveia Martins, *Os acordos qudro e os contratos celebrados ao seu Abrigo: em especial, o regime da sua modificaçao*, in: M. Assis Raimundo, *Centralizaçao e Agregaçao de Compras Pùblicas*, Almedina, Coimbra, 2019, pp. 207–274.

34 Socha, cit.

Framework Agreements, one might ask whether there is still room for Parallel Framework Agreements, given that they are clearly limited in the event that each individual Framework Agreement carries a minimum amount, in addition to the maximum, and are in any case excluded when the individual Framework Agreement carries an exclusivity clause.[35]

2. IMPROVEMENT PROPOSALS

The imposition of the maximum value of Framework Agreements through the *Autorità* and *Simonsen* rulings and the consequent start of the tendency to contractualize Framework Agreements created a situation of great uncertainty among economic operators and contracting authorities,[36] the main aspects of which have been illustrated in the preceding paragraphs. From an operational point of view, contracting authorities have often reacted to the obligation imposed by the CJEU by setting strongly overestimated maximum amounts of the Framework Agreement, in fact nullifying the practical scope of this upper limit but with the consequence of inducing unfounded expectations in economic operators and thus producing further uncertainty.[37]

In essence, the CJEU introduced a substantial change to the legal nature of the Framework Agreements but left the work half done, lacking all the consequent systematic adjustments required by this choice, because of course this is not the competence of the Court but of the legislator.

Therefore, it is now up to the European Legislator to decide whether to restore the non-contractual nature of Framework Agreements, by removing the obligation of a maximum amount, or to follow the approach of the CJEU and regulate the legal consequences of this new Framework Contract configuration.

In the first case, the European legislator should reiterate what has already been established in recitals 60–62 of Directive 2014/24/EU concerning the balance between the protection of transparency and competition, on the one hand, and the need to maintain the legal technique of Framework Agreements,

---

[35] Socha, cit., in ch. 9 (pp. 250–276) examines cases where Framework Agreements concluded by Central Purchasing Bodies oblige contracting authorities to a minimum amount of purchases or exclusivity and analyzes the consequences on the practicability of Parallel Framework Agreements.

[36] Among the many comments to this effect, one should note for interesting observations from an operational point of view, O. Giannoni, *Stratégie et techniques de l'achat public*, Berger Levrault, Boulogne, 2022, p. 119: "la multiplication de ces incertitudes risque soit de dissuader les acteurs économiques, soit de peser sur les performances des marchés publics." See also Socha, cit., pp. 77–78.

[37] Giannoni, cit., p. 119; Socha, cit., p. 79.

on the other hand, clearly stating that no maximum amount is imposed by EU law on Framework Agreements. As it is well known, the Directive considers the inclusion of a maximum duration of four years and the obligation to indicate in advance the contracting authorities as well as the economic operators to be sufficient elements to ensure compliance with transparency and competition. The CJEU, on the other hand, has ruled that it is also necessary to impose an upper limit on the amount of the Framework Agreement, because otherwise transparency and competition would be impaired. The legislator could then insert further limitations to ensure this balance – which the CJEU considered insufficient – but without distorting the Framework Agreement and thus without inserting a maximum amount. It could, for example, establish that the Framework Agreement is not allowed in the case of a single economic operator (following what the CJEU decided in the *EPIC* case), it could introduce mandatory exclusivity clauses for contracting authorities using Framework Agreements,[38] it could perhaps even provide for the obligation to establish a *minimum* guaranteed amount for each economic operator, in order to encourage participation and remunerate their availability.[39] This solution could lend itself to two criticisms:[40] on the one hand, it could be argued that in any case it violates the principle of transparency, even with the additional expedients suggested; on the other hand, that the return to a very flexible Framework Agreement would blur the difference with the Dynamic Purchasing System. As to the first objection, it has already been said that the balancing judgment is up to the legislator, and moreover, contracting authorities have often reacted to the obligation imposed by the CJEU by setting strongly overestimated maximum amounts of the Framework Agreement, which has effects contrary to transparency. As to the second objection, it has been mentioned that the difference between a Framework Agreement and a Dynamic Purchasing System is already blurred in the original text of Directive 2014/24/EU and thus would not change much.

[38] This option was highlighted by Professor François Lichère during the EPLG Meeting held in Lyon, on April 2 and 3, 2025, with the awareness that exclusivity clauses will exclude the possibility of using Parallel Framework Agreements.

[39] This imposition would not have the effect of transforming the Framework Agreement into a Framework Contract because uncertainty would still remain as to the subject matter of the Framework Agreement, as the maximum amount would not be defined.

[40] I am grateful for these critics to Professors Dacian Dragos and Albert Sanchez Graells, who raised these issues during the EPLG Meeting held in Lyon, on April 2 and 3, 2025.

In the latter case, it would be necessary to address at least the main problem set out in the preceding paragraphs and thus to regulate the legal consequences of exceeding the ceiling, in the case of Framework Agreements managed by the CPB with more than one contracting authority, by allocating the risk and consequent liability between the contracting authority who carried out the Framework Agreement and the contracting authority that concluded the contract exceeding the overall limit and by protecting the *bona fide* economic operator's reliance.

One could then imagine a third hypothesis, in which both types would be allowed: both with and without a binding maximum amount – where perhaps it would be more correct to speak of Framework Contracts and Framework Agreements. The latter (without a binding maximum amount) could be reserved for cases in which the contracting authority or the CPB has to deal with situations characterized by uncertainty as to the quality and quantity of the purchase requirements, as pointed out by Filipon's comparative analysis.

An example is that of emergency purchases: the contracting authority knows that statistically there will be emergencies (floods, earthquakes), but does not know when, nor of what intensity, and therefore concludes a Framework Agreement without a maximum amount, with several operators, to guarantee security and flexibility of supply. Among other things, it can be noted that in this case, recourse to the Framework Agreement would in any case have pro-competitive effects because the alternative would be a negotiated procedure without prior publication, for reasons of extreme urgency (Article 32(2)(c) of Directive 2014/24/EU), and therefore through the Framework Agreement without a maximum amount the extreme urgency is in some way "harnessed" so as to ensure transparency and competition.

Finally, it seems worth mentioning two more potential improvement proposals.

The first is the one, already mentioned in the ECA Report, to enter a search key in TED so that Framework Agreements can be selected and analyzed. Access to proper data would be indispensable for checking how Framework Agreements are used and what their effects are on competition.

The second is to investigate the relationship between Framework Agreements and cross-border procurements. This is an extremely interesting field of analysis, especially in a context in which there is an increasing need for cross-border procurements in very sensitive sectors such as defense, energy, and health.[41]

---

[41] M. Draghi (ed.), *The Future of European Competitiveness*, September 2024. See also Socha, cit., p. 284.

The structure of Framework Agreements seems to be particularly suitable for cross-border procurements, but the issue seems to be still highly unexplored, lacking a steady data analysis and a clear regulation which is necessary to provide guidance, both from a substantive point of view[42] and in terms of remedies[43] to contracting authorities wishing to use such techniques.

---

[42] For the main issues pending regulation on cross-border procurements, see Lombardi – Rossa, cit.; for the interaction between cross-border procurements and Framework Agreements, see Comba, *Framework Agreements for Cross-border Procurements* ..., cit.

[43] Recently, the CJEU addressed the issue of procedural rules and jurisdiction in cross-border procurements (C-480/22, *EVN Business Services*, ECLI:EU:C:2023:918), leaving many issues still unresolved.

9. Digitalisation and competition

Proposals for upcoming public procurement reform

Gabriella M. Racca

REFORM PROPOSALS

With the future revision of Public Procurement Directives up for discussion, the following proposals should be considered:[1]

- new EU provisions for a set of mandatory rules to reduce the legal and administrative barriers resulting from the 27 different implementations and other provisions to be implemented according to national choices;
- the introduction of a European 28th legal regime providing a common set of rules for small and medium-sized enterprises (SMEs) and innovative companies and related EU compliant platform for public procurement of innovation[2] (or the platform for the EU institutions public procurement);
- the extension of European provisions to cover contract execution and management, in order to check the final outcome of the contract (public spending) throughout the procurement cycle, at least in the main phases, including e-invoice and payment, through digital instruments, and also

1 See the contribution from the University of Turin research group (coordinator Prof. Racca) in response to the consultations launched by the European Commission on revising the Public Procurement Directives (Ref. Ares(2024)8928678; feedback reference no. F3525461), and in response to the proposal for a Regulation establishing the European Business Wallet (Ref. Ares(2025)3928207; feedback reference no. F3565847).

2 European Commission, 'Communication from the Commission to the European Parliament, the Council, the European Economic and Social Committee and the Committee of the Regions: The EU Startup and Scaleup Strategy – Choose Europe to Start and Scale', COM(2025) 270 final, 28 May 2025.

adopting the Building Information Modeling approach (at least for work procurement);

- the evolution of the European Single Procurement Document (ESPD) into a Virtual Company Dossier, to be integrated within the forthcoming "European Business Wallet" (according to the EU Commission proposal)[3] for economic operators and suppliers. Such a system, updated in real time through interoperable public databases (that collect information at a national level), could both assess the absence of exclusion grounds and a number of standardised qualification criteria. Contracting authorities could then define the levels they require, in accordance with the proportionality principle, based on this digital preliminary evaluation (a "green light" should be provided or "yellow" if self-cleaning is needed);
- a different set of rules for work procurement should be provided, due to the need for connection among e-procurement platforms and the dataset related to the Building Information Modeling in order to adapt to the specific sector (e.g. also specific set of provisions and platforms should be provided for healthcare, energy, security, social and third-sector procurement, etc.);
- the adoption and development of public e-commerce platforms at the national level but that are interoperable cross-border, to provide the possibility to have an "Amazon-like" experience for public buyers, supporting framework agreements or dynamic purchasing systems on the relevant subject matter and the related logistics;
- the implementation of similar platforms with simplified and streamlined tender requirements and fast-track procedures for innovative SMEs and start-ups and for below threshold contracts (thus out of the scope of the next reform).[4]

---

3 European Commission, *The EU Startup and Scaleup Strategy*, 5; already mentioned in the Regulation (EU) No. 2024/1183 of 11 April 2024, amending Regulation (EU) No. 910/2014 as regards establishing the European Digital Identity Framework (EIDAS 2).

4 This is also specified in the context of the future establishment of a "European Innovation Act", which is expected to promote regulatory sandboxes and enable innovators to develop and trial innovative projects. This new framework will, in particular, contain "a common legal definition and basic principles regarding the establishment of regulatory sandboxes, including cross-border or place-based regulatory sandboxes, while ensuring sector-specific needs". See European Commission, *The EU Startup and Scaleup Strategy*, 5.

1. FROM CURRENT LACK OF PARTICIPATION TO INCREASED COMPETITIVENESS IN THE PROCUREMENT MARKET

Lack of competition in the procurement market has been identified as a key challenge by the European Court of Auditors, with recent reports indicating a growing trend of concentration among major economic operators to the detriment of SMEs and innovative start-ups, highlighting insufficient action by Member States to address such barriers to competitive tendering.[5]

Public procurement procedures have become lengthier and more bureaucratic, making them less attractive compared to private procurement, and high administrative costs and requirements penalise SMEs, in particular.[6] Current regulations do not adequately incentivise competition or consider strategic aspects such as innovation or environmental and social sustainability (and effective digital transformation). The scarcity of reliable data hinders the effective monitoring of procedures to prevent the risk of maladministration and corruption, which undermines the competitiveness of the market.[7]

---

5 As noted by the European Court of Auditors, market concentration in the EU public procurement sector has resulted in significantly reduced competition, with "few activities used by Member States to address obstacles". Between 2011 and 2021, the average number of participants per tender declined from six to three, and 42% of contracts were awarded through direct awards, often following a single bid. The Court further emphasised that the frequent use of direct awards, which should remain exceptional, has further limited competition. European Court of Auditors, *Special Report 28/2023: Public Procurement in the EU – Less Competition for Contracts Awarded for Works, Goods and Services in the 10 Years up to 2021* (Publications Office of the European Union 2023), 42.

6 See: Laurence Folliot-Lalliot, 'Digital Transformation for SMEs' (intervention at the International Conference *Public Contracts and Digital Transformation: EU and American Evolutions*, University of Turin, 28 March 2025), organised in collaboration with the *Ius Publicum Network Review*, the International Network *Public Contracts in Legal Globalisation*, and George Washington University Law School.

7 See Sope Williams, 'Fighting Corruption with AI and Digital Tools' (intervention at the International Conference *Public Contracts and Digital Transformation: EU and American Evolutions*, University of Turin, 28 March 2025), organised in collaboration with the *Ius Publicum Network Review*, the International Network *Public Contracts in Legal Globalisation*, and George Washington University Law School; see also Gabriella M. Racca and Christopher R. Yukins, 'Emergency Procurement and Corruption' in Sope Williams and Jessica Tillipman (eds), *Routledge Handbook of Public Procurement Corruption* (Routledge, London 2024) 76 ff.

To overcome competition barriers and foster broader participation by SMEs and innovative start-ups, the EU Commission has highlighted key reforms, such as the establishment of a 28th EU regime for innovative companies, the development of the European Business Wallet, and the adoption of a European Innovation Act. All these measures should be integrated into the forthcoming reform of the Public Procurement Directives, with the aim of fostering innovation and making procurement rules less risk-averse and more accessible to innovative SMEs.[8]

To address and overcome the legal and administrative fragmentation, promote competition and open the single market, the next European procurement provisions might contain clearly defined mandatory rules (directly applicable) and some provisions to be implemented by the different Member States.

Indeed, in recent years, experience has demonstrated the need to minimise differences among the 27 national transpositions of the Public Procurement Directives, as these have created legal barriers to the opening of the procurement market, hence the possible idea also of a 28th legal regime for innovative procurement, alongside the EU Commission's proposal of a 28th legal regime for innovative companies (and possibly also for the EU Institutions instead of the Financial Regulation). A specific platform might be provided for quick and transparent joint procurement based on this common regime. Digital transformation is a key enabler of this broader set of reforms, with the aim of enhancing also the EU's technological competitiveness.

Further deployment of digital instruments and interoperable platforms will simplify access and participation in the procurement market. To this purpose, a strategic proposal is to enhance the ESPD 4.0 with the Virtual Company Dossier or with the EU digital Business Wallet, the "electronic identification" for legal persons, which should provide a harmonised digital identification enabling authentication and sharing of data, to access public and private services securely.[9]

In the context of public procurement, the progressive implementation of the Business Wallet for economic operators may enhance the efficiency of cross-border transactions, reduce administrative burdens, and foster greater trust in the digital single market. In the e-procurement system, the Business Wallet should be integrated with the Virtual Company Dossier, resulting from the necessary digital evolution of the European Single Procurement Document 4.0, overcoming the need for self-certification and the subsequent checks, according to EU or national choices (in Italy still quite complex). Digital tools,

---

8 European Commission, *The EU Startup and Scaleup Strategy*, 5.

9 See Recital 7, Regulation (EU) 2024/1183, (eIDAS 2), cit. See the Call for evidence – Ares(2025)3928207, European Business Wallet, and the response by the University of Turin research group (Feedback reference no. F3565847).

including AI, could streamline qualification grounds as well as tender requirements and enable fast-track procedures for low value, R&D and innovation procurement, while ensuring oversight and flagging potential distortions during deployment and execution phases.

Moreover, despite EU rules encouraging the consideration of non-price factors, such as environmental and social clauses, a large number of contracts are still awarded based solely on price, due in part to the lack of binding sustainability obligations and the plurality of national practices.[10] These criticalities clearly emerged in the responses to the Call for evidence on the reform of the Procurement Directives, as public entities viewed the current legislation (56%) as effectively promoting green and sustainable procurement, whereas a smaller and less convinced proportion of companies and economic operators agreed (46%).[11]

Digital tools, such as interoperable e-procurement systems and AI-assisted evaluation mechanisms, may support contracting authorities in the effective and consistent application of green and social criteria, such as eco-labels or life-cycle costing, by enabling objective assessment of environmental impacts and facilitating compliance with the EU climate objectives. Furthermore, establishing a 28th legal regime for innovative companies could introduce harmonised requirements, including environmental and social criteria which could be verified more efficiently by contracting authorities using targeted digital tools (a "green light" provided by interoperable platforms).

Digital transformation could also overcome the problem of single tendering, the rate of which is constantly increasing (in some countries, nearly one-third of contracts exceeding EU thresholds receive only one or no bids).[12] Single tendering can lead to higher prices, as data show that contracts with only one tender tend to cost almost 10% more, which is always to the detriment of the

---

[10] See OECD, *Harnessing Public Procurement for the Green Transition – Good Practices in OECD Countries* (OECD Publishing, Paris 2024) https://doi.org/10.1787/e551f448-en accessed 8 December 2025.

[11] European Commission, Directorate-General for Internal Market, Industry, Entrepreneurship and SMEs, *Factual Summary Report on the Public Consultation on Evaluation of the Public Procurement Directives*, Ref Ares(2025)3894320, 14 May 2025.

[12] For example, in Hungary, where a "Single Bid Reporting Tool" and the Public Procurement Performance Measurement Framework were created to monitor and reduce single bids. See OECD, *Improving Competitive Practices in Hungary's Public Procurement: Reducing Single-Bids and Enhancing Supplier Participation, OECD Public Governance Reviews* (OECD Publishing, Paris 2024) https://doi.org/10.1787/5d1c1ec1-en accessed 8 December 2025.

contracting entity, which must bear the additional costs.[13] Several legal and structural factors contribute to these challenges, including overly complex regulatory frameworks, insufficient advertising periods for tenders and extensive use of negotiated procedures without prior publication, as pointed out by the EU Court of Auditors.[14]

Moreover, high market concentration and the risk of collusion further undermine competitive procurement, particularly in critical sectors characterised by a limited number of suppliers, such as healthcare, where the acquisition of highly specialised pharmaceuticals and medical devices is often constrained by a limited pool of suppliers, potentially restricting market access and distorting competitive dynamics.[15]

Therefore, future reforms should focus on increasing market engagement, and promoting greater participation of innovative SMEs. Procurement processes should be streamlined through digital transformation and integration of e-procurement systems to mitigate distortions through digital monitoring.[16]

---

13 For instance, in Slovenia, single-bid procedures accounted for 51% of all procurement cases in 2022, up from 44% in 2021, as evidenced by the OECD. See OECD, *Maximising the Benefits of Effective Competition in Public Procurement in Slovenia, OECD Public Governance Reviews* (OECD Publishing, Paris 2025) https://doi.org/10.1787/c1e5d31f-en accessed 8 December 2025.

14 As highlighted by the European Court of Auditors, single bidding remains one of the main challenges to competition in public procurement, as also acknowledged in the replies of the European Commission. See European Court of Auditors, *Special Report 28/2023: Public Procurement in the EU. Less Competition for Contracts Awarded for Works, Goods and Services in the 10 Years up to 2021*, 38, and the *Replies of the Commission* (Publications Office of the European Union 2023).

15 The medical, IT, and construction sectors are among those most affected by high single-bid rates, as evidenced by the OECD. OECD, *Improving Competitive Practices in Hungary's Public Procurement. Reducing Single-bids and Enhancing Supplier Participation*, 26 ff. See also European Commission, *Proposal for a Regulation of the European Parliament and of the Council Laying a Framework for Strengthening the Availability and Security of Supply of Critical Medicinal Products as Well as the Availability of, and Accessibility of, Medicinal Products of Common Interest, and Amending Regulation (EU) 2024/795*, COM(2025) 102 final, 2025/102 (COD), Strasbourg, 11 March 2025. See Gabriella M. Racca, 'Digital Transformation in Healthcare Procurement' (2023) 23(2) *HealthManagement.org – Medical Devices and AI Regulations* 98 ff.

16 See also: European Commission, Directorate-General for Regional and Urban Policy, Central European University, and the Government Transparency Institute, *Single Bidding and Non-competitive Tendering Procedures in EU Co-funded Projects*, Report by Mihály Fazekas (Publications Office of the European Union 2019) https://data.europa.eu/doi/10.2776/751156 accessed 8 December 2025.

The upcoming revision of the European Directives on Public Procurement should address the issues highlighted by the European Court of Auditors and define a comprehensive strategy to promote fairer and more effective competition, modernising and simplifying the rules, facilitating access for start-ups and innovators, and strengthening transparency and monitoring of public procurement data.[17]

Specifically, it is important to consolidate data into accessible and structured platforms, which would facilitate data collection and in-depth analysis. Thus, data might provide market analysis and predictions of the economic operators interested and more suitable to perform a specific contract.

2. DIGITALISATION AND COMPETITION: THE POSSIBLE DIGITAL REFORM

Future provisions on European public procurement should therefore address the identified issues regarding the low level of participation and competition in the European public procurement market, despite the existence of common rules for decades.[18] Many barriers to the opening of the single market are still there, and the digital transformation should help to overcome them. Indeed, the European Commission has also reaffirmed its commitment through a significant digital transformation to increase competition and transparency in the procurement sector.[19]

E-procurement platforms, with e-forms, should support the entire digital procurement lifecycle to guarantee fair competition, not only in the award phase, but also in contract execution.[20] As recognized by the CJEU, and in the

---

17 Paulo Magina, 'AI in Procurement for Integrity and Efficiency' (intervention at the International Conference *Public Contracts and Digital Transformation: EU and American Evolutions*, University of Turin, 28 March 2025), organised in collaboration with the *Ius Publicum Network Review*, the International Network *Public Contracts in Legal Globalisation*, and George Washington University Law School.

18 European Court of Auditors, *Special Report 28/2023: Public Procurement in the EU. Less Competition for Contracts Awarded for Works, Goods and Services in the 10 Years up to 2021*, 5.

19 European Commission, *Replies of the European Commission to the Special Report 28/2023: Public Procurement in the EU. Less Competition for Contracts Awarded for Works, Goods and Services in the 10 Years up to 2021* (28 November 2023).

20 Gabriella M. Racca, 'Digital Transformation for an Effective E-Procurement' in Carina Risvig Hamer, Marta Andhov, Erik Bertelsen and Roberto Caranta (eds), *Into the Northern Light. In memory of Steen Treumer* (Ex Tuto Publishing, Copenhagen 2022) 215 ff (article awarded the TED Ambassador Award 2023);

recent EU Commission strategy for innovative SMEs, this would also facilitate the participation of the smallest economic operators.[21] Taking into account the entire procurement cycle would facilitate monitoring the effective outcome of public spending for the benefit of citizens, and dealing with e-invoice and payment could help to overcome the lack of knowledge for the economic operators of this phase. This is one of the reasons for the absence of cross-border participation in the procurement market.

The updated Tenders Electronic Daily (TED) database might become the reference point for European public demand (Public Procurement Data Space). It is envisaged that the national e-senders identified by the Member States (e.g. for Italy, ANAC's National Public Contracts Database) will send contract e-notices to the TED through structured native digital documents (e-forms) for contracts above the European threshold (as is already the case) but also, potentially, for contracts below the threshold.

This evolution may enhance the creation of the European Procurement Data Space,[22] as part of the wider European Data Space, reinforced by native digital

---

Anna Corrado, Elena Griglio and Gabriella M. Racca (eds), *La digitalizzazione dei contratti pubblici. Manuale delle nuove procedure telematiche – Piattaforme, fiducia e innovazione* (Dike Giuridica, Naples 2025).

[21] Recent CJEU case law also highlights several competition-related issues in public procurement, progressively limiting the scope of mandatory public disclosure of procurement and beneficial ownership data, as evidenced in two relevant cases (C-54/21, *Antea Polska* and the joined cases C-37/20 and C-601/20, *Luxembourg Business Registers*). In *Antea Polska*, the CJEU emphasised that transparency, which serves the "principle of good administration" (points 50, 64, 66, and 76 of the ruling), must support procurement integrity without harming competition. See: EU Court of Justice, Judgment of the Court, fourth chamber, 17 November 2022, Case C-54/21, *Antea Polska S.A., Pectore-Eco sp. z o.o., Instytut Ochrony Środowiska – Państwowy Instytut Badawczy*. Similarly, though not directly related to the procurement sector, in the *Luxembourg Business Registers* case the Court invalidated provisions of the Anti-Money Laundering Directive that mandated unrestricted public access to beneficial ownership data, finding them incompatible with the EU Charter of Fundamental Rights—particularly Articles 7 and 8, which guarantee the rights to privacy and data protection. While the Court acknowledged the directive's objective of combating money laundering, it found the interference excessive and not strictly necessary, concluding that the provisions failed to adequately balance public transparency with fundamental rights. See: EU Court of Justice, Judgment of the Court, Grand Chamber, 22 November 2022, Joined Cases C-37/20 and C-601/20, *WM, Sovim SA v. Luxembourg Business Registers*. See: European Commission, *The EU Startup and Scaleup Strategy*, 5.

[22] Chaire de droit des contrats publics, *Digitalisation de la commande publique* (Université Jean Moulin Lyon 3) https://chairedcp.univ-lyon3.fr/rapport

documents,[23] which can provide fluxes of data, representing a privileged perspective for monitoring the internal market and public resources spending by means of artificial intelligence tools, and also provide market analysis and foster the participation of SMEs.[24]

The entire digital public procurement procedure on interoperable platforms will include e-notification (i.e. the electronic publication of tender notices), e-access (i.e. electronic access to public procurement documents), e-submission (i.e. the submission of tenders in electronic format), with the provision of the personal identification codes necessary to operate on the relevant electronic platform. The recalled evolution of Virtual Company Dossiers into Business Wallets updated in real time would quickly provide the necessary knowledge of the capacity and qualification of economic operators (green hook to relevant data).

As the European Commission has highlighted, the efforts to fight fraud and corruption would employ AI-driven semantic analysis, machine learning and data mining of structured electronic invoices, with the aim of improving monitoring and accuracy. Data from electronic invoices could also be used as the most accurate dataset regarding business transactions, thus reducing administrative burdens. Additionally, (blockchain-enabled) e-invoice financing could effectively address the risk of duplicate invoice financing across borders by creating a unique digital fingerprint for each invoice.[25] Moreover, the evolution of the e-Certis IT system should enable the exchange not of certificates and attestations themselves but rather of data relating to the most frequently requested qualification criteria. In a future perspective, this might be overcome by a complete and interoperable set of data from the Virtual Company Dossier or the Digital Business Wallet for each economic operator.

The ESPD should strategically evolve from a self-certification to an automatic check of the fulfilment of requirements with native digital data that give a green light to the economic operator through interoperable databases, without asking or sending certificates. This would guarantee an effective digital

-digitalisation-de-la-commande-publique accessed 8 December 2025.

23 European Commission, *Communication from the Commission to the European Parliament, the Council, the European Economic and Social Committee and the Committee of the Regions: A European Strategy for Data*, COM(2020) 66 final, 19 February 2020.

24 European Commission, Communication of 16 March 2023, *Public Procurement: A Data Space to Improve Public Spending, Boost Data-driven Policy-making and Improve Access to Tenders for SMEs*, 2023/C 98 I/01.

25 European Commission, *Report on the Effects of Directive 2014/55/EU on the Internal Market and on the Uptake of Electronic Invoicing in Public Procurement*, COM(2024) 72 final, 19 February 2024.

economic operators' qualification to overcome the current "paper-based" or "pdf certificate-based" approach and manual verifications by public officials.[26]

The upcoming reform on public procurement should therefore be in synergy with the evolution of the Virtual Company Dossier of the economic operators, in line with the EU Commission's proposal for a "European Business Wallet",[27] aiming at facilitating the exchange of information relating to legal persons in different EU countries.

From this perspective, the new procurement provisions should integrate verified data and credentials of economic operators to enable and facilitate their qualification and exclusion (whenever a self-cleaning would not be possible). The information exchange and data re-use will open up the prospect of exploiting risk management strategies in procurement, overcoming the mere formalisms of the current systems of self-certification and control of enterprises' capacity (the ultimate beneficiary, the effective capacity and integrity) for effective competition and transparent evaluation.[28]

3. FOSTERING COLLABORATIVE PROCUREMENT AND INNOVATION THROUGH DIGITAL PLATFORMS

The future reform of procurement should aim to develop and promote a system of interoperable EU-compliant national platforms, managed by Central Purchasing Bodies or other qualified contracting authorities.[29] Such a system could facilitate the effective opening of the single market by enabling the development of public e-commerce platforms, possibly specialised (or with specific market analysis) in different sectors (e.g. healthcare and social

[26] European Commission, Directorate-General for Internal Market, Industry, Entrepreneurship and SMEs, *Interoperability in End-to-End eProcurement* (Publications Office of the European Union 2020) https://data.europa.eu/doi/10.2873/991386 accessed 8 December 2025. See also Anna Corrado, Elena Griglio and Gabriella M. Racca (eds), *La digitalizzazione dei contratti pubblici. Manuale delle nuove procedure telematiche – Piattaforme, fiducia e innovazione* (Dike Giuridica, Naples 2025).

[27] European Commission, *The EU Startup and Scaleup Strategy*, 5.

[28] OECD, *Managing Risks in the Public Procurement of Goods, Services and Infrastructure*, OECD Public Governance Policy Papers No. 33 (OECD Publishing, Paris 2023) https://doi.org/10.1787/45667d2f-en accessed 8 December 2025.

[29] Gabriella M. Racca, 'Central Purchasing Bodies in Italy: Reluctance and Challenges' in Carina Risvig Hamer and Mario Comba (eds), *Centralising Public Procurement* (Edward Elgar Publishing, Cheltenham 2021), 220 ff.

services, energy, technology) based on transparent market analysis and networks of qualified and reliable suppliers.

The development of specialised platforms at EU level could promote the use of specific model contracts or standard contractual clauses for specific sectors, such as healthcare, with special provisions for the implementation of cross-border cooperation, among qualified contracting authorities, as well as through collaborative and digital models. This can also take the form of specific "alliances" (such as the Big Buyers' Initiative of the EU Commission) developed for specific cross-border cooperation[30] and innovation procurement in specific sectors.[31] Such platforms may also operate as "communities of practice", providing best or next practices to foster innovation. Such advanced forms of digital cooperation could enable supply chains in strategic sectors, such as medical devices or essential medicines, to overcome current fragmentation and evolve towards collaborative models ensuring the traceability of production chains from manufacture to final distribution.[32]

These platforms could be shared with other interested contracting authorities through framework agreements or dynamic purchasing systems, awarded by national or local Central Purchasing Bodies according to the relevant market.

---

[30] Gabriella M. Racca and Christopher R. Yukins (eds), *Joint Public Procurement and Innovation: Lessons Across Borders* (Droit Administratif / Administrative Law Collection, dir Jean-Bernard Auby, Bruylant, Brussels 2019).

[31] Gabriella M. Racca and Silvia Ponzio, 'Next Challenges for the EU Public Procurement Reform: Digitalisation and Cooperation' (2024) 2 *Ius Publicum Network Review*; Gabriella M. Racca, 'La digitalizzazione necessaria dei contratti pubblici: per un'Amazon pubblica' (2021) 45(4) *DPCE online* 4669–4706; Olivier Giannoni, 'Faut-il «amazonifier» la commande publique?' (2022) *AJDA* 26. One example is the establishment of the Critical Medicines Alliance in January 2024, which brings together over 300 public bodies, private organisations, and representatives of the pharmaceutical industry, with the aim of identifying vulnerabilities and defining strategic interventions to reduce the risk of shortages in the supply chain of essential medicines. See Critical Medicines Alliance, *Strategic Report* (28 February 2025) https://health.ec.europa.eu/document/download/3da9dfc0-c5e0-4583-a0f1-1652c7c18c3c_en?filename=hera_cma_strat-report_en.pdf accessed 8 December 2025.

[32] See European Commission, *Proposal for a Regulation of the European Parliament and of the Council Laying a Framework for Strengthening the Availability and Security of Supply of Critical Medicinal Products as Well as the Availability of, and Accessibility of, Medicinal Products of Common Interest, and Amending Regulation (EU) 2024/795*, which emphasises the need to establish a harmonised framework to enhance the security of supply and availability of critical medicinal products, in response to the vulnerabilities exposed by the pandemic and the evolving geopolitical context.

The activities might thus be fully traceable inside the different platforms, and the choice for the buyers might be wider. The suppliers, especially SMEs, will greatly benefit from such a system entering directly into any platform providing business opportunities (through a shared model of qualification) for the benefit of EU citizens.

4. DIGITAL TRANSFORMATION FOR FAIR COMPETITION IN THE ENTIRE PROCUREMENT CYCLE

Forthcoming reform of EU directives should cover not only the award phase but also the execution of public contracts, the transition to effective e-procurement and the completion of the EU e-invoicing system. The US pragmatic experience requires considering the whole procurement process to prove the effective outcome of the contract, giving much less attention to the selection than to the execution (not even awarding damages for the violation during the awarding phase).[33] This would enable the digital monitoring of the outcome of public spending and effectively implement the principle of competition throughout the entire lifecycle of the public contract. Thus, it would also allow the direct acquisition of information on the promptness, quality of execution and the coherence with the e-award and the subsequent contract, for an effective qualification for further procurements. Reputation might be more effectively evaluated. This approach is also in line with the evolution of CJEU case law, which has highlighted that bidders, including unsuccessful ones, have a "right to fairness and competition" under mandatory European and national rules, including during the execution phase.[34]

The execution phase of the public procurement cycle is normally considered outside the scope of the Public Procurement Directives. The award phase has been considered the most relevant phase for the application of the EU principles, with regard to the principle of competition among economic operators. Until now, Member States have considered it sufficient intervention to deal with the award phase to ensure non-discrimination, transparency and the opening of the EU procurement market. Because of the choice to focus EU intervention on the award phase, the execution phase of the procurement is left

33 Gabriella M. Racca and Christopher R. Yukins, 'Introduction. The Promise and Perils of Innovation in Cross-Border Procurement' in Gabriella M. Racca and Christopher R. Yukins (eds), *Joint Public Procurement and Innovation: Lessons Across Borders* (Droit Administratif / Administrative Law Collection, dir Jean-Bernard Auby, Bruylant, Brussels 2019), 1 ff.

34 CJEU, *Pressetext Nachrichtenagentur GmbH* v *Republik Österreich* in Case C-454/06, ECR I-4401, 19 June 2008.

to the national choices of Member States, and only material changes have been addressed; otherwise, it is considered an award without notice.

As recognised, a public contract must pursue the public interest throughout its entire cycle and requires that the performance respects certain quality standards, as promised in the award and specified in the subsequent contract, in pursuit of the public interest of citizens.[35] Therefore, it is a matter of public interest to know how the public contract is executed, and it is the reason why it cannot be considered a purely private issue between the two parties to the contract and why transparency is required, for example, in Italy, throughout the execution phase.[36] It seems clear that if the public contract were a normal private contract, after the award it could be modified by mutual agreement as is commonly the case in private law. However, the European Court of Justice, and later the Directive, have clearly limited such possibility, safeguarding fair competition primarily in the interest of unsuccessful tenderers in respect of the competitive selection outcome (material changes are limited).

Therefore, a minimum level of transparency is required, as otherwise suspicion of discrimination, favouritism, unfair arrangements and lack of integrity during the execution of the contract may arise and would possibly discourage participation and trust in public administrations (fairness of competition in the award should be respected during the execution too).[37]

The role of third parties (economic operators interested in the award of the contract, media, social witnesses, academia, NGOs, civil society) is of outstanding importance to guarantee the correct award of the contract but also its correct subsequent contract performance (as "watchdogs").[38] Their role can greatly vary in different legal systems, considering their characteristics and the effectiveness of other monitoring systems on the contract award,

---

35 Gabriella M. Racca, Roberto Cavallo Perin and Gian Luigi Albano, 'Competition in the Execution Phase of Public Procurement' (2011) 41(1) *Public Contract Law Journal* 89 ff.

36 See: Italian State Council, Plenary Session, No. 10 of 2 April 2020.

37 European Court of Auditors, *Special Report 28/2023: Public Procurement in the EU. Less Competition for Contracts Awarded for Works, Goods and Services in the 10 Years up to 2021*, 5.

38 Gabriella M. Racca, 'The Role of Third Parties in the Execution of Public Contracts' in Laurence Folliot-Lalliot and Simone Torricelli (eds), *Contrôle et Contentieux des Contrats Publics – Oversight and Remedies in Public Contracts* (Bruylant, Brussels 2017) 415 ff.; Gabriella M. Racca and Roberto Cavallo Perin, 'Corruption as a Violation of Fundamental Rights: Reputation Risk as a Deterrent Against the Lack of Loyalty' in Gabriella M. Racca and Christopher R. Yukins (eds), *Integrity and Efficiency in Sustainable Public Contracts. Balancing Corruption Concerns in Public Procurement Internationally,* 2014, 23 ff.

management and execution. It depends on many factors, and monitoring tasks could be assigned to different subjects and authorities (anti-corruption, antitrust, audit systems, unsuccessful tenderers, media, civil society, and now also digital tools). Nonetheless, the idea that the fairness of the competition during the award procedure cannot be jeopardised after the signing of the contract allowing material amendments is a key issue as it relates to trust in any procurement system.[39]

The CJEU recognised such principles, considering that material amendments during the execution must be considered ineffective, obviously except in the limited cases provided by the Directives. As well known, material amendments are considered as an award without notice and thus a violation of the principle of transparency, participation and fair competition.[40] These principles allow the CJEU to examine the performance of an amended procurement (which would otherwise fall outside the EU competence) and declare it ineffective with the aim "to restore competition and to create new business opportunities for those economic operators which have been deprived illegally of their opportunity to compete".[41] As a consequence, limits to material amendments are clearly set out in the 2014 EU Directives.[42]

---

39 Gabriella M. Racca and Christopher R. Yukins, 'Introduction: Steps for Integrity in Public Contracts' in Gabriella M. Racca and Christopher R. Yukins (eds.), *Integrity and Efficiency in Sustainable Public Contracts. Balancing Corruption Concerns in Public Procurement Internationally*, 2014, 2 ff.

40 See Directive 2014/23/EU, Art. 43; Directive 2014/24/EU, Art. 72; Directive 2014/25/EU, Art. 89, according to the previous CJEU case law: CJEU, 19 June 2008, *Pressetext Nachrichtenagentur GmbH v Republik Österreich* in Case C-454/06, ECR I-4401. The Court maintained that material amendments are those modifications beyond the scope of the awarded contract that tenderers could not have reasonably anticipated at the time of the original award when they joined the competition, and also in the case of a settlement agreement, with both parties agreeing to mutual waivers, designed to bring an end to a dispute the outcome of which is uncertain, which arose from the difficulties encountered in the performance of that contract: CJEU, 7 September 2016, *Finn Frogne A/S v Rigspolitiet ved Center for Beredskabskommunikation*, in C-549/14. See Gabriella M. Racca and Roberto Cavallo Perin, 'Material Changes in Contract Management as Symptoms of Corruption: A Comparison between EU and US Procurement Systems' in Gabriella M. Racca and Christopher R. Yukins (eds.), *Integrity and Efficiency in Sustainable Public Contracts. Balancing Corruption Concerns in Public Procurement Internationally*, 2014, 247 ff.

41 Directive 2007/66/EC, recital No. 14.

42 Directive 2014/23/EU, Art. 43; Directive 2014/24/EU, Art. 72; Directive 2014/25/EU, Art. 89. Gabriella M. Racca and Roberto Cavallo Perin, 'Material Amendments of Public Contracts during their Terms: From Violations of

Any means of monitoring the procurement cycle (mainly digital) and particularly the adequate performance of the contract, not only by the contracting authorities but also by any "third party", can favour the goal of an effective, timely and good execution of the contract, which is the ultimate goal of any procurement system.

A very relevant change in the future procurement provisions might be the use, in both the award and execution phases, of digital platforms integrated with the digital modeling approach. This permits monitoring the activities of any member of the framework alliance in any phase through sensors, drones and the integration of data-based approaches at various stages of the procurement process. This will provide transparency, fairness and accountability, thus more participation due to a renewed confidence in the procurement system.

Competition therefore must be safeguarded until the end of the performance phase so that "promised quality" (as defined in the competitive award) aligns with the "delivered quality".[43] This implements the idea that the goal is the prompt execution of public procurement and contracts through digital tools for the benefit of EU citizens and not merely to ensure compliance with the provisions of the award procedure.[44]

5. FUTURE PERSPECTIVE OF DIGITAL AND COLLABORATIVE TRANSFORMATION

The fundamental principles of equality, non-discrimination, transparency and proportionality could therefore be implemented by designing an effective e-procurement system that can digitally monitor the entire public contract lifecycle. In this perspective, the interoperable platforms, together with the collection of data sets of all the phases of the award, execution and payment of contracts, would be correct and prompt, based on a reciprocal "digital trust", which is key to encouraging and fostering participation, especially among SMEs and innovative companies.[45] The Public Procurement Data Space initiative might be one of the developing points of the reform strategy, together with the new Digital Business Wallet, to facilitate the evaluation either of exclusion

Competitions to Symptoms of Corruption' *European Procurement & Public Private Partnership Law Review* (2013) No. 4, 279 ff.

43 Gabriella M. Racca, Roberto Cavallo Perin and Gian Luigi Albano, 'Competition in the Execution Phase of Public Procurement', 89 ff.

44 Gabriella M. Racca and Christopher R. Yukins (eds.), *Integrity and Efficiency in Sustainable Public Contracts. Balancing Corruption Concerns in Public Procurement Internationally*, 2014.

45 Gabriella M. Racca, 'La "fiducia digitale" nei contratti pubblici tra piattaforme e data analysis' (2023) 2 *Istituzioni del Federalismo* 357 ff.

grounds or of qualification grounds, thus also favouring direct participation of SMEs.

The specific provisions providing Building Information Modeling especially for works and facility management might also be applied to services procurement with framework alliances, in which the roles of all stakeholders and subcontractors (that will enter directly in the digital framework) should be defined, along with their respective obligations and incentives for prompt and correct execution.[46] It seems necessary to consider alternative models to those traditionally recognised, which have been based on a purely competitive logic, with a consequent reduction of competition observed over the last ten years (notably by the European Court of Auditors).

Such an evolution towards a collaborative approach in public procurement, with tangible benefits for both public and private parties, would allow contracting authorities to establish cooperation agreements (framework alliances) with qualified suppliers (also applying Virtual Company Dossier or possibly the next digital Business Wallet).[47] Thus ensuring that procurement processes are not only competitive but also efficient, thanks to information modeling (and digital twins). The new European provisions should reconsider a public–private cooperative model capable of responding to collective needs and addressing sustainability and social inclusion objectives. This could be achieved through specific digital and cross-border platforms also for SMEs to scale up or third sector operators, that can digitally pursue and control the best approach for any specific sector and scale of public interests. Finally, these deep modifications of the procurement landscape in the next reform process would ultimately reach the goal of efficiency, integrity and opening of the EU markets in the interest and benefit not only for market integration but mainly for innovation and European social integration.

---

46 Article 22, ar. 4, Directive 2014/24/EU: "For public works contracts and design contests, Member States may require the use of specific electronic tools, such as building information electronic modelling tools or similar. In such cases, the contracting authorities shall offer alternative means of access, as provided for in paragraph 5, until such time as those tools become generally available within the meaning of the second sentence of the first subparagraph of paragraph".

47 European Commission, *The EU Startup and Scaleup Strategy*, 5.

10. (Choice of) award procedures

Past, present and future

Steven Van Garsse

REFORM PROPOSALS

- Clarify the scope of the competitive procedure with negotiations versus the competitive dialogue.
- Remove Innovation Partnership.
- Include ex-ante checks for direct awards.
- Focus on professionalization of public buyers.
- Include PCP in the new Directive.

1. INTRODUCTION

Public procurement is seen as a key driver of economic growth and employment in the European Union. Ensuring competition is seen as a crucial condition in this regard.[1] In order to organize competition, Procurement Directives provide for public procurement procedures. The result of the public procurement procedure aims to obtain the most economically advantageous tender.[2] Competition should, as it were, lead to innovative, cost-effective solutions as a result of market forces. In other words, public spending is minimized, and companies are encouraged to offer competitive and innovative solutions.

[1] European Commission, Directorate-General for Enterprise and Industry, 'Public Procurement as a Driver of Innovation in SMEs and Public Services', Publications Office (data.europa.eu, 2014) https://data.europa.eu/doi/10.2769/40468 accessed 17 June 2025.

[2] Cf '[f]or public authorities, procurement is a powerful tool for spending public money in an efficient, sustainable and strategic manner, especially in times of strained national budgets': European Commission, Communication from the Commission to the European Parliament, the Council, the European Economic and Social Committee and the Committee of the Regions: Making Public Procurement Work in and for Europe COM(2017) 572 final (2017) 2.

The public procurement procedures frame this process by considering general principles such as equality, transparency, and proportionality. The choice of the public procurement procedure determines which rules apply and the degree of flexibility to engage with market participants.

Over the years, the public procurement rules were oftentimes changed and modernized.[3] The review of the 2004 Public Procurement Directives, resulting in the 2014 Directives, focused on diversification and flexibility. In this contribution, we take stock of the 2014 regime and look critically ahead. As is known, in the last months before publication of this book, steps are being undertaken to revise the 2014 Public Procurement Directives.[4] Following, therefore, we first review the state of the current rules, followed by a brief assessment.[5] We also discuss the report of the Court of Auditors and its relevance for the topic of public procurement procedures. The contribution concludes with some final reflections on the way forward.

The focus of this chapter is on public procurement in the classic sectors. The award of public contracts in the special sectors and in the defense and security sector is therefore out of scope.

2. DIRECTIVE 2014/24/EU

Public procurement has been regulated at the European level for many decades.[6] In 2014, as we know, a thorough review of the European Public

---

[3] At present, the rules can be found in Directive 2014/24/EU of the European Parliament and of the Council of 26 February 2014 on public procurement Directive 2004/18/EC [2014] OJ L94/65; Directive 2014/23/EU of the European Parliament and of the Council of 26 February 2014 on the award of concession contracts [2014] OJ L94/1; Directive 2014/25/EU of the European Parliament and of the Council of 26 February 2014 on procurement by entities operating in the water, energy, transport and postal services and repealing Directive 2004/17/EC [2014] OJ L94/243.

[4] European Commission, 'Public Procurement Directives – Evaluation' (ec.europa.eu, 2024) https://ec.europa.eu/info/law/better-regulation/have-your-say/initiatives/14427-Public-procurement-directives-evaluation_en accessed 2 June 2025.

[5] A must-read on this topic is also: Pedro Telles and Luke Butler, 'Public Procurement Award Procedures in Directive 2014/24/EU' in François Lichere, Roberto Caranta and Steen Treumer (eds), *Novelties in the 2014 Directive on Public Procurement* (Djof Publishing 2014).

[6] See Sue Arrowsmith, *The Law of Public and Utilities Procurement* (3rd edn, vol 1, Sweet & Maxwell 2014) 150; Sue Arrowsmith, 'Purpose of the EU Procurement Directives: Ends, Means and the Implications for National Regulatory Space for Commercial and Horizontal Procurement Policies' (2011) *CYELS* 14,

Procurement Directives took place. The idea was to simplify public procurement procedures, improve access for small and medium-sized enterprises (SMEs), and promote transparency and strategic procurement. A key trend of 2014 was the wider choice that was created when choosing an appropriate public procurement procedure. Indeed, more and modernized procedures were created as a result of the revision. In fact, after the 2014 revision, contracting authorities can use – depending on the circumstances – the traditional open and restricted procedures, the competitive dialogue procedure, the competitive procedure with negotiation, the negotiated procedure without prior notice, as well as innovation partnerships. The most common procedures are the open and restricted ones. The benefit of an open procedure is that all economic operators can put in an offer. Conversely, a restricted procedure is divided into two steps: in the first step, the economic operators submit a request for qualification, and in the second step, the contracting authority invites the selected economic operators to submit a tender. The other procedures can only be used in special and some cases even (very) exceptional circumstances.

In some countries, additional procedures are implemented for public contracts below the European thresholds. In Belgium, for example, reference can be made to the simplified negotiated procedure with publication.[7] This is a negotiated procedure with prior publication and without a prequalification stage. It is therefore a procedure that combines characteristics of the open procedure and the competitive procedure with negotiation. It should also be noted that countries remain free, within the limits of the Directive, to further specify the procedures. This happened, for example, in Portugal for the competitive

1. See already in the seventies: Council Directive 71/305/EEC of 26 July 1971 concerning the coordination of procedures for the award of public works contracts [1971] OJ L185/5; Council Directive 77/62/EEC of 21 December 1976 coordinating procedures for the award of public supply contracts [1977] OJ L13/1; See also: Council Directive 93/37/EEC of 14 June 1993 concerning the coordination of procedures for the award of public works contracts [1993] OJ L199/54; Council Directive 92/50/EEC of 18 June 1992 relating to the coordination of procedures for the award of public service contracts [1992] OJ L209/1; Directive 2004/17/EC of the European Parliament and of the Council of 31 March 2004 coordinating the procurement procedures of entities operating in the water, energy, transport and postal services sectors [2004] OJ L134/1; Directive 2004/18/EC of the European Parliament and of the Council of 31 March 2004 on the coordination of procedures for the award of public works contracts, public supply contracts and public service contracts [2004] OJ L134/114.

[7] Article 41 of the Belgian Public Procurement Law of 17 June 2016, Official Gazette 14 July 2016. See also Steven Van Garsse (ed), *Wet 17 juni 2016. Artikelsgewijze commentaar (nieuwe) wetgeving overheidsopdrachten* (Politeia 2025).

dialogue.[8] Rather than focusing on diversity, we want to focus on what is common at the EU level and therefore concerns all EU member states.

Whereas Directive 2004/18/EU still very much emphasized the use of traditional procedures, a paradigm shift took place in 2014 regarding the use of negotiated procedures.[9] There was a growing realization that, by their very nature, negotiated procedures with prior publication were not necessarily anti-competitive and therefore harmful. On the contrary, better results could often be obtained through negotiation than through traditional procedures. Directive 2014/24/EU thus opened the way for the more flexible use of negotiated procedures with prior publication, and it did so in two ways. First, it significantly broadened the use of so-called special procedures such as the competitive dialogue and the competitive procedure with negotiations (hereafter A). However, the use of negotiated procedures without prior publication remained exceptional (hereafter B). Second, a new procedure was created, namely the innovation partnership (hereafter C).

2.1 The Broadening of the Use of Negotiated Procedures with Prior Publication

The competitive dialogue and the competitive procedure with negotiation – certainly since the 2014 Directives – have a much broader scope than before. The procedures can be used, inter alia, because: (i) the needs of the contracting authority cannot be met without adaptation of readily available solutions; (ii) they include design or innovative solutions; (iii) the contract cannot be awarded without prior negotiations because of specific circumstances related to the nature, complexity, or the legal and financial make-up, or because of the risks attached to them; or (iv) the technical specifications cannot be established

8 See Pedro Telles and Luke Butler, 'Public Procurement Award Procedures in Directive 2014/24/EU' in François Lichere, Roberto Caranta and Steen Treumer (eds), *Novelties in the 2014 Directive on Public Procurement* (Djof Publishing 2014).

9 See Kris Wauters, 'De onderhandelingsprocedures: is er sprake van een paradigmaverschuiving in 2016?' (2018) 16 *Tijdschrift voor Bouwrecht en Onroerend goed* (TBO) 110; compare with art. 11 of Council Directive 92/50/EEC of 18 June 1992 relating to the coordination of procedures for the award of public service contracts [1992] OJ L209/1, referring to "exceptional cases" and stating inter alia "in all other cases, Contracting Authorities shall award their public service contracts by the Open Procedure or by the Restricted Procedure"; compare also art. 7(2)(c) of Council Directive 93/37/EEC of 14 June 1993 concerning the coordination of procedures for the award of public works contracts [1993] OJ L199/54.

with sufficient precision by the contracting authority. Consequently, in a lot of cases, contracting authorities will be able to use these procedures.

This increased scope has led to criticism in legal scholarship.[10] First, it could prejudice competition. Second, as stated, as far as the competitive dialogue is concerned, the increased scope was achieved by opening up the grounds of application within which the competitive procedure with negotiations can be used. According to certain authors, this would make the competitive dialogue superfluous.[11] After all, the competitive procedure with negotiations as a procedure would be very flexible, allowing it to be shaped like a competitive dialogue and thus achieve similar results. Also, the need for the competitive dialogue has disappeared since it has become clear over the years that prior involvement in a technical dialogue does not necessarily lead to exclusion.

However, these positions cannot be endorsed. The implementation of both procedures was accompanied by several requirements to promote transparency and equality. Both procedures contain good safeguards for competition.[12] For example, measures were introduced by the legislature to preserve competition at a final stage.[13] In the competitive procedure with negotiations, it no longer seems possible to negotiate exclusively with a preferred bidder.[14] In practice, such negotiations could give rise to "deal creep" and thus distort competition. In the competitive dialogue procedure, the ability to negotiate after the closing of the dialogue is strictly limited and well framed.[15] Consequently, in our opinion, the procedures and their increased scope do not themselves appear to be such that their use leads to restrictions on or distortions of competition. If competition in these procedures would be more limited than in other procedures at all, this seems to be caused rather by the complexity of the underlying

---

10 See Albert Sanchez-Graells, *Public Procurement and the EU Competition Rules* (2nd edn, Hart Publishing 2015) 272–278.

11 Pedro Telles, 'Rethinking the Public Procurement Directives: How Many are Too Many?' (Telles.eu., 18 February 2025) https://www.telles.eu/rethinking-the-procurement-directives-how-many-procedures-are-too-many/ accessed 2 June 2025.

12 Cf art 84(2), Directive 2014/24/EU of the European Parliament and of the Council of 26 February 2014 on public procurement and repealing Directive 2004/18/EC [2014] OJ L94/65.

13 Art. 29 *in fine*, ibid.

14 Nonetheless, discussion remains in legal scholarship on this point. See in Belgium Tim Bruyninckx, 'Wat met de voorkeursbieder in mededingingsprocedures met onderhandeling?' in Constant De Koninck et al (eds), *Jaarboek Overheidsopdrachten 2019–2020* (EBP 2020) 601–619.

15 Art. 30(7), Directive 2014/24/EU of the European Parliament and of the Council of 26 February 2014 on public procurement and repealing Directive 2004/18/EC [2014] OJ L94/65.

project, by the scope of the contract, the selection criteria, and the technical specifications that cause that rather than the fact that few market participants can participate in such procedures. Thus, it is not the type of procedure itself, but the subject matter and specific circumstances that relate to the subject matter or the behavior of the contracting authority that is at the root of the fact that in practice fewer parties participate in these procedures.

The view that the competitive dialogue would be redundant cannot be supported. After all, the procedures still have a different nature and purpose, and they do not – as explained – proceed in a similar manner. In fact, the subtle differences make the procedures easily distinguishable from one another, and one cannot be replaced by the other.

To understand the distinction well, it is necessary to go back to the origins of competitive dialogue.[16] This public procurement procedure was – inter alia – created because in complex projects the need was felt to engage in an early dialogue with the market.[17] A prior technical dialogue was seen by some as anti-competitive, and the discussion soon arose as to whether parties who were involved prior to the award procedure could still be included in the award procedure. The solution at the time was to integrate the dialogue into the public procurement procedure. Today, as has been said, prior involvement does not necessarily lead to exclusion. This position is correct. However, the situation is not substantially different from before. In fact, excluding market parties has to be proportionate. The mere fact that parties were involved before does not per se lead to falsification of competition. Moreover, it's up to contracting authorities to take action to eliminate possible advantages. This idea was also implemented in Directive 2014/24/EU.[18] Under Article 40(1), contract-

---

[16] See Steven Van Garsse (ed), *De concurrentiedialoog* (Die Keure 2014) 159; Sue Arrowsmith and Steen Treumer (eds), *Competitive Dialogue in EU Procurement* (Cambridge University Press 2012).

[17] Albert Sanchez-Graells, *Public Procurement and the EU Competition Rules* (2nd edn, Hart Publishing 2015) 273. See for other reasons Steven Van Garsse, 'Een inleidende situering' in Steven Van Garsse (ed), *De concurrentiedialoog* (Die Keure 2014) 5; Steven Van Garsse, 'Artikel 162' in Steven Van Garsse (ed), *Artikelsgewijze commentaar wetgeving overheidsopdrachten. KB van 15 juli 2011* (Politeia n.d.); Neil Braeckevelt, Anthony Logghe and Frederik Ongena, 'De concurrentiedialoog: uitdagingen voor klassieke overheidsopdrachten en PPS-projecten' in Constant De Koninck et al (eds), *Jaarboek overheidsopdrachten 2011–2012* (EBP 2012) 879–904. See also critically Adrian Brown, 'The Impact of the New Procurement Directive on Large Public Infrastructure Projects: Competitive Dialogue or Better the Devil You Know?' (2004) 4 *PPLR* 160 et seq.

[18] Dacian C. Dragos, 'Article 40 Preliminary Market Consultations' in Roberto Caranta and Albert Sanchez-Graells (eds), *European Public Procurement: Commentary on Directive 2014/24/EU* (Edgar 2021) 448.

ing authorities may conduct market consultations to prepare the procurement and inform economic operators of their procurement plans and requirements before launching a procurement procedure. Article 40(2) further details that in this scenario, contracting authorities can seek or accept advice from different stakeholders, namely independent experts or authorities or from market participants. If the advice doesn't distort competition nor violate the non-discrimination and transparency principles, it can be used in the planning and conduct of the procurement procedure. Hence, the advice can help the contracting authorities prepare the procedure, yet the principles of procurement must be complied with. Article 41 furthermore stresses that if a candidate or tenderer or an undertaking has advised the contracting authority or has otherwise been involved in the preparation of the procurement procedure, the contracting authority shall take appropriate measures to ensure that competition is not distorted by such advice or involvement. Such measures include sharing information, postponing deadlines for the offers or, in *extrema ratio*, after having adequately assessed that no other means are possible, even excluding the candidate or tenderer.

Consequently, the competitive dialogue still meets a need, namely to make it possible, within a legally secure framework, to maintain an intensive technical dialogue on the fulfillment of the contracting authority's needs and without the risk for economic operators to be excluded. In fact, the competitive dialogue is probably one of the most important instruments in organizing Early Contractor Involvement (ECI).[19] ECI is a procurement technique where a contractor becomes involved at an early stage in a construction project, before the design is fully finalized. This allows the market to contribute to the design process, improve collaboration, and identify and mitigate risks early on in the process compared to traditional contracting. ECI is considered to be beneficial for complex or high-risk projects, as it helps to reduce and mitigate risks and enhance collaboration.[20]

Thus, the competitive dialogue starts from the idea that a contracting authority has a certain need, but does not yet fully know how to fulfill this need.[21] This

---

[19] PIANC, *Marcom WG 194: A Framework for Early Contractor Involvement in Infrastructure Projects* (2022). See also Paulos A. Wondimu, Ole Jonny Klakegg and Ola Lædre, 'Early Contractor Involvement (ECI): Ways to Do it in Public Projects' (2020) 20 *JPP* 62; Marijke Valkenburg, Sander Lenferink, Roel Nijsten and Jos Arts, 'Early Contractor Involvement: A New Strategy for Buying the Best in Infrastructure Development in the Netherlands' (2012) 12 *JPP* 1.

[20] Ibid.

[21] For this reason, there is also no need to make binding offers in a competitive dialogue during the dialogue. However, once the dialogue is closed, mature procurement documents are sent out, and tenderers will submit their offers.

idea, which was at the origin of competitive dialogue and was more explicitly enshrined during its launch in 2004,[22] was not explicitly restated in the Classic Directive. On the contrary, as seen, the grounds of application of the competitive procedure with negotiations were opened to the competitive dialogue. This gives the impression that both procedures can be used in similar cases, but nothing could be further from the truth. This is obviously unfortunate, and it would be good if the legislator could make some clarification on this in the new Directive. The purpose and the design of the two procedures remain different. In a competitive dialogue, one knows one's needs but is not sufficiently able to translate the needs into decent solutions and well-drafted public procurement documents. A collaborative approach is then used to further develop the project and identify solutions in close collaboration. Once the solutions are identified, the dialogue is closed and offers are requested. In a competitive procedure with negotiations, one is able to identify its needs and solutions; however, further negotiations are needed to improve the offers. Therefore, the focus of negotiations/dialogue is different in the two procedures.

As seen earlier, the course of the two procedures is also different. A competitive dialogue culminates in an offer after closing the dialogue. This offer can still be negotiated with the preferred bidder to a limited extent.[23] As Article 30(7) *in fine* states, at the request of the contracting authority, negotiations with the tenderer identified as having submitted the tender presenting the best price-quality ratio in accordance with Article 67 may be carried out to confirm financial commitments or other terms contained in the tender by finalizing the terms of the contract provided this does not have the effect of materially modifying essential aspects of the tender or of the public procurement, including the needs and requirements set out in the contract notice or in the descriptive document and does not risk distorting competition or causing discrimination. These negotiations are clearly justified by the complexity of the project.

In the competitive procedure with negotiations, the situation is different. Several rounds of bidding can be organized. Where the contracting authority intends to conclude the negotiations, it shall inform the remaining tenderers and set a common deadline to submit any new or revised tenders. At the final stage, final negotiations with (only) one (selected) economic operator no longer seem possible in this regard.

---

22 See also European Commission, *Explanatory Note on Competitive Dialogue-Classic Directive*, CC/2005/04_rev 1 (5 October 2005).

23 See before also Sue Arrowsmith, *Law of Public and Utilities Procurement* (Sweet & Maxwell 2006) para 8.42; Ciara Kennedy-Loest, 'What can be Done at the Preferred Bidder Stage in Competitive Dialogue' (2006) 6 *PPLR* 316 et seq.

The choice for one or the other procedure will therefore have to be made considering the needs, and the choice will also have to be justified.[24] Obviously, both procedures have a number of things in common – which wrongly creates the impression that they are interchangeable. For example, both procedures are complex and require thorough preparation. Likewise, the legislature has seen fit to make the grounds of application identical. However, as explained, the focus and conduct is quite different, so when deciding on the award procedure, these differences should be kept in mind.

2.2 The Exceptional Use of the Negotiated Procedure Without Prior Publication

While it has been explained earlier that the scope of certain procedures has been significantly increased, this does not apply to negotiated procedures without prior publication. As a result, the use of this procedure remains very exceptional. This is obviously due to the negative impact that such a procedure has on competition. Indeed, depending on the ground for application, only limited competition will be organized or even no competition will be organized. The case law of the CJEU has consistently made clear over the years that the grounds for application should be interpreted restrictively. The European Commission also follows this line, although it appeared willing to give contracting authorities more guidance in crisis situations.

For example, in full Covid crisis, the European Commission recalled the exceptional application conditions to use a negotiated procedure without prior publication for reasons of urgency:

> All the conditions have to be met cumulatively and are to be interpreted restrictively (see, for instance cases C-275/08, Commission v Germany, and C-352/12, Consiglio Nazionale degli Ingegneri). A 'negotiated procedure without publication' allows contracting authorities to negotiate directly with potential contractors; a direct award to a preselected economic operator remains the exception, applicable if only one undertaking is able to deliver within the technical and time constraints imposed by the extreme urgency. Each contracting authority will have to evaluate whether the conditions for using such a 'negotiated procedure without prior publication' are met. It will have to justify its choice of such a procedure in an individual report.[25]

---

[24] Cf art 84(2), Directive 2014/24/EU of the European Parliament and of the Council of 26 February 2014 on public procurement and repealing Directive 2004/18/EC [2014] OJ L94/65.

[25] European Commission, 'Guidance from the European Commission on Using the Public Procurement Framework in the Emergency Situation Related to the COVID-19 Crisis' (2020/C 108 I/01) (eur-lex.europa.eu, 2020)

However, when applied to purchases of all kinds of products, such as oral masks and ventilation, equipment, all the conditions for making purchases under this procedure seemed to be met during the Covid crisis.[26] Nevertheless, the many scandals that surfaced after Covid show that, in practice, restricting competition and initiating direct negotiations with self-selected market participants pose very serious risks.[27] Thus, in practice, the direct negotiations without competition seem to give rise to abuses, corruption, and fraud very quickly.

Contracting authorities should therefore reasonably do everything they can to avoid the use of this procedure. Very recently this was also confirmed by a judgment of the CJEU in 2025.[28] The judgment concerned the old Public Procurement Directive 2004/18/EU. Under Article 31(1)(b) of this Directive, the procedure without prior publication could be applied, among other things, "when, for technical or artistic reasons or reasons connected with the protection of exclusive rights, the contract may be awarded only to a particular economic operator." According to previous case law of the Court, application was open if two conditions must be cumulatively fulfilled.[29] Namely, first, there must be technical or artistic reasons or reasons to protect exclusive rights connected with the subject matter of the contract; and second, for these reasons it must be absolutely necessary to award the contract to a particular economic operator.

With the judgment of January 9, 2025, the CJEU added an additional condition to the application, in particular by explicitly requiring that the existence of technical or artistic reasons or reasons of protection of exclusive rights should not be attributable to the contracting authority. By doing so, the Court seems to align the conditions to the condition that already existed for the application ground of urgency and with Article 32, 2., b) of the later Directive 2014/24/EU, the successor of Article 31, 1., b) of the old Directive 2004/18/EC. Indeed, this Directive has specified that the public procurement procedure may be used for artistic or technical reasons and situations in which exclusive rights must be protected "if there is no reasonable alternative or substitute and the absence of competition is not due to artificial restrictions on the terms of the contract." Fully in line with this new provision, the Court considered in its judgment

---

https://eur-lex.europa.eu/legal-content/EN/TXT/PDF/?uri=CELEX:52020XC0401(05) accessed 2 June 2025.

26 Ibid.

27 See, for example: Steve Goodrich (ed), *Behind the Masks: Corruption Red Flags in COVID-19 Public Procurement* (Transparency International UK 2024).

28 C-578/23 *Česká republika – Generální finanční ředitelství v Úřad pro ochranu hospodářské soutěže* [Judgment of 9 January 2025].

29 C-57/94 *Commission v Italy* [1995] ECR I-1249 and Case C-394/02 *Commission v Greece* [2005] ECR I-04713.

that contracting authorities must make every reasonable effort to avoid the application of the exceptional procedure and thus use procedures that are more open to competition (rec. 31). Contracting authorities also may not themselves create or actively or passively maintain a state of exclusivity (recital 33) and, relatedly, the exclusivity must not be intentionally created or maintained to constitute an illegal application of the procedure (cont. 34).

This judgment is furthermore in line with an idea enshrined in Article 18 of the Directive stating that "[c]ontracting authorities shall treat economic operators equally and without discrimination and shall act in a transparent and proportionate manner" and "[t]he design of the procurement shall not be made with the intention of excluding it from the scope of this Directive or of artificially narrowing competition. Competition shall be considered to be artificially narrowed where the design of the procurement is made with the intention of unduly favoring or disadvantaging certain economic operators."

2.3 The Creation of a New Procedure: The Innovation Partnership

Quite interesting was the creation of a new procedure in the Classic Directive, specifically the innovation partnership.[30] This procedure attempted to bring together the production, development, and procurement of innovative solutions in one tiered procedure. The Directive incorporates a comprehensive set of rules to frame the procedure.

Moreover, the use of the innovation partnership is very strictly regulated by Article 31(1) of the Classic Directive. The procedure is only open if there is an innovative product, service, or works that "cannot be met by purchasing products, services, or works already available on the market." Thus, the procedure is not open if whatever is proposed does not meet the definition of innovation as described in Article 2(1)(22).[31] Innovation is rather strangely defined in the Directive as "the implementation of a new or significantly improved

[30] See Pedro Gomez, *EU Procurement and Innovation. The Innovation Partnership Procedure and Harmonization Challenges* (Edward Elgar 2021); Christoph Krönke, 'Innovation Partnerships: Purpose, Scope of Application and Key Elements of a New Instrument of Strategic Procurement' in Gabriella Racca and Christopher Yukins (eds), *Joint Public Procurement and Innovation: Lessons Across Borders* (Bruylant 2019); Vitalii Pashkov and Andrii A. Olefir, 'Innovative Partnership as New Form of Public Procurement in the European Union' (2017) 2(8) *RECoL* 66.

[31] See Pedro Telles and Luke Butler, 'Public Procurement Award Procedures in Directive 2014/24/EU' in François Lichere, Roberto Caranta and Steen Treumer (eds), *Novelties in the 2014 Directive on Public Procurement* (Djof Publishing 2014).

product, service, or process, including but not limited to production, building, or construction processes, a new marketing method, or a new organizational method in business practices, workplace organization, or external relations inter alia with the purpose of helping to solve societal challenges or to support the Europe 2020 strategy for smart, sustainable, and inclusive growth."[32] If and when an innovation partnership can be used is therefore unclear. Furthermore, as scholars state, the instrument has limited practical applicability.[33] Innovation partnerships seem particularly useful to develop an innovative product that does not yet exist but which meets the needs of a contracting authority. Nevertheless, in that case, a competitive dialogue also seems to be an option. As authors have stated, "solutions requiring a high degree of innovation, Competitive Dialogue can also be used to include the opportunity to test prototypes before final development of products and services."[34]

Consequently, the procedure does not seem to have a lot of added value. In addition, to the extent that the intention of the contracting authority was merely to encourage the development of innovative solutions through public procurement, a technique that is called "pre-commercial procurement" can also be used.[35] Pre-commercial procurement is a process to procure exempted R&D services under Article 14 of the Directive. In PCP, contracting authorities buy research and development from several competing suppliers in parallel to compare alternative solution approaches and identify the best value for money solutions that the market can deliver to address their needs. Research and development is split into phases (solution design, prototyping, original development and validation/testing of a limited set of first products) with the number of competing research and development providers being reduced after

---

[32] Art. 2(22), Directive 2014/24/EU of the European Parliament and of the Council of 26 February 2014 on public procurement and repealing Directive 2004/18/EC [2014] OJ L94/65.

[33] See also Pedro Telles, 'Rethinking the Public Procurement Directives: How Many are Too Many?' (Telles.eu., 18 February 2025) <https://www.telles.eu/rethinking-the-procurement-directives-how-many-procedures-are-too-many/> accessed 2 June 2025.

[34] Michael Burnett and Martin Oder, 'Competitive Dialogue: A Tool with Many Uses' (eipa.eu, 13 May 2021) <https://www.eipa.eu/blog/competitive-dialogue-a-tool-with-many-uses/> accessed 1 June 2025.

[35] Charles Edquist and Jon Mikal Zabala-Iturriagagoitia, 'Pre-commercial Procurement: A Demand and Supply Policy Instrument in Relation to Innovation?' (2015) 45 *R&D Management* 147; see also Ramona Apostal, *Trials and Tribulations in the Implementation of Pre-Commercial Procurement in Europe* (TMC Asser Press 2017).

each phase.[36] PCP is therefore not intended to procure commercial volumes of end products.

The procedure has been embraced by several contracting authorities, and numerous innovation projects have been launched at the European level.[37] Best practices describing the procedure and modalities of the PCP procedure are being disseminated by the European Commission.[38]

3. THE 2014 REFORM ONE STEP FORWARD?

The Classic Directive of 2014 had the merit of broadening the choice of public procurement procedures that contracting authorities can use. It also had the merit of broadening the scope of application of the competitive procedure with negotiations and competitive dialogue. That this would have a negative impact on competition cannot, in our opinion, be endorsed as explained. The recent report of the European Court of Auditors does not change our view.[39] That report looked very critically at developments in public procurement between 2011 and 2021. The Court points to a worrying trend of declining competition in public procurement. Anyone reading the report even gets the impression that the 2014 reform was a complete failure. However, in our opinion, the reduced competition is not per se tied to the choice or use of certain procurement procedures.[40] For example, in an open procedure, potentially many bidders can participate. This creates high costs with a very limited chance of success. Consequently, companies will hesitate to incur these costs. Strict selection requirements or technical specifications can also substantially reduce competition, as seen. Similarly, participating in an award procedure is very burdensome from an administrative point of view. This was also confirmed in the report: "The administrative burden of public procurement procedures is generally perceived as heavy, by both bidders and contracting authorities.

---

[36] NCP Flanders, 'Infosheet on Pre-commercial Procurement' (ncpflanders.be, 13 July 2021) <https://ncpflanders.be/infosheets/pre-commercial-procurement-and-public-procurement-of-innovation> accessed 2 June 2025.

[37] See, for example, European Commission, 'Precommercial Showcases' (research-and-innovation.ec.europa.eu) <https://research-and-innovation.ec.europa.eu/strategy/support-policy-making/shaping-eu-research-and-innovation-policy/new-european-innovation-agenda/innovation-procurement/pre-commercial-procurement/showcases_en> accessed 2 June 2025.

[38] Ibid.

[39] European Court of Auditors, *Special Report 28/2023: Public Procurement in the US – Less Competition for Contracts Awarded for Works, Goods and Services in the 10 Years up to 2021* (Luxembourg 2023).

[40] With the exception of direct awards explained following.

More than half of survey respondents also pointed to lengthy administrative procedures constituting a key deterrent to businesses participating in public procurement.'[41] It also states: "Our interviewees indicated that procedures are overly complicated and less flexible than procurement in the private sector, and there has been no significant simplification that might have made public contracts more attractive to companies." Thus, there seems to be a more general problem. However, the comparison with private procedures is difficult to make and not fair. After all, contracting authorities have to consider all kinds of principles and interests that are much less involved in private purchases. Consequently, the higher degree of red tape is at least partly explained by the specific capacity of the purchaser (working in the general interest) and the fact that tax money is involved. Moreover, public procurement procedures, such as the negotiated procedure, and the competitive dialogue seems to be closer to the kind of procedures companies organize when tendering out for projects.[42] It would therefore be in the interest of contracting authorities not to tinker with them as there is no good reason to take away flexible procedures meeting compelling actual social and economic needs. The same is true for the negotiated procedure without prior notice (but see *infra*). That competition is more limited when working with direct negotiations in those exceptional cases is beyond dispute. However, the regulations were not relaxed in this regard in 2014; on the contrary, they were tightened.

Having said that, some improvements to the Directive(s) could be made. For example, in public–private partnerships, some contracting authorities launch their project, after careful analysis, as a concession using the specific rules that were enacted for concessions. It then happens that during negotiations, risks are shifted from the contractor to the contracting authority. The result is that the public procurement procedure fails. If the project no longer qualifies as a concession, the public procurement procedures and rules of the public contracts should be used. This is something the legislature could easily fix. If at inception the project qualifies as a concession, the contracting authority should be able to close the contract under the rules of the Concession Directive unless it is clear that the contracting authority was trying to escape the rules related to public contracts.

Another thing that should be considered is better regulating the procedure of the negotiated procedure without prior notice.[43] As already seen, this pro-

41 Ibid.

42 Compare Edward W. Merrow, *Contract Strategies for Major Projects: Mastering the Most Difficult Element of Project Management* (Wiley 2022).

43 See also Sarah Schoenmaekers, 'Art. 32' in *Evaluation of the 2014 Public Procurement Directives. Answer to the Call of Evidence,* Ref. Ares(2024)8928678, PCLG Network, https://www.public-contracts.org/ accessed 2 June 2025.

cedure is prone to corruption. Whereas the legislature should not touch the grounds of application to use this procedure, it should consider regulating the procedure a bit more as it did for other public procurement procedures, enhancing transparency and objectivity. Furthermore, what could be considered is to build in additional checks and balances when awarding contracts based on direct awards. For example, an *ex ante* check (before award) on the existence of the grounds for exception and the process could be objectified by involving external auditors or probity advisers during the public procurement procedure/negotiations.[44]

Last but not least, while we think the 2014 reform was an important step forward, the biggest problems seem to be caused by the actual use of (running the) procedures. The European legislature should encourage member states to put greater effort into professionalizing contracting authorities. For example, using a negotiated procedure requires a lot of skills and expertise that are not always present today. This obviously contributes to an increased probability of failure.

4. SOME CONCLUDING REMARKS

In 2014, the European legislator set out to make public procurement procedures more flexible by creating more choice and allowing wider use of the competitive dialogue and competitive procedure with negotiations. This can be endorsed. One might even consider continuing this trend by, for example, further expanding the scope of the competitive procedure with negotiations by making it a standard procedure as in Directive 2014/25/EU. It is indeed difficult to understand why there should be a distinction between the two directives on that point. Moreover, in practice, even when purchasing off-the-shelf products, there may be good reasons to negotiate with tenderers.

That the competitive dialogue is sometimes considered unnecessary is unfortunate. The specific objective of this procedure has not been sufficiently expressed, which may give the wrong impression that this procedure is easily interchangeable with the competitive procedure with negotiations. The reality is different. It would be good if the legislature could clarify this and highlight the specificity of the procedures more. Should it still be considered to eliminate the competitive dialogue, the competitive procedure with negotiations should be redesigned. In very complex projects, there is a need to conduct final

[44] Compare: Office of the Chief Advisor, 'Use of Probity Auditors and Advisors' (buyingfor.vic.gov.au.) <https://www.buyingfor.vic.gov.au/probity-procurement-goods-and-services-guide and https://www.hpw.qld.gov.au/__data/assets/pdf_file/0014/3353/procurementguideprobityauditorsadvisors.pdf> (hpw.qld.gov.au., 4 November 2018) accessed 2 June 2025.

negotiations with a preferred bidder and to request confirmation of commitments made previously – certainly in terms of financing. Today, as seen, arguably that possibility exists only for competitive dialogue. Furthermore, if the idea of negotiations with a preferred bidder would be considered in the competitive procedure with negotiations, the legislature is also advised to regulate the position of economic operators that are put in a waiting room as explained in another recent publication.[45]

What else could be improved? We think the process of the negotiated procedure without prior notice could be improved as this procedure is very prone to corruption. Moreover, more attention should be paid to the professionalization of public buyers. We think this is key to better manage risks and reduce failures. Furthermore, as we have explained, the legislature should fix the legal issues that arise when, during negotiations, a concession becomes a public contract because of a shift in the risks.

Last but not least, we think the innovation partnership procedure offers little added value. It is hardly used. It would be better to remove this procedure from the Directive. On the other hand, consideration should be given to including the PCP procedure in the new Directive. This procedure appears to be very useful for developing innovation using public procurement. This procedure has developed a certain maturity in recent years and has added value, but the fact that the R&D contracts subject to this procedure fall outside the scope of public procurement legislation creates legal uncertainty. For example, the legal protection regime for public procurement does not apply. Consequently, the standstill period also does not apply, and bidders do not have the same safeguards on obtaining information and justifications as in classic public procurement. This is unfortunate. The better option therefore is to include excluded R&D services in the scope of the new Directive and to incorporate and formally regulate the PCP procedure.

---

45 The waiting room technique is regularly used in the procurement practice in combination with the notion of "preferred bidder." After a round of negotiations, the contracting authority will draw up a ranking based on an assessment against the award criteria. The first-ranked tenderer will be the preferred bidder, while the other tenderers will be sent to the waiting room. Negotiations will be continued with the preferred bidder only, with a view to awarding the contract. If the negotiations are not successful, the contracting authority does not have to stop the procedure but can resort to tenderers in the waiting room to continue the procedure. See Steven Van Garsse, Simon Verhoeven and Ellen Wouters, 'Second-ranked tenderers and the principle of the "waiting room" in EU procurement law' (2025) EPPPL (forthcoming).

11. Of many sticks and one mutant carrot

The new external dimension of EU public contracts

Roberto Caranta

REFORM PROPOSALS

- EU rules should clearly indicate whether participation of non-covered economic operators is allowed or not; and if so, under which conditions contracting authorities or entities may diverge from the default position.
- Following the example from both the International Procurement Instrument (IPI) Regulation and the Anti-Coercion Instrument, they should provide for score adjustments in case participation is allowed.
- Alternatively, as it is the case under both the IPI Regulation and the Net-Zero Industry Act, the Commission should be mandated to define both the public contracts that are closed to the participation of the concerned third-country bidders and any score adjustment to be applied to the other contracts.
- To avoid the elusion of the new provisions, rules of origin for both the suppliers and the goods and services supplied should be enacted following the model in Article 3 of the IPI Regulation and in Article 16 and Annex II of the Anti-Coercion Instrument.

1. INTRODUCTION: THE EXTERNAL DIMENSION OF EU PUBLIC PROCUREMENT

EU public procurement (and concessions) law is normally approached from its huge internal (market) dimension. However, the EU public contracts market also has an external dimension. Estimated at two trillion euros,[1] this

[1] Public Procurement, https://single-market-economy.ec.europa.eu/single-market/public-procurement_en, accessed July 2025.

market is of obvious interest for economic operators from third countries. Reciprocally, foreign procurement markets are of interest to EU-based economic operators.

Today, the Government Procurement Agreement (GPA), a plurilateral agreement concluded in the framework of the World Trade Organisation (WTO), is the most relevant text for the opening of the European public contracts market to economic operators from third countries. A specific trade agreement on public procurement has been vouchsafed since Article III:8 of the General Agreement on Tariffs and Trade (GATT) 1994 and Article XIII of the General Agreement on Trade in Services (GATS) excluded government procurement from the main multilateral WTO disciplines.[2] Only those procuring entities listed by each party in its Annexes I to III are covered under the GPA. Objective coverage is not only limited by thresholds. The parties have committed to open to foreign competition only those supplies and services contracts listed in Annexes IV and V.[3] Economic operators whose country is party to a trade agreement with the EU are not granted access to all and every procurement or concession in the EU, as the relevant schedules of commitments (e.g. GPA Annexes) will apply.[4] The GPA and other international agreements to which the EU is a party do not cover economic operators from many countries, including, for instance, Turkey and the People's Republic of China.[5]

The external dimension of EU public procurement is regulated under Article 25 of the Classic Directive. Article 25 is mirrored in Article 43 of the Utilities Directive. However, the Utilities Directive has additional provisions on third countries' content in tenders. The Concessions Directive instead has no corresponding provisions, even if some works concessions are covered in the EU

---

[2] Laurence Folliot Lalliot and Christopher R. Yukins, "Will Protectionism Prevail in Global Public Procurement?" (2024) 2 Concurrences 1, 2. As recalled by Recital 4 of Regulation (EU) 2022/1031 on the access of third-country economic operators, goods and services to the Union's public procurement and concession markets and procedures supporting negotiations on access of Union economic operators, goods and services to the public procurement and concession markets of third countries [2022] OJ L 173/1 (International Procurement Instrument – IPI). However, Wolfgang Weiß and Cornelia Furculita, *Open Strategic Autonomy in EU Trade Policy. Assessing the Turn to Stronger Enforcement and More Robust Interest Representation* (Cambridge University Press 2024) esp. 295 ff., argue that the carve-out from WTO obligations is far from complete; see also Rika Koch, *Green Public Procurement under WTO Law* (Springer 2020) 59.

[3] See Recital 10 Regulation (EU) 2022/1031 (IPI).

[4] For a full list of the relevant agreements, see Public Procurement, https://policy.trade.ec.europa.eu/help-exporters-and-importers/accessing-markets/public-procurement_en, accessed July 2025.

[5] See Article 2(1)(k) Regulation (EU) 2022/1031 (IPI).

Annex 6 to the WTO-GPA and the WTO-GPA is recalled in Articles 9 and 53 of that directive.

When the 2014 Public Procurement Directives were passed, unchallenged (neo-)liberalism allocated different productions around the world according to "efficiency", that is, where costs were lower, either because of higher productivity or lower production costs or simply because externalising costs on the environment, workers and communities was easier. Seamless global supply chains then delivered (mainly) goods where the demand was greatest. The WTO-GPA ensured – and still ensures – a measure of reciprocal opening of procurement markets. The Public Procurement Directives were an incarnation of public procurement market opening – and market making – harmonisation instruments.[6]

The EU and most of its Member States have in the past been quite welcoming to economic operators from third countries, including those not benefiting from reciprocal market opening agreements.[7] This open attitude has changed markedly in the past few years, for many reasons. At a very basic level, EU institutions realised that third countries have failed to reciprocate and to grant EU-based economic operators access to their public contract markets. Moreover, some third countries have been actively supporting the efforts by their own companies to penetrate the EU public contracts market with subsidies coming on top of more lenient regulatory environments allowing for lower production costs.[8] By 2019, the Commission had adopted the *Guidance on the participation of third-country bidders and goods in the EU procurement market*.[9] The toolbox, however, boiled down to the potential exclusion of abnormally low tenders and a passionate call to use strategic procurement.[10]

---

[6] Roberto Caranta, "Never Secondary, Forever Horizontal: The Promises of Sustainable Public Procurement" in Annamaria La Chimia – Martin Trybus (eds), *Reforming Public Procurement Law – Liber Amicorum in Honour of Sue Arrowsmith* (Hart 2024) 139–154.

[7] Lalliot and Yukins (n 2).

[8] See, for example, European Commission, "Joint Communication to the European Parliament, the European Council and the Council setting out an EU-China – A strategic outlook" JOIN (2019)5 final; see Giacomo Gattinara and Petr Ondrusek, "Un nouvel instrument dans le droit européen des marchés publics et des concessions: le règlement (UE) 2022/2560 sur les subventions étrangères faussant le marché intérieur" (2024) 1 Rev Droit UE 217, 219 f.

[9] European Commission, "Communication from the Commission – Guidance on the Participation of Third-country Bidders and Goods in the EU Procurement Market" C/2019/5494.

[10] Ibid., 13 ff and 17 ff, respectively.

At a deeper level, COVID and the consequences of the Russian invasion of Ukraine made it clear that blindly relying on international products/inputs left the EU exposed to breakdowns in global supply chains and to the ensuing price shocks. These events have taught us that global supply chains are far from being seamless. They are delicate things prone to sudden disruption.[11] And to blackmail. The recent Competitiveness Compass argues that "In a context where other major players impose access restrictions to their markets and seek to boost manufacturing capacity in critical technologies, Europe must safeguard its own capacities."[12] The various conflicts raging in the Middle East have compounded the need to buttress the resilience of EU supply chains, including with reference to public contracts.[13] Finally, at a wider political level, the realisation of the social impact on European workers of offshoring production outside of the EU together with the fact that the externalisation of environmental and even social costs is ultimately bound to bounce back, for example through climate change or immigration, have together caused some in the EU to reconsider the benefits of production delocalisation or offshoring.[14]

In this chapter, the measures enshrined in the Foreign Subsidies Regulation (FSR)[15] to protect EU bidders from unfair competition from subsidised economic operators from third countries will be analysed first (§ 2). The procurement provisions of the Net-Zero Industry Act (NZIA)[16] enacted to ensure the resilience of supply chains vital for the green transition will be analysed next (§ 3). The above provisions tend to restrict the participation of third-country

---

11 See, for example, European Commission, "Communication from the Commission to the European Parliament, the Council, the European Economic and Social Committee and the Committee of the Regions Trade Policy Review – An Open, Sustainable and Assertive Trade Policy" COM(2021) 66 final.

12 European Commission, "Communication from the Commission to the European Parliament, the European Council, the Council, the European Economic and Social Committee and the Committee of the Regions Communication from the Commission – A Competitiveness Compass for the EU" COM(2025) 30 final 14.

13 See the analysis by Michael Bowsher et al., "International Procurement Developments in 2022: New Perspectives in Global Procurement" (2022) Gov. Contr. Year in Rev 59, 61 ff. (Part II authored by Pascal Friton).

14 Roberto Caranta, "Sustainability Takes Centre Stage in Public Procurement" (2023) 85(1) Ruch Prawniczy Ekonomiczny i Socjologiczny 41.

15 Regulation (EU) 2022/2560 of the European Parliament and of the Council of 14 December 2022 on foreign subsidies distorting the internal market [2022] OJ L 330/1.

16 Regulation (EU) 2024/1735 of the European Parliament and of the Council of 13 June 2024 on establishing a framework of measures for strengthening Europe's net-zero technology manufacturing ecosystem [2024] OJ L 2024/1735 (NZIA).

economic operators in the EU public procurement market. The IPI[17] is instead intended to entice third countries to open their public procurement market to EU-based economic operators, but it goes well beyond nudging (§ 4). An assessment of the changed interpretation of Article 25 of the Classic Directive in a very different EU framework for the international dimension of public procurement will follow (§ 5). The conclusions will reflect how this new international trade law framework could be consolidated in the soon-to-be-reformed Public Procurement Directives (§ 6).

2. THE FOREIGN SUBSIDIES REGULATION

The Foreign Subsidies Regulation (FSR), enacted late in 2022, aims to tackle distortions in the EU internal market caused by foreign subsidies, thereby ensuring fair competition.[18] Limiting the attention here to public procurement, according to Article 27, the focus of the legislative intervention is "Foreign subsidies that cause or risk causing a distortion in a public procurement procedure shall be understood as foreign subsidies that enable an economic operator to submit a tender that is unduly advantageous."[19] Two elements are relevant here: a distortion caused by the subsidy and an unduly advantageous tender. Gattinara and Ondrusek have shown how the notion and the treatment of the latter notion are inspired by the well-known public procurement rules on abnormally low tenders.[20]

Under Articles 28 and 29 of the FSR, when the thresholds for both the contract value (at least EUR 250 million) and the subsidies received at group level (EUR 4 million) are met, economic operators participating in a public procurement procedure shall notify the contracting authority or entity of all foreign financial contributions meeting the above threshold. Otherwise, economic operators shall "list in a declaration all foreign financial contributions received and confirm that the foreign financial contributions received are not

[17] Regulation (EU) 2022/1031 (IPI).

[18] See Gattinara and Ondrusek (n 8); the proposal was analysed in depth by Ondrej Blažo, "A New Regime on Protection of Public Procurement against Foreign Subsidies Distorting the Internal Market: Mighty Paladin or Giant on the Feet of Clay?" (2021) 21 International and Comparative Law Review 138–161; Weiß and Furculita (n 2) ff.

[19] Article 27 refers back to Article 4; see also European Commission, "Commission Staff Working Document Initial clarifications on the application of Article 4(1), Article 6 and Article 27(1) of Regulation (EU) 2022/2560 on foreign subsidies distorting the internal market" SWD(2024) 201 final.

[20] Gattinara and Ondrusek (n 8) 223 ff.

notifiable".[21] The notification or declaration is submitted to the Commission by the contracting authority or entity, which must also communicate their suspicions in case they think the information submitted to them is not trustworthy. Under Article 30(2) and (3), the Commission is tasked with carrying out a preliminary review no later than 20 working days after it receives a complete notification. In case it decides to initiate an in-depth investigation, it shall inform the economic operator concerned and the contracting authority or the contracting entity without delay.[22] Under Articles 9 and 29(8), the Commission can also start an investigation *ex officio*, including for below the notification threshold, but only with reference to concluded contracts.[23]

In case the Commission finds that the subsidies received have negatively distorted the competition in the public contracts market, the concerned economic operator has the possibility to offer commitments "appropriate and sufficient to fully and effectively remedy the distortion" (Articles 11 and 31). Otherwise, the Commission shall adopt an implementing act in the form of a decision prohibiting the award of the contract to the economic operator concerned ("decision prohibiting the award of the contract").[24]

An implemented regulation has been adopted,[25] and the Commission has launched a consultation to start working towards guidelines for the application of the FSR.[26] So far, the Commission has received notification concerning more than 300 public procurement procedures and opened three in-depth investigations, one concerning procurements for trains in Bulgaria and involving CRRC

---

21 For a critical appraisal of the administrative burden on economic operators – and a not-too-veiled fear that investigations might end targeting US firms, including in the defence sector – see Pascal Friton, Max Klasse and Christopher R. Yukins, "The EU Foreign Subsidies Regulation: Implications for Public Procurement and Some Collateral Damage" (2023) 65 Government Contractor 63.

22 See also European Commission, "Communication pursuant to Articles 4(2), 8(1), 15, 17(2) and 25 of Implementing Regulation (EU) 2023/1441 on detailed arrangements for the conduct of proceedings by the Commission pursuant to Regulation (EU) 2022/2560 of the European Parliament and of the Council on foreign subsidies distorting the internal market" (2023/C 246/02).

23 See Gattinara and Ondrusek (n 8) 229 ff.

24 See Weiß and Furculita (n 2) 332 f.

25 Commission Implementing Regulation (EU) 2023/1441 on detailed arrangements for the conduct of proceedings by the Commission pursuant to Regulation (EU) 2022/2560 of the European Parliament and of the Council on foreign subsidies distorting the internal market [2023] OJ L 177/1.

26 Commission launches consultations on guidelines under the Foreign Subsidies Regulation, https://ec.europa.eu/commission/presscorner/detail/en/ip_25_685, accessed July 2025.

Qingdao Sifang Locomotive Company[27] and two others concerning the design, construction and operation of a photovoltaic park in Romania.[28] In all cases, the tenders were withdrawn after the launch of the preliminary investigations. Two *ex officio* investigations are currently pending, concerning wind turbines and security equipment.[29]

While a very small percentage of the notifications are actually leading to in-depth investigations, the Commission is clearly focusing on some strategic technology, and this is confirmed by *ex officio* investigations. The withdrawal of all tenderers suspected of having received subsidies is clearly signalling an impact of the FSR on public procurements across (especially Eastern) Europe.

Finally, the Commission has opened a consultation on a possible revision of the FSR as foreseen under Article 52(2) and published update guidelines.[30]

3. THE NZIA AND THE CONCERN FOR RESILIENCE

The Net-Zero Industry Act (NZIA) was announced in the Commission Communication "A Green Deal Industrial Plan for the Net-Zero Age"[31] in early 2023 and was rapidly adopted.[32] The NZIA is interesting here for two

[27] Summary notice concerning the initiation of an in-depth investigation in case FSP.100147 pursuant to Articles 10(3)(d) of Regulation (EU) 2022/2560 (C/2024/1913), https://eur-lex.europa.eu/eli/C/2024/1913/oj/eng, accessed July 2025.

[28] Summary notices concerning the initiation of an in-depth investigation in Case FSP. 100151, pursuant to Articles 10(3)(d) of Regulation (EU) 2022/2560 (C/2024/2830) and (C/2024/2832),https://eur-lex.europa.eu/legal-content/EN/TXT/PDF/?uri=OJ:C_202402830 and https://eur-lex.europa.eu/legal-content/EN/TXT/PDF/?uri=OJ:C_202402832, accessed July 2025.

[29] Concerning the latter case, see the recently launched in-depth investigation announced at https://ec.europa.eu/commission/presscorner/detail/en/ip_25_3019, accessed December 2025; see also Case C-720/24 P(R) *Nuctech Warsaw Company Limited* ECLI:EU:C:2025:205; T-284/24 R *Nuctech Warsaw Company Limited and Nuctech Netherlands v Commission* EU:T:2024:564.

[30] https://ec.europa.eu/commission/presscorner/detail/en/ip_25_1954, accessed September 2025, and Guidelines on the application of certain provisions of Regulation (EU) 2022/2560 on foreign subsidies distorting the internal market C(2026) 42 final.

[31] European Commission, "Communication from the Commission to the European Parliament, the European Council, the Council, the European Economic and Social Committee and the Committee of the Regions Green Deal Industrial Plan for the Net-Zero Age" COM(2023) 62 final.

[32] Michael Fruhmann and Julia Meszaros, "Der neue Net-Zero Industry Act (NZIA)" (2024) 7 *ZVB – Zeitschrift für Vergaberecht und Bauvertragsrecht* 296,

related aspects. First, the NZIA makes the resilience of the EU economy a central concern in public procurement law. Second, it introduces specific additional "adjustments" compared to the FSR to buttress – or to allow the reconstruction of – EU industry by limiting the competitive advantages enjoyed by economic operators hailing from third countries without the need to establish the existence and effects of possible subsidies. The green transition required to meet the ambitious climate goals of the EU needs a reliable supply of those technologies covered under the NZIA and listed in its Annex (e.g. solar thermal and wind technologies).[33]

Public procurement has a role to play. Article 25 of the NZIA is dedicated to "Sustainability and resilience contribution in public procurement procedures".[34] Focusing here on resilience, under Article 25(7), contracting authorities and entities acquiring covered technologies must take into account "tender's resilience contribution" when contracts or framework agreements are covered under one of the public procurement directives. More specifically, if the Commission has established that a huge proportion of a specific net-zero technology or its main specific components originates in a third country, public buyers must include a number of conditions in the procurement documents to bind future contractors not to supply more than 50% of the specific net-zero technology or of its main specific components from any of the third countries listed by the Commission.[35] Contractors are bound to provide evidence of their compliance with that condition and must pay a "proportionate charge" in case of breach of their obligations.[36]

Under Article 25(8), those obligations do not apply to contracts covered by the GPA or any other relevant international agreements by which the Union is bound.[37] Unlike with the "sustainability contribution", higher costs, even exceeding 20%, are not an excuse to forgo the "resilience contribution". However, under Article 25(11), where the application of the resilience contribution has led to "a situation where no suitable tenders or no suitable requests to participate have been submitted in response to a public procurement procedure", the contracting authorities or contracting entities may, on an exceptional basis, either use a negotiated procedure without prior publication or not take into account the resilience contribution in a subsequent procedure addressing the same aims. The provision diverges from the approach in Article 32(2)(a)

296.

[33] Recital 16.

[34] Fruhmann and Meszaros (n 32) 298 ff.

[35] See also Recital 57.

[36] As Recital 58 indicates, this is "in order to ensure that the mechanism is complied with".

[37] See also Recital 57.

of the Classic Directive as recourse to negotiated procedures is here only one possibility, the other being forgoing the resilience criterion in following "regular" procedure.[38]

Compared with the FSR (and the IPI), which might be considered as protective or reactive measures to shield EU producers from unfair competition from abroad, the NZIA is the first proactive measure targeted at strengthening EU producers and, more generally, to reduce the dependence of the EU on third countries. It is expected to be followed by a Critical Medicines Act and possibly by a wider but not necessarily general "European preference" (see §6).

4. THE INTERNATIONAL PROCUREMENT INSTRUMENT

The history of the adoption of the IPI represents well the seismic changes that have affected and are affecting the external dimension of EU public procurement.[39] The Commission tabled its first proposal in 2012,[40] but, because of the opposition from some Member States, the proposal was revised in 2016.[41] Although it was only in early 2019 that the legislative process restarted in earnest. Facing increased competition from Chinese companies harming EU industry, the Council decided that "the EU must also safeguard its interests in the light of unfair practices of third countries, making full use of trade defence instruments and our public procurement rules, as well as ensuring effective reciprocity for public procurement with third countries" and called "for resuming discussions on the EU's international procurement instrument".[42] In

[38] See further Fruhmann and Meszaros (n 32) 304.

[39] See Weiß and Furculita (n 2) 287 ff.

[40] European Commission, "Proposal for a Regulation of the European Parliament and of the Council on the access of third-country goods and services to the Union's internal market in public procurement and procedures supporting negotiations on access of Union goods and services to the public procurement markets of third countries" COM(2012) 124 final.

[41] European Commission, "Amended proposal for a Regulation of the European Parliament and of the Council on the access of third-country goods and services to the Union's internal market in public procurement and procedures supporting negotiations on access of Union goods and services to the public procurement markets of third countries" COM(2016) 34 final.

[42] European Council, "European Council meeting (21 and 22 March 2019)" EUCO 1/19; see also European Commission, "Joint Communication to the European Parliament, the European Council and the Council EU-China – A strategic outlook" JOIN(2019) 5 final.

its New Industrial Strategy,[43] the Commission wrote of "a time of moving geopolitical plates which affect the nature of competition".[44] Therefore, "A swift agreement on the proposed International Procurement Instrument will also be essential to address lack of reciprocity and to give the EU further leverage in negotiations".[45]

According to Recital 5, the "Union advocates an ambitious opening of the international public procurement and concession markets of the Union and its trading partners, in a spirit of reciprocity and mutual benefit". On its face, the IPI Regulation is an instrument for market opening, not for market closure.[46] Lacking reciprocity, the EU market might be closed to put additional negotiating pressure on non-cooperative third countries.

Under Articles 1(1) and 5 of the IPI Regulation, the Commission is charged with investigating – of its own motion or because of a "substantiated complaint" – whether specific measures or practices exist in a third country that limit the access of EU economic operators, goods or services to that country's public procurement or concession markets.[47] Participatory rights of the third country are guaranteed under Article 5 with the aim of achieving reciprocal market opening through corrective measures adopted by the relevant country.[48] Consultation with the Member States and written participation of interested parties are also foreseen. If an acceptable *modus vivendi* is not achieved, based on a balance of all relevant interests, including the EU's broader interests and those of EU economic operators, the Commission may adopt an IPI measure (Article 6(1) to (3)).[49] IPI measures can be applied only to procurement procedures where the estimated value of the tender is equal to or above EUR 15,000,000 net of VAT for works and concessions and equal to or above EUR 5,000,000 net of VAT for goods and services (Article 6(4)).

The procedure has been deployed for the first time with reference to measures and practices in the Chinese procurement market for medical devices, which have been considered by the Commission to discriminate unfairly against European companies and products. The report from the Commission evidenced both the widespread application of "Buy China" rules and of centralised procurement practices favouring subsidised local producers. For its part, the Republic of China, while downplaying market closure measures and

---

43 European Commission, "Communication from the Commission: A New Industrial Strategy for Europe" COM(2020) 102 final.

44 § 1.

45 § 3.2.

46 Lalliot and Yukins (n 2) 8.

47 Recital 14 Regulation (EU) 2022/1031 (IPI).

48 Ibid., Recitals 17 ff.

49 Ibid., Recital 20.

practices, insisted on the need for starting negotiations either in the framework of its accession to the WTO-GPA or bilaterally.[50]

Under Article 6(6) of the IPI Regulation, an IPI measure may either consist of a "score adjustment" penalising tenderers from the concerned third country or in their outright exclusion from public procurement or concession procedures throughout the EU. According to the definition in Article 2(1)(d):

> "score adjustment" means the relative diminution by a given percentage of the score of a tender, resulting from its evaluation by a contracting authority or a contracting entity, on the basis of the contract award criteria defined in the relevant public procurement documents. In cases where price or cost is the only contract award criterion, the score adjustment means the relative increase, for the purpose of the evaluation of tenders, by a given percentage of the price offered by a tenderer.

Each IPI measure details its scope of application and, where appropriate, the percentage values of the score adjustment (Article 6(8)). Under Article 1(4), contracting authorities and entities must refer to the IPI measure in the contract documents.[51] A breach of such an obligation would not make the IPI measure inapplicable; rather, it would be a reason for competitors to challenge the contract documents and the award.[52] Under Article 9, contracting authorities and entities might forgo the application of an IPI measure if there is no alternative source of supply or for overriding reasons in the general interest, but they must notify the Commission about this decision and the reasons supporting it. In order to limit the risk that IPI measures are circumvented through subcontracts, Article 8 provides that penalty clauses need to be inserted in public contracts.[53]

---

50 European Commission, "Report from the Commission pursuant to Article 5(4) of Regulation (EU) 2022/1031 on the investigation under the International Procurement Instrument concerning measures and practices of the People's Republic of China in the public procurement market for medical devices" COM(2025) 5; see also for more information on the evidence gathered, European Commission, "Commission Staff Working Document Factual findings of the IPI investigation on the procurement market for medical devices in the People's Republic of China Accompanying the document Report from the Commission pursuant to Article 5(4) of Regulation (EU) 2022/1031 on the investigations under the International Procurement Instrument concerning measures and practices of the People's Republic of China in the public procurement market for medical devices" SWD(2025)2.

51 See Bowsher et al. (n 13) 64.

52 Article 10 of Regulation (EU) 2022/1031 (IPI); see also Recital 27.

53 Ibid., Recital 23.

Rules of origin are an important aspect for the application of the IPI Regulation. They are needed to avoid that third-country economic operators may circumvent the rules too easily by acquiring the status of EU operators (or the status of operators from third countries benefiting from market access).[54] A distinction is drawn between goods, on the one hand and services, including works, on the other hand.[55] Concerning the former, Article 3(4) refers to Article 60 of Regulation (EU) 952/2013 laying down the Union Customs Code. Concerning services, under Article 3, the origin is determined with reference to the "origin" – that is, establishment – of the natural or legal person providing it. "Permanent residence" is referred to in the case of natural persons (Article 3(1)(a)). Under Article 3(1)(b)(i), the origin of a legal person should be considered to be the country under the laws of which a legal person is constituted or otherwise organised and in the territory of which the legal person is engaged in substantive business operations. However, legal persons constituted or otherwise organised under the laws of a Member State should only be considered to have their origin in the Union if they have a direct and effective link with the economy of a Member State. To avoid a possible circumvention of an IPI measure, in case a legal person is "not engaged in substantive business operation" in the EU, the reference is to the person or persons having a decisive influence on the legal person concerned (Article 3(1)(b)(ii)).[56] The Commission "Guidance on the participation of third-country bidders and goods in the EU procurement market provides contracting authorities and entities with further information on how to apply rules of origin provisions."[57]

While the FSR and the NZIA aim at limiting unfair or otherwise undesirable competition on the EU public procurement market from third-country economic operators and act as sticks, the IPI aims at prying open foreign markets to the benefit of EU economic operators, and therefore it represents the carrot in the external public procurement dimension of the EU. If enticing fails, however, the temporary fallback position is to close the EU market, so the carrot may turn into a stick. This is well illustrated by the first Commission decision closing an IPI investigation and restricting the access of economic operators and medical devices originating in the People's Republic of China to the EU public procurement market for medical devices.[58] The measure excludes

54 Ibid., Recitals 11 ff; see Gattinara and Ondrusek (n 8) 220.

55 Ibid., Article 2(2).

56 Ibid., Recital 13.

57 European Commission C/2019/5494 (n 9) 8 ff.

58 Commission Implementing Regulation (EU) 2025/1197 of 19 June 2025 imposing an International Procurement Instrument measure restricting the access of economic operators and medical devices originating in the People's Republic of China to the European Union public procurement market for medical devices

Chinese tenders from all procurement procedures concerning all categories of medical devices organised by all Union contracting authorities and contracting entities with a value equal to or above EUR 5,000,000. As the Commission itself stressed in the conclusions to its report on the application of the IPI regulation, an IPI measure is hoped to be conducive to more negotiation with the concerned third country.[59]

5. THE INTERPRETATIVE TRANSFORMATION OF ARTICLES 25 AND 43: *KOLIN* AND *QINGDAO*

As already mentioned, on the face of it, Article 25 of the Classic Directive (and Article 43 of the Utilities Directive) does not do much more than recall the obligations flowing from the WTO-GPA and from other international agreements. Early on, however, La Chimia argued that the provision should also be read as a "bargaining tool" to lure more third countries to enter into reciprocal agreements to ensure that their economic operators can benefit from access to the EU procurement market.[60] This instrumental function of Articles 25 and 43 has been much strengthened by the Court of Justice of the European Union (CJEU) in the recent *Kolin* case,[61] which was reaffirmed in *Qingdao*.[62]

According to the CJEU in *Kolin*, Article 43 of the Utilities Directive "reflects" the EU international commitments to give equal participation rights to economic operators hailing from third countries benefiting from international commitments signed by the EU.[63] However, the CJEU read more into the Utilities Directive. According to the Court, in the absence of exclusion measures adopted by the EU, although the Directive does not preclude those third-country economic operators

pursuant to Regulation (EU) 2022/1031 of the European Parliament and of the Council 2025/1197 [2025] OJ L 2025/1197.

59 Report pursuant to Article 13 of Regulation (EU) 2022/1031 on the application of this Regulation and on the progress made in international negotiations, regarding access for Union economic operators to the public procurement or concession markets of third countries, undertaken under this Regulation (COM(2025) 430 final).

60 Annamaria. La Chimia, "Comment to Article 25" in Roberto Caranta and Albert Sanchez Graells (eds), *European Public Procurement Commentary to Directive 2014/24/EU* (Hart 2021) at 275.

61 Case C-652/22 *Kolin Inşaat Turizm Sanayi ve Ticaret AŞ* ECLI:EU:C:2024:910.

62 Case C-266/22 *CRRC Qingdao Sifang* ECLI:EU:C:2025:178.

63 Case C-652/22 *Kolin* (n 61) para 43, referring to Recital 27 of the Directive.

> from being allowed to participate in a public procurement procedure governed by Directive 2014/25, it does, however, preclude those economic operators from being able, in the context of their participation in such a procedure, to rely on that directive and thus to require that their tender be treated equally to those submitted by tenderers from Member States and by the tenderers from third countries referred to in Article 43 of that directive. (paragraph 45)

Reasoning otherwise would indeed mean that the same benefits reflected in Article 43 would be accorded to economic operators from all third countries, regardless of whether they are covered by an international agreement.[64] The conclusion is further supported by reference to the IPI Regulation discussed previously (§ 4).[65] The IPI Regulation confirms that economic operators that do not benefit from international commitment may be excluded from public procurement procedures in the EU as they do not enjoy market access rights.[66]

To rebut the argument advanced by some of the Member States to the effect that the Utilities Directive does not stand in the way of national law according access to economic operators from all third countries, even those not bound by international agreements, the CJEU referred to the EU exclusive competence in matters of international trade.[67] The Court held that only the EU is competent to decide in general terms which economic operators *do* have access to the European procurement markets. The decision takes place through the negotiation and conclusion of international agreements. The exclusive competence of the EU in this area is grounded in Article 3(1)(e) and (2) of the TFEU. Therefore,

> Any act of general application specifically intended to determine the arrangements under which economic operators from a third country may participate in public procurement procedures in the European Union is such as to have direct and immediate effects on trade in goods and services between that third country and the European Union, with the result that it falls within the exclusive competence of the European Union (...).[68]

The CJEU again refers to the IPI Regulation to strengthen its conclusion about the exclusive competence of the EU with reference to the adoption of "measures of general application that may be taken with regard to economic operators of a third country which has not concluded an international agreement

64 Ibid., paras 46 and 47; see also Case C-266/22 *Qingdao* (n 62) para 58.

65 The link between the two is stressed by Christopher Bovis, "Editorial" (2024) 4 *EPPPL* 229.

66 Case C-652/22 *Kolin* (n 61) para 49; see Bovis (n 65), 230.

67 Opinion 2/15 (EU-Singapore Free Trade Agreement) ECLI:EU:C:2017:376.

68 Ibid., para 57.

with the European Union".[69] In *Qingdao*, the CJEU further deduced from the exclusive EU competence a prohibition against domestic legislation that excludes economic operators who do not benefit from market opening measures from participating in award procedures.[70]

The EU exclusive competence to adopt measures of general application does not pre-empt contracting authorities and entities from accepting bids from third-country economic operators. While the default position is the exclusion of economic operators hailing from third countries not benefiting from reciprocal market access,[71] contracting authorities or entities are, however, left to assess whether the concerned economic operators "should be admitted to a public procurement procedure and, if it decides to admit them, whether provision should be made for an adjustment of the result arising from a comparison between the tenders submitted by those operators and those submitted by other operators".[72] Moreover, since the economic operators concerned do not enjoy market access rights,

> it is open to the contracting entity to set out, in the procurement documents, arrangements for treatment intended to reflect the objective difference between the legal situation of those operators, on the one hand, and that of economic operators of the European Union and of third countries which have concluded such an agreement with the European Union, within the meaning of Article 43 of that directive, on the other hand.[73]

It is not clear from the judgment what these "arrangements" might be. The possibility for an "adjustment" is simply mentioned but not elaborated upon.

Arguably, a reference may be made to "score adjustments" as regulated under Article 6(8) of the IPI Regulation. However, Article 6(8) leaves to the Commission only the power to detail the scope of application and, where appropriate, the percentage values of the score adjustment. Lacking EU-wide rules, this task must be shouldered by each and every contracting authority or entity. Since the CJEU has denied the Member States the power to introduce general rules in this matter, it does not seem possible for any of them to bind public buyers to a specific approach to "score adjustment".

The *Kolin* judgment is also less than straightforward concerning the law applicable to the possible participation of third countries' economic operators in procurement procedures. There is indeed some tension between paragraphs

---

69 Ibid., para 59.

70 Case C-266/22 *Qingdao* (n 62) paras 62 and 64.

71 Bovis (n 65) 230.

72 Case C-652/22 *Kolin* (n 61) para 63; see also Case C-266/22 *Qingdao* (n 62) para 63.

73 Ibid., para 64.

65 and 66 of the judgment – and this in both the English, the French and the Croatian versions. In the former paragraph, the CJEU stresses that the national provisions implementing EU public procurement and concession law cannot be applied to those economic operators.[74] In the latter, it concedes that certain "requirements", "such as transparency or proportionality" might be applicable, but any infringement thereof could be only examined "in the light of national law and not of EU law".[75]

It is already worth pointing out that the CJEU refers here to "transparency and proportionality" as simple "requirements" instead of as principles, as is customary in the case law consolidated in Article 18 of the Classic Directive.[76] The big problem here is that in many EU Member States, most rules concerning public procurement are those implementing EU law, and they apply to procedures whether or not the procurement is formally covered by EU law. While in some Member States purely "national" provisions may regulate the award of contracts not covered under the Public Procurement Directives nor falling under the general principles of EU law, such as some below the threshold contracts, the approach devised by the CJEU might not in practice be workable in other countries.[77]

For reasons of transparency, the participation of third-country bidders should, in principle, be introduced *ex ante* in the contract documents. Still, lacking any specific rule in the contract documents, some legal rules must *perforce* be found. The rule of law is one of the founding values of the EU *and* the Member States under Article 2 of the Treaty on European Union. Contracting authorities and entities cannot act freely towards economic operators who do not benefit from market access, and vague "requirements" cannot be considered enough to meet the standards demanded by the rule of law. Finally, it seems that rights of access to justice under Article 13 of the European Convention on Human Rights cannot be excluded. Here again, the concerned third-country economic operators will benefit from whatever judicial protection is available generally under national law but not from specifically EU redress mechanisms

---

74 Ibid., para 65; this is repeated in Recital 67 referring again to "national provisions transposing the rules contained in Directive 2014/25".

75 Ibid., para 66.

76 See Carina Risvig Hamer, "Comment to Article 18(1)" in Caranta and Sanchez Graells (n 60), 187–198.

77 See the chapters collected by Roberto Caranta and Dacian C. Dragos (eds), *Outside the EU Procurement Directives – Inside the Treaties?* (DJOF Publishing 2012); see also Dacian C. Dragos and Roxana Vornicu, "Public Procurement below Thresholds in the European Union. EU Law Principles and National Responses" (2013) 3 EPPPL 187 ff.

and tools, including the preliminary reference and remedies, such as ineffectiveness and damages.[78]

To try and address the question left open by the CJEU case law, the Commission services simply issued a non-paper outlining the conditions for possible participation in the EU procurement market by bidders from non-covered third countries, following *Kolin* and *Qingdao*.[79] That is already not the most committal sort of legal act. The Commission was not ready for a communication, and the document very closely follows the judgments. The Commission did not even say firmly that the rules for non-covered economic operators must be set in the contract documents. Somewhat more helpful is the non-paper in its final published version concerning adjustments. Here, the Commission clearly indicates that contracting authorities and entities might take inspiration from Article 6(8) of IPI Regulation (EU) 2022/1031 or "decide to apply any adjustment mechanism it may consider appropriate for a specific public procurement procedure".[80]

Kolin and *Qingdao* will require giving precise indications in the forthcoming revision of the 2014 Public Procurement Directives to guide the contracting authorities and entities in dealing with bidders from third countries. These indications will have to clarify whether the default position for non-covered economic operators is exclusion or admission and the duty of public buyers to clearly indicate in the public procurement documents whether they want to reverse the default position and how to set adjustments in case of non-covered economic operators' admission to the procedure.

6. CONCLUSIONS

Reliance on the public procurement lever to either make international trade fairer, if not fully reciprocal, or to close the EU public procurement market is not limited to the FSR, the IPI or the NZIA. A recent addition is the

[78] Roberto Caranta and Vítězslava Fričová, "EU public procurement and concessions law" in Miroslava Scholten (ed), *Research Handbook on the Enforcement of EU Law* (Edward Elgar 2023) 415–430.

[79] Communications and guidance documents, https://single-market-economy.ec.europa.eu/single-market/public-procurement/communications-and-guidance-documents_en, accessed July 2025.

[80] See critically Bordering the Irresponsible: Commission's Q&A on the Third Country Access to EU Procurement Post Kolin/Qingdao, https://www.howtocrackanut.com/blog/2025/5/20/bordering-the-irresponsible-commission-non-paper-on-third-country-access, accessed July 2025.

Anti-Coercion Instrument.[81] Among the measures provided for therein, once again we find the exclusion from EU procurements of goods, services or suppliers from the third country concerned or the imposition of a score adjustment.

However, the external dimension of EU public contracts is no longer limited to trying to restore a fair competitive balance with trading partners. In her political guidelines for the new term, Commission President Ursula von der Leyen has indicated that she "will propose a revision of the Public Procurement Directive. This will enable preference to be given to European products in public procurement for certain strategic sectors. It will help ensure EU added value for our citizens, along with security of supply for vital technologies, products and services."[82] The Competitiveness Compass confirms the intention of reforming the procurement directives, aiming at "reinforcing technological security and domestic supply chains, as well as simplifying and modernising rules, in particular for start-ups and innovative companies", but it also adds that "The Commission will propose the introduction of a European preference in public procurement for strategic sectors and technologies."[83] The same tune is being played in the recent resolution of the European Parliament.[84]

The "European preference" is going to be deployed in the forthcoming Critical Medicines Act.[85] The Commission is calling for both incentivising resilience, sustainability and positive social impacts in public procurement of critical medicinal products and for joint procurement of medical products of common interest.[86]

To different extents, the FRS, the NZIA, the IPI and other recently enacted instruments must be read as aspects of a new trend towards friend-shoring that is not exclusive to the EU.[87] Still, this trend might lead to the fragmentation of

---

81 Regulation (EU) 2023/2675 on the protection of the Union and its Member States from economic coercion by third countries.

82 Europe's Choice, Political Guidelines for the Next European Commission 2024–2029, https://commission.europa.eu/document/e6cd4328-673c-4e7a-8683-f63ffb2cf648_en, accessed July 2025.

83 European Commission, "A Competitiveness Compass for the EU" (n 12) 14 f.

84 European Parliament resolution of 9 September 2025 on public procurement (2024/2103(INI)), esp. § 69, but with the caution in § 13.

85 European Commission, "Proposal for a Regulation of the European Parliament and of the Council laying a framework for strengthening the availability and security of supply of critical medicinal products as well as the availability of, and accessibility of, medicinal products of common interest, and amending Regulation (EU) 2024/795" COM(2025) 102 final.

86 See Articles 18 ff and 21 ff, respectively.

87 With reference to the US, see Lalliot and Yukins (n 2) ff; see also in a wider context European Parliament, "EU-China relations: De-risking or de-coupling

international law as applicable in the EU and to EU contracting authorities and entities, making procurement more complex.[88] Also, doubts have been raised concerning the consistency of some of the new provisions with WTO law.[89] Finally, it is all but certain that the new course of EU public procurement law to engage with third countries will actually lead to more market openings to the benefit of EU economic operators.[90]

More general international law issues aside, the forthcoming reform will have to link the future Public Procurement Directives with the numerous legal texts that differently address the external dimension of EU public procurement law, providing contracting authorities and entities with clear indications about who can participate in public procurement procedures in the EU and what adjustments might be necessary for non-covered third-country economic operators. Moreover, any "European preference" should be articulated in the Public Procurement Directives, with a delegation to the Commission to change or update the list of preferred products or services and/or of any "adjustement".

– the future of the EU strategy towards China", https://www.europarl.europa.eu/RegData/etudes/STUD/2024/754446/EXPO_STU(2024)754446_EN.pdf, accessed July 2025.

88 Fruhmann and Meszaros (n 32) 305.

89 For a very analytical discussion, see Weiß and Furculita (n 2) esp. 294 ff (IPI) and 336 ff (FSR); see also M. Frank, "The EU's New Foreign Subsidy Regulation on Collision Course with the WTO" (2023) 60(4) Common Market Law Review 925.

90 Michael Bowsher et al. (n 13) (part II authored by Pascal Friton) 71.

PART III

The instrumental use of public procurement

12. Environment and public procurement

Proposals for aligning EU law with the European Green Deal

Penelope Giosa

REFORM PROPOSALS

- Introduction of minimum mandatory sustainability and procedural requirements in Green Public Procurement (GPP).
- Integration of environmental due diligence requirements for economic operators.
- Utilization of sustainability reports as selection criteria and contract performance conditions.
- Optimization and broad adoption of life-cycle costing (LCC) methodologies and tools.
- Mandatory use of environmental third-party labels.
- Establishment of a flexible framework for prioritizing environmental objectives.

1. INTRODUCTION

Public procurement in the EU represents approximately 14% of its GDP, or EUR 2 trillion annually, involving over 250,000 public authorities.[1] As major purchasers in sectors like energy, transport, healthcare, and education, public authorities can significantly advance environmental policy goals, including climate change mitigation, resource efficiency, and sustainable consumption through Green Public Procurement (GPP).

While GPP, Sustainable Public Procurement, and Socially Responsible Public Procurement are powerful tools for societal goals, environmental

1 European Commission, "Public Procurement" (2024) <https://single-market-economy.ec.europa.eu/single-market/public-procurement_en>.

objectives can conflict or require prioritization. The European Court of Auditors' December 2023 report (pr28/2023) underscored the need for an environmental objective hierarchy within the new public procurement legal regime.[2] This chapter explores current provisions and proposes reforms to better integrate environmental considerations into EU public procurement law.

2. ENVIRONMENTAL PROVISIONS IN THE 2014 DIRECTIVE: NOVEL BUT ALSO CONTROVERSIAL

The 2014 Public Procurement Directive introduced environmental provisions to facilitate better integration of green considerations. This section critically discusses these rules, analyzing their impact and outlining steps to align EU procurement law with contemporary green objectives. This chapter focuses on specific provisions, acknowledging that green considerations apply throughout the public procurement procedure.

2.1 Mandatory Horizontal Clause

The 2014 Directive's Article 18(2) mandates Member States to ensure compliance with applicable environmental laws. This clause allows exclusion of economic operators (Article 57(4)(a)) and subcontractors (Article 71) for non-compliance and rejection of abnormally low tenders linked to environmental non-compliance (Article 69(1)(d)).

However, the clause's effectiveness is questionable. Most EU stakeholders believe its impact has been limited due to lack of clarity on enforcement authority, "appropriate measures," its broad scope, and difficulties in enforcing performance throughout the contract lifecycle.[3]

---

2 European Court of Auditors, "Special Report 28/2023: Public Procurement in the EU – Less Competition for Contracts Awarded for Works, Goods and Services in the 10 Years up to 2021" <www.eca.europa.eu/ECAPublications/SR-2023-28/SR-2023-28_EN.pdf> accessed 18 January 2025.

3 Valentina Caimi and Silvia Sansonetti, "The Social Impact of Public Procurement – Can the EU Do More?" (2023) for the European Parliament's Committee on Employment and Social Affairs <www.europarl.europa.eu/RegData/etudes/STUD/2023/740095/IPOL_STU(2023)740095_EN.pdf> accessed 18 January 2025; Willem Janssen, "Shifting Towards Mandatory Sustainability Requirements in EU Public Procurement Law: Context, Relevance and a Typology" in W. Janssen and R. Caranta (eds), *Mandatory Sustainability Requirements in EU Public Procurement Law: Reflections on a Paradigm Shift* (Hart Publishing, 2023); Carina Risvig Hamer and Marta Andhov, "Article 18

2.2 Labels

The 2014 Directive permits contracting authorities to reference specific labels or eco-labels in technical specifications, award criteria, or contract performance clauses without specifying underlying criteria.[4] Article 43(1)(a) demands all label requirements be linked to the purchased works, goods, or services. Labels cannot be used in selection criteria related to the tenderer's general corporate policy, aligning with the CJEU's Max Havelaar (C-368/10) ruling, which permitted detailed eco-label specifications but not the eco-label itself.[5] This aims to reduce administrative burden by removing repeated assessment of label relevance.[6]

Nevertheless, strict interpretation of the subject-matter link raises concerns. It can discourage public purchasers from referencing general certification schemes that include requirements not directly linked to the specific purchase.[7] This is significant because many sustainability criteria are best enforced at the organizational level, not per product or service.[8]

Also, labels must be established transparently by independent bodies, with participation from all relevant stakeholders.[9] Criteria must be objective, non-discriminatory, and accessible.[10] To avoid limiting competition, equivalent

Public Procurement Principles" in Caranta and Sanchez-Graells (eds), *European Public Procurement – Commentary on Directive 2014/24/EU* (Edward Elgar, 2021).

[4] Birna Guðrún Magnadóttir and others, *Nordic Guideline – Green Public Procurement: How to Use Environmental Management Systems and Ecolabels in EU Tenders* (Nordic Council of Ministers, 2017).

[5] Max Havelaar (C-368/10) EU:C:2012:284.

[6] Vilhelmiina Ihamäki et al., "Green Public Procurement in the European Union and the Use of Eco-labels IER 4114" <www.maastrichtuniversity.nl/sites/default/files/2023-03/green_public_procurement_in_the_european_union_and_the_use_of_eco-labels.pdf> accessed 18 January 2025; Roberto Caranta, "The Changes to the Public Contract Directives and the Story They Tell About How EU Law Works" (2015) 6(52) Common Market Law Review 391–460.

[7] Ibid.

[8] Abby Semple, "The Link to the Subject Matter – A Glass Ceiling for Sustainable Public Contracts?" in B. Sjåfjell and A. Wiesbrock (eds), *Sustainable Public Procurement Under EU Law – New Perspectives on the State as Stakeholder* (1st ed., Cambridge University Press, 2015), 50–74

[9] Ibid.

[10] Article 43, paragraph 1(c) of the 2014/24/EU Directive; European Commission, "Public Procurement Reform Factsheet No. 7: Green Public Procurement" (2014) <https://ec.europa.eu/docsroom/documents/15509?locale=en> accessed 18 January 2025.

labels or other proof must be accepted if an economic operator cannot obtain the label on time.[11] While this shifts the burden of proof from the 2004 Directives, the investigation and verification process for labels often exceeds award procedure timelines, especially with reduced minimum deadlines.[12] Hence, it is argued that in most cases the burden of proof is easily met.[13] Additionally, by accepting a manufacturer's own dossier, the public purchaser can no longer insist on third-party certification regarding the environmental characteristics of the product in question. Hence, in practice there is no progression from the 2004 Directives, and confusion is caused by the seemingly contradictory wording of Article 43.[14]

2.3 Life-Cycle Costing

A key novelty of the 2014 Directive is allowing the Most Economically Advantageous Tender (MEAT) award criterion to be based on LCC. This means offers can be selected based on LCC, encompassing all costs over a contract's lifecycle, including internal costs (e.g., R&D, production, transport, energy, maintenance, disposal) and environmental externality costs (e.g., greenhouse gas emissions, pollution from raw material extraction, or product use).[15] LCC can be applied at various stages: market consultation, technical criteria, award criteria, label use, and performance requirements.[16] The 2014 Directive's promotion of LCC shifts focus beyond initial purchase price

---

11 Ibid.

12 Roberto Caranta, "Labels as Enablers of Sustainable Public Procurement" in B. Sjåfjell and A. Wiesbrock (eds), *Sustainable Public Procurement Under EU Law – New Perspectives on the State as Stakeholder* (1st ed., Cambridge University Press, 2015), 99–113.

13 Ibid.

14 Bogdana Neamtu and Dacian Dragos, "Sustainable Public Procurement: The Use of Eco-Labels" (2015) 2(10) European Procurement and Public Private Partnership Law Review 92–101; Abby Semple, "Reform of the EU Procurement Directives and WTO GPA: Forward Steps for Sustainability?" in G. L. Albano, K. F. Snider and K. V. Thai (eds), *Charting a Course in Public Procurement Innovation and Knowledge Sharing* (1st ed., Academics Press, 2013).

15 Commission (fn 10).

16 Dacian Dragos and Bogdana Neamtu, "Life-cycle Thinking in EU Public Procurement – Moving Beyond a Simple 'Buzz Word'" in A. Castelli, G. Piga, S. Saussier and T. Tátrai (eds), *The Challenges of Public Procurement Reforms* (Routledge, 2020).

to include indirect costs of non-environmentally preferable assets throughout their operational and use phases.[17]

Environmental externality costs can only be considered if their monetary value is quantifiable and verifiable.[18] If no common EU method exists, national, regional, or local methods can be established.[19] However, localized carbon footprint calculations raise concerns about increased national preferences. Any methods used for the environmental externality cost assessment should be objective, not specific to one procedure, and require data that is providable with reasonable effort by enterprises.[20] However, LCC application by procurement officers remains limited[21] due to several challenges, such as absence of clear methodologies,[22] lack of competence and knowledge to assess/verify bidder information,[23] and insufficient reliable data, especially for environmental cost drivers difficult to monetize.[24] Addressing these challenges is crucial to increase procurement officers' confidence in using LCC.

---

17 Stéphane Saussier and Christopher H. Bovis, "Life-cycle Costing in Public Procurement: Colloquium" in A. Castelli, G. Piga, S. Saussier and T. Tátrai (eds), *The Challenges of Public Procurement Reforms* (Routledge, 2020).

18 Article 68, para. 1(b) of the 2024/24/EU Directive.

19 Commission (fn 10).

20 Article 68, para. 2.

21 Please read the survey carried out on a sample of 119 public administrations from different countries in Benedetta Nucci, Fabio Iraldo and Maria Rosa De Giacomo, "The Relevance of Life Cycle Costing in Green Public Procurement" (2016)(1) Economics and Policy of Energy and the Environment 91–109.

22 Marta Andhov, Roberto Caranta and Anja Wiesbrock, "The European Union Law of Life-cycle Costing" in M. Andhov, R. Caranta and A. Wiesbrock (eds), *Cost and EU Public Procurement Law Life-Cycle Costing for Sustainability* (Routledge, 2021); Raquel Carvalho, "Life-cycle Costing in the Member States" in M. Andhov, R. Caranta and A. Wiesbrock (eds), *Cost and EU Public Procurement Law Life-Cycle Costing for Sustainability* (Routledge, 2021).

23 Benedetta Nucci, Fabio Iraldo and Maria Rosa De Giacomo, "The Relevance of Life Cycle Costing in Green Public Procurement" (2016)(1) Economics and Policy of Energy and the Environment 91–109; Andhov, Caranta and Wiesbrock (fn 22); Carvalho (fn 22).

24 Áurea Adell Querol, Bettina Schaefer and Josep Esquerrà i Roig, "LCC and GPP Competing or Complementary Approaches?" in A. Castelli, G. Piga, S. Saussier and T. Tátrai (eds), *The Challenges of Public Procurement Reforms* (Routledge, 2020); Oshani Perera, Barbara Morton and Tina Perfrement, "Life Cycle Costing in Sustainable Public Procurement: A Question of Value" IISD, Winnipeg, Manitoba, Canada <www.iisd.org/system/files/publications/life_cycle_costing.pdf> accessed 10 December 2024; Aure Adell et al., "Existing Approaches to Encourage Innovation Through Procurement" ICLEI – Local Governments for Sustainability, European Secretariat, Freiburg, Germany;

3. GREEN PUBLIC PROCUREMENT: THE WAY AHEAD

Given the 2014 Directive's novel yet controversial environmental provisions, several changes and additions are necessary. These reforms aim to better promote GPP in the EU, aligning it with the European Green Deal and recent EU sustainability and due diligence standards, specifically the EU Corporate Sustainable Due Diligence Directive (2024/1760) and the Corporate Sustainability Reporting Directive (2022/2464), which establish a coherent framework for understanding companies' sustainability profiles.

3.1 Introduction of Minimum Mandatory Sustainability and Procedural Requirements

Since 2014, the EU Public Procurement Directive has offered opportunities to integrate environmental objectives, yet this has led to considerable legal uncertainty for public procurers, especially those new to environmental factors.[25] Despite existing EU GPP criteria, their voluntary nature offers insufficient incentives for contracting authorities and Member States to procure green.[26] Indeed, GPP implementation varies widely across Member States, with only a third mandating it for specific sectors or contracts.[27]

In this context, the Commission's new Circular Economy Action Plan commits to proposing minimum mandatory GPP criteria and targets in sectoral

---

UNEP-SETAC, "Towards a Life Cycle Sustainability Assessment: Making Informed Choices on Products" United Nations Environment Programme, Paris; Elisabeth Hochschorner and Maria Noring, "Practitioners' Use of Life Cycle Costing with Environmental Costs—a Swedish Study" (2011)16 The International Journal of Life Cycle Assessment 897–902; Jason J. Czarnezki and Steven Van Garsse, "What is Life-Cycle Costing?" in M. Andhov, R. Caranta and A. Wiesbrock (eds), *Cost and EU Public Procurement Law: Life-Cycle Costing for Sustainability* (Routledge, 2021).

[25] Commission, "Green Public Procurement Criteria and Requirements" <https://green-business.ec.europa.eu/green-public-procurement/gpp-criteria-and-requirements_en> accessed 10 December 2024.

[26] Jonas Tallberg, "Paths to Compliance: Enforcement, Management, and the European Union" (2002) 56(3) International Organization; Kleoniki Pouikli, "Towards Mandatory Green Public Procurement (GPP) Requirements Under the EU Green Deal: Reconsidering the Role of Public Procurement as an Environmental Policy Tool" (2021) 21 ERA Forum.

[27] Commission, "Implementation and Best Practices of National Procurement Policies in the Internal Market" (Report from the Commission) COM (2021) 245 final 9.

legislation, coupled with compulsory reporting.[28] Also, the 2022 Communication stated that contracting authorities would be required to use green procurement criteria for specific product groups.[29] As a result, over 46 sector-specific mandatory requirements already exist at an EU level (e.g., Energy Star Regulation, Clean Vehicles Directive, Energy Performance of Buildings Directive, Energy Efficiency Directive), with eight more pending. This signifies a shift towards mandating, not just encouraging, GPP. Despite this proliferation of sectoral legislation, many commentators advocate for GPP's comprehensive mandatory uptake.[30] We likewise contend the Commission should propose minimum EU-recognized mandatory criteria and explore competition rule relaxation where necessary, while ensuring targeted sustainability requirements continue in sectoral legislation. Therefore, the new Directive needs a clear provision obligating, not merely allowing, GPP requirements for contracting authorities and Member States.[31] This reinforces the "how to buy" framework of the Public Procurement Directives, crucial for leveraging public spending for

---

[28] Commission, "A New Circular Economy Action Plan for a Cleaner and More Competitive Europe" COM(2020) 98 final.

[29] Commission, "On Making Sustainable Products the Norm" (Communication from the Commission to the European Parliament, the Council, the European Economic and Social Committee and the Committee of the Regions) COM(2022) 140 final.

[30] Enrique Carreras and Davide Vannoni, "Mandatory Requirements in Sustainable Procurement: The Economic Perspective" in W. Janssen and R. Caranta (eds), *Mandatory Sustainability Requirements in EU Public Procurement Law: Reflections on a Paradigm Shift* (Hart Publishing, 2023); Willem Janssen, "Shifting Towards Mandatory Sustainability Requirements in EU Public Procurement Law: Context, Relevance and a Typology" in W. Janssen and R. Caranta (eds), *Mandatory Sustainability Requirements in EU Public Procurement Law: Reflections on a Paradigm Shift* (Hart Publishing, 2023); Marta Andhov and Federica Muscaritoli, "Climate Change and Public Procurement: Are We Shifting the Legal Discourse?" in W. Janssen and R. Caranta (eds), *Mandatory Sustainability Requirements in EU Public Procurement Law: Reflections on a Paradigm Shift* (Hart Publishing, 2023); Marta Andhov, "Contracting Authorities and Strategic Goals of Public Procurement – A Relationship Defined by Discretion?" in S. Bogojević, X. Groussot and J. Hettne (eds), *Discretion in EU Public Procurement Law* (Hart Publishing, 2019) 134; Kleoniki Pouikli, "Towards Mandatory Green Public Procurement (GPP) Requirements Under the EU Green Deal: Reconsidering the Role of Public Procurement as an Environmental Policy Tool" (2021) ERA Forum 699; Lela Mélon, "More Than a Nudge? Arguments and Tools for Mandating Green Public Procurement in the EU" (2020) 12 Sustainability 988.

[31] This was also suggested by Kleoniki Pouikli, "Towards Mandatory Green Public Procurement (GPP) Requirements Under the EU Green Deal: Reconsidering

green objectives and providing a coherent basis for increasing sustainability requirements from other EU laws.[32]

Also, a general mandatory provision would clarify existing Public Procurement Directive provisions, such as Article 57(4) on discretionary exclusion for environmental non-compliance, and incentivize "further market developments in providing environmentally friendly solutions" and "a strong and efficient incentive for public procurers to engage in GPP".[33] Regarding procedural requirements, the new Directive should include a "comply or explain" principle, requiring justification when GPP criteria are not integrated.[34]

Mandatory GPP criteria should be adopted in the most appropriate form, such as mandatory technical specifications, selection[35] and award criteria, or contract performance clauses and targets. Minimum binding environmental procurement targets are particularly welcome given varying institutional quality and public sector capacity among Member States. According to a survey, properly motivated bureaucrats need more discretion and require fewer rules.[36] Therefore, such targets, general and cross-sectoral, would allow strong bureaucracies' discretion while ensuring purchases meet specified environ-

---

the Role of Public Procurement as an Environmental Policy Tool" (2021) ERA Forum 699.

[32] Laura Treviño-Lozano and Ezgi Uysal, "Bridging the Gap Between Corporate Sustainability Due Diligence and EU Public Procurement" (2023) 30(5) Maastricht Journal of European and Comparative Law.

[33] Lela Mélon, "More Than a Nudge? Arguments and Tools for Mandating Green Public Procurement in the EU" (2020) 12 Sustainability 988. See also Commission, "Proposal for a Regulation of the European Parliament and of the Council Establishing a Framework for Setting Ecodesign Requirements for Sustainable Products and Repealing Directive 2009/125/EC" COM (2022) 142 final, 2022/0095 (COD).

[34] ClientEarth, "Sustainable Public Procurement in the European Union – Briefing in Support of Mandatory Requirements" <www.clientearth.org/latest/documents/briefing-sustainable-public-procurement-in-the-european-union/> accessed 18 January 2025; Fredo Schotanus and Ruben Nicolas, "Coercive, Mimetic and Normative Influences on the Uptake of Sustainable Public Procurement: An Institutional Perspective" in W. Janssen and R. Caranta (eds), *Mandatory Sustainability Requirements in EU Public Procurement Law: Reflections on a Paradigm Shift* (Hart Publishing, 2023).

[35] Indicatively, the Net-Zero Industry Act (NZIA) and the Ecodesign for Sustainable Products Regulation (ESPR) mandate specific selection criteria for green public procurement and renewable energy auctions, focusing on sustainability, resilience, and other non-price factors.

[36] Erica Bosio et al., "Public Procurement in Law and Practice" (2022) 112 American Economic Review 1091.

mental thresholds. "Minimum" implies basic targets with scope for derogation *in melius*.[37] Achieving sustainability targets could be added to the Directive's aims via a Recital.[38]

Furthermore, environmental criteria should be independent award criteria, not solely part of LCC. Monetizing environmental externalities is difficult, and even when feasible, it doesn't guarantee the greenest option.[39] Amending Article 67 of Directive 2014/24 to award contracts to the "most economically and sustainably advantageous offer" would address this. A General Court judgment affirmed that award criteria need not be purely economic, as non-economic factors can affect an offer's value.[40]

3.2 Introduction of Environmental Due Diligence Requirements

Improved implementation and enforcement of the mandatory environmental horizontal clause is achievable by linking it to environmental due diligence requirements for economic operators. This would mandate tender participants to conduct environmental due diligence, identifying, preventing, mitigating, and accounting for environmental risks or impacts within their operations, subsidiaries, contractors, and subcontractors. Non-compliance would lead to exclusion from tendering, mirroring Germany's supply chain due diligence

---

[37] M. Andhov, R. Caranta, W. A. Janssen and O. Martin-Ortega, "Shaping Sustainable Public Procurement Laws in the European Union – An Analysis of the Legislative Development from 'How to Buy' to 'What to Buy' in Current and Future US Legislative Initiatives" <www.greens-efa.eu/en/article/study/shaping-sustainable-public-procurement-laws-in-the-european-union> accessed 21 February 2025; See also the Action Plan for the Environmental Sustainability of Consumption in the Public Administration, published by the Italian Ministry of Environment and cited by Aura Iurascu, "How Will the Adoption of Mandatory GPP Criteria Change the Game? Lessons from the Italian Experience" (2023)1 EPPPL 10.

[38] Marta Andhov et al., "Sustainability Through Public Procurement: The Way Forward – Reform Proposals" (2020) <https://researchprofiles.ku.dk/da/publications/sustainability-through-public-procurement-the-way-forward-reform-> accessed 21 February 2025.

[39] Aurea Adell Querol et al., "LCC and GPP: Competing or Complementary Approaches?" in A. Castelli, G. Piga, S. Saussier and T. Tátrai (eds), *The Challenges of Public Procurement Reforms* (Routledge, 2020), 55.

[40] *Sophia Group v Parliament* (T-578/19); See also Grith Skovgaard Ølykke and Susie Smith, "Use of Labels and Certificates as Award Criteria: *Sophia Group v Parliament* (T-578/19)" (2021) 5 P.P.L.R., NA136-NA140.

law.[41] This shifts EU public procurement rules from solely focusing on the award procedure to prioritizing preferred products/services and avoiding certain suppliers.[42]

However, for EU applicability, Recital 97 of the 2014 Directive's subject-matter requirement should be redefined. This redefinition is not wholesale abandonment but a clarification to integrate broader due diligence from recent EU legislation like the Corporate Sustainable Due Diligence Directive (2024/1760) (CSDDD) and Corporate Sustainability Reporting Directive (2022/2464) (CSRD) into public procurement. This would allow consideration of a company's comprehensive sustainability performance, even if it touches on general operations, while maintaining proportionality and relevance to the contract, thereby ensuring coherence between EU legislative instruments.

Recital 97 states, "the condition of a link with the subject-matter of the contract excludes criteria and conditions relating to general corporate policy, which cannot be considered as a factor characterising the specific process of production or provision of the purchased works, supplies or services. Contracting authorities should hence not be allowed to require tenderers to have a certain corporate social or environmental responsibility policy in place."

The rationale, from the Commission's Green Paper, was to prevent contracting authorities from influencing undertaking behavior regardless of the purchased product or service, ensuring efficient use of public money.[43] Also,

---

41 Section 22 of Deutscher Bundestag (2021), Gesetz über die unternehmerischen Sorgfaltspflichten in Lieferketten (German Supply Chain Due Diligence Act), 2021; Claire Methven O'Brien and Roberto Caranta, "Should EU Public Procurement Law Integrate Sustainability Due Diligence Requirements? EU Institutions' Procurement as a Case Study" in C. M. O'Brien and R. Caranta (eds), *The Economics and Law of Public Procurement* (Routledge, 2024); Anna Burghardt-Kaufmann et al., "Due Diligence in Supply Chains – Update on Corporate Human Rights and Environmental Due Diligence Requirements in the EU and Germany" (2023) <www.whitecase.com/insight-alert/due-diligence-supply-chains-update-corporate-human-rights-and-environmental-due> accessed 21 February 2025.

42 Willem Janssen and Roberto Caranta, *Mandatory Sustainability Requirements in EU Public Procurement Law Reflections on a Paradigm Shift* (Hart Publishing, 2023); Claire Methven O'Brien and Roberto Caranta, "Should EU Public Procurement Law Integrate Sustainability Due Diligence Requirements? EU Institutions' Procurement as a Case Study" in C. M. O'Brien and R. Caranta (eds), *The Economics and Law of Public Procurement* (Routledge, 2024).

43 European Commission, "Green Paper on the Modernisation of EU Public Procurement Policy: Towards a More Efficient European Procurement Market" COM (2011) 15 final.

meeting the various requirements could disproportionately burden small and medium-sized enterprises (SMEs) lacking economic and human resources.[44]

However, no evidence supports the alleged effects of loosening, maintaining, or expanding the subject-matter test.[45] Also, improving SMEs' environmental performance is crucial for greener growth, as they account for 60–70% of industrial pollution in Europe.[46] Green procurement can incentivize SMEs to comply with environmental regulations and support their greening efforts by expanding the green product market.[47] Therefore, integrating suppliers' environmental due diligence requirements into the new Public Procurement Directive is warranted, supported by complementary programs for SMEs. Alternatively, economic operators already subject to environmental due diligence under other EU legislation, such as the CSDDD, should be excluded from public contracts if non-compliant.[48]

3.3 Sustainability Reports as Selection Criterion and Contract Performance Condition

If the subject-matter requirement is redefined, contracting authorities should consider economic operators' sustainability performance, not just product/service performance. Data from the EU Corporate Sustainability Reporting Directive (2022/2464) should assess bidders' sustainability. However, this raises concerns about public administrations' capacity and competence to analyze and verify such comprehensive data.

Therefore, it is suggested the sustainability reporting requirements of the Corporate Sustainability Reporting Directive should serve as selection criteria for participation. Reports should detail how bidding companies address

---

44 Ibid.

45 Semple (fn 8).

46 Karen Miller et al., "First Assessment of the Environmental Compliance Assistance Programme for SMEs (ECAP)" (2011) <https://www.ecologic.eu/15980> accessed 8 March 2025.

47 OECD, "Environmental Policies and SMEs" in *SME Policy Index: ASEAN 2018: Boosting Competitiveness and Inclusive Growth* (OECD Publishing, 2018) <https://doi.org/10.1787/9789264305328-9-en> accessed 8 March 2025.

48 Claire Methven O'Brien and Amy Weatherburn, "Commission Proposal for a Regulation on Prohibiting Products Made with Forced Labor on the Union Market: The Issue of Remedies" European Parliament, <www.europarl.europa.eu/thinktank/en/document/EXPO_BRI(2023)702583> accessed 8 March 2025; Claire Methven O'Brien and Roberto Caranta, "Due Diligence in EU Institutions' Own-Account Procurement: Rules and Practices" (2024) <www.europarl.euopa.eu/thinktank/en/document/IPOL_STU(2024)758335> accessed 8 March 2025.

potential negative sustainability impacts and how sustainable investments monitor, measure, and assess their impact. This would aid contracting authorities in assessing environmental and societal benefits or impacts from their practices, and evaluating bidders' integration of sustainable public procurement into their culture.

Addressing administrative burden and ensuring SME access is paramount when extending CSRD and CSDDD reporting and due diligence obligations to public procurement. While these Directives primarily target large undertakings, similar detailed requirements could disproportionately burden SMEs. To mitigate this, the detail and complexity of sustainability reports for procurement should be proportionate to the bidder's size and capacity. Simplified or "light" reporting templates, focusing on key, material sustainability aspects relevant to the contract, could be implemented for SMEs.

Additionally, sustainability reports should be contract performance conditions, contrary to Recital 104's stance against general corporate policy requirements. Regular sustainability reports offer transparency on supplier performance, promoting accountability for non-performance and demonstrating sustainable procurement policy impact. Access to detailed performance metrics drives improvement and innovation in ongoing public contracts, based on evidence. Thus, consistent submission of sustainability reports by nominated suppliers ensures sustainable procurement accountability and implementation success.

3.4 Optimization of LCC Monetization Calculations

As the previous discussion has shown, challenges in LCC application significantly impact environmentally friendly procurement choices. LCC use is relatively low, except in construction.[49] For broader adoption, life-cycle costs must have clear monetary value.

In this context, several academics suggest a common EU (or national) mandatory LCC methodology could encourage use by reducing fragmentation and increasing legal certainty.[50] While Directive 2009/33 (Clean Vehicles Directive) mandated LCC, its ex-post evaluation showed it failed to drive

49 OECD, "Life-Cycle Costing in Public Procurement in Hungary: Stocktaking of Good Practices" in *OECD Public Governance Reviews* (OECD Publishing, 2022), <https://doi.org/10.1787/8d90f627-en> accessed 10 April 2025.

50 Dragos and Neamtu (fn 16); Abby Semple, "Mixed Offerings for Sustainability in a New European Union Procurement Directive" (2012) 21 Public Procurement Law Review 106–108.

cleaner vehicles.[51] Consequently, Directive (EU) 2019/1161, which amended it, removed the mandatory methodology, allowing contracting authorities to choose any LCC approach for MEAT criteria. On the contrary, "contracting authorities and contracting entities should be able to choose any life-cycle costing methodology in order to support their procurement processes on the basis of the most economically advantageous tender ('MEAT') criteria."[52]

However, recent developments, notably the Clean Industrial Deal,[53] signal potential renewed openness towards mandating LCC methods. This initiative, part of the broader EU industrial strategy, could leverage LCC as a key tool for ensuring public investments genuinely support sustainable industrial transformation.

Given that the quality of a common EU methodology is not always guaranteed (as seen with the old Clean Vehicles Directive), mandating an LCC calculation is not ideal. Instead, the new Public Procurement Directive should facilitate a participatory procedure for LCC methodology development, involving industry.[54] This addresses contracting authorities' lack of expertise, time, and funds, and alleviates concerns about LCC flexibility leading to abuses favoring specific undertakings.[55]

The creation of user-friendly LCC tools is also crucial for simplifying and universalizing LCC in daily procurement operations. OECD surveys indicate tools are mostly available for standardized products, leaving a "vast spectrum of products non-covered".[56] This means that there is a pressing need for user-friendly LCC tools for performing calculations, as this would ensure their widespread use in public procurement. The OECD's mapping identified features contributing to user-friendliness: clear input distinction for buyers/suppliers, calculation transparency, embedded guidance, reference data availability, result visualization, appropriate support tools (e.g., Excel), basic investment explanations, and means of proof for input data. Based on these findings, contracting authorities should be equipped with user-friendly LCC tools, and the new Procurement Directive should reference them to promote their use.

51 Commission, "Ex-Post Evaluation of Directive 2009/33/EC on the Promotion of Clean and Energy Efficient Road Transport Vehicles", COM 2015.

52 Recital 24 of the Directive (EU) 2019/1161.

53 European Commission, "Clean Industrial Deal – A Plan for EU Competitiveness and Decarbonisation" <https://commission.europa.eu/topics/eu-competitiveness/clean-industrial-deal_en> accessed 10 April 2025.

54 This was also highlighted by Andhov, Caranta and Wiesbrock (fn 22).

55 Regarding these concerns, please read Dragos and Neamtu (fn 16), 36–39.

56 OECD, "Life-Cycle Costing in Public Procurement" in *Hungary: Stocktaking of Good Practices, OECD Public Governance Reviews* (OECD Publishing, 2022) <https://doi.org/10.1787/8d90f627-en> accessed 10 April 2025.

3.5 Mandatory Environmental Third-Party Labels

Based on the previous discussion, it also is apparent that translating environmental issues into monetary terms remains challenging.[57] Even LCC tool creation is labor-intensive, requiring extensive stakeholder and research body involvement. Furthermore, some items are impossible to price, or monetary calculations for environmental costs are incomplete.[58] Hence, LCC cannot be a substitute for quality criteria and proper technical specifications.

Against this background, environmental third-party labels certifying goods/services' environmental characteristics offer a viable LCC alternative. This requires labels to adopt LCC methodologies and be based on standards considering durability, repairability, recyclability, and environmental footprint. This recommendation assumes mandatory use of third-party certified labels or equivalents, disallowing alternative proof if labels aren't obtained in time. Implementing this would require revising the 2014 Directive and overturning the Max Havelaar principle, which prohibited contracting authorities from referencing specific labels for MEAT selection. Mandatory label use would benefit contracting authorities by reducing costs and simplifying sustainability criteria and verification.[59] Portugal has adopted such a measure, and Japan mandates green public procurement for government agencies, strongly recommending certified products.[60] Nonetheless, concerns exist regarding competitive implications, particularly for SMEs and start-ups, due to high certification and third-party verification costs.[61]

---

57 Pernilla Gluch and Henrikke Baumann, "The Life Cycle Costing (LCC) Approach: A Conceptual Discussion of its Usefulness for Environmental Decision-making" (2004) 39(5) Building and Environment; Helena Estevan, Bettina Schaefer and Aure Adell (Ecoinstitut SCCL), "Life Cycle Costing State of the Art Report" <https://iclei-europe.org/publications-tools/?c=search&uid=JVTB5WYD> accessed 10 April 2025.

58 Gluch and Baumann (fn 57).

59 One Planet Network – EcoAdvance, "Sustainable Public Procurement Policies That Use Ecolabels and Environmental Certifications – Good Practices in the Use of Ecolabelling and Sustainable Public Procurement" <www.oneplanetnetwork.org/sites/default/files/2024-11/English%20-%20Sustainable%20public%20procurement%20policies%20that%20use%20ecolabels%20and%20environmental%20certifications.pdf> accessed 12 April 2025.

60 João Sequeira Sena-Cuatrecasas, "Green Public Procurement" <www.cuatrecasas.com/resources/lf-eng-653fd8d38af31075579219.pdf?v1.82.3.20241213> accessed 12 April 2025; One Planet Network – EcoAdvance (fn 59).

61 Pedro Telles, "Portugal's Plan for Mandatory Green Public Procurement (II)" <www.telles.eu/portugals-plan-for-mandatory-green-public-procurement-ii/> accessed 12 April 2025.

To address this, the new Directive could introduce a grace period for certification fees and third-party verification, facilitating SME/startup access, similar to Thailand's two-year grace period for its "Green Cart" catalog, which relies on self-declaration with random verification and sanctions for false claims.[62] Concurrently, SMEs and startups should receive financial support via eco-innovation funds, SME promotion, or eco-design competitions. These align with Recital 7 of Directive (EU) 2024/825 on empowering consumers, which emphasizes public authorities promoting access to sustainability labels for SMEs.

3.6 How to Better Connect Public Procurement and Competition Law

As the Commission emphasizes, "public authorities, including the EU institutions, should lead by example and ensure that their procurement is green."[63] To achieve this goal, the current legal framework attempts to elevate sustainability to the same level as economic efficiency. However, provisions within Directive 2014/24/EU, such as Recital 91, still impose restrictions on contracting authorities. This Recital highlights that while contracting authorities can contribute to environmental protection and sustainable development, they must simultaneously "ensure that they can obtain the best value for money for their contracts". This inherent tension, where ambitious green criteria might be perceived as unduly restricting competition, demands a governance shift in EU green public procurement. It necessitates balancing broader environmental benefits against negative effects on competition and economic efficiency.

Balancing environmental and economic objectives remains challenging, with no "one-size-fits-all" approach. From the perspective of public procurement officials, who act in the broader public interest of climate protection and future generations rather than for profit, introducing complex legal defenses against competition infringement could be perceived as an undue burden, actively disincentivizing green procurement efforts. Public purchasers, unlike private undertakings, are not incentivized by commercial gain to defend such complex legal positions.

Therefore, instead of a reactive "defense", a proactive mechanism is proposed to provide greater legal certainty and reduce the risk of competition

[62] Siddharth Prakash, Tobias Schleicher, Mirja Michalscheck and Öeko Institut e.V, "Barrier Analysis and Strategies for Ecolabels and Sustainable Public Procurement Implementation" <www.oeko.de/fileadmin/oekodoc/Barrier-Analysis-report.pdf> accessed 12 April 2025.

[63] Commission, The European Green Deal (Communication) COM(2019) 640 FINAL.

challenges for contracting authorities genuinely pursuing environmental objectives. Inspired by the approach to sustainability agreements in competition law, a new provision should be introduced into Directive 2014/24/EU to outline a "Green Procurement Safe Harbor" or "Sustainability Compliance Framework". This framework would clarify the conditions under which contracting authorities' choices, driven by ambitious environmental considerations, would be presumed compliant with competition rules, thereby minimizing the risk of challenges.

This framework could establish cumulative conditions, akin to Article 101(3) TFEU exemptions, offering clear guidance and protection for contracting authorities:

a) environmental standards or specifications of contracting authorities must demonstrably contribute to protecting health, life, or the environment;
b) the public (current and future generations) must receive a fair share of resulting environmental and societal benefits; and
c) environmental standards or specifications of contracting authorities must be genuinely necessary and proportionate to achieving these objectives.

The burden of proof for challenging the application of this safe harbor should be placed on the undertakings making the accusation. Thus, in cases of ambitious environmental standards or demanding environmental specifications, contracting authorities would operate with increased legal certainty, confident that their actions are unlikely to be challenged for artificially narrowing competition, contrary to Article 18 of Directive 2014/24/EU. This suggestion comes amid a growing focus on sustainability issues in competition law both at the EU and national level. Indicatively, the European Commission has included guidance on sustainability agreements in the new Guidelines on horizontal cooperation agreements,[64] while the national competition authorities in the Netherlands and Greece have recently published draft guidance and adopted competition law sustainability "sandboxes".[65]

[64] European Commission, "Communication from the Commission – Guidelines on the applicability of Article 101 of the Treaty on the Functioning of the European Union to horizontal co-operation agreements, 2023/C 192/01" <https://eur-lex.europa.eu/legal-content/EN/TXT/?uri=oj:JOC_2023_259_R_0001> accessed 27 May 2025.

[65] Johan Ysewyn, Laura van Kruijsdijk and Eirini Marnera, "Building a Sustainability Strategy – What Companies Can (Not) Do from a Competition Law Perspective" <https://www.covcompetition.com/2023/01/building-a-sustainability-strategy-what-companies-can-not-do-from-a-competition-law-perspective/> accessed 27 May 2025.

13. Public procurement as a stronger leverage for social justice

Nicolas Gabayet

REFORM PROPOSALS

Please note that the italic style marks the change of phrasing of the current articles:

- Rephrasing Article 18(2) from 'Member States shall take appropriate measures (...)' to '*Contracting authorities* shall take appropriate measures (...).'
- Introducing social inclusion among the public procurement principles stated at Article 18 of the Directive, in a third paragraph which would state: Article 18(3): Subject to compliance with Article 18(1), contracting authorities shall take appropriate measures at any stage of the public procurement procedures in order to favor social inclusion.
- Rephrasing Article 56(1)(b): 'Contracting authorities *shall* decide not to award a contract to the tenderer submitting the most economically advantageous tender where they have established that the tender does not comply with the applicable obligations referred to in Article 18(2).'
- Rephrasing Article 57(4)(a): 'Contracting authorities *shall* exclude or shall be required by Member States to exclude from participation in a procurement procedure any economic operator (...) where the contracting authority can demonstrate by any appropriate means a violation of applicable obligations referred to in Article 18(2).'
- Rephrasing of Article 67(2): 'The most economically advantageous tender (...) shall be identified on the basis of the price or cost (...) and may include the best price-quality ratio, which shall be assessed on the basis of criteria, including qualitative, environmental and/or social aspects, linked to the *life-cycle* of the public contract in question.'
- Codification of the *RegioPost* Case at Article 70, which would amount to deleting the part of the sentence 'linked to the subject-matter of the contract

within the meaning of Article 67(3) and' from Article 70: 'Contracting authorities may lay down special conditions relating to the performance of a contract, provided that they are indicated in the call for competition or in the procurement documents. Those conditions may include economic, innovation-related, environmental, social or employment-related considerations.'

- Article 20: 'Member States may reserve the right to participate in public procurement procedures to *women or disadvantaged persons owned SMEs*, sheltered workshops and economic operators whose main aim is the social and professional integration of disabled or disadvantaged persons or may provide for such contracts to be performed in the context of sheltered employment programs, provided that at least 30 % of the employees of those workshops, economic operators or programmes are disabled or disadvantaged workers.'
- Recital 36: 'Employment and occupation contribute to integration in society (...). The same is true for other social businesses whose main aim is to support the social and professional integration or reintegration of disabled and disadvantaged persons, such as the unemployed, members of disadvantaged minorities *(such as minority ethnic groups)* or otherwise socially marginalised groups (...).'

1. CONTEXT

Advocate General Kokott's landmark opinion in the *Max Havelaar* case cogently articulated the fundamental tension at the heart of EU public procurement law. She highlighted the challenge of reconciling the core principles of the internal market—non-discrimination and market access—with the growing desire to advance social and environmental objectives. As she stated:

> Whether and to what extent environmental and social considerations may be taken into account and, in particular, reference may be made to environmental and fair-trade labels, is a question of fundamental importance for the further development of the public procurement law. In giving its answer, the Court is faced with the challenge of finding an equitable balance between the requirements of the internal market and environmental and social concerns, without, however, ignoring the practical requirements of award procedures. On the one hand, there can be no discrimination between potential tenderers or partitioning of markets. On the other hand, contracting authorities must be allowed to procure environmentally friendly, organic and fair-trade products without excessive administrative burdens.[1]

[1] Case C-368/10, *European Commission v Kingdom of the Netherlands* [2012] ECR 1–28, Opinion of Advocate General J. Kokott, 3.

Almost three decades after the seminal judgment in *Beentjes*[2] in 1988, the 2014/24 EU Directive provides a framework that allows contracting authorities to consider social factors at various stages of the public procurement process. Specifically, the Directive permits the inclusion of social considerations within:

Exclusion grounds (Article 57);
Technical specifications (Article 42);
Award criteria (Article 67(3)); and
Contract performance conditions (Article 70).

Furthermore, to specifically promote the integration of persons with disabilities or other disadvantaged individuals, the Directive includes an affirmative action measure. It allows for 'reserved contracts' to be awarded to social enterprises or similar entities (Article 20).

Despite these provisions, the reforms introduced by the 2014 Directives appear to have been inefficient in leveraging public procurement to advance social justice. A 2023 report by the European Court of Auditors highlighted that social aspects are still rarely considered in public tenders.[3] The report also noted that 'the promotion of strategic procurement with the goal to encourage greater consideration of environmental, social or innovative aspects has had a limited impact overall; the share of procedures using award criteria other than price is very limited despite the 2014 reform'.[4]

The reasons for the infrequent use of these social levers in public procurement are not readily apparent, and notably, the Court of Auditors' report does not identify them. Yet, this is a crucial element for determining how to improve the effectiveness of the directives in this area. Is the low uptake of these tools a result of contracting authorities making a deliberate political choice not to use procurement as a lever for social justice? Or is it that, even with the political will to do so, the provisions of the EU Directives are perceived as difficult to apply? If the latter is true, is it because the provisions are unclear, not specific enough, or are seen as carrying a legal risk, such as a potential breach of the principle of equal treatment? These questions are challenging to answer from a purely academic standpoint without an extensive empirical survey of a significant number of contracting authorities across multiple Member States.

---

2 Case 31/87, *Gebroeders Beentjes BV v State of the Netherlands* [*1988*] ECR 4635.

3 European Court of Auditors, *Special Report: Public Procurement in the EU. Less Competition for Contracts Awarded for Works, Goods and Services in the 10 Years up to 2021*, 5, 30.

4 Ibid., 48.

It is also worth considering whether the EU institutions simply did not go far enough in shaping effective tools for strategic public procurement in 2014.[5] The purpose of this chapter is to offer some initial insights and proposals aimed at enhancing the opportunities for contracting authorities to utilise public procurement as a tool for social leverage.

2. ISSUES WITH THE CURRENT EUROPEAN LEGISLATION

The social considerations that may be incorporated into public procurement policies, or 'social linkages',[6] can be broadly categorised into two main groups. As Cravero distinguishes them, these are, on the one hand, policies aimed at implementing 'core human and labour rights' and on the other, 'socially inclusive policies as a further step of the social-oriented approach'.[7]

The former category, those concerning fundamental rights, seems to require less debate. Their inclusion in public procurement procedures and clauses largely ensures Member States' compliance with international labour and human rights conventions. Although there is some uncertainty regarding the binding effect of the provision, compliance with applicable national, European, and international social and labour law has been enshrined in Article 18(2) of Directive 2014/24 as a principle of EU public procurement law.[8] As this chap-

[5] It is worth keeping in mind that most of the amendments to the 2004/18 EC Directive drafted to favour social and environmental considerations in public procurement have been rejected by the Council and the Commission. See M. Andhov, "Contracting Authorities and Strategic Goals of Public Procurement – A Relationship Defined by Discretion", in S. Bogojević, X. Groussot, J. Hettne (eds), *Discretion in EU Public Procurement Law* (Hart Publishing, 2019), 119.

[6] C. McCruden, "Buying Social Justice: Equality and Public Procurement", [2007] 60 *Current Legal Problems* 121, 121: "how governments combine two functions of government at the same time: participating in the market as purchaser, and regulating it by using its purchasing power to advance conceptions of social justice".

[7] C. Cravero, "Promoting Supplier Diversity in Public Procurement: A Further Step in Responsible Supply Chain" [2018] 2(1) *European Journal of Sustainable Development Research* 8.

[8] Due to the wording of Article 18(2) ('Member States shall *take appropriate measures* to ensure that in the performance of public contracts economic operators comply with applicable obligations in the fields of environmental, social and labour law', instead of 'shall ensure'), the provision has been regarded as having a 'facultative nature', (M. Andov, "Contracting Authorities and Strategic Goals of Public Procurement – A Relationship Defined by Discretion", at 128) and therefore not being 'an effective mandatory sustainability requirement directing at

ter—and indeed the entire work—aims to propose ways to improve the EU Directives, it appears more useful to focus primarily on socially inclusive policies. This area, with the notable exception of exclusion grounds, seems to be the one where there is the most significant room for improvement.

2.1 Efficiency of Socially Responsible Public Procurement

The relevance of Socially Responsible Public Procurement[9] has been a topic of intense debate over the past two decades.[10] One might question whether instrumentalising public procurement as a lever for social justice amounts to an acknowledgment of states' failures to perform welfare functions and to implement social inclusion and protection rules through primary or secondary legislation. This could lead to a perception of 'social washing', where public procurement is used to create a socially friendly image despite an overall policy framework that is not truly supportive of social goals. Conversely, there is no reason why using public procurement as an additional tool, alongside more traditional social policies, could not make a valuable contribution to social justice, even if its impact is less significant than that of dedicated legislation.

This raises a fundamental public policy question: does the EU want to maintain a purely economic approach to public procurement, prioritising cost efficiency, or does it also want to use procurement as a lever for social inclusion, even if this occasionally comes at a greater economic cost? This is ultimately a matter of societal choice and, thus, a political issue. On this matter, the EU has made its position clear in recent years: public procurement is considered a strategic tool for developing a social economy.[11] Consequently, it is highly

---

contracting authorities' (W. Janssen, "Shifting Towards Mandatory Sustainability Requirements in EU Public Procurement Law: Context, Relevance and Topology", in W. Janssen, R. Caranta (eds), *Mandatory Sustainability Requirements in EU Public Procurement Law: Reflections on a Paradigm Shift* (Hart Publishers, 2023), 3, 11).

[9] European Commission (2021) 3573 final, *Buying Social – A Guide to Taking Account of Social Considerations in Public Procurement* (2nd edition).

[10] For an overview, see C. McCruden, "Buying Social Justice: Equality and Public Procurement"; "EC Public Procurement Law and Equality Linkages: Foundations for Interpretation", in S. Arrowsmith, P. Kunzlik (eds), *Social and Environmental Policies in EC Procurement Law: New Directives and New Directions* (Cambridge University Press, 2009), 271.

[11] Council Recommendation (C/2023/1344), 27 November 2023, *Developing Social Economy Framework Conditions*, Recital 20, Section 15, Section 23 (a) (xi); E. Letta, *Much More than a Market – Speed, Security, Solidarity Empowering the Single Market to Deliver a Sustainable Future and Prosperity for All EU Citizens*, 2024, 45: "Public procurement must be harnessed to advocate for a "high road" to

unlikely—and arguably undesirable—that the Commission and the Parliament would consider withdrawing social considerations from the directives during the revision process. The relevant question regarding the directives' role as a lever for social justice is therefore not 'how to do less?' but rather 'how to do more?'.

However, the EU only holds shared competence with the Member States in this area.[12] Leveraging this competence alongside its competence regarding the internal market, the EU has adopted significant pieces of social legislation with both direct effects (such as Article 9 of the Directive on adequate minimum wages in the EU[13]) and indirect effects (such as the Directive on posted workers,[14] which contains no explicit provisions on public contracts). Yet, even in the case of specific social legislation, compelling Member States to implement social policies through public procurement directives remains politically sensitive, which limits the binding force of such provisions. For example, Article 9 of Directive 2022/2041 on adequate minimum wages merely notes that 'Member States shall take appropriate measures to ensure that ... economic operators and their subcontractors comply with the applicable obligations regarding wages' and other connected rights. This phrasing is similar to that in Article 18(2) of Directive 2014/24/EU, and it leaves Member States with considerable room for manoeuvre. So far, no binding duties toward either the Member States or contracting authorities can be inferred from it.

It appears, therefore, that the EU's approach in the area of public procurement is primarily to provide Member States with harmonised legal tools for social linkages. These tools enable procuring authorities to discretionarily choose to use public procurement as a lever for social justice,[15] while infringing as little as possible on the core principles and primary purposes of EU public procurement law (e.g., implementing economic freedoms, equal treatment,

---

development. This involves focusing on policies and practices that aim for more than just the minimum requirements in terms of wages and working conditions. Such an approach aligns public spending with a broader agenda of social advancement and economic inclusivity", 106.

12 Art. 4(2)(b) TFEU.

13 Directive (EU) 2022/2041 of the European Parliament and of the Council of 19 October 2022 on adequate minimum wages in the European Union (OJ L 275, 25.10.2022, 33).

14 Directive (EU) 2018/957 of the European Parliament and of the Council of 28 June 2018 amending Directive 96/71/EC concerning the posting of workers in the framework of the provision of services ELI: http://data.europa.eu/eli/dir/2018/957/oj.

15 M. Andhov, "Contracting Authorities and Strategic Goals of Public Procurement – A Relationship Defined by Discretion", 118–137.

and transparency). Bearing this 'enabling approach'[16] in mind, the issue of political accountability concerning the cost/benefit balance of using public procurement as a social lever primarily rests with the Member States and their contracting authorities.

2.2 Improving the Existing Rules

The Classic Directive outlines five types of tools: exclusion grounds, reserved contracts, the use of technical specifications, award criteria, and performance conditions. With the exception of exclusion grounds, all these tools are intended to serve as levers for social inclusion. Before examining potential improvements to them, it is essential to first advocate for the enshrinement of social inclusion as a core principle of EU public procurement law.

2.2.1 Strengthening the legal impact of Article 18 as the ground for social justice in the Classic Directive

As its title suggests, Article 18 of Directive 2014/24/EU contains the 'principles of procurement' and should be regarded as the core of the Classic Directive's framework. In legal science, a principle is defined as 'a primary concept [or] assumption … that is held to be true and fundamental for a particular field, procedure, knowledge [and that] is used to predict the course of related entities.'[17] Consequently, most of the Directive's legal provisions are based on Article 18, and none of them should contradict its scope.

If Article 18 is the core of the Classic Directive, then Article 18(1) is arguably the 'core of the core', as it contains the essential principles of the EU's internal market as applied to public procurement: equal treatment, non-discrimination, transparency and proportionality.[18]

The social principles of public procurement are then addressed in Article 18(2). The issue, however, is that this paragraph aims to protect only one aspect of social considerations in public procurement—namely, the 'core human and

---

[16] This EU policy has clearly been acknowledged as merely "enabling". See COM (2011) 896 final, 2; M. Andhov, R. Caranta, A. Wiesbrock, "The European Union Law of Life-cycle Costing", in M. Andhov, R. Caranta, A. Wiesbrock (eds.), *Cost and EU Public Procurement Law: Life-Cycle Costing for Sustainability* (Routledge, 2020), 20, 22.

[17] *The Law Dictionary, featuring Black's Law Dictionary* (2nd edition) https://thelawdictionary.org/?s=principle.

[18] Directive 2014/24/EU, Article 18(1): "Contracting authorities shall treat economic operators equally and without discrimination and shall act in a transparent and proportionate manner".

labour rights'—with no mention of social inclusion.[19] In the *Tim SpA* case,[20] the Court of Justice of the European Union (CJEU) held that in enacting the rule set out in Article 18(2)—which requires Member States to '[ensure] that ... economic operators comply with applicable obligations in the fields of environmental, social and labour law ...'[21]—the Union legislature sought to establish that requirement as a 'principle'[22] and a 'cardinal value'.[23] These statements have sometimes been analysed with caution regarding their actual effect on strengthening the legal impact of Article 18(2).[24] This is partly because the Court's emphasis on the importance of Article 18(2) in that case seemed primarily intended to verify whether a national provision automatically excluding a subcontractor for non-compliance with standards regarding the employment of persons with disabilities was proportionate.[25] Separately—and without any direct link to *Tim*—it has also been well established that the phrasing of Article 18(2) addresses Member States, who are only required to 'take appropriate measures', rather than placing direct obligations on contracting authorities.[26].

Nevertheless, the *Tim* case demonstrates that the importance of Article 18(2) has not gone unnoticed by the Court. The statements in *Tim* may have therefore opened the door for a future, stronger acknowledgment of sustainability's cardinal value as a public procurement law principle. For instance, in his opinion in the recent *AESTE* case,[27] Advocate General (AG) Biondi, in acknowledging that 'the provision in Article 18(2) is particularly noteworthy, in that it requires economic operators to comply with applicable legal obligations,

[19] C. Cravero, "Promoting Supplier Diversity in Public Procurement: A Further Step in Responsible Supply Chain".

[20] Case C-395/18, *Tim SpA v Consip SpA* [2020] ECLI:EU:C:2020:58.

[21] Directive 2014/24/EU, Article 18(2).

[22] Ibid.

[23] Ibid.

[24] W. Janssen, "Shifting Towards Mandatory Sustainability Requirements in EU Public Procurement Law: Context, Relevance and Topology", in W. Janssen, R. Caranta (eds), *Mandatory Sustainability Requirements in EU Public Procurement Law: Reflections on a Paradigm Shift* (Hart Publishers, 2023) 10.

[25] Ibid.

[26] M. Andhov, "Contracting Authorities and Strategic Goals of Public Procurement – A Relationship Defined by Discretion", 129; M. Andhov, A. Biondi, L. Rubini, *Regulating for a Sustainable and Resilient Single Market. Challenges and Reforms in the Areas of State Aid, Competition, and Public Procurement Law*, European Trade Union Institute, Report 2023.01, 56.

[27] Case C-210/24, *Asociación de Empresas de Servicios para la Dependencia (AESTE) v Ayuntamiento de Ortuella* [2025] Opinion of AG Biondi ECLI:EU:C:2025:529. The judgment in that case is not yet available at the time of the writing of this chapter.

specifically social and labour law, when performing contracts',[28] quoted the Court's formula from *Tim* to emphasise this 'cardinal value'.[29] Going further, AG Biondi asserted that in *Tim*, the Court 'establish[ed] it as a principle on the same footing as the other principles set out in paragraph 1 of the same article',[30] concluding that 'that cardinal value should therefore guide the interpretation of the entire directive'.[31] According to AG Biondi, Article 18(2) thus holds the same weight as Article 18(1) and should not necessarily be subordinated to the principles of equal treatment, non-discrimination, transparency and proportionality.

To strengthen Article 18 as a guarantee of the effectiveness of using public procurement as a lever for social justice, I propose two key changes: first, substituting 'Contracting Authorities' for 'Member States' in Article 18(2) and second, giving social inclusion the same status as compliance with social and labour law within Article 18.

Social inclusion is not explicitly mentioned in Article 18, although the recitals refer to the goal of the 'integration or reintegration of disabled and disadvantaged persons, disadvantaged minorities or otherwise socially marginalized groups',[32] the 'favouring of social integration of disadvantaged persons or members of vulnerable groups'[33] and the promotion of gender equality at work and female employment.[34] While all these objectives are oriented towards social inclusion, unlike compliance with labour law and social rights, social inclusion does not yet enjoy the status of a 'principle of procurement'. It is difficult to see how social inclusion can become effective if it remains a mere objective confined to the recitals. Enshrining social inclusion as a principle of European public procurement law in Article 18 could therefore significantly enhance its status as an enforceable rule and improve the use of public procurement law as a lever for social justice in the EU.

Reform proposal regarding Article 18:

---

28 Ibid., para. 31.

29 Ibid.

30 Ibid.

31 Ibid.

32 Directive 2014/24/EU, Recital 36.

33 Ibid., Recital 99.

34 Directive 2014/24/EU, Recital 98: 'Contract performance conditions might also be intended to favour the implementation of measures for the promotion of equality of women and men at work, the increased participation of women in the labour market and the reconciliation of work and private life'.

1) Changing the phrasing of Article 18(2) from 'Member States shall take appropriate measures (…)' to 'Contracting authorities shall take appropriate measures (…)'.
2) Introducing social inclusion among the public procurement principles stated at article 18 of the Directive, in a third paragraph which would state:

> Article 18 (3): 'Subject to compliance with art. 18(1), contracting authorities shall take appropriate measures at any stage of the public procurement procedures in order to favor social inclusion'.

2.2.2 Extending the mandatory character of the exclusion (Art. 57) and of the possibility not to award a contract (Art. 56(1)(b)) for infringement to labour and social laws

Exclusion of economic operators from a public procurement procedure under Article 57 of Directive 2014/24/EU and the possibility of not awarding a contract under Article 56 appear to be means of ensuring that the final contract holder complies with obligations 'established by Union law, national law, collective agreements or by the international environmental, social and labour law provisions', as required by Article 18(2).[35]

However, as has been previously noted,[36] the facultative nature of the decision not to award the contract under Article 56(1)(b) and the decision to exclude an economic operator under Article 57(4)(a) in cases of non-compliance with labour and social laws present two key problems.

First, it weakens the legal impact of Article 18(2). The absence of a mandatory obligation to exclude or not award a contract directly undermines the

[35] Directive 2014/24/EU, Article 57(1): 'Contracting authorities shall exclude an economic operator from participation in a procurement procedure where they (…) are otherwise aware that that economic operator has been the subject of a conviction by final judgment for one of the following reasons: (f) child labour and other forms of trafficking in human beings as defined in Article 2 of Directive 2011/36/EU of the European Parliament and of the Council'; Directive 2014/24/EU, Article 57(4): 'Contracting authorities may exclude or may be required by Member States to exclude from participation in a procurement procedure any economic operator in any of the following situations: (a) where the contracting authority can demonstrate by any appropriate means a violation of applicable obligations referred to in Article 18(2)'.

[36] M. Andhov, R. Caranta, W.A. Janssen, O. Martin-Ortega, *Shaping Sustainable Public Procurement Laws in the European Union – An Analysis of the Legislative Development from 'How to Buy' to 'What to Buy' in Current and Future EU Legislative Initiatives* (Report for the Greens/EFA in the European Parliament, 2022), 56, 56–58.

authority of Article 18(2) by implying that it is legally permissible to award a contract to an economic operator that infringes labour and social laws. This permissive approach contradicts the principle that such obligations are fundamental.

Second, it distorts competition. The discretionary power granted to contracting authorities by these articles creates a risk of competition distortion. When some contracting authorities choose not to sanction non-compliant economic operators, they place these operators in a more advantageous position than their competitors who adhere to the rules. This inconsistent application of the rules can create an uneven playing field, undermining the fairness and integrity of the procurement process.

I consequently propose to rephrase Article 56(1)(b) in replacing 'may' with 'shall':

> Contracting authorities *shall* decide not to award a contract to the tenderer submitting the most economically advantageous tender where they have established that the tender does not comply with the applicable obligations referred to in Article 18(2).

And likewise in Article 57(4)(a):

> Contracting authorities *shall* exclude or *shall* be required by Member States to exclude from participation in a procurement procedure any economic operator (...) where the contracting authority can demonstrate by any appropriate means a violation of applicable obligations referred to in Article 18(2).

2.2.3 Award criteria

Article 67(2) of Directive 2014/24/EU enables awarding authorities to be able to integrate social considerations into the criteria taken into account to determine the most economically advantageous offer, providing that the 'social aspects' are linked to the subject-matter of the contract:

> The most economically advantageous tender from the point of view of the contracting authority shall be identified on the basis of the price or cost, using a cost-effectiveness approach, such as life-cycle costing in accordance with Article 68, and may include the best price-quality ratio, which shall be assessed on the basis of criteria, including qualitative, environmental and/or social aspects, linked to the subject-matter of the public contract in question. Such criteria may comprise, for instance:
>
> (a) quality, including technical merit, aesthetic and functional characteristics, accessibility, design for all users, social, environmental and innovative characteristics and trading and its conditions.[37];

[37] Directive 2014/24/EU, Article 67(2); Concordia Bus Finland (C-513/99) [2002], para. 61 and *Commission v Netherlands* (C-368/10) [2012].

The requirement of a link between a social or environmental condition and the subject-matter of the contract in Article 67(2) of Directive 2014/24/EU reflects a form of 'legal scepticism'[38] towards social criteria. This scepticism is based on the concern that such criteria could be used to 'artificially narrow competition'.[39]

The core issue is that this link-to-the-subject-matter (LtSM) condition inhibits the legal effectiveness of social criteria. Consequently, it has been widely regarded as a significant barrier to the development of comprehensive sustainability policies in public procurement.[40] However, since the enactment of Directive 2014/24/EU, there have been few judgments on this matter from the CJEU.

In their report, Shaping Sustainable Public Procurement Laws in the European Union, M. Andhov et al. proposed the concept of a 'life-cycle' as an alternative to the LtSM condition.[41] Under this approach, social requirements would need to be linked to the life-cycle of the service or good, which is defined in Article 2(20) of the Classic Directive as:

> all consecutive and/or interlinked stages, including research and development to be carried out, production, trading and its conditions, transport, use and maintenance, throughout the existence of the product or the works or the provision of the service, from raw material acquisition or generation of resources to disposal, clearance and end of service or utilization.

---

38 E. Manuza, N. Meershoek, 'Fostering the Social Market Economy through Public Procurement? Legal Impediments for New Types of Economy Actors' [2020] 6 *PPLR* 343, 347.

39 A. Sanchez-Graells, "Some Reflections on the 'Artificial Narrowing of Competition' as a Check on Executive Discretion in Public Procurement", in S. Bogojević, X. Groussot, J. Hettne (eds), *Discretion in EU Public Procurement Law* (Hart Publishing, 2019) 79.

40 "The Link to the Subject-Matter: A Glass Ceiling for Sustainable Public Contracts?", in B. Sjåfjell, A. Wiesbrock (eds.), *Sustainable Public Procurement under EU Law* (Cambridge University Press, 2015), 50–70; M. Andhov, R. Caranta, A. Wiesbrock, "The European Union Law of Life-cycle Costing", 33; L. Rodgers, "The Operation of Labour Law as the Exception: The Case of Public Procurement", in A. Sanchez-Graells (ed), *Smart Public Procurement and Labour Standards* (Hart Publishing, 2020), 141–163, at 152; M. Andhov, R. Caranta, W.A. Janssen, O. Martin-Ortega, *Shaping Sustainable Public Procurement Laws in the European Union – An Analysis of the Legislative Development from 'How to Buy' to 'What to Buy' in Current and Future EU Legislative Initiatives*, 58–59.

41 M. Andhov, R. Caranta, W.A. Janssen, O. Martin-Ortega, *Shaping Sustainable Public Procurement Laws in the European Union – An Analysis of the Legislative Development from 'How to Buy' to 'What to Buy' in Current and Future EU Legislative Initiatives.*

This definition makes it clear that the notion of a life-cycle covers all stages of a good or service, including its production and performance. Accordingly, it would be easier for a contracting authority to demonstrate that social criteria (e.g., salary rates, wage increases, employment of disadvantaged workers) required in procurement documents are linked to the life-cycle of the good or service, rather than having to prove a direct link to the subject matter of the contract.

Reform proposal: Replacing the requirement of a LtSM in Article 67(2) by the requirement of a link to the life-cycle.

The new writing of the first sentence of Article 67(2) would consequently be:

> The most economically advantageous tender from the point of view of the contracting authority shall be identified on the basis of the price or cost, using a cost-effectiveness approach, such as life-cycle costing in accordance with Article 68, and may include the best price-quality ratio, which shall be assessed on the basis of criteria, including qualitative, environmental and/or social aspects, linked to the *life-cycle* of the public contract in question.

2.2.4 Performance conditions

Article 70 of the Directive 2014/24/EU permits contracting authorities to include social considerations, such as 'social or employment-related' conditions, during the contract performance phase, provided these conditions are linked to the subject-matter of the contract.[42] Article 70 specifies that the conditions may be *inter alia* 'social or employment related'.[43]

In contrast to the strict interpretation of the link between social award criteria and the subject matter, case law has loosened this requirement for performance conditions. Since the *RegioPost* case,[44] which was adjudicated before the enactment of Directive 2014/24/EU, it is permissible for contracting authorities, at the stage of selecting participants, to require bidders and their subcontractors to commit to paying a minimum wage. The possibility established by this case law also extends to the requirement of employing a

---

42 Article 70 of the Directive 2014/24/EU: 'Contracting authorities may lay down special conditions relating to the performance of a contract, provided that they are linked to the subject-matter of the contract within the meaning of Article 67(3) and indicated in the call for competition or in the procurement documents. Those conditions may include economic, innovation-related, environmental, social or employment-related considerations'.

43 Ibid.

44 Case C-115/14, *RegioPost* EU:C:2015:760.

percentage of disadvantaged persons (e.g., workers with disabilities, the long-term unemployed).

Suggested evolution: Codifying *RegioPost* and therefore loosening the link to the subject matter for social performance conditions. This raises a question of compliance with the requirement in the performance phase of the contract.

Proposed reform: Deleting the part of the sentence 'linked to the subject-matter of the contract within the meaning of Article 67(3) and' from Article 70:

Article 70: Contracting authorities may lay down special conditions relating to the performance of a contract, provided that they are indicated in the call for competition or in the procurement documents. Those conditions may include economic, innovation-related, environmental, social or employment-related considerations.

2.2.5 Reserved contracts

Article 20 of Directive 2014/24/EU provides contracting authorities with the option to reserve certain public procurement procedures for 'economic operators whose main aim is the social and professional integration of disabled or disadvantaged persons'.[45] This provision should be interpreted in light of Recital 36, which explicitly links employment to the 'integration or reintegration of disabled and disadvantaged persons, disadvantaged minorities or otherwise socially marginalised groups'.[46]

Reserved contracts thus represent a form of affirmative action within the public procurement framework, using it as a lever for social justice.

However, while notable within EU public procurement law, this legal framework for reserved contracts appears to lack ambition when compared to other affirmative action schemes designed to promote the inclusion of minority

[45] Article 20 of Directive 2014/24/EU: 'Member States may reserve the right to participate in public procurement procedures to sheltered workshops and economic operators whose main aim is the social and professional integration of disabled or disadvantaged persons or may provide for such contracts to be performed in the context of sheltered employment programs, provided that at least 30 % of the employees of those workshops, economic operators or programs are disabled or disadvantaged workers'. See also I. Baciu, 'The Possibility to reserve a Public Contract under the New European Public Procurement Legal Framework' [2018] *EPPPL* 307.

[46] Recital 36 of Directive 2014/24/EU.

ethnic groups or women in public procurement law, such as those found in the US.[47]

The concept of positive action is not inherently contrary to EU Treaties, including the fundamental principle of non-discrimination (Article 18 TFEU), which is a cornerstone of European public procurement law. A strong analogy can be drawn between affirmative action as a tool for achieving gender equality in employment under EU law and positive action as a mechanism for social inclusion in EU public procurement law. Article 157 (4) TFEU states that:

> with a view to ensuring full equality in practice between men and women in working life, the principle of equal treatment shall not prevent any Member State from maintaining or adopting measures providing for specific advantages in order to make it easier for the underrepresented sex to pursue a vocational activity or to prevent or compensate for disadvantages in professional careers.

In *Kalanke*,[48] the CJEU held that regarding positive measures to guarantee gender equality concerning employment:

> A national rule that, where men and women who are candidates for the same promotion are equally qualified, women are automatically to be given priority in sectors where they are under-represented, involves discrimination on grounds of sex.
>
> It must, however, be considered whether such a national rule is permissible under Article 2(4), which provides that the Directive[49] 'shall be without prejudice to measures to promote equal opportunity for men and women, in particular by removing existing inequalities which affect women's opportunities'.
>
> That provision is specifically and exclusively designed to allow measures which, although discriminatory in appearance, are in fact intended to eliminate or reduce actual instances of inequality which may exist in the reality of social life.

---

[47] See the US *Federal Acquisition Regulation*, Section 19, Small Businesses Programmes, Subpart 19.5 – Small Business Total Set-Asides, Partial Set-Asides, and Reserves, 19.504 Orders under multiple-award contracts: '(3) When setting aside an order above the simplified acquisition threshold, the contracting officer shall first consider setting aside the order for the small business socioeconomic contracting programs (i.e., 8(a), HUBZone, service-disabled veteran-owned small business, and women-owned small business) before considering a small business set-aside'.

[48] Case C-450/93, *Eckhard Kalanke/Freie Hansestadt Bremen* [1995] ECR I-03051, para. 16 to 18.

[49] Directive (EC) 2006/54 of the European Parliament and of the Council of 5 July 2006 on the implementation of the principle of equal opportunities and equal treatment of men and women in matters of employment and occupation (recast), O.J. L 2006/204, 23.

Affirmative action as a means of reducing inequalities between men and women is also consistent with EU policies. The European Commission recommends that EU institutions and Member States introduce legal duties to implement positive action measures where necessary to achieve full equality in practice.[50]

The reasoning adopted to permit affirmative action in employment sectors where women are underrepresented demonstrates that these types of measures are not entirely contrary to the EU Treaties. The same rationale could be applied in public procurement, particularly when women or 'disadvantaged minorities' are underrepresented as economic operators in a given sector.

Reform proposals:

- Article 20: 'Member States may reserve the right to participate in public procurement procedures to women or disadvantaged persons owned SMEs, sheltered workshops and economic operators whose main aim is the social and professional integration of disabled or disadvantaged persons or may provide for such contracts to be performed in the context of sheltered employment programs, provided that at least 30 % of the employees of those workshops, economic operators or programmes are disabled or disadvantaged workers.'
- Recital 36: 'Employment and occupation contribute to integration in society and are key elements in guaranteeing equal opportunities for all. In this context, sheltered workshops can play a significant role. The same is true for other social businesses whose main aim is to support the social and professional integration or reintegration of disabled and disadvantaged persons, such as the unemployed, members of disadvantaged minorities (e.g., minority ethnic groups) or otherwise socially marginalised groups. However, such workshops or businesses might not be able to obtain contracts under normal conditions of competition. Consequently, it is appropriate to provide that Member States should be able to reserve the right to participate in award procedures for public contracts or for certain lots thereof to such workshops or businesses or reserve performance of contracts to the context of sheltered employment programmes.'

A decade after the EU sought to make public procurement more socially responsible through Directive 2014/24/EU, it appears the European legislator did not

[50] European Commission: Directorate-General for Employment, Social Affairs and Inclusion, *International Perspectives on Positive Action Measures – A Comparative Analysis in the European Union, Canada, the United States and South Africa* (Publications Office of the EU, 2009).

go far enough to effectively leverage public procurement for social rights and social inclusion. This was likely due to a prevailing concern that social considerations in procurement procedures could jeopardise core principles such as non-discrimination, equal treatment, transparency and proportionality.

However, as demonstrated by the *Tim* case and Advocate General Biondi's conclusions in *AESTE*, social considerations now seem to be regarded by the Court of Justice as a principle of equal importance to those previously mentioned.

Consequently, the reforms proposed in this chapter aim to enhance the effectiveness of social considerations in public procurement procedures. Specifically, these reforms include:

- Making the obligations in Article 18(2) directly incumbent upon contracting authorities, rather than Member States.
- Adding a new principle of social inclusion to Article 18.
- Rendering the exclusion of an economic operator in breach of social or labour laws mandatory.
- Replacing the 'link to the subject-matter' condition in Article 67(2) with the notion of 'life-cycle'.

14. Access for start-ups and small and medium-sized enterprises and subcontracting

François Lichère and Cédric Bernard

REFORM PROPOSALS

- Introduce an allotment obligation to encourage access by small and medium-sized enterprises (SMEs).
- Set up a minimum share of public procurement contracts for SMEs.
- Generalise the right to direct payment for subcontractors.
- Prohibit the rejection of a start-up's candidature for the sole reason of a lack of references in the execution of a previous public contract.
- Make variants admissible as a matter of principle and require contracting authorities to justify any departure from this principle.

1. INTRODUCTION

The European economy relies heavily on the activity of small and medium-sized enterprises (SMEs).[1] They represent 99% of European companies and employ nearly 100 million people across the European Union.[2] Moreover,

---

[1] In accordance with the Commission Recommendation of 6 May 2003 concerning the definition of micro, small and medium-sized enterprises (C(2003) 1422), SMEs are enterprises which employ fewer than 250 persons and which have an annual turnover not exceeding 50 million euros, and/or an annual balance sheet total not exceeding 43 million euros.

[2] Communication from the Commission to the European Parliament, the Council, the European Economic and Social Committee and the Committee of the Regions, 'SME Support Package', 12 September 2023, COM(2023) 535. See also the annual report on the performance of European SMEs of 4 July 2024 available online: https://single-market-economy.ec.europa.eu/smes/sme-strategy-and-sme-friendly-business-conditions/sme-performance-review_en?prefLang=fr.

due to their local influence and their contribution to innovation, diversity and equality,[3] SMEs have been at the heart of the European Union's economic, social and environmental strategy since the early 2000s, particularly since the 2008 'Small Business Act'.[4]

In addition to various measures to simplify administrative procedures,[5] the support of the public authorities for SMEs is illustrated in particular by the revision of public procurement Directives in 2014.[6] While it is difficult to accurately assess their direct (as contractor) or indirect (as first- or second-tier subcontractor) participation in public procurement,[7] the observation that SMEs have difficulty accessing public procurement motivated the adoption of European Directives 2014/23/EU, 2014/24/EU and 2014/25/EU.[8] A change in 'formal perspective'[9] is taking place since, for the European Commission, 'the

---

3 Ibid.

4 Communication from the Commission to the European Parliament, the Council, the European Economic and Social Committee and the Committee of the Regions, 'Think Small First: A Small Business Act for Europe', SEC(2008) 2101.

5 For example: the reduction of payment terms to 30 days by public bodies (Directive 2011/7/EU of the European Parliament and of the Council of 16 February 2011 on combating late payment in commercial transactions), recognition of electronic invoicing (Directive 2014/55/EU of the European Parliament and of the Council of 16 April 2014 on electronic invoicing in public procurement), the simplification of financial reporting obligations and the reduction of administrative burdens for SMEs (Directive 2013/34/EU of the European Parliament and of the Council of 26 June 2013 on the annual financial statements, consolidated financial statements and related reports of certain types of undertakings), or the addition of an exemption in the area of state aid (Commission Regulation (EU) No 651/2014 of 17 June 2014 declaring certain categories of aid compatible with the internal market).

6 Stéphane Braconnier, 'PME et marches publics: totems...' (2014) 148 *Contrats publics* 3.

7 The average share of SMEs in public procurement contracts exceeding the thresholds set by the public procurement directives was estimated at 64% in number and 42% in value by the European Commission in 2008 (*European Code of Best Practices*, 2008, p. 4), while a study from 2014 estimated this share at 56% in number and 29% in value (Wessel Thomassen et al., *SMEs' Access to Public Procurement Markets and Aggregation of Demand in the EU* (2014, pp. 24–42)).

8 This is confirmed by the numerous references to improving SME access in the parliamentary debates of 15 January 2014. These are available online: https://www.europarl.europa.eu/doceo/document/CRE-7-2014-01-15-ITM-011-09_FR.html.

9 François Lichère, 'L'accès aux PME dans la Directive 2014/24' in Yseult Marique and Kris Wauters (eds), *EU Directive 2014/24 on Public Procurement: A New Turn for Competition in Public Markets?* (Ed. Larcier 2016, p. 110).

public procurement rules [...] should be revised and modernised in order to increase the efficiency of public spending, facilitating in particular the participation of small and medium-sized enterprises (SMEs) in public procurement',[10] and 'particular importance should be given to improving the access opportunities of SMEs throughout the Union concession markets'.[11]

In this respect, the recitals of Directive 2014/24/EU emphasise 22 times the need to ensure or facilitate access to public procurement for SMEs. These include, for example, preserving market access opportunities for SMEs (rec. 59), increasing opportunities for SMEs to participate in a dynamic purchasing system (rec. 66), encouraging the division of contracts into lots and limiting the number of lots awarded to candidates (rec. 78 and 79), the adaptation of time limits for participation (rec. 80), the relaxation of requirements on the financial capacity of SMEs (rec. 83) and administrative burdens (rec. 84), the establishment of a single European platform to simplify administrative procedures for public procurement (e-certis, rec. 87), the design contest to optimise support for SMEs (rec. 120), the monitoring of national initiatives to increase SME participation (rec. 124) and the task assigned to the Commission to examine the effects on the internal market resulting from the application of the SME thresholds (rec. 134).[12]

Paradoxically, SMEs are only expressly mentioned in the enacting terms of Directive 2014/24/EU in Article 83, with the obligation to report on the participation of SMEs in public procurement (para. 3) and the role of Member States in ensuring that 'information and guidance on the interpretation and application of the Union public procurement law is available free of charge to assist contracting authorities and economic operators, in particular SMEs, in correctly applying the Union public procurement rules' (para. 4). However, four amendments were initially proposed to emphasise support for SMEs in three other articles: Article 44 of the draft on division into lots[13] (Article

[10] Directive 2014/24/EU of the European Parliament and of the Council of 26 February 2014 on public procurement and repealing Directive 2004/18/EC, recital 2.

[11] Directive 2014/23/EU of the European Parliament and of the Council of 26 February 2014 on the award of concession contracts, recital 1.

[12] It should be noted, with regard to the legislative file on the proposal for Directive 2014/24/EU, that numerous amendments have been proposed to place even greater emphasis on the accessibility of SMEs. See: Report on the proposal for a directive of the European Parliament and of the Council on public procurement, available online: https://www.europarl.europa.eu/doceo/document/A-7-2013-0007_FR.html?redirect.

[13] With the addition of the following words at the beginning of the article: 'In order to stimulate competition and improve access for SMEs' (parliamentary

46 of the directive), Article 19 of the draft on electronic communications[14] (Article 22 of the directive) and Article 67 of the draft on the method used for life-cycle costing[15] (Article 68 of the directive). The fact remains that, even in the absence of express references, several measures in the directive favour (in theory[16]) SME access to public procurement, such as minimum time limits for procedures,[17] multi-supplier framework agreements[18] and subcontracting.[19]

The results produced by the application of the 2014 directive are, however, questionable with regard to the objective of increasing SME participation in public procurement. In its Special Report No 28/2023 of 4 December 2023, the European Court of Auditors notes the lack of real progress in this area, except in Austria, Lithuania and Poland, where an increase has been observed.[20] In the majority of cases, the situation remained similar from 2016 to 2021, with occasional decreases in participation and grants, particularly in Sweden

amendment). Another amendment (by the Committee on Industry, Research and Energy) proposed a similar wording: 'In order to strengthen competition and help SMEs access procurement'.

14 The Committee on Industry, Research and Energy recommended specifying that the obligation to proceed electronically should be 'insofar as this does not represent an insurmountable obstacle for SMEs and micro-enterprises'.

15 A parliamentary amendment sought to add in the second paragraph of the article that the method used to calculate the life-cycle cost 'should, if possible, be simplified to make it accessible to SMEs'.

16 One provision may be perceived as unfavourable to SMEs: the social and environmental qualification requirements of Article 62 of Directive 2014/24/EU. However, as Abby Semple emphasises in her commentary on this provision, the corollary of the principle of equality (treating economic operators differently when they are in different situations) would apply to SMEs in this area, as soon as they enter the public procurement market for the first time. See: Abby Semple, 'Article 62 – Quality Assurance Standards and Environmental Management Standards' in Roberto Caranta and Albert Sanchez-Graells (eds), *European Public Procurement. Commentary on Directive 2014/24/EU* (Edward Elgar Publishing 2021, p. 676). See also: CJEU, 3 March 2005, Fabricom SA, case C-21/03 and C-34/03, para. 27; CJEU, 14 December 2004, Arnold André, case C-434/02.

17 See the justifications for certain amendments in the aforementioned legislative file.

18 Martha Andhov, 'Article 33 – Framework Agreements' in Roberto Caranta and Albert Sanchez-Graells (eds), *op. cit.*, p. 373.

19 Johannes Stalzer, 'Article 71 – Subcontracting' in Roberto Caranta and Albert Sanchez-Graells (eds), *op. cit.*, p. 759 and p. 767.

20 European Court of Auditors, Public procurement in the EU – Less competitive award of works, goods and services contracts between 2011 and 2021, Report No 28/2023, pp. 32–33, available online on the institution's official website: https://www.eca.europa.eu/fr/publications?ref=SR-2023-28.

and Finland.[21] In response to the publication of this report, the European Commission merely reiterated its action in favour of SMEs and the possibilities offered by the directive promoting their access to public procurement, such as allotment.[22] However, the contributions to the public consultation launched by the Commission between December 2024 and March 2025 confirm the conclusions of the European Court of Auditors, with 89 out of 949 participants emphasising their need for simplification of administrative procedures and more effective support mechanisms for SMEs in public procurement.[23]

Therefore, on the eve of a review of Directive 2014/24/EU, several avenues for reflection can be considered to strengthen the effective participation of SMEs in public procurement, without hindering the objective of competition. SME access can be strengthened by various measures aimed at re-establishing real equality among candidates (Section 2), better supervision of subcontracting (Section 3) and taking into account the specific characteristics of start-ups (Section 4).

2. MEASURES AIMED AT REINFORCING REAL EQUALITY AMONG CANDIDATES

The strengthening of the direct participation of SMEs in public procurement can result from an obligation to divide contracts into lots (2.1), a reduction in administrative formalities (2.2)[24] and from the share of the execution to be reserved for SMEs (2.3).

---

21 Ibid. In France, data from the Economic Observatory of public procurement confirms this stagnation in French public procurement. See the data published between 2014 and 2023 on the website of the French Ministry of the Economy: https://www.economie.gouv.fr/daj/oecp-analyse-economique-part-des-pme-dans-commande-publique.

22 European Commission, Response of the European Commission to the Special Report of the European Court of Auditors, December 2023, pp. 4–5, available online: https://www.eca.europa.eu/Lists/ECAReplies/COM-Replies-SR-2023-28/COM-Replies-SR-2023-28_FR.pdf.

23 The contributions are available online: https://ec.europa.eu/info/law/better-regulation/have-your-say/initiatives/14427-Directives-sur-les-marches-publics-evaluation/feedback_fr?p_id=33227589. The same is true for start-ups, as evidenced by the contributions to another call for a European strategy for start-ups and scale-ups open from 17 February to 17 March 2025. See, online: https://ec.europa.eu/info/law/better-regulation/have-your-say/initiatives/14530-Strategie-de-lUE-en-faveur-des-jeunes-pousses-et-des-entreprises-en-expansion_fr.

24 Other avenues for reflection are sometimes proposed, such as the use of sustainable development selection criteria to promote SME access to public procurement. A recent study states that: '[...] environmental clauses have a positive impact

2.1 Mandatory Division into Lots

The only real measure directly aimed at favouring SMEs,[25] Article 46 of Directive 2014/24/EU allows for the 'division of contracts into lots' in order to guarantee access for SMEs.[26] The objective is to give contracting authorities considerable leeway with a view to public economic support for SMEs.[27] However, the division of public procurement into lots remains optional and, in this sense, Directive 2014/24/EU constitutes a 'minimum harmonisation'.[28] Thus, it is not surprising that, in the absence of in-depth harmonisation (which the obligation of division would have implied), access for SMEs has not been strengthened. In the absence of an obligation in national legislation, the practices of the contracting authorities may not have evolved.

Indeed, Article 46 of the Directive leaves the contracting authorities free to decide whether or not to divide the contract into lots, as well as the number and value of the lots, at the risk, however, of compromising its ability to meet the objective of access for SMEs to public procurement.[29] However, the methods of division into lots considerably affect the rate of participation of micro-enterprises and SMEs, as well as the chances of being awarded contracts.[30] In short, it has been empirically evidenced that the more lots a contract has, the greater the chances of success for SMEs in obtaining a share of the contract.[31] On the other hand, although the division into lots is optional, the contracting authorities are required to state the reasons for the absence of subdivision of the contract into lots. A few authors emphasise the imprecision of the

---

on the likelihood of an SME being awarded a contract. In other words, all other things being equal, the introduction of an environmental clause in a public contract increases the likelihood that it will be awarded to an SME rather than to a larger company. This impact on the probability of awarding a contract to an SME is around +7%' (Adrien Deschamps, *Développement durable et accès des PME aux marchés publics* (Report to the Direction des achats de l'État 2024, p. 18).

[25] François Lichère, *op. cit.*, p. 111.

[26] Dir. 2014/24/EU, recit. 78.

[27] François Lichère, *op. cit.*, p. 119. See also: Ignacio Herrera Anchustegui, Lisa Margrethe Nes and Tor Sikkeland, 'Article 46 – Division of Contracts into Lots' in Roberto Caranta and Albert Sanchez-Graells (eds.), *op. cit.*, p. 500.

[28] Martin Trybus, 'The Division of Public Contracts into Lots under Directive 2014/24: Minimum Harmonisation and Impact on SMEs in Public Procurement?' (2018) 3 *European Law Review* 313.

[29] Dir. 2014/24/EU, art. 46(1) and recit. 78.

[30] Johan Stake, *SME Participation and Success in Public Procurement* (Södertörn University 2014, p. 23).

[31] Ibid.: SME participation increases when the contract is divided into 2 to 4 lots, and the rate of award to an SME increases when the contract has more than 10 lots.

provisions of the directive as to the extent of this obligation to provide reasons concerning the possible justifications (recital 78 of the directive gives only a few examples[32]) and the methods of their control.[33] This question therefore falls within the national margin of discretion of the Member States, which may either adopt the 'default approach' adopted by the text, as in the United Kingdom,[34] or, on the contrary, raise the rule of allotment as a principle,[35] as in Germany and France. In this regard, the French legislator has chosen to restrict the grounds justifying the absence of subdivision of contracts,[36] while the judge exercises full control over the decision not to subdivide and a simple manifest error test on the definition of lots.[37]

By making subdivision mandatory, the European legislator would offer SMEs a fair chance of participating in a public procurement contract.[38] Admittedly, this obligation had been discussed during the parliamentary work on Directive 2014/24/EU. Moreover, an opinion was issued against the adoption of an amendment that intended to make it mandatory. The rapporteur considered, in this sense, that:

> Although there is a clear need to promote SME access to public procurement, imposing an almost absolute obligation on contracting authorities to subdivide contracts into lots is not the right approach. Furthermore, it is likely that leaving contracting authorities free to limit the number of lots that can be obtained by a tenderer runs counter to the objective of rewarding innovative or competitive SMEs and carries a significant risk of abuse aimed at discriminating against third parties. It is preferable to opt for more flexible measures.

---

32 Dir. 2014/24/EU, recit. 78: 'the contracting authority could, for example, argue that it considers that such division could restrict competition or render the execution of the contract excessively costly or technically difficult, or that the need to coordinate the contractors of the various lots could seriously compromise the proper execution of the contract'.

33 Ignacio Herrera Anchustegui, Lisa Margrethe Nes and Tor Sikkeland, *op. cit.*, p. 501 et seq.; François Lichère, *op. cit.*, p. 114; Martin Trybus and Marta Andrecka, 'Favouring Small and Medium Sized Enterprises with Directive 2014/24/EU?' (2017) 3 *EPPPL* 229; Martin Trybus, *op. cit.*, p. 329.

34 Martin Trybus, *op. cit.*, p. 317.

35 Dir. 2014/24/EU, art. 46, par. 4.

36 In this sense, the public procurement and concessions contracts code stipulates that 'the buyer may decide not to divide a contract into lots' in two specifically identified cases: '1° It is not in a position to carry out the organisation, management and coordination tasks itself; 2° The division into separate lots is likely to restrict competition or make the performance of the services technically difficult or financially more costly' (art. L. 2113–10).

37 CE, 21 May 2010, *Commune d'Ajaccio* [2010] No. 333737.

38 Ignacio Herrera Anchustegui, Lisa Margrethe Nes and Tor Sikkeland, *op. cit.*, p. 505.

This is the classic debate, which some authors admit,[39] on the dangers inherent in the division of markets in terms of protectionism,[40] collusion[41] and possible additional costs during contractual execution.[42] However, there are many measures that can be taken to reduce these risks[43] and, above all, these potential disadvantages are largely offset by the advantages of having a genuine pro-SME policy, particularly in an increasingly competitive and commercial environment at international level. Furthermore, the allotment requirement would ensure the same level of competition throughout the European Union, as the lack of harmonisation could lead to SMEs being favoured in certain Member States only.

Beyond the requirement for allotment, it is possible to provide, in addition to maintaining the possibility of limiting the number of lots awarded to the same economic operator,[44] for a ban on discounts in the case of multiple award of lots.[45] Such a practice has in fact been banned in France in order not to favour large companies: even if it may increase the overall cost for public purchasers on a given contract, it preserves SMEs and thus competition in the long run.

2.2 The Reduction of Administrative Formalities

To alleviate the administrative and financial burdens inherent in public procurement, which constitute a real 'repellent for companies, especially SMEs',[46] which do not always have the human and financial capacities to meet the formal requirements imposed by the public procurement procedures, a European Single Procurement Document (ESPD) has been introduced in Article 59 of Directive 2014/24/EU. The aim was to enable economic operators

---

39 For a contrary view, see: Miguel Assis Raimundo, '"Aiming at the Market You Want": A Critical Analysis of the Duties on Division into Lots under Directive 2014/24/EU' (2018) 4 *PPLR* 167.

40 François Lichère, *op. cit.*, p. 120; Martin Trybus and Marta Andrecka, *op. cit.*, p. 217; Martin Trybus, *op. cit.*, p. 260.

41 Ignacio Herrera Anchustegui, Lisa Margrethe Nes and Tor Sikkeland, *op. cit.*, p. 498.

42 Ibid.; Martin Trybus and Marta Andrecka, *op. cit.*, p. 226.

43 Bertrand Dacosta, 'L'accès des PME aux marchés publics dans la nouvelle directive Marchés publics' (2014) 96 *BJCP* 325.

44 Dir. 2014/24/EU, art. 46, para. 2.

45 Code de la commande publique, art. L. 2151–1.

46 European Court of Auditors, Public procurement in the EU. Decline in competition for works, goods and services contracts awarded between 2011 and 2021, 2023, p. 52. In the same vein: Dir. 2014/24/EU, recit. 84.

to produce certificates and other documents for the assessment of certain exclusion and selection criteria only once, in the manner of a European Digital Passport.[47] In practice, the ESPD is a pre-completed solemn declaration in which the tenderer certifies that they are not subject, nor is the third party on whose capacity they rely where applicable, to any grounds for exclusion but also that they meet the selection and award criteria established by the contracting authority.[48]

The ESPD is supposed to be a simplifying factor insofar as SMEs can reuse it in a subsequent procedure, provided that they confirm the validity of the information it contains. However, the number of supporting documents required does not facilitate access for SMEs, which do not necessarily have the resources, time and knowledge to provide all the information requested. Admittedly, the contracting authority can obtain certificates or relevant information free of charge and directly through national databases, and the economic operator is exempted from producing supporting documents, in particular with regard to criminal record.[49] However, this information is not necessarily easily accessible. Ultimately, it is a question of transferring the administrative and financial burdens of procurement to the contracting authorities (verifications also lengthen the procedural deadlines).[50] This explains the low level of interest shown in practice in the ESPD.[51]

Consequently, it would be advisable not necessarily to abolish the ESPD but to rethink e-Certis and the ESPD by simplifying the user experience (for filling in the declaration) and the number of supporting documents requested in order to make it easier for SMEs to apply for public contracts.[52]

2.3 The Share of Contract Performance to be Reserved for SMEs

If SMEs have difficulty obtaining a contract with a contracting authority, they can be supported by stipulating that a minimum share of the work will be reserved for SMEs. In this respect, it would not be a question of reserving public

---

47 Name initially planned, in French, during parliamentary proceedings.

48 Dir. 2014/24/EU, art. 59, para. 1.

49 Dir. 2014/24/EU, art. 59.

50 Martin Trybus and Marta Andrecka, *op. cit.*, p. 232; Pedro Telles, 'Article 59. European Single Procurement Document' in Roberto Caranta and Albert Sanchez-Graells (eds.), *op. cit.*, p. 651.

51 François Lichère, Laurent Richer and Marion Ubaud-Bergeron (eds.), *Bilan et réforme des directives de 2014* (Chaire de droit des contrats publics, 2025, forthcoming).

52 This request for a reduction in formalities is a recurring theme in the 89 contributions to the public consultation that closed in March 2025.

contracts for SMEs but of requiring that the execution of certain contracts be carried out in part by SMEs. Indeed, reserving contracts for SMEs would have an immediate impact on cross-border public procurement since it is quite obvious that the contracts would be awarded to domestic SMEs.

This is why it would be wise for a reform concerned with SME access to public procurement to allow for a mandatory sharing, with exceptions duly justified by the subject matter of the contract, or considerations of a technical nature, as it may happen that in certain areas no SMEs have the required competences. It could be stipulated, for example, that in principle 10% of contracts must be awarded to SMEs for works and services (as such a requirement would make no sense when it comes to supply).

It could also be stipulated that the share of the execution may be subject to a criterion for the selection of bids, this criterion being able to be combined with the minimum share previously mentioned.

This would also make it possible to validate the compatibility with European law of the SME reservation mechanisms provided for by certain national laws. For example, French law requires a minimum of 20% of the share to be entrusted to SMEs (it was 10% before Decree No. 2024-1251 of 30 December 2024) for global contracts with private financing (R 2213–5 of the Code de la commande publique (CCP)) or public financing (R 2171-23 CCP). In addition, it makes it a mandatory award criterion for privately funded contracts, that is, public–private partnership contracts (Article L 2222-4 CCP), which can be combined with the aforementioned minimum share.

It should be noted that the share reserved for SMEs could take any form, whether the SMEs are members of a group of economic operators or subcontractors.

On the subject of subcontracting, it would be beneficial to provide better supervision, as SMEs often work through subcontractors.

3. BETTER SUPERVISION OF SUBCONTRACTING

Article 71 of Directive 2014/24/EU gave concrete form to the wish expressed by the European legislator 10 years previously: to enact provisions on subcontracting with the aim of promoting access to public procurement for SMEs.[53] The framework for subcontracting, meanwhile, helps to 'ensure that

[53] Directive 2004/18/EC of the European Parliament and of the Council of 31 March 2004 on the coordination of procedures for the award of public works contracts, public supply contracts and public service contracts, recital 32.

the process of selecting the contractor is not rendered meaningless by an uncontrolled recourse to subcontracting'.[54]

In this context, Article 71 of the Directive stipulates that the contracting authority may require or may be obliged by a Member State to ask the tenderer to indicate in the tender the share of the contract intended to be subcontracted to third parties/subcontractors, together with the proposed subcontractors.[55].

However, to avoid restricting SMEs' access to subcontracting, a review of certain limits set by Article 71 would be relevant, in particular those concerning the refusal, from the award phase, of the use of subcontracting to carry out certain 'essential tasks'.[56] By recognising a high degree of discretion on the part of the contracting authority, such a limit 'could bring subcontracting to a sudden halt [...] despite having been widely promoted in recent years, particularly with a view to facilitating SME access to public procurement'.[57] The unclear definition of the concept of 'essential tasks' also complicates the analysis of the scope of this provision,[58] the meaning of which depends mainly on the subject of the contract, leaving considerable leeway for contracting authorities.[59] Therefore, the scope of this prohibition should be reduced to make it compatible with the obligation to reserve a portion of subcontracting for SMEs. In addition, clarification is needed of the concept of 'essential tasks' in order to secure subcontracts and promote subcontracting.

Another subcontracting mechanism would require a revision to promote the indirect participation of SMEs in public procurement: the generalisation of direct payment from contracting authorities to subcontractors.

The direct payment mechanism provided for in public procurement is supposed to be effective in promoting access for SMEs.[60] However, it remains an incentive[61] and is subject to conditions that limit direct payment to the subcontractor. National legislation may introduce measures to oppose the main contractor. Firstly, direct payment must relate to services already provided,

---

54 Rozen Noguellou, 'Les nouvelles directives et l'exécution des contrats' [2014] *AJDA* 858.

55 Dir. 2014/24/EU, art. 71 para. 2.

56 Dir. 2014/24/EU, art. 62 para. 2.

57 Stéphane Braconnier, *Précis du droit de la commande publique* (5th edn, Le Moniteur 2017, p. 249).

58 Hélène Hoepffner, *Droit des contrats administratifs* (Dalloz 2022, p. 604).

59 In this sense, see. Ministry of the Economy, Directorate of Legal Affairs, Observatoire économique de la commande publique, *La sous-traitance*, Technical sheet, updated on 01/04/2019, p. 3.

60 Martin Trybus and Marta Andrecka, *op. cit.*, p. 237; Johannes Stalzer, *op. cit.*, p. 757.

61 François Lichère, *op. cit.*, p. 117.

which excludes the awarding of advances by the contracting authority to the subcontractor. Secondly, direct payment must, in principle, be made at the request of the subcontractor and only when 'the nature of the contract permits', which suggests that all contracts could be targeted, provided that the services concerned are clearly identifiable.[62] Finally, the direct payment terms must be set out in the contract documents.

Furthermore, Article 71, paragraph 7, authorises national legislation to make the direct payment mechanism compulsory.[63]

This measure, if put in place, undoubtedly prevents the cash flow difficulties to which SMEs are particularly prone, especially as economic doctrine deplores the late payments of contractors to subcontractors.[64] This is not insignificant for SMEs, since one in four SME bankruptcies is reportedly attributable to late payments.[65] While it is true that a recent reform of the 2011 directive[66] on combating late payment helps to reduce the consequences of these difficulties,[67] a generalisation of direct payment would make subcontracting public contracts more attractive for SMEs by guaranteeing them payment for their services. It would be advisable to go further than what is provided for in Article 71 where direct payment is a simple possibility for Member States.

That being said, in order to preserve Member States' room for manoeuvre, but also to prevent the risk of late payment by public purchasers, the future directive could provide that subcontractors have the choice between direct payment by the public purchaser or payment by the main contractor.

62 Johannes Stalzer, *op. cit.*, p. 766.

63 Directive 2014/24/EU, recital 105.

64 Stéphane Saussier and Jean Tirole, 'Renforcer l'efficacité de la commande publique' (2015) 22 *Notes du conseil d'analyse économique* 3; Lucien Rapp, 'Sept solutions pour améliorer l'accès des PME aux contrats de la commande publique' (2014) 148 *Contrats publics* 55.

65 European Commission, 'Questions and Answers: The Regulation on Late Payments', available online: https://ec.europa.eu/commission/presscorner/detail/fr/qanda_23_4412.

66 Directive 2011/7/EU of the European Parliament and of the Council of 16 February 2011 on combating late payment in commercial transactions.

67 European Parliament legislative resolution of 23 April 2024 on the proposal for a regulation of the European Parliament and of the Council on combating late payment in commercial transactions (COM(2023)0533 – C9-0338/2023 – 2023/0323(COD)).

4. START-UPS, THE FORGOTTEN ONES OF PUBLIC PROCUREMENT

As special SMEs,[68] start-ups could be the subject of a separate review to facilitate their access to public procurement. In 2016, the European Commission stated that:

> Public procurement, worth two trillion euros, represents an immense potential for growth for start-ups and scale-ups. At present, this potential is still not sufficiently exploited. In relation to their weight in the economy, start-ups and scale-ups do not obtain a proportional share of public procurement.[69]

Better support for contracting authorities to enable them to use procurement opportunities and modernised procurement tools is needed to improve market penetration of innovative start-ups and scale-ups. In particular, preliminary market consultations and innovation partnerships can be powerful means for start-ups and scale-ups to present their innovative products to public buyers. This will make it easier for start-ups and scale-ups to succeed in public procurement. The widespread use of electronic procurement is essential in this respect,[70] at least if the start-ups are fully equipped and their internet network efficient enough.

In this context, as part of the work on a European Union strategy for start-ups and scale-ups, some public contributions propose to promote public procurement to support research and development of new solutions put forward by start-ups. Public procurement can 'serve as a showcase for start-up offerings; the market will enable public authorities to face challenges, calls for collaboration and calls for tenders, which will promote direct engagement between the private and public sectors'.[71]

The establishment of a European-level platform dedicated to commercial relations with start-ups would thus be recommended,[72] as would the generalisation of innovation partnerships, particularly to facilitate innovation by

---

68 There is no legal definition of start-ups (or scale-ups). In practice, they are relatively young SMEs that have not yet entered a market or are in the process of expanding in a given market. They generally develop innovative solutions and operate in technological fields (IT, robotics, engineering, biochemistry, etc.).

69 European Commission, COM(2016) 733 final, p. 8.

70 Ibid.

71 See, for example, online: https://ec.europa.eu/info/law/better-regulation/have-your-say/initiatives/14530-Strategie-de-lUE-en-faveur-des-jeunes-pousses-et-des-entreprises-en-expansion/F3522373_fr.

72 Ibid.

start-ups of sustainable development solutions.[73] The European Commission has also emphasised the usefulness of innovation partnerships in supporting start-ups.[74] However, the innovation partnership procedure, which has been very rarely used by contracting authorities, should be simplified.

It is also possible to consider reversing the principle with regard to variants, (i.e. to stipulate that consultation documents must prohibit variants and must justify this prohibition).

Finally, according to Directive 2014/24 (Article 58(4)), 'with regard to technical and professional abilities, contracting authorities may impose conditions to ensure that economic operators possess the necessary human and technical resources and experience to perform the contract to an appropriate quality standard. The contracting authorities may require, in particular, that economic operators have a sufficient level of experience, demonstrated by suitable references from contracts performed in the past'. But nothing is said about whether this experience can come from the operator's employees. It is therefore impossible for a start-up to demonstrate experience as an economic operator. It would be advisable to add, as has been the case in French law since 2006, that 'However, the absence of references relating to the execution of contracts of the same nature cannot, on its own, justify the elimination of a candidate'.

Beyond that, other expectations are shared that are in line with those of traditional SMEs, particularly with regard to the simplification of administrative procedures[75] or the reservation for start-ups of shares of the performance of contracts (to reduce the allocation to large established companies).[76]

---

[73] See, for example, online: https://ec.europa.eu/info/law/better-regulation/have-your-say/initiatives/14530-Strategie-de-lUE-en-faveur-des-jeunes-pousses-et-des-entreprises-en-expansion/F3522300_fr.

[74] European Commission, COM(2016) 733 final, p. 8. It should be noted that the European Commission has published two guides on innovation partnership and access to public procurement for start-ups in 2022 for economic operators and contracting authorities: https://ec.europa.eu/docsroom/documents/54276?locale=fr; https://ec.europa.eu/docsroom/documents/54254?locale=fr.

[75] See, for example, online: https://ec.europa.eu/info/law/better-regulation/have-your-say/initiatives/14530-Strategie-de-lUE-en-faveur-des-jeunes-pousses-et-des-entreprises-en-expansion/F3522124_fr; https://ec.europa.eu/info/law/better-regulation/have-your-say/initiatives/14530-Strategie-de-lUE-en-faveur-des-jeunes-pousses-et-des-entreprises-en-expansion/F3522029_fr

[76] See, for example, online: https://ec.europa.eu/info/law/better-regulation/have-your-say/initiatives/14530-Strategie-de-lUE-en-faveur-des-jeunes-pousses-et-des-entreprises-en-expansion/F3522029_fr; https://ec.europa.eu/info/law/better-regulation/have-your-say/initiatives/14530-EU-strategy-for-start-ups-and-scale-ups/F3523624_en.

15. Innovation and public procurement

The need for the law to match the policy demands

Pedro Cerqueira Gomes

REFORM PROPOSALS

- Establish a centralised EU Service for Innovation Procurement (EUSIP) to provide legal, technical, and economic guidance, ensuring consistent support and reducing legal uncertainty across Member States.
- Simplify and clarify rules for the innovation partnership procedure to enhance its usability, focusing on grounds of use, selection of economic operators, intellectual property rights, and contract modifications.
- Introduce an EU preference regime for start-ups and SMEs in strategic sectors, with clear definitions and safeguards to promote innovation while complying with EU Treaty principles.

1. INNOVATION AND PUBLIC PROCUREMENT – THE RECENT PAST AND THE NEW MOMENTUM

Since 2002, public procurement has been recognised as a demand-side tool to drive innovation.[1] With the 2004 Public Procurement Directives and the 2007 Commission Communication on the exclusion of pre-commercial procurement,[2] it became evident that the nexus between public procurement and innovation encompassed two distinct yet mutually reinforcing approaches: (i) the public procurement of innovative solutions (PPI) encompassing both

[1] P Cerqueira Gomes, *EU Public Procurement and Innovation – The Innovation Partnership Procedure and Harmonisation Challenges* (Edward Elgar Publishing 2021) 7.

[2] European Commission, *Pre-commercial Procurement: Driving Innovation to Ensure Sustainable hHigh-quality Public Services in Europe, Brussels*, COM(2007) 799 final, 14 December 2007.

the development and the acquisition phases, throughout award procedures; and (ii) pre-commercial procurement, which pertains to the commissioning of research and development (R&D) services, excluded from the procurement Directives.[3]

Despite the opportunities afforded by the 2004 Public Procurement Directives and the 2007 Commission Communication, these frameworks proved largely ineffective, namely due to risk aversion and lack of expertise.[4] To increase the innovation levels, several changes in the 2014 Directives were introduced. The Public Procurement Directives not only provide for the first time a definition of innovation (Article 2(22)),[5] but also introduce a new tailored procedure—the innovation partnership—specifically designed for the procurement of innovative goods, services, and works.[6] Nevertheless, as acknowledged in the Guidance on Innovation Procurement, the incorporation of this novel procedure does not preclude the promotion of innovation through alternative public procurement procedures, namely by preliminary market consultations, technical specifications, the adoption of functional requirements, variants, award criteria, and more flexibility on using special procedures, such as competitive procedure with negotiation, competitive dialogue, and design contests or even beyond formal public procurement procedures, via pre-commercial procurement.[7]

Data disseminated in 2020 revealed a pronounced underachievement and underinvestment in both PPI and pre-commercial procurement across all European Member States. In response, the Commission has issued soft law instruments, including the innovation guidance seeking to reduce legal uncertainty by providing a qualified interpretation of EU law, and has financed a range of initiatives (EAFIP, Big Buyers, Procure2innovate) that promote

---

[3] European Commission, *Public Procurement as a Driver of Innovation in SMEs and Public Services* (European Union 2014).

[4] European Commission, *Europe 2020, Flagship Initiative. Innovation Union Brussels,* COM(2010) 546 final, 6 October 2010, point 3.2. R Caranta and P Cerqueira Gomes, "Public Procurement and Innovation" (2021) 22 *ERA Forum* 371–385. European Commission, *Green Paper on the Modernisation of EU Public Procurement Policy Towards a More Efficient European Procurement Market Brussels,* COM(2011) 15 final, 27.1.2011, point 4.3.

[5] Gomes (n 1) 148–153.

[6] On the innovation partnership procedure please see S Arrowsmith, *The Law of Public and Utilities Procurement*, vol I (3rd edn, Sweet & Maxwell 2014) 1040–1060; Gomes (n 1) 107–143; P Cerqueira Gomes, "Article 31" in R Caranta and A Sanchez Graells (eds), *European Public Procurement – Commentary on Directive 2014/24/EU* (Edward Elgar 2021) 335–49.

[7] European Commission, *Guidance on Innovation Procurement* C(2021) 4320 final.

professionalisation and support the creation of a network of national competence centres to facilitate knowledge sharing and best practices in innovation procurement.[8] The 2022 New European Innovation Agenda has further emphasised the role of public procurement in fostering experimental approaches to the regulation of nascent technologies and also vaguely highlighting the potential of its purchasing power in driving innovation procurement.[9] The latter Agenda advocates for the formation of an innovation procurement advisory service to help Member States and public buyers become more innovative, but its impact is almost minimal.[10] In September 2023, the European Commission launched a new European Observatory dedicated to monitoring, analysing, and disseminating the information related to the implementation of public services using Artificial Intelligence (AI), blockchain, and other emerging technologies.[11] In the same month, the EU published a proposal for a Model of contractual clauses for AI, published on the Public Buyers Community, which has been recently revised in alignment with the EU regulations on Artificial Intelligence[12] and consequently divided into AI clauses for high-risk AI and AI clauses for non-risk AI.[13]

The Special Report of the Court of Auditors (2023) on Public Procurement also notes that public buyers rarely consider innovation in their procurement activities.[14] The continued underachievement of innovation public procurement is acutely problematic given the new political *momentum* within the European Union. At present, the significance of innovation within the European strategic paradigm has acquired renewed impetus, heralding a prospective regulatory

---

[8] European Commission, *Benchmarking of R&D Procurement and Innovation Procurement Investments in Countries across Europe* (DG GNECT, F – Digital Single Market 10 October 2020). For more details and explanations of the initiatives mentioned, see Gomes (n 1) 16.

[9] European Commission, *A New European Innovation Agenda* COM(2022) 323 final.

[10] Ibid., 10.

[11] European Commission, *Public Sector Tech Watch. Mapping Innovation in the EU Public Services* (Publications Office of the European Union 2024).

[12] Regulation (EU) 2024/1689 of the European Parliament and of the Council of 13 June 2024 on harmonised rules on artificial intelligence (Artificial Intelligence Act) [2024].

[13] European Commission, *Proposal for Standard Contractual Clauses for the Procurement of Artificial Intelligence (AI) by Public Organisations* (September 2023).

[14] European Court of Auditors, *Special Report Public Procurement in the EU – Less Competition for Contracts Awarded for Works, Goods and Services in the 10 Years up to 2021* (2023) 48.

transformation. Both the Draghi Report[15] and the European Commission's strategy, "A Competitiveness Compass for the EU,"[16] have identified the establishment of a new competitiveness model predicated on innovation-led productivity as a critical catalyst for reinvigorating the European project. This model envisions Europe as a preeminent global hub where tomorrow's technologies are conceived, manufactured, and marketed in a carbon-neutral manner. In pursuit of this agenda, the Commission intends to propose a revision of the Public Procurement Directives, infusing them with a more robust innovation focus compared to the antecedent 2014 Directives, which were already oriented towards innovation.

The EU proposes to amend the 2014 Directives to incorporate a European preference for strategic sectors and technologies, prioritising innovative solutions in areas such as artificial intelligence, renewable energy, and cybersecurity to drive technological advancement and strengthen domestic supply chains. This preference directly links to innovation by incentivising public procurement of cutting-edge goods, services, and works developed by EU-based firms, particularly start-ups and SMEs, thereby fostering research and development (R&D) and aligning with the EU's innovation-driven competitiveness goals, as outlined in the Draghi Report and the New European Innovation Agenda.[17] This development reflects not only an escalating demand for innovation but also the EU's imperative to counter extraterritorial protectionist measures with its own strategic and defensive policies,[18] as exemplified by the Foreign Subsidies Regulation 2022/2560, which highlights the geopolitical ramifications on the future legislative process.[19] The Commission also advocates for the simplification and modernisation of the European public procurement legal framework to better accommodate start-ups and innovative enterprises.[20] Clearly, there is an intention for the revision of the Directives with a quasi-survival focus on innovative EU public procurement.

---

15 M Draghi, *The Future of European Competitiveness – Part A: A Competitiveness Strategy for Europe* (European Commission 2024) 51–52.

16 European Commission, *A Competitiveness Compass for the EU* COM(2025) 30 Final, 9, 14–15.

17 Ibid., 14–15.

18 For the same perspective of the adoption of certain protectionism in global public procurement markets, see the inspiring paper of L Folliot Lallitot and CR Yukins, "Will Protectionism Prevail in Global Public Procurement?" (2021) 2 *Concurrences* 1–13.

19 It is interesting to analyse if the case-law of the Court of Justice is also showing this tendency, mainly with the Case C-652/22 *Kolin Inşaat Turizm Sanayi ve Ticaret AŞ* [2024] ECLI:EU:C:2024:910.

20 European Commission (n 16) 15.

More recently, the Commission's evaluation of the 2014 Directives confirms this trend, finding that the uptake of public procurement of innovation remains limited in practice. This study highlights that the specific innovation partnership procedure has been used only for 199 contracts across the EU between 2016 and 2023. These data suggests that current legislative framework has not yet fully succeeded in its objective to drive innovation.[21] In my opinion, EU public procurement law can still align with the EU's holistic policy to promote innovation, provided some strategic reforms are implemented within the new revised Directive.

2. THE CREATION OF THE EU SERVICE FOR INNOVATION PROCUREMENT – A LAW THAT MATCHES THE POLITICAL AND TECHNICAL DEMANDS OF INNOVATION

Innovation can be promoted in any award procedure. However, in the eyes of the European legislature in 2014, the innovation partnership procedure surpasses other public procurement procedures covered by the Directive because it provides greater flexibility, discretion, and room for negotiation—all essential ingredients for the R&D of innovative goods, services, and works in close cooperation with the public sector, particularly during the contract execution phase.[22] One element that distinguishes the innovation partnership is the fact that the innovation occurs not during the procedural phase but rather during the execution of the contract. This element aims to avoid the typical inflexibility of the procedural phase of public procurement procedures.[23]

However, this call for substantial flexibility, discretion, and negotiation, which are vital for innovation, still represents a harmonisation challenge. Contracting authorities operating in Member States with structural disadvantages and national administrative law traditions that have not fully embraced procedural discretion or negotiation will face even greater challenges in using the innovation partnership procedure or other procedures with more room for

21 European Commission, *Evaluation of Directive 2014/23/EU on Concessions, Directive 2014/24/EU on Public Procurement and Directive 2014/25/EU on Utilities* SWD (2025) 332 final, 39, 66.

22 Gomes (n 1) 136–137.

23 Ibid., 137; C Edquist and L Hommen, 'Public Technology Procurement and Innovation Theory' in C Edquist, L Hommen and L Tsipouri (eds), *Public Technology Procurement and Innovation* (Kluwer Academic Publishers 2000) 5–70.

negotiations,[24] particularly considering the inadequate capacity of public officials to manage these types of procedures. Furthermore, the uncertainty about what constitutes innovation for the public sector poses a significant challenge for all contracting authorities, leading to reluctance in prioritising innovative solutions, namely in using innovation as award criteria.

To mitigate these harmonisation challenges, effective and co-responsible legal advice is essential. While Article 83(4) mandates that Member States ensure free legal advice and guidance on the implementation of EU public procurement law, relying solely on national structures to do it is inadequate. This chapter proposes a system of greater 'co-responsibility' between Member States and European actors, such as the European Commission, to meet the demands of increasingly programmatic public procurement rules and the respect of the EU consistency principle within the public procurement legal framework.[25]

The heightened importance of promoting innovation through public procurement in the Commission's new political agenda calls for a more proactive role from the Commission itself. Although the EAFIP initiative, funded by the Directorate-General Connect, provides guidance and local assistance to public procurers, it remains insufficient. The Commission should integrate a new EU Service for Innovation Procurement (EUSIP) within its internal structure (e.g., through Directorates-General, services, or agencies)[26] rather than outsourcing them, ensuring centralised and consistent support in all the different dimensions of innovation in the public sector. This will increase legal certainty regarding compliance with EU law and reduce the risk of regulatory capture for specific technologies.[27]

---

24 For a deep analysis of the fact that the mere harmonisation of laws alone cannot guarantee the same level of effectiveness in promoting innovation via public procurement where structural differences and certain administrative law traditions, such as those related to procedural discretion and the ability to negotiate, see Gomes (n 1) 63–106.

25 P Cerqueira Gomes, "Article 83" in R Caranta and A Sanchez Graells (eds), *European Public Procurement – Commentary on Directive 2014/24/EU* (Edward Elgar 2021) 335–349.

26 For a discussion of the administrative organisation of the Commission and the phenomenon of EU agencies, M Ruffert, *Law of Administrative Organisation of the EU – A Comparative Approach* (Edward Elgar 2020) 77–133.

27 For deep analysis and risks of acquiring technology, such as inefficiency and regulatory capture see, A Sanchez-Graells, *Digital Technologies and Public Procurement – Gatekeeping and Experimentation in Digital Governance* (OUP 2024).

Alternately, Sanchez-Graells proposes the creation of an independent regulatory body called AI in the Public Sector Authority (AISPSA) in each Member State tasked with monitoring the public sector digitalisation, reducing the risk of regulatory capture by certifying standards, licensing, and the adoption of technology in the public sector.[28]

This proposal offers significant strengths, such as enhanced oversight of high-risk technologies like AI and alignment with the EU's regulatory frameworks (e.g., the EU AI Act and NIS 2 Directive), ensuring responsible technology adoption in the public sector. However, it may face challenges, including the risk of fragmentation across Member States, which could undermine harmonisation efforts, and a limited focus on the procedural complexities of innovation procurement.

The two solutions can nonetheless coexist and are complementary. While the AISPSA would ensure governance and compliance in technology adoption, the EUSIP would address the specific needs of innovation procurement by providing contracting authorities with centralised legal, technical, and economic guidance. Together, these mechanisms would reduce the fragmentation of procurement practices across Member States, enabling the EU to meet its innovation-driven competitiveness goals, as outlined in the Draghi Report and the New European Innovation Agenda, while maintaining a level playing field in the internal market. An alternative path that will not be explored could be the creation of a specific directorate under the AI office regulated under Article 64 of the EU AI Act.[29]

A new provision should be included in the revised Public Procurement Directive to guarantee that contracting authorities have access to legal, technical, and economic advice specifically for innovation procurement issues, above the thresholds. This is critical because increasing innovation in procurement is a matter of survival for the European project. Such a service would incentivise contracting authorities to seek guidance, conduct lawful procedures—especially via the innovation partnership—and ultimately enhance cross-border trade and joint procurement in critical sectors such as renewable energy, cybersecurity, and advanced healthcare technologies, thereby fostering a harmonised approach to innovation procurement that strengthens the EU's competitive edge against other global innovation leaders.

---

28 Ibid., 106–113.

29 See Commission Decision C/2024/1459 of 24 January 2024 establishing the European Artificial Intelligence Office.

3. SIMPLIFICATION AND CLARIFICATION OF THE LEGAL RULES OF THE INNOVATION PARTNERSHIP

This section will focus merely on the innovation partnership procedure, and I will propose concrete changes that could be made within the revised Classic Directive that could foster the use of this given procedure, working towards simplification of the use and clarification of certain procedural and contract execution issues, regarding the (i) grounds of use; (ii) selection of economic operators; (iii) Intellectual Property (IP) rights and state aid; and (iv) contract modifications within the innovation partnership procedure.

3.1 Grounds of Use

Under Article 31(1) and (2), the innovation partnership procedure may be initiated when a contracting authority identifies a need for an innovative product, service, or work that cannot be satisfied by solutions currently available on the market. This provision establishes two key criteria for initiating an innovation partnership: (i) the necessity for innovation and (ii) the unavailability of suitable solutions on the market.[30]

To address uncertainties in assessing market availability for innovation partnerships, the revised Directive should mandate preliminary market consultations to ensure transparency and reduce legal risks.[31] I propose requiring mandatory preliminary market consultations, as outlined in Article 40, before launching the procedure.[32] The European Commission has emphasised that, when conducted effectively, such consultations play a critical role in assessing the state of the art and clarifying market uncertainties. Additionally, the use of a Prior Information Notice (PIN) under Article 48 is also an effective mechanism to publicise these consultations.[33]

The European legislator should therefore amend the Directive to include a specific provision or recital stipulating that market availability must be evaluated through preliminary market consultations, which would enhance transparency and reduce legal risks by ensuring a robust evidence base for the decision to pursue an innovation partnership. These consultations should be conducted in an open, online format—such as on the contracting authority's

---

[30] Gomes (n 1) 143–145.

[31] A Sanchez-Graells explains the potential danger of the limited knowledge of public officials through the lens of agency theory, while also stressing the specific dangers of the procurement of digital technologies, Sanchez-Graells (n 27) 61–65.

[32] Gomes (n 6) 340–341.

[33] European Commission, *Guidance on Innovation Procurement* (n 7) 37.

institutional website—for a minimum of 15 days to ensure broad participation. To simplify the grounds of use for the innovation partnership, the Directive could further provide a simplified assessment framework, such as a checklist of criteria for determining market unavailability. Alternatively, the use of a PIN could be mandated as a standardised approach.

Moreover, there is also a need to define innovation in the context of the grounds of use of this procedure. Article 2(22) defines innovation,[34] but its discretionary nature leaves Member States and contracting authorities to determine the specific objectives of innovation in meeting public needs. To provide more clarity, the recitals of the Directive should be refined with a non-exhaustive list illustrating the intended scope of public sector innovation, drawing on the European Commission's Guidance on Innovation Procurement to offer contracting authorities clearer direction.[35]

In light of recent EU policy developments, the grounds for using the innovation partnership procedure should be broadened to include goods, services, and works not yet available on a large-scale commercial basis,[36] rather than limiting it strictly to those unavailable in the market. This adjustment would ease the market unavailability criterion, potentially increasing the adoption of innovation partnerships.

Additionally, the innovation partnership procedure should also be made available for the acquisition of emerging technology solutions requiring adaptation for the public sector context. Given the procedure's inherent flexibility during the contract execution phase and its less stringent application of the EU equal treatment and competition principles—particularly in the possible scenario of the innovation partnership being awarded to more than one economic operator—it is well-suited to support the procurement of such technologies, which often necessitate flexibility and close collaboration between suppliers and public entities for effective implementation.[37]

---

34 For a detailed debate on the issue, see Gomes (n 1) 143–53.

35 European Commission (n 7) 5.

36 In the same vein, Regulation (EU) 2021/695 of the European Parliament and of the Council of 28 April 2021 establishing Horizon Europe – the Framework Programme for Research and Innovation [2021] OJ L170/1, Article 2 (8).

37 Development of innovation in the contract execution phase, rather than in the procedural phase, is one of the unique features of the innovation partnership as compared with the other public procurement procedures regulated under close cooperation and flexibility between the contracting authority and the economic operators throughout the innovation process, which occurs more effectively during the contract execution phase than during the award phase, when stricter procedural rules apply Directive 2014/24/EU; see Gomes (n 1) 180–181.

To ensure consistency in this expanded application, the Directive should provide guidance on the scope of "emerging technologies for the public sector" by describing their key characteristics rather than a fixed legal definition. These technologies can be understood as innovative digital or technological solutions with the potential to transform public administration and service delivery, particularly those not yet widely available on the market but capable of addressing pressing public sector challenges. Examples include artificial intelligence, blockchain, the Internet of Things, big data analytics, quantum computing, high-performance computing, or software, with the potential to improve efficiency, interoperability, transparency, and citizen engagement in public services, while addressing challenges like sustainability, digital inclusion, and cybersecurity enhancement.[38]

3.2 Selection of Economic Operators

Recital 49 indicates that the procedural rules for the innovation partnership should be based on those applicable for the competitive procedure with negotiation. However, distinctions exist, particularly in the selection phase. Article 31(6) deviates from Article 58 by emphasising that contracting authorities in the selection phase should pay special attention to the candidates' capacity in the field of R&D of innovative solutions.[39]

The wording of Article 31(6) underscores that the selection phase should focus primarily on the tenderers' R&D capacity and their ability to develop and apply innovative solutions effectively, encouraging the participation of innovative SMEs and start-ups. This suggests that when evaluating a tenderer's technical and professional ability for an innovation partnership, the criterion of R&D expertise should take precedence over other elements listed in Article

[38] This definition was inspired by several EU sources, namely Regulation (EU) 2024/903 of the European Parliament and of the Council of 13 March 2024 laying down measures for a high level of public sector interoperability across the Union (Interoperable Europe Act); Regulation (EU) 2021/694 of the European Parliament and of the Council of 29 April 2021 establishing the Digital Europe Programme and repealing Decision (EU) 2015/2240; Decision (EU) 2022/2481 of the European Parliament and of the Council of 14 December 2022 establishing the Digital Decade Policy Programme 2030 [2022]; Regulation (EU) 2021/695 of the European Parliament and of the Council of 28 April 2021 establishing Horizon Europe – the Framework Programme for Research and Innovation, laying down its rules for participation and dissemination and repealing Regulation (EU) N.º 1290/2013.

[39] For a different view advocating that Article 31(6) cannot be seen as a specific selection criterion when compared to Article 58, see Arrowsmith (n 6) 1054–1055.

58(4), which may still be considered but should play a secondary role compared to the requirements of Article 31(6).[40] However, the legislator has not provided sufficient clarity in how Articles 31(6) and 58(4) should be interpreted together. Nor has it adequately addressed how an economic operator can demonstrate its R&D capacity without relying solely on experience. For example, would it be legally permissible and proportionate for a contracting authority to allow public procurement documents to demonstrate R&D capacity through alternative means, such as staff qualifications (as per Article 60(4)), awards, research grants, or publications in scientific journals, rather than requiring a decade of experience in a specific field, provided the principles of equal treatment and non-discrimination are safeguarded? Annex XII, Part II of Directive 2014/24/EU, which outlines acceptable means of proof, does not currently recognise awards, research grants, or scientific publications as valid evidence of technical ability.[41]

This highlights a clear need for legislative amendment or, at the very least, the inclusion of additional guidance in the recitals and Annex XII to outline best practices for assessing R&D capacity in a way that attracts start-ups and innovative companies—an explicit political objective of the EU. Such changes would ensure that the selection process better aligns with the goal of fostering innovation while maintaining fairness and transparency.

3.3 Intellectual Property Rights and State Aid

Article 31(6) gives contracting authorities the discretion to establish in the public procurement documents how they want to define the agreements applicable to intellectual property rights. The issue of ownership and assignment of intellectual property has been partially regulated by the EU, since there is national autonomy and divergences on the matter.[42]

The revised Directive should advocate for a balanced model of IP allocation that ensures fairness, incentivises innovation, and mitigates state aid risks. IP rights arising from R&D activities and inventions developed by public employees (or others) during the innovation partnership would primarily belong to the public entity ensuring that the outcomes of publicly funded R&D remain accessible for the contracting authority. However, to encourage participation

---

40 Gomes (n 1) 172–176.

41 Gomes (n 6) 343.

42 The differences in this context are justified not by the lack of legal competence for the EU to regulate this field of law but mainly because of divergences in national law approaches, especially in the case of common law copyright and *droit d'auteur*; J Pila and P Torremans, *European Intellectual Property Law* (2nd edition, OUP 2019) 39–71.

and fairly compensate inventors, the model grants the inventor the right to share in the economic benefits derived from the public entity's exploitation of the innovation. For instance, if the public entity licenses the IP to third parties or uses it commercially, the inventor will receive a predefined percentage of the resulting revenues.[43]

Furthermore, the model allows the public entity to assign ownership of the IP to the inventor under specific conditions, in exchange for a non-exclusive, non-transferable, royalty-free licence for the public entity to use the IP. This ensures that the public sector retains access to the innovation for its purposes, such as implementing the technology in public administration, while enabling the inventor to commercialise the IP in other markets. Should the inventor subsequently generate economic benefits from exploiting the innovation—through licensing or direct commercialisation—the public entity would be entitled to a percentage of those profits. This reciprocal benefit-sharing mechanism not only promotes fairness but also reduces the risk of the partnership being classified as state aid, as it minimises the perception of an unbalanced advantage granted to the private party.[44]

This proposed model aligns with the EU's broader objectives of fostering innovation while maintaining a level playing field. By embedding such provisions in the procurement documents, as permitted under Article 31(6), contracting authorities can mitigate legal uncertainties surrounding IP ownership and ensure compliance with state aid regulations, such as those outlined in the General Block Exemption Regulation (GBER, Regulation (EU) 651/2014).[45]

To further support this approach, the revised Directive should include specific provisions or recitals addressing IP rights in innovation partnerships. These could mandate the inclusion of standardised IP clauses in procurement documents, drawing on the European Commission's 2023 proposal for Model Contractual Clauses for Innovation, published on the Public Buyers Community. Such clauses should be adaptable to the specific needs of the partnership but provide a default framework for IP allocation, benefit sharing, and state aid compliance. For instance, they could stipulate that any public funding provided through the partnership must adhere to market terms—such as fair

43 Gomes (n 6) 348–349.

44 A Sanchez-Graells points out the dangers of the innovation partnership procedure, regarding the compliance of point 33(d)(ii) of the Commission communication on state aid for R&D and innovation, A Sanchez-Graells, "State Aid and EU Public Procurement: More Interactions, Fuzzier Boundaries" in L Hancher and JJ Piernas López (eds), *Research Handbook on European State Aid Law* (2nd edn, Edward Elgar 2020).

45 Commission, "Framework for State Aid for Research and Development and Innovation" [2014] OJ C198/1, para. 33.

royalty rates or competitive pricing for IP licences—to avoid conferring an unfair advantage.

Moreover, the proposed EUSIP (in section 2) could play a pivotal role in supporting contracting authorities by offering legal and economic expertise on IP arrangements. This centralised service could provide guidance on drafting IP clauses, assessing the market value of IP to ensure state aid compliance, and navigating national differences in IP law. Such support would be particularly valuable in partnerships involving emerging technologies like artificial intelligence or blockchain, where IP rights are often complex and contested.

3.4 Contract Modifications

The innovation partnership procedure, by its nature, requires significant flexibility during the contract execution phase to accommodate the uncertainties inherent in developing innovative goods, services, or works. However, this need for adaptability creates tension with the contract modification rules outlined in Article 72.[46] This issue is not unique to innovation partnerships, as the need to modify contracts to incorporate innovation can arise in any public procurement procedure. The specific legal provisions governing innovation partnerships in Article 31 of the Directive should take precedence when interpreting and applying Article 72, as the former reflects a legislative intent to prioritise flexibility in such cases, though similar flexibility should be considered for all procurement contracts to support innovation more broadly. Nevertheless, reconciling these two legal frameworks poses challenges.

One key issue arises with Article 72(4), which sets out conditions under which contract modifications are not permitted. The rigidity of these conditions does not align well with the demands of innovation partnerships, where the development process—often involving lengthy R&D phases—requires ongoing adjustments during the successive phases of the innovation partnership procedure or even as a result of the intermediate targets (Article 31(2)). These adjustments may include changes to the scope, timeline, or deliverables of the contract, driven by the unpredictable outcomes of innovation. A strict interpretation of Article 72(4) risks stifling the very flexibility that the innovation partnership procedure is designed to provide, potentially discouraging contracting authorities from using this mechanism.

Another challenge relates to Article 72(2), which outlines exceptions to the obligation to re-tender when modifying a contract. Specifically, Article 72(1)(a) allows modifications without re-tendering if they are provided for in a clear, precise, and unequivocal review clause or option within the original public

[46] Gomes (n 1) 181–185.

procurement documents.[47] However, this expectation is often unrealistic in the context of innovation partnerships. The R&D process in such projects is inherently uncertain and unpredictable, making it nearly impossible for even the most diligent contracting authority to foresee all potential outcomes at the outset. The European legislator acknowledges this unpredictability by allowing contracting authorities to terminate the innovation partnership—either partially with specific partners or entirely—after evaluating R&D results at predefined intermediate stages. This provision underscores the need for flexibility, which conflicts with the strict predictive requirements of Article 72(1)(a).

A further complexity arises when considering whether new discoveries during the R&D phase qualify as an exception to re-tendering under Article 72(2)(b). This provision permits contract modifications without re-tendering if the changes are due to unforeseen circumstances that a diligent contracting authority could not have anticipated, provided the modifications do not alter the overall nature of the contract. The question is whether a new discovery during R&D can be classified as such an unforeseen circumstance. While there is no definitive answer, as each case must be assessed individually, if the discovery is genuinely unpredictable and directly results from the R&D activities, it could potentially fall within this exception. For instance, if an unexpected technological breakthrough emerges that requires adjusting the contract but does not fundamentally change its purpose, Article 72(2)(b) might apply, provided the contracting authority can demonstrate that the outcome was unforeseeable at the time of tendering.[48]

To address these challenges, the revised Directive must provide clearer guidance on how Article 72 applies to innovation partnerships. This could include a specific recital or provision clarifying that the flexibility inherent in Article 31 takes precedence over the stricter modification rules in Article 72, particularly for changes driven by the unpredictable nature of R&D. Additionally, contracting authorities should be encouraged to include broad, adaptable review clauses in their public procurement documents, acknowledging the likelihood of unforeseen developments while still adhering to the principles of transparency and equal treatment.

---

[47] Case C-549/14 *Finn Frogne A/S v Rigspolitiet ved Center for Beredskabskommunikation* [2016] ECLI: EU: C: 2016: 634.

[48] Gomes (n 1) 197.

4. EU PREFERENCE REGIME FOR INNOVATIVE START-UPS AND SMEs

The European Union's renewed emphasis on innovation, as outlined in the Draghi Report and the "A Competitiveness Compass for the EU" strategy, highlights the critical role of start-ups and SMEs in driving innovation. Therefore, the EU is considering a preference regime within the revised EU Public Procurement Directives that favours innovative start-ups and SMEs in strategic sectors. However, implementing such a regime—especially the reservation of contracts for start-ups—presents significant legal and practical complexities, particularly in ensuring compatibility with EU principles of non-discrimination and equal treatment under the Treaty on the Functioning of the European Union.

Favouring start-ups may lack a specific justification to discriminate among economic operators. The European legislator must try to find any justification under the European Treaties. To ensure compliance, the possibility to reserve contracts to specific sectors with high innovation, such as AI, and contracts below certain new—to be introduced—EU thresholds, accommodates a possible justification under the internal market exceptions, namely concerning public policy or even public security for high-risk technologies.

Another critical challenge in implementing this regime is the lack of a uniform EU definition of "start-up." Unlike SMEs, which are defined by the European Commission Recommendation 2003/361/EC, the term "start-up" is not legally codified in EU procurement law. However, the EU has provided informal guidance through initiatives like the European Innovation Council work programme[49] and others.

To support the preference regime, the revised Directive should adopt a working definition. A start-up could be defined as an economic operator established for less than seven years with a low turnover or staff that spends at least 15% of revenue on R&D.[50] This definition could be supplemented by evidence, such

---

[49] European Commission, *EIC Work Programme 2024* C(2023) 8849.

[50] Alternately, in the United States, the Small Business Innovation Research (SBIR) and Small Business Technology Transfer (STTR) programmes define eligible small businesses as for-profit entities with fewer than 500 employees, generally requiring at least 51% US ownership, and prioritise funding for high-risk, innovation-driven R&D projects. These programmes, integrated into federal funding mechanisms, enable small businesses to contribute significantly to technological innovation through government grants and contracts, also offering a potential model for a definition of start-up at EU level that is capable of enhancing the European Union's public procurement strategy; see 15 USC §638 (2022), as amended by Pub L No 117–328, 29 December 2022.

as participation in EU-funded innovation programmes or registration with national innovation registries, where available. Such a definition would provide clarity for contracting authorities while remaining flexible enough to adapt to diverse Member State contexts. Recognising the legal constraints of contract reservations and their compatibility with the European Treaties, namely for discriminating among types of enterprises, I propose an alternative strategy of preference to enhance start-up and SME involvement: by increasing the use of design contests for innovation under certain participation requirements—permitted under Article 78 of Directive 2014/24/EU—which could encourage start-ups to showcase their innovative ideas without the competitive pressure of traditional tenders.[51]

Nonetheless, to operationalise the reserve contracts regime, the revised Directive should include a specific recital or article authorising limited contract reservations for start-ups, with clear safeguards to ensure compliance with non-discrimination principles and other Treaty-based provisions. The proposed EU Service for Innovation Procurement (section 2) could provide guidance on defining start-ups, assessing their eligibility, and designing reservation criteria, thereby supporting harmonisation across Member States.

5. CONCLUSION

This chapter has argued that the EU's public procurement framework, despite incremental advancements through the 2014 Directives, remains underutilised as a catalyst for innovation due to persistent barriers such as risk aversion, legal uncertainty, and insufficient expertise among contracting authorities. A revised Directive with a centralised EUSIP, simplified and clarified innovation partnership rules, and a start-up preference regime can align procurement with the EU's innovation agenda.

---

[51] As an example, the US National Aeronautics and Space Administration (NASA) uses open innovation approaches, including prizes or challenges, as a procurement method. This could be a good strategy within the EU Directive; see J Gustetic, J Crusan, S Rader and S Ortega "Outcome-driven open innovation at NASA" (2015) 34 *Space Policy* 11–17.

16. Reforming procurement for crisis

Proposals for simplified, collaborative and equity responses

Annamaria La Chimia

REFORM PROPOSALS

A comprehensive ad hoc crisis framework is needed covering pre, during, and post-crisis phases. This framework should include:

- Straightforward definition of crises, avoiding farraginous and exclusionary definitions based on level of harm, or the foreseeability of events in favour of pragmatic definitions that link crisis to any external event that hinders the fulfilment of public functions.
- Mandating equality impact and risk assessments to ensure procurement practices do not have an adverse effect on certain individuals because of the characteristics they share.
- Use of more flexible and simplified procedures (from extended frameworks to streamlined competitive negotiated procedures).
- Simplified conditions for the use of the negotiated procedure but also the introduction of express safeguards such as the publication of notices and the requirement to conduct mini competitions with the use of a rated-supplier system created ad hoc for crises.
- Ad hoc programmes to strengthen business capacity and the professionalisation of the procurement workforce.
- Establishment of a European star-rating system for companies to improve selection of reliable suppliers during crises.
- Enhancing transparency through detailed and continuous reporting (including the collection of gender-disaggregated data) during all phases of a crisis.
- Identify specific sectors where EU collaborative action is strengthened through regulatory sandboxes.

- Embed the principles of solidarity and collaboration within the Directive to always guide the actions of contracting authorities.

1. INTRODUCTION

Since March 2020, the terms "crisis" and "procurement" have been associated with procuring during the COVID-19 pandemic.[1]

Yet procurement officials regularly encounter different types of crises and emergencies. These might be linked to natural or other disasters, such as earthquakes, cyclones, floods, wars, or even administrative failures caused by bad planning, lack of capacity, or inadequate resource structures.[2]

The process to reform the Classic Directive provides a timely opportunity to reassess the Directive's approach to crises and investigate whether it adequately considers the various risks and interests at stake. Addressing these questions is essential, given that both the extent and frequency of crises are expected to increase in the coming years due to the worsening of climate change and conflictual geopolitical scenarios that threaten global peace and security, and the stability of the global economy and trading system.

Building on this author's previous work and existing literature on procuring during COVID-19, the chapter engages with recent EU initiatives and considers the procurement regulatory instruments available at the EU level to deal with crises. It discusses the risks and trade-offs involved, focusing on some gaps (i.e. regulatory blind spots) that have emerged during and after COVID-19. Finally, it proposes new regulatory approaches to ensure that procurement officials can adequately prepare for, respond to, and reconstruct after crises, leaving no one behind during the process.

---

[1] We are referencing the first edited collection to address procurement during COVID-19, Sue Arrowsmith, Luke Butler, Annamaria La Chimia and Cris Yukins (eds), *Public Procurement Regulation in (a) Crisis?: Global Lessons from the COVID-19 Pandemic* (Bloomsbury 2021); see also Annamaria La Chimia, 'Procuring for COVID-19: Housebound Reflections on a Procurement Earthquake' (2020) 29 *Public Procurement Law Review*.

[2] To respect the editors' guidelines on economy of exposition, this chapter does not deal with administrative crises (those caused by bad planning, budget constraints, or delays within the administration) since these present different characteristics that require ad hoc solutions targeting systemic public management failures.

2. INTERESTS AT STAKE AND REGULATORY BLIND SPOTS

As widely discussed in the literature—including by the present author—during crises, procurement officials face a trade-off between competing interests: acquiring goods and services quickly and minimising risks of fraud and corruption, as well as the potential for procuring inadequate or low-quality goods and services.[3] Some of these risks, as explained by Yukins and Schwarz, are linked to the methods employed to procure during crises, such as direct purchasing, which undermines transparency and competition.[4]

Other risks, such as artificial price inflation and price gouging, also emerge during crises, particularly when multiple countries are involved, which results in a sudden surge in demand for certain essential goods and services, exacerbating the supply security risks associated with lengthy global supply chains.[5] The mentioned risks were evident during COVID-19 and have reemerged amid the energy crises stemming from Russia's unlawful invasion of Ukraine. As the Draghi report highlights, lack of coordination between countries resulted in competing demands for the same goods, leading to "artificially increased price divergence and altered cross-border trading patterns".[6]

Emphasis on coordination has been placed by both the Draghi and Letta Reports. For example, Draghi encourages coordination and a common governance structure in the energy sector,[7] while the Letta Report recommends a 'unified approach to health.'[8]

---

[3] Christopher R Yukins and Joshua Schwartz, 'Katrina's Continuing Impact on Procurement: Emergency Procurement Powers in H.R. 3766' (21 September 2005) 47(35) *Gov't Contractor* par. 397.

[4] Ibid.

[5] Albano and La Chimia, 'Emergency Procurement and Responses to Covid 19: the Case of Italy' in Arrowsmith et al. (eds) (n 1) ch 14, 331–354.

[6] Mario Draghi, *The Future of European Competitiveness: In-depth Analysis and Recommendations: Part B* (Report for the European Commission, 9 September 2024) 39 https://commission.europa.eu/topics/eu-competitiveness/draghi-report_en.

[7] Ibid.

[8] Enrico Letta, *Much More than a Market – Speed, Security, Solidarity: Empowering the Single Market to Deliver a Sustainable Future and Prosperity for All EU Citizens* (Council of the European Union, April 2024) 51 https://www.consilium.europa.eu/media/ny3j24sm/much-more-than-a-market-report-by-enrico-letta.pdf.

Concerns for future crises have accelerated discussions to strengthen and broaden the scope of the EU's strategic autonomy,[9] focusing on how the EU ought to reinforce specific sectors to lessen its dependency on third countries,[10] "reshoring production to Europe" for a more resilient and independent Union, addressing supply chain vulnerabilities.[11] Ad hoc initiatives have been pursued,[12] such as the critical raw materials, Regulation (EU) 2024/1252[13] and the EU Health Security Framework.[14]

Enhanced coordination among member states is also relevant for procurement,[15] and it should be pursued to strengthen preparation for, response to, and post-reconstruction after crises. Notably, with Regulation (EU) 2024/2747 establishing a framework of measures applicable during crises—the Internal Market Emergency and Resilience Act (IMERA)[16]—the Union has embraced greater coordination in times of crisis. Title V is dedicated to public procurement and reinforces the possibilities to coordinate member states' actions, although no obligation to purchase collectively is imposed.

---

9 The scope of EU strategic autonomy "has been widened to virtually all EU policy areas"; see Mario Damen, *EU Strategic Autonomy Monitor: EU Strategic Autonomy 2013–2023: From Concept to Capacity* (European Parliamentary Research Service, July 2022) 1 https://www.europarl.europa.eu/thinktank/en/document/EPRS_BRI(2022)733589.

10 Ibid.

11 Ibid., 3; also see Josep Borrell and Thierry Breton, 'For a United, Resilient and Sovereign Europe' (EEAS, Brussels, 8 June 2020) https://www.eeas.europa.eu/eeas/united-resilient-and-sovereign-europe-thierry-breton_und_en.

12 See European Commission, 'Joint Communication to the European Parliament, the European Council and the Council on "European Economic Security Strategy"' (JOIN (2023) 20 final, 20 June 2023) https://eur-lex.europa.eu/legal-content/EN/TXT/PDF/?uri=CELEX:52023JC0020.

13 Regulation (EU) 2024/1252 of the European Parliament and of the Council of 11 April 2024 establishing a framework for ensuring a secure and sustainable supply of critical raw materials and amending Regulations (EU) No 168/2013, (EU) 2018/858, (EU) 2018/1724 and (EU) 2019/1020 (OJ L, 2024/1252, 3.5.2024.

14 Regulation (EU) 2022/2371 of the European Parliament and of the Council of 23 November 2022 on serious cross-border threats to health and repealing Decision No 1082/2013/EU (OJ L 314, 6.12.2022, p. 26).

15 See Aris Georgopoulos, 'The EU's Joint Procurement Agreement in Light of COVID-19: Learning the Correct Lessons from the Pandemic and Identifying Actions for Improvement' in Arrowsmith et al. (eds) (n 1) ch 6, 176–194.

16 Regulation (EU) 2024/2747 of the European Parliament and of the Council of 9 October 2024 establishing a framework of measures related to an internal market emergency and to the resilience of the internal market and amending Council Regulation (EC) No 2679/98 (Internal Market Emergency and Resilience Act).

Member states can request the Commission to procure on their behalf or in their name (art. 36) and can participate in joint procurement procedures (art. 39). In such cases, an exclusivity clause can be imposed (the article states "shall, where appropriate") (art. 41) that binds member states not to procure the crisis-relevant goods/services through other channels and not to run parallel negotiations. Individual procurement for supplementary goods shall be conducted "in a manner that does not undermine the ongoing procurement" (art. 41). When the internal market emergency mode has been activated (ex. art. 18), individual procurement by the member states needs to be conducted in a collaborative manner and guided by "the spirit of solidarity between Member States" (art. 40). Coordination includes best efforts to inform each other and the Commission about ongoing procedures, share information before launching any new procedures, and consult about the most appropriate manner to procure (art. 40). Time will tell how effective and practically enforceable such measures are. In this author's view, the IMERA alone does not suffice, the principles of coordination and solidarity should be embedded within the Classic Directive itself to consolidate and strengthen the EU's more general approach to crises.

While enhanced crises and disaster risk management coordination beyond the scope of Title V may require a revision of the distribution of competencies between the EU and its member states,[17] it is suggested that regulatory sandboxes could be explored, enabling new approaches for individual procurement to be tested for limited periods and in specific sectors to explore enhanced coordination and new solutions for crises, especially to enhance the capacity of more vulnerable regions to face crises.

Indeed, the COVID-19 crisis has evidenced that crises do not affect countries and individuals in the same way. Structural inequalities within and between countries result in unequal access to essential supplies and services. The lack of resources in deprived regions, including insufficient professionalisation as a key resource for procurement systems, aggravates the effects of crises, denying the most vulnerable access to essential services.[18] The interplay of various factors, such as gender, race, ability, and class also intensifies the detrimental effects of crises.[19] Recent studies have shown that procurement

---

17 See Georgopoulos (n 15).

18 La Chimia (n 1).

19 The risk management literature has demonstrated that crises exacerbate pre-existing inequalities and gender disparities, resulting in increased gender-based violence, biases and inequity. See Elisabeth Ferris, Daniel Petz and Chareen Stark, *The Year of Recurring Disasters: A Review of Natural Disasters in 2012* (Brookings Institution Press 2013) https://www.brookings.edu/wp-content/uploads/2016/06/ND-Review-Chapter-4.pdf; Stéphane Hallegatte, Adrian

can be a valuable tool for addressing inequality risks.[20] This requires conducting gender and human rights impact assessments of purchases to prepare for, respond to, and reconstruct during and after crises,[21] strengthening contractual clauses and imposing due diligence obligations on companies to ensure adequate working conditions and prevent gender-based violence as well as ensuring crises do not lead to the loss of business opportunities for SMEs and women-led businesses.[22]

Disparities in access to public services, especially during crises, necessitate new measures to enhance access to and quality of services of general interest, to avoid, as Letta argues, the single market becoming a source of inequality and poverty.[23] This should be a vital consideration when procuring for crises and may require reconsidering procurement principles and priorities. Letta's Report, for example, advocates for preventing a race to the bottom in social standards; arguably, this approach should also apply to crisis management and procurement rules to prioritise people's needs during and after crises.

Existing EU procurement rules designed to expedite the procurement process in urgent and extremely urgent situations and the newly enacted IMERA fail to incorporate mechanisms to mitigate the negative social, gender, and human rights impacts of crises. This leads to regulatory blind spots that adversely affect more vulnerable individuals. Targeted responses are needed

Vogt-Schilb, Julie Rozenberg and Jérémy Lecocq, 'From Poverty to Disaster and Back: A Review of the Literature' (2020) 4 *Economics of Disasters and Climate Change* 223 https://doi.org/10.1007/s41885-020-00060–5; Ben Brunckhorst, Ruth Hill, Ghazala Mansuri, Trang Nguyen and Miki Doan, 'Climate and Equity: A Framework to Guide Policy Action' (World Bank Poverty and Equity Global Practice 2023) http://documents.worldbank.org/curated/en/099521007052323208.

[20] World Bank, *Gender Responsive Public Procurement in the Caribbean with a Spotlight on Emergency Considerations* (World Bank, March 2024) https://documents1.worldbank.org/curated/en/099041624155026994/pdf/P1722671f7a1170 9d192f81322e1c10506c.pdf.

[21] World Bank, ibid. It is worth pointing out that as emphasisd in the cited World Bank report, this is also in line with the UN approach and broad international consensus necessitating the incorporation of gender considerations into disaster risk management, see the *Hyogo Framework for Action on Disaster Risk Reduction 2005–2015* (UNISDR, 2005); the *Sendai Framework for Disaster Risk Reduction 2015–2030* (UNISDR, 2015); and the *Beijing Agenda for Global Action on Gender-Sensitive Disaster Risk Reduction* (adopted at the International Conference on Gender and Disaster Risk Reduction 2015). See UNISDR, UNDP and IUCN, *How Natural Disasters Affect Women* (IUCN, 2009) https://www.unisdr.org/files/9922_MakingDisasterRiskReductionGenderSe.pdf.

[22] For the gender-related aspects of crises, see extensively World Bank (n 20).

[23] Letta (n 8).

to account for the different impacts of crises based on people's intersectional characteristics. When reforming the Directive, these issues will need to be addressed.

3. CRISES AND THE EU DIRECTIVE 2014/24/EU: SHORTCOMINGS OF THE CURRENT REGULATORY FRAMEWORK AND PROPOSALS FOR REFORM

The existing Directive 2014/24/EU does not provide a specific framework for crises. Contracting authorities can rely on the rules for urgent and extremely urgent situations to respond to crises.[24] Such rules allow a certain degree of flexibility; however, they focus on immediate responses *during* urgent events, neglecting the pre- and post-crisis phases, which are as important as the immediate response.

The absence of a specific regulatory framework for crises calls into question the Directive's suitability to adequately deal with crises and to account for all interests at stake.

3.1 Definition of Crises

Unlike Regulation 2024/2747 and other EU procurement instruments—such as the Defence Procurement Directive[25] and the EU 2024 (recast) Budget Regulation,[26] which define crises in Articles 3, 1(10), and 2(22), respectively—Directive 2014/24/EU fails to define crises. However, the Directive refers to urgency and extreme urgency, which allow, under certain conditions, the use of expedited procedures (see following). Nevertheless, no definitions are provided for urgency or extreme urgency, nor is it extremely clear what differentiates urgent from extremely urgent situations, except for the presence of

---

[24] On the existing framework, see extensively Arrowsmith, 'Recommendations for Urgent Procurement in the EU Directives and GPA: COVID-19 and Beyond' in Arrowsmith et al. (eds) (n 1) ch 3, 63–106.

[25] Directive 2009/81/EC of the European Parliament and of the Council of 13 July 2009 on the coordination of procedures for the award of certain works contracts, supply contracts and service contracts in the fields of defence and security [2009] OJ L 216/76, Art 1(10) https://eur-lex.europa.eu/legal-content/EN/TXT/HTML/?uri=CELEX:32009L0081.

[26] Regulation (EU, Euratom) 2024/2509 of the European Parliament and of the Council of 23 September 2024 on the financial rules applicable to the general budget of the Union (recast) [2024] OJ L 2509, Art 2(22) https://commission.europa.eu/publications/eu-financial-regulation_en.

additional requirements for extreme urgency, such as the foreseeability of the event.[27] This is problematic because, as will be further explained, only in cases of extreme urgency can contracting authorities use more flexible procedures such as the negotiated procedure without publication (art. 32).

While the absence of a definition of crises may be intended to allow discretion for contracting authorities and to allow flexibility to account for events not yet known, this absence may create uncertainties hindering rather than assisting procurement authorities, especially when authorities are unaccustomed or hesitant to exercise discretion.

When examining how crises are defined in other EU procurement instruments and how urgency and extreme urgency have been characterised by recent doctrine, one common approach that emerges is the definition of crises—or urgency—associated with the level and extent of harm.[28]

For example, Article 1(10) of the Defence Directive links crisis to "a *harmful* event 'which clearly *exceeds* the dimensions of harmful events *in everyday life* and *which* substantially *endangers or restricts the life and health* of people, or has a substantial impact on *property values*" (emphasis added). To qualify as a crisis, the degree of harm must exceed that of everyday harmful events, and a causality link is necessary. However, what an everyday harmful event is and how significant the excess of harm should be is not clarified.

Article 3 of the recently enacted 2024/2747 regulation noted previously defines "crisis" as an "exceptional, unexpected and sudden, natural or man-made event of extraordinary nature and scale that takes place within or outside of the Union, that has or may have a severe negative impact on the functioning of the internal market and that disrupts the free movement of goods, services and persons or disrupts the functioning of its supply chains". In our opinion, this definition would not be suitable in the procurement field because it is too restrictive, adding further elements of uncertainty (i.e. the extraordinary nature of the events and the severity of the impact) that would unduly constrain the actions of procurment entities. It should therefore be limited to the exceptional cases of disruption of the internal market for which it is intended.

---

27 Extreme urgency is linked to the possibility of using the procedure in Article 32 of Directive 2014/24/EU; other requirements include non-attribution of the event to the contracting authority, impracticability of expedited procedures and use solely as strictly necessary. As these requirements relate to the use of Article 32 rather than to the definition of extreme urgency per se, they will be dealt with in Section 3.3. See Arrowsmith, 'Reccomandations for Urgent Procuremnt in the EU Directives and GPA: COVID-19 and Beyond' in Arrowsmith et al. (Eds) (n1) ch 3, 63–106.

28 See extensively Arrowsmith (n 27) 66–67.

Within the doctrine, Arrowsmith suggests that urgency requires "consideration of the nature, extent and likelihood of harm"[29] and that "any type of harm may give rise to 'urgency'", but warns that "*the extent and risk* of harm are important" (emphasis added).[30]

In our opinion, however, a definition centred on harm and its extent is problematic as it involves subjective and discretionary decisions that may be affected by limited information and unconscious biases. This is especially the case when a limited number of individuals are disproportionately affected by the event, or when the situation worsens for some individuals due to the intersection of specific characteristics they share. The apparent neutrality of a definition based on harm and the absence of any gender and human rights considerations when defining harm and its extent risks creating negative consequences for vulnerable groups more exposed to crises. These considerations are crucial, particularly given the increasingly strong connections emerging between crises and intersectionality, as recently emphasised by the UN Special Rapporteur on climate change and exemplified by the Klimaseniorinnen case before the ECtHR.[31]

Establishing the causal link between the event and the harm could also be problematic when the situation is complex or new, and its effects, consequences, or the extent of damage are not yet fully understood. Also problematic is whether only the harm caused during the event qualifies as harm that gives rise to a crisis and justifies the use of urgent procedures, or if harm related to the post-crisis/reconstruction phase is also eligible.

Similar considerations can be made regarding another requirement associated with situations of extreme urgency and, by extension, crises—namely, the foreseeability of the event. The Court of Justice of the European Union and national courts are usually very strict in applying this criterion, especially when the foreseeability claimed by contracting authorities is linked to administrative decisions made by other administrations.[32] With catastrophic events

---

[29] See Arrowsmith (n 27), 66.

[30] Ibid., 67.

[31] See Elisa Morgera, Report of the Special Rapporteur on the Promotion and Protection of Human Rights in the Context of Climate Change (UN Doc A/HRC/56/46, 21 June 2024) https://www.ohchr.org/en/documents/thematic-reports/ahrc5646-scene-setting-report-report-special-rapporteur-promotion-and; *Verein KlimaSeniorinnen Schweiz and Others v Switzerland* (Grand Chamber, ECtHR, Application No 53600/20, 9 April 2024) [2024] ECHR 304.

[32] See, for example, Cour Administrative d'Appel Paris, 31 octobre 1995, N° 94PA01442, *SARL Debruyne Ruling 'The Arrival of 141 Families Following the Completion of a Social Housing Project ...[omissis] Cannot be Considered an Unforeseeable Circumstance*; Case C-352/12 Consiglio Nazionale degli Ingegneri

becoming ever more predictable, especially thanks to new technologies, defining the boundaries of this criterion might become ever more difficult, leading to suboptimal solutions.

The questions raised are not just theoretical disagreements with current approaches but questions of justice that require careful consideration, especially in light of the stringent approach taken by the Court of Justice of the European Union and by national courts when deciding on the legitimacy of using fast procedures, such as the negotiated procedure without competition.

In our view, the definition of crises in the procurement context needs to be determined with regard to the ultimate goal of public procurement itself. It should be centred on beneficiaries and outcomes, prioritising the public interest to be fulfilled through the purchase. Hence, any external event that prevents authorities from fulfilling their functions in the interest of citizens should qualify as a crisis and allow deviation from ordinary procurement rules.

In this respect, the definition of procurement given by Edquist and Quinot is helpful. The authors argue that "With the help of the products procured, public organisations intend to achieve a goal or a mission, satisfy human needs, solve a societal or climate problem, etc. The public agencies want to be able to address and meet challenges, i.e. have a function fulfilled. And this is done in the interest of the citizens. In fact, this is a core distinction between public procurement and private acquisition of products. While private acquisition of products is only that, i.e. obtaining the product, public procurement necessarily involves both the acquisition of the product and the public function to be served by the product" (footnote omitted).[33]

Any definition of crises should centre on fulfilling the mission of public authorities, the public function the product/service was meant to serve. When this mission is obstructed by an external event, regardless of its foreseeability and irrespective of any assessment of harm, the crisis procedures should be applicable. This is necessary to quickly respond to crises and avoid restrictive and exclusionary approaches. The proposed interpretation helps overcome the limitations highlighted. Too many times the provision of public services, public works, and public goods has suffered major setbacks because the expedited procurement procedures could not be used for failure to prove one of the requirements linked to the application of faster procedures.[34]

EU:C:2014:202 (affirming the strict interpretation of the unforeseeability and causal-link requirements under Article 32(2)(c) of Directive 2014/24/EU).

[33] Charles Edquist and Ginette Quinot, 'Functional Public Procurement and Innovation' (2005) 1 *Public Procurement Law Review* 40–41.

[34] See SARL Debruyne ruling above (n 32).

Strengthened transparency, auditing, monitoring, and accountability systems—including individual performance reviews that align with organisational outcomes—can then be used to ensure contracting authorities act in accordance with good administration principles and the internal market is not unduly distorted.

While recognising that previous interpretations by other authors are valid if considered in light of the existing law, a *de lege ferenda* perspective that embraces the Commission's and the Council's calls to simplify the existing public procurement framework needs not only to recognise the limitations and constraints of *de lex lata*, but to overcome them with new solutions that put the needs of Contracting Authorities and the beneficiaries of public goods, services, and works at the centre of the procurement framework.

3.2 Territorial Impact of Crises and Solidarity as a Ground Principle

Another gap left by the Directive is linked to the absence of any reference to the geographical impact of crises. The Directive does not distinguish between different geographical types of urgent situations. It does not differentiate between localised, national, or global states of urgency and crises—whether the state of urgency is due to a worldwide or local crisis or affects single or multiple procurement entities. As we have learned during COVID-19, such differences are significant. As explained in Section 2, global crises could significantly impact the capacity of contracting authorities to procure. Lack of coordination can result in price gouging and irrational market distortions.

Collaboration and solidarity between member states are essential for addressing crises that impact multiple regions. This is true not only from an economic and efficiency perspective but also, as Letta argues, because solidarity is a fundamental union principle.[35] Therefore, solidarity should guide the actions of contracting authorities and become a core principle within the reformed Classic Directive.[36] Regulatory sandboxes could be foreseen, at least as experimental measures, where in certain sectors collaboration is mandated at the EU level when crises affect more regions/states .

---

[35] Letta (n 8) 101.

[36] See Georgopoulos (n 15) for the EU approach to collaboration during the COVID-19 pandemic.

3.3 The Directive's Instruments for Speeding the Procurement Process

As Drabkin and Thai argue, legislators traditionally employ deregulatory techniques to address emergencies and crises.[37] These techniques include rules that directly shorten the process duration, such as reduced time limits for tendering or indirectly expedite the procedure by relaxing certain requirements, such as certification requirements.[38]

The EU regulator employs various deregulatory techniques to manage procurement during urgent and extremely urgent situations. As the Commission's COVID-19 Communication outlines, the Directive permits purchasing authorities to "substantially reduce the deadlines to accelerate open or restricted procedures". In extreme urgency cases, such as COVID-19, they may, subject to certain conditions, use the negotiated procedure without publication per Article 32 of Directive 2014/24/EU.[39] However, as extensively discussed in the literature, these procedures carry risks related to reduced transparency, increased potential for corruption, and speculation, which may lead to higher costs.[40]

Article 27, which pertains to the open procedure, allows contracting authorities to shorten the minimum time limit for receiving tenders from 35 days to 15 (from the date the contract notice is sent) when a "state of urgency, duly substantiated by the contracting authority" makes it impossible to adhere to the established time limit.

Article 28(6) foresees similar provisions for the restricted procedure, indicating that "in cases of duly substantiated urgency, the time limit for the receipt of requests to participate can be reduced to no less than 15 days (instead of 30) from the date the contract notice was sent. The time limit for the receipt of tenders can also be reduced to no less than 10 days [instead of 30] from the date the invitation to tender was sent. The state of 'duly substantiated' urgency must make it 'impracticable to adhere to the time limits laid down in this Article.'"

---

37 David Drabkin and Khi V Thai, 'Emergency Contracting in the US Federal Government' (2007) 7(1) *Journal of Public Procurement* 84.

38 La Chimia (n 1).

39 Communication from the Commission, 'Guidance from the European Commission on Using the Public Procurement Framework in the Emergency Situation Related to the COVID-19 Crisis' (2020/C 108 I/01) OJ C 108 I/1 (1 April 2020) art 32.

40 Drabkin and Thai (n 37).

(art. 28.6).[41] This shortened timeframe also applies in case of urgency for the competitive procedure with negotiation (art. 29).

Both articles emphasise that the urgency must be "duly substantiated" but do not specify *how* this should be done in practice. Arguably, any means can be employed. Any event, whether natural or man-made, can lead to a state of urgency; potentially, even events caused by the contracting authority, such as inadequate planning, could justify a state of urgency under Articles 27 and 28.[42] Article 27 further requires a causal link between urgency and the impracticability of the ordinary time limit—indeed, the article uses the term "renders".

As the literature indicates, even if a reduced timeline could help contracting authorities expedite procedures, open and restricted processes are often impractical during crises.[43] As Totis argues, due to the numerous requirements that authorities and suppliers must fulfil, even with a shorter timeframe, the duration for completing such procedures remains lengthy, hindering a prompt response to a crisis.[44] In cases of *extreme* urgency, the Directive allows the use of the negotiated procedure without prior publication. Article 32 states that "*in so far as is strictly necessary* where for reasons of *extreme urgency* brought *about by events unforeseeable by the contracting authority* ... [omissis]. The *circumstances invoked to justify extreme urgency shall not, in any event, be attributable to the* contracting authority." (art. 32.2.c, emphasis added).

Consolidated case law, at both national and European levels, as well as official government guidance and doctrine, have made clear that this procedure can be used in extremely urgent cases only when further conditions are met: 1) the non-foreseeability of the event, 2) the causal link, 3) the event is external and not attributable to the contracting authority, 4) the measures are used only as far as it is strictly necessary, and 5) other procedures are not suitable.[45]

These are essential qualifications of this procedure, intended to limit the regulatory trade-off between acquiring goods swiftly and ensuring transparency, non-discrimination, and equal treatment, which, as explained in other chapters

41 In the circumstances where Arts 27(3) and 28(6) apply—that is, substantiated urgency—other requirements can be derogated, such as those in Arts 53(1)(2) and 53(1)(3).

42 See Arrowsmith (n 27) 67.

43 See Totis Kotsonis, 'EU Procurement Legislation in the Time of COVID-19: Fit for Purpose?' [2020] 4 *Public Procurement Law Review*.

44 Ibid.

45 In this respect, see the Réponse du Gouvernement français à la question écrite no 23726 de Mme Christine Pirès-Beaune (Journal Officiel, Assemblée nationale, Question écrite no 23726, 20 October 2020) 7283, recalling the jurisprudence of the Court in C-275/08.

of this book, are foundational principles within the Directive. However, as it has been explained above in Section 3.1, restrictive intrepretations of some of these requirements have led to less than optimal solutions for the beneficiaries of the public goods, services, and works to be purchased. Hence, these requirements should be considered no longer adequate for procuring for crises. For example, with regard to the unpredictability of events, it is worth remembering that with advancements in new technologies and the exacerbation of climate change, crises are becoming increasingly predictable—or foreseeable—yet they remain beyond the contracting authority's control. When revising the Directive's rules, the EU legislator should consider removing references to the foreseeability of events and instead focus, as suggested prior, on whether the event hampers the authority's capacity to fulfil its tasks.

A restrictive approach may also limit the use of this procedure for prolonged crises or for the post-reconstruction phase when situations might be classified as urgent rather than extremely urgent. In this respect, it is interesting that the Defence Directive follows a different approach and allows the use of the negotiated procedure without publication in "urgent cases linked to a crisis" (art. 28).

One important issue highlighted by the doctrine is whether this procedure allows negotiating with one supplier only (single source) or requires negotiations with more suppliers.[46] As extensively debated in the literature, the Directive is not prescriptive on this point and both mechanisms are allowed.[47] This author agrees with this position and with those that—drawing from the example of countries where a similar system was in place—suggest that reforms of this procedure could include a requirement to conduct negotiations with a small number of suppliers (three to five suppliers).[48] This approach was used in Italy during COVID[49] and, it is submitted, could be beneficial particularly for managing prolonged crises and the post-reconstruction phases. However, crucial issues that have emerged from the Italian experience need to be addressed, such as suppliers' selections for participating in the negotiation. Italy, for instance, applies a rotation principle,[50] yet the usefulness of this

---

[46] Butler L, regulating single source procurement in emergencies, in Arrowsmith et al. (n 1) Chapter 4, and Arrowsmith (n 27) 76–77.

[47] Arrowsmith (n 27).

[48] See for further details Arrowsmith (n 27) 46.

[49] See Gian L Albano and Annamaria La Chimia, 'Emergency Procurement and Responses to COVID-19: The Case of Italy' in Arrowsmith et al. (eds) (n 1) ch 14, 331–354.

[50] See Luca Bertonazzi, 'La rotazione degli affidamenti negli appalti sotto soglia' (2024) 11(2) *Il Foro Amministrativo* 261.

principle and the risks it entails, such as potential collusion between bidders, need careful assessment.

In this author's view, a mini competitive negotiation system should be combined with a European suppliers' rating system for crises, whereby suppliers are rated for their compliance with environmental and labour standards as well as past performance, and only those with a high rating should be invited to participate in the mini competitions. This would help minimise the risk of contracting with rogue suppliers while heping to incorporate environmental and human rights standards in the selection criteria. The interoperability of electronic qualification platforms could facilitate the establishment of the rated system. To avoid undue restriction of competition, the rating could be limited to specific sectors and apply only to procuring for crises. Arguably, a rating system would be better than a normal qualification system because it would allow contracting authorities to sieve through suppliers, facilitating selection by providing an objective system of classification among suppliers (i.e. the rating), while incentivising suppliers to improve their standards and exceed minimum requirements.

For example, Italy introduced a legality rating mechanism with L. 27/2012 whereby companies receive a rating of 1 to 3 stars according to their compliance with legal obligations (legality rating). A similar rating (company rating) linked to companies' past performances and other standards was introduced by the former procurement code (art. 83(10) of Legislative Decree 50/2016, then modified by d.lgs. 19 April 2017, n. 56). In its original design, the rating could be taken into consideration by contracting authorities during the procurement process.[51] However, the system suffered many setbacks due to its limited scope to Italian companies only and was later abandoned. Nonetheless, the idea of rewarding contractors who comply with certain norms has merit and, as this author has argued elsewhere, should be considered at the European level.[52] A common European rating used in targeted sectors for crises would facilitate adherence to high legal standards when procuring for crises, while its uniform application to all European companies would ensure a level playing field for EU companies, i.e. it would not disadvantage companies from one member state vis-à-vis other EU countries. At the same time, if its application was limited to specific sectors and in situations of crises there would be limited

---

[51] Consiglio di Stato (Commissione speciale), Parere No 782 (30 March 2017) 67 https://www.giustizia-amministrativa.it.

[52] See Annamaria La Chimia, 'Development Aid Procurement & the UNGPs on Business & Human Rights: Challenges and Opportunities to Move Towards "The New Frontier of Buying Justice"' in Sope Williams-Elegbe and Geo Quinot (eds) *Public Procurement Regulation for the 21st Century Africa* (Juta & Co, 2018) 31–78.

disruption to competition, proportionate to the need to provide faster selection of suppliers, protecting contracting authorities against rough and unethical suppliers and guaranteeing respect of high environmental and human rights standards.

Finally, this author agrees with those suggesting that enhanced transparency mechanisms should be foreseen in the form of compulsory ex-ante notifications and fuller disclosure of ex-post information.[53] The enhanced transparency would facilitate monitoring and accountability as well as the identification of weaknesses within public administrations that would benefit from further ad hoc training.

3.4 Temporal Element: Pre, During, and Post Crises

In the Directive, the terms urgency and extreme urgency are frequently linked to the adverb "when" or "immediately" (see para 80 of the preamble), creating the impression that the Directive focuses solely on procurement during urgent or extremely urgent situations. The Directive overlooks the pre- and post-crisis phases, despite these being crucial for effective crisis management and should hold significance from a procurement perspective.[54]

While the procurement literature has emphasised the importance of using instruments like frameworks and dynamic purchasing systems to prepare for crises,[55] it has generally overlooked post-crisis management. Yet flexible procedures and tailored solutions may also be as crucial to quickly meet the needs of the affected population. However, as explained in the previous section, it is questionable whether the Directive procedures for extremely urgent situations can be used during the reconstruction phase when demonstrating urgency and extreme urgency might be more difficult. This also seems to be confirmed by the consolidated case-law of the Court of Justice of the EU (EUCJ), which has found against the renewal of contracts beyond the immediate emergency.[56]

---

[53] Arrowsmith (n 27) 90–92.

[54] See World Bank (n 20), which emphasises that effective crisis procurement requires both robust pre-crisis preparedness (risk and capacity assessments, supplier pre-qualification) and dedicated post-crisis recovery planning (impact reviews, lessons-learned exercises).

[55] Schwartz, 'Katrina's Lessons for Ongoing UK Procurement Reform Efforts' (2006) 6 *Public Procurement Law Review* 2006 362–363. See also Arrowsmith (n 27).

[56] See Order of 27 September 1988, *Commission v Italy* (Case 194/88 R) EU:C:1988:462, para 17 (holding that contracts cannot be renewed beyond the period originally foreseen by the contracting authority); *Commission v Germany* (Case C-318/94) EU:C:1996:149, para 18 (refusing to allow renewal where the need

3.5 Other Regulatory Instruments

The literature highlights alternative procurement instruments for addressing emergencies and crises. As Schwartz contends, authorities should prioritise "preparedness" and facilitate the use of procurement instruments, such as frameworks, that enable them to anticipate key procurement steps such as selection, specification, and contract terms.[57] Others, have clarified that procurement instruments like frameworks, dynamic purchasing systems, e-marketplaces, and qualification lists are extremely beneficial during such crises, providing practical alternatives to negotiated procedures without publication for crisis management.[58]

These instruments are also foreseen within the Directive and have proved vital during the first phase of the response to COVID-19.[59] Some authors have indicated specific changes that should be introduced to several of these procedures to ensure they are used more efficiently during crises. For example, Arrowsmith suggests that frameworks should be reformed to allow entities not initially included in a framework to participate.[60] This is undoubtedly a sound recommendation that, in this author's view, should be endorsed and extended to allow entities from other countries to benefit from existing frameworks when crises are global or affect more than one member state. Other useful suggestions made in the doctrine also include the shortening of the timeframe for bidding within the Dynamic Purchasing Systems (DPS).[61] Expanding the use of e-marketplaces for off-the-shelf products should be encouraged as this could enable fast purchases without compromising strategic procurement objectives, such as sustainability and transparency.[62]

---

had been anticipated and the contracting authority had delayed); and Opinion of 2 June 2005, *Commission v Italy* (Case C-525/03) EU:C:2005:343, para 67 (finding inadmissible a challenge to expired emergency legislation permitting renewed procurements).

57 Schwartz (n 55).

58 Steven Kelman, *Procurement and Public Management: The Fear of Discretion and the Quality of Government Performance* (AEI Press 1990).

59 Gian L Albano, 'Homo Homini Lupus: On the Consequences of Buyers' Miscoordination in Emergency Procurement for the COVID-19 Crisis in Italy' (2020) 29 *Public Procurement Law Review* 161.

60 Arrowsmith (n 27) 69–70.

61 See Arrowsmith (n 27) 66–71.

62 In general on e-marketplaces, see Desiree Klingler, 'Amazon.gov: Benefits and Risks of E-Marketplaces in Public Procurement' (seminar presentation, eProcurement for Domestic and Cross-Border Trade: Experience of GPA Parties from Transition Economies, EBRD/WTO, 25 March 2025) https://lawreform.glueup.com/event/137596/#home.

Finally, other rules that might indirectly speed up procuring should be considered: for example, exemption from bid guarantees or payments before delivery. During COVID-19, EU member states adopted different approaches to these rules, often competing by lowering the standards that suppliers had to meet when delivering goods.[63] Currently, no common approach is envisaged on some of the "deregulatory norms" that might indirectly speed up the procurement process. In this author's opinion, a common and unified approach would be beneficial not only to avoid member states competing against each other but also to ensure that whenever goods are bought within the EU, these are safe and, in case of crises, can be used by other authorities.

Finally, rules should be established to strengthen contract monitoring during the execution phase—including enhanced transparency and data sharing—allowing for speedy contract termination when labour, environmental, or other law violations are detected.

4. CONCLUSIONS

The global economy is facing an "unprecedented polycrisis"[64] driven by climate change and geopolitical turmoil. In this context, it is crucial for the Directive to provide a specific framework for procurement for crises that better accounts for the pre, during, and post-crisis phases and facilitates the use of more flexible purchasing procedures, which should be exempted from farraginous requirements. Procurement officials should receive ad hoc training to implement such a framework which, together with stronger capacity performance and monitoring mechanisms, enhanced transparency, and accountability, would help minimise risks of corruption and fraud.

The existing regulatory framework risks overshadowing critical interests, such as human rights, social considerations, and gender implications of purchasing for crises. Reforms should include an obligation to conduct HR and gender impact assessments of the purchase as soon as it is practicable. The information acquired can then be used to address existing risks and inform future practice. Procurment for crises needs to put the individual at the centre, prioritising the delivery of public goods, services, and works for the beneficiary. Most authors agree that enhancing data collection and transparency could help mitigate some risks associated with purchasing during crises. This author supports this position but further recommends data should include information

63 See La Chimia PPLR (n 1).

64 WTO, 'DDG Ellard Addresses the Role of Multilateralism in a World of Polycrisis' *WTO News* (Geneva, 24 June 2022) https://www.wto.org/english/news_e/news22_e/ddg_ellard_24jun22_e.htm.

on gender and human impact of crises and be gender-disaggregated, covering primary contractors as well as subcontractors, down to the supply chain.

The temporal and spacial dimensions of crises should gain new relevance. When crises affect multiple member states or the entire EU, coordination must be ensured at the EU level beyond the existing internal market emergency framework.[65] This is essential, considering the likelihood of crises becoming increasingly global in the coming years.

65 As argued by Georgopoulos this might require a revision of the division of competences between EU and Member states. See Georgopoulos (n 15).

PART IV

Expanding the rules on contract performance

17. Modification of directives and contract modifications

Article 72 of Directive 2014/24/EU revisited

Piotr Bogdanowicz

REFORM PROPOSALS

- [New section in Article 72] distinguishing the notions of the overall nature of the contract and the substantial modification and defining the former.
- [Change in Article 72(1)] extending the obligation to publish a notice in the *Official Journal of the European Union* to at least some substantial modifications provided for in a review clause (Article 72(1)(a)) and the replacement of the economic operator (Article 72(1)(d)).
- [Change in Article 72(1)] providing sanctions for failure to publish a notice in the *Official Journal of the European Union.*
- [Change in Article 72(1)(d)] clarifying the grounds for the replacement of the economic operator.
- [Change in Article 72(4)] merging the first two sentences of Article 72(4).
- [Change in Article 72(4)] providing an exhaustive list of substantial modifications.
- [Change in Article 72(4)] clarifying the grounds for substantial modifications.

1. CONTEXT AND RELEVANCE

The modification (change) of a contract was regulated for the first time in the history of European Union public procurement law in directives adopted in 2014.[1] Regulation was no surprise[2] as it sought to codify the Court of Justice of the European Union ("Court" or "CJEU") case-law on the topic,[3] which had in many instances been inconsistent, too rigid, and at times even self-contradictory.[4]

The result was "a new and elaborate provision" in Article 72 of Directive 2014/24/EU.[5] The overall assessment of the regulation of contract modification in Directive 2014/24/EU should in my view be positive. As noted by Caranta and Halonen, in many ways the provision in question clarified the legal regime on contract modifications and, to some extent, made them more flexible than before.[6] Also, the structure of the provision, setting forth situations when a modification is permissible, including a substantial one, if only conditions specified in Article 72(1) and (2) are met, seems right.

This does not mean that the provision does not have any weaknesses. The main downsides are as follows:

---

1 See Directive 2014/23/EU of the European Parliament and of the Council of 26 February 2014 on the award of concession contracts (OJ 2014 L 94/1); Directive 2014/24/EC of the European Parliament and of the Council of 26 February 2014 on public procurement and repealing Directive 2004/18/EC (OJ 2014 L 94/65) as well as Directive 2014/25/EC of the European Parliament and of the Council of 26 February 2014 on procurement by entities operating in the water, energy, transport and postal service sectors and repealing Directive 2004/17/EC (OJ 2014 L 94/243). In this chapter, I focus on Directive 2014/24/EU, unless otherwise explicitly stated. In any case, Directive 2014/23/EU, Directive 2014/24/EU and Directive 2014/25/EU are hereinafter referred to as "Public Procurement Directives".

2 Kirsi-Maria Halonen, 'Fundamentals of Contract Modifications in EU Procurement Law' in Dacian C. Dragos, Kirsi-Maria Halonen, Bogdana Neamtu, Steen Treumer (eds), *Contract Changes. The Dark Side of EU Procurement Law* (Edward Elgar Publishing 2023) 18.

3 See recital 107 of Directive 2014/24/EU: "It is necessary to clarify the conditions under which modifications to a contract during its performance require a new procurement procedure, taking into account the relevant case-law of the Court of Justice of the European Union."

4 See Piotr Bogdanowicz, *Contract Modifications in EU Procurement Law* (Edward Elgar Publishing 2021) 29–74.

5 Steen Treumer, 'Into the Grey Area: Implementation of the Public Procurement Directive in Denmark' in Steen Treumer, Mario Comba (eds), *Modernising Public Procurement. The Approach of EU Member States* (Edward Elgar Publishing 2021) 27.

6 Roberto Caranta, Kirsi-Maria Halonen, 'Foreword' in Dacian C. Dragos, Kirsi-Maria Halonen, Bogdana Neamtu, Steen Treumer (eds), *Contract Changes. The Dark Side of EU Procurement Law* (Edward Elgar Publishing 2023) xi. Similarly, Tobias Indén in Michael Steinicke, Peter L. Vesterdorf (eds), *Brussels Commentary on EU Public Procurement Law* (Nomos 2018) 766.

i. the unclear notion of the overall nature of the contract, which applies to modifications provided for in review clauses (Article 72(1)(a)), modifications due to unforeseen circumstances (Article 72(1)(c)) and modifications *de minimis* (Article 72(2));
ii. limiting the information obligations (publishing a notice in the *Official Journal of the European Union*) to modifications for works, services or supplies (Article 72(1)(b)) and modifications due to unforeseen circumstances only and no negative consequences associated with non-publications;
iii. insufficiently clear concept of the substantial modification (Article 72(4)); and
iv. certain ambiguities concerning the situation of the replacement of the economic operator.

Below I will point out why and how potential reforms can take place.

2. REFORM PROPOSALS FOR ARTICLE 72 OF DIRECTIVE 2014/24/EU

2.1 Unclear Notion of the Overall Nature of the Contract

It may be considered quite surprising that the notion of the overall nature of the contract has not, in principle, been set out in more detail in the Directive. It is only in the recitals that the EU legislator indicated, while discussing contract modifications due to unforeseen circumstances, that alteration of the nature of the overall procurement may consist, for example, in "replacing the works, supplies or services to be procured by something different or by fundamentally changing the type of procurement since, in such a situation, a hypothetical influence on the outcome may be assumed".[7]

Consequently, as noted by Halonen, the concept of the overall nature of the contract has puzzled practitioners and academics alike.[8] Advocate General Rantos pointed out in this context that the wording of Article 72 of Directive 2014/24/EU is not "a model of clarity in that regard".[9] Indeed, the notion gives rise to significant doubts and the said recital does not dispel them at all.[10] For

7 Recital 109.

8 Halonen (fn 2), 23.

9 Opinion delivered on 30 April 2025 in Case C-282/24 *Polismyndigheten*, ECLI:EU:C:2025:305, para. 20.

10 Leaving aside the discussion of whether this should not take place in the body of Directive 2014/24/EU rather than in a recital which creates the situation of *provisions in disguise*, as once called by Treumer and Comba (Steen Treumer, Mario Comba, 'Introduction' in Steen Treumer, Mario Comba (eds), *Modernising Public*

instance, there is a discussion in legal literature whether the mere increase or decrease in the amount of works, supplies or services acquired could result in alteration of the overall nature of the contract. Given the wording of Article 72(1)(a), which allows for modifications "irrespective of their monetary value", or Articles 72(1)(c) and 72(2), according to which pure change in price could not be considered as such as long as it does not exceed thresholds set forth therein, it is unlikely that this is the case. However, Arrowsmith seems not to exclude such a possibility.[11] Similarly, Kotsonis provides that consecutive, significant price amendments could be considered to change the overall nature of the contract.[12] Another issue is the relationship between the alteration of the overall nature of the contract and the substantial modification of the contract. Semple aptly notes that changes altering the overall nature of the contract go beyond substantial changes, which may be justified in certain circumstances.[13] Basically, these two notions apply in different contexts and do not overlap. Whilst each alteration of the overall nature of the contract will probably constitute a substantial modification, it won't be like that the other way around. Nonetheless, there are views that the notion of "overall nature" refers to the economic balance and the essential terms of the contract,[14] which may

---

Procurement. The Approach of EU Member States (Edward Elgar Publishing 2021) 3).

[11] Sue Arrowsmith, *The Law of Public and Utilities Procurement: Regulation in the EU and UK. Volume 1* (Sweet & Maxwell 2014) 600.

[12] Totis Kotsonis, 'EU Procurement Legislation in the Time of COVID-19: Fit for Purpose?' (2020) 4 *Public Procurement Law Review* 199, 207.

[13] Abby Semple, *A Practical Guide to Public Procurement* (Oxford University Press 2014) 140. This is seconded by Halonen (fn 2). See also the opinion of Advocate General Rantos, who considers, by way of example, that the broader concept of "substantial modifications" includes, in principle, significant modifications to the price, duration or subject matter of a contract, whereas the narrower concept of "alterations of the overall nature" of a contract includes modifications that more profoundly affect the very essence of the contract (for example, adding the supply of goods to a service contract or changing the place of supply) (para 23) (fn 9).

[14] Vincent P. Wangelow, 'EU Public Procurement Law: Amendments of Public Works Contracts After the Award Due to Additional Works and Unforeseeable Circumstances' (2020) 2 *European Procurement & Public Private Partnership Law Review* 107, 110. See also François Lichère, Valentin Lamy, 'Contract changes in France' in Dacian C. Dragos, Kirsi-Maria Halonen, Bogdana Neamtu, Steen Treumer (eds), *Contract Changes. The Dark Side of EU Procurement Law* (Edward Elgar Publishing 2023) 153, who note that it is difficult to differentiate the overall nature of the contract from a substantial modification of the contract.

bring to mind substantial modifications.[15] What is more, in Case C-282/24 *Polismyndigheten*, the Commission submitted before the CJEU that the two concepts are the same.[16]

As we know, the CJEU did not follow the Commission's position and held in the judgment that "the concept of an alteration of the overall nature of a framework agreement is distinct from that of a substantial modification thereto and that the former concept covers only the most significant substantial modifications which entail a fundamental change in the subject matter of the framework agreement or in the type of framework agreement concerned or a fundamental change in its balance, with the result that they may be regarded as being of such a kind that they result in the transformation of the framework agreement in its entirety" (para. 41).

Following the judgment, the abovementioned lack of clarity should be removed from Directive 2014/24/EU, and the notion of the overall nature of the contract should be clarified in Article 72. The current provision leaves too wide a discretion for contracting authorities and, consequently, too much uncertainty for economic operators. This could be fixed by adding a new section in Article 72 which would say that the requirement of not changing the overall nature of the contract referred to in Article 72(1)(a), Article 72(1)(c) and Article 72(2) is applied without prejudice to Article 72(4), that is, substantial modification of the contract,[17] and refers to: [18]

i. a fundamental change in the type of the contract (such as replacing the type of the contract by a different one, e.g. a service into a works contract or a concession contract into a public contract);

---

15 Actually, in France the words "materially different in character", which can be found in the first sentence of Article 72(4), dealing with substantial modifications, have been transposed to "a change in the overall nature of the contract". See the apt criticism from Francois Lichère, 'Transposition of the Public Procurement Directive in France: Between Overimplementation and Questionable Implementation' in Steen Treumer, Mario Comba (eds), *Modernising Public Procurement. The Approach of EU Member States* (Edward Elgar Publishing 2021) 107.

16 Case C-282/24 *Polismyndigheten* (fn 9), para 18.

17 This clarification is necessary in order to dispel the abovementioned doubts about the relationship between the notions of the alteration of the overall nature of the contract and the substantial modification.

18 Although creating an exhaustive list of such alterations may not be an easy task, it is assumed that the notion of the overall nature of the contract is limited to the most significant substantial modifications and, as such, it should be defined. See also the opinion of Advocate General Rantos (fn 9), para 29.

ii. a fundamental change in the subject matter of the contract (such as replacing the procured works, supplies or services with other works, supplies or services, not related to the original subject matter of the contract);
iii. a fundamental change in the duration of the contract (such as replacing a fixed-term contract with a contract without a fixed term);[19] or
iv. a fundamental change in balance of the contract.

2.2 Limited Information Obligations

The issue with the lack of transparency of contract modifications was addressed by Treumer in 2012, that is, before Directive 2014/24/EU was adopted and we only knew the Commission's draft thereof. He aptly noted that competitors will typically not know of a breach of the duty to retender as it is difficult or perhaps impossible to obtain exact insight into the details of the original contract and the subsequent changes, which will discourage most competitors from complaining.[20]

From this perspective, expanding the duty of transparency by Directive 2014/24 to at least some contract modifications was a right direction. In accordance with Article 72(1), contracting authorities that have modified a contract in the cases set out under points (b) and (c) (i.e., for additional works, services or supplies and due to unforeseen events, respectively) shall publish a notice to that effect in the *Official Journal of the European Union*. Such notice shall contain the information set out in Annex V part G and shall be published in accordance with Article 51. However, it is not clear why the EU lawmaker has chosen to limit the information obligations only to these two cases of contract modification.[21] In particular, it is surprising that the contracting authority is not required to publish a notice of any modification provided for in a review clause. Such an obligation would make it possible for competent authorities or other economic operators to verify whether the relevant modification has

---

[19] This will not be relevant for concession contracts which by definition are fixed-term contracts. See the first sentence of Article 18(1) of Directive 2014/23/EU: "The duration of concessions shall be limited."

[20] Steen Treumer, 'Regulation of Contract Changes Leading to a Duty to Retender the Contract: The European Commission's Proposals of December 2011' (2012) 5 *Public Procurement Law Review* 153, 153.

[21] Even if some authors point out that regulation alone is not enough and it is necessary to promote the ethics of the "good contracting authority"; see Francisco Javier Vázquez Matilla, 'The Modification of Public Contracts: An Obstacle to Transparency and Efficiency' in Gabriella M. Racca, Christopher R. Yukins (eds), *Integrity and Efficiency in Sustainable Public Contracts Balancing Corruption Concerns in Public Procurement Internationally* (Bruylant 2014), 296.

been provided for in the contract in a clear, precise and unequivocal manner and thus whether it is consistent with the contract and does not alter its overall nature. Similarly, the replacement of the economic operator should be publicised.[22] The absence of such information may effectively prevent any challenging of modification as unlawful.[23] This is particularly important given that the number of judgments regarding the interpretation of relevant provisions of Public Procurement Directives adopted in 2014 is still relatively low.[24] Greater transparency could change it.[25]

It is submitted though that the provisions of Directive 2014/24/EU on publishing contract modification notices seem not that effective for increasing transparency as there are no negative consequences associated with non-publication.[26] This may lead to situations where contracting authorities avoid publishing contract modification notices. In fact, they do not have any incentive to do so. As noted by Halonen, from a contracting authority's perspective, publishing contract modification notices can even be risky as such notices flag the potentially problematic and unlawful modifications to the public and render the contract vulnerable to legal disputes and claims for ineffectiveness.[27]

---

22 See also Dacian C. Dragos, Bogdana Neamtu, 'Introduction: Why the Dark Side of Procurement' in Dacian C. Dragos, Kirsi-Maria Halonen, Bogdana Neamtu, Steen Treumer (eds), *Contract Changes. The Dark Side of EU Procurement Law* (Edward Elgar Publishing 2023) 12–13 who opt for "wider transparency during contract execution [...] in order to ensure the effectiveness of EU law".

23 Access to information about a contract, including its modifications, is a necessary prerequisite for the right to an effective remedy, in line with Article 47 of the Charter of Fundamental Rights of the European Union. Carri Ginter, Nele Parrest, Mari Ann Simovart, 'Access to the Content of Public Procurement Contracts: The Case for a General EU-law Duty of Disclosure' (2013) 4 *Public Procurement Law Review* 156, 160.

24 There are the following judgments of the Court: of 26 March 2020, *HUNGEOD* (C-496/18 and C-497/18); of 14 May 2020, *T-Systems Magyarország* (C-263/19); of 2 September 2021, *Sisal* (C-721/19 and C-722/19); of 3 February 2022, *Advania Sverige and Kammarkollegiet* (C-461/20); of 7 December 2023, *Obshtina Razgrad and Obshtina Balchik* (C-441/22 and C-443/22); of 7 November 2024, *Adusbef* (C-683/22); of 20 March 2025 (Joined Cases C-728/22 to C-730/22); of 20 March 2025, *Anib and Play Game* (C-728/22 to C-730/22); of 29 April 2025 (C-452/23, *Tesla and Fastned Deutschland*); and of 16 October 2025, *Polismyndigheten* (C-282/24).

25 In some Member States, such as Portugal, the information obligations relate to all cases of contract modifications. The author thanks Miguel Assis Raimundo for providing this information.

26 Dragos, Neamtu (fn 22) 13.

27 Halonen (fn 2) 30.

There are several possible solutions to this problem. One of them could be mandatory publication of a VEAT (voluntary ex ante transparency) notice – before making a change, the contracting authority could publish such a notice, which would not only enhance transparency, but also, in the absence of a challenge to the intended change, give the contracting parties more certainty about compliance with EU law. This would be a big change, given that under current rules contracting authorities shall publish notices concerning made contract modifications only.[28] However, it seems that such a solution could go too far and would unnecessarily make the entire contract modification process more formal. Another approach could therefore be to remain with the current status quo (publication of the modification made) but to indicate that in the absence of publication, a modification is ineffective (i.e., by its very absence, regardless of whether the change met the conditions provided for in Article 72). Parties to the contract should have the right to justify the modification on one of the grounds set forth in Article 72. Consequently, the best way forward could be to impose fines in case of non-publication. Such solutions already exist in some Member States (Italy, Austria).[29]

To sum up, Article 72(1) and the obligation to publish a notice in the *Official Journal of the European Union* should be changed to cover at least some substantial modifications provided for in a review clause (such as an increase in remuneration, a change in the duration of the contract or the deadline for performance of the works, etc.) and the replacement of the economic operator on a basis of Article 72(1)(d). At the same time, failure to publish a notice in the *Official Journal of the European Union* should be associated with certain sanctions.

2.3 Insufficiently Clear Concept of the Substantial Modification

The first sentence of Article 72(4) of Directive 2014/24 provides that, "[a] modification of a contract or a framework agreement during its term shall be considered to be substantial within the meaning of point (e) of paragraph 1,

---

28 See judgment of 7 November 2024, *Adusbef* (C-683/22): "modification notice must be published after the planned modification, not before. The wording of the second subparagraph of Article 43(1) of the directive unequivocally refers to the contracting authorities 'having modified' a concession during its term." (para. 68).

29 See B. Biancardi, R. Caranta, P. Patrito, 'Contract Changes in Italy' in Dacian C. Dragos, Kirsi-Maria Halonen, Bogdana Neamtu, Steen Treumer (eds), *Contract Changes. The Dark Side of EU Procurement Law* (Edward Elgar Publishing 2023) 191–192; and in the same book, Christoph Krönke, Valentina Neubauer, 'Contract Changes in Germany and Austria' 175.

where it renders the contract or the framework agreement materially different in character from the one initially concluded." The reference to point 1(e) in point 4 is not the most fortunate, since Article 72(1)(e) in turn refers to ... Article 72(4).[30] But the main issue with Article 72(4) is that it is not clear when a modification should be deemed material. The second sentence of Article 72(4) points out that a modification shall be considered substantial if one or more of the conditions are met: hypothetical change in the terms and conditions of the procedure, modification of the economic balance in favour of the economic operator, considerable extension of the scope of the contract and impermissible replacement of the economic operator. Doubts may arise as to whether the second sentence of Article 72(4) and situations specified therein should be read in isolation from the first sentence of Article 72(4), or in conjunction with it, and whether these conditions in the second sentence create an exhaustive list of substantial modifications. These doubts are fuelled by the analysis of the outcome of the implementation of Article 72 into national legal orders which shows that the Member States have adopted different approaches in this respect.[31]

In my opinion, situations specified in the second sentence of Article 72(4) in principle at least exemplify the material change described in the first sentence of that article; however, this should be clarified. This could be done by greatly simplifying the wording of the provision, for example by saying that "a modification of a contract or a framework agreement during its term shall be considered to be substantial, where it renders the contract or the framework agreement materially different in character from the one initially concluded, including where one or more of the following conditions is met […]."[32]

---

[30] In accordance with Article 72(1)(e), contracts and framework agreements may be modified without a new procurement procedure in accordance with this Directive where the modifications, irrespective of their value, are not substantial within the meaning of paragraph 4.

[31] Steen Treumer, Mario Comba (ed), *Modernising Public Procurement. The Approach od EU Member States* (Edward Elgar Publishing 2021). For instance, in some Member States, the list of criteria for the assessment of whether a change is to be considered substantial is non-exhaustive (e.g. Denmark, Italy, Sweden), whilst in others the list is considered just a definition of substantial modification (e.g. Finland).

[32] This would be in line with the views already presented by the Court. See, for example, judgment of 2 September 2021, *Sisal* (C-721/19 and C-722/19) providing that "[Article 43(4) of the Directive 2014/23 being an equivalent of Article 72(4)] lays down a general rule according to which a modification of a concession contract during its term is to be considered to be substantial where it renders the concession materially different in character from the one initially concluded. That

Thus, on this occasion, it is proposed to create an exhaustive list of substantial modifications.

Notwithstanding this, some specific changes to Article 72(4)(a) and (c) should be considered.

As far as Article 72(4)(a) is concerned, its wording has already been criticised in literature as too hypothetical.[33] Pursuant to this provision, "without prejudice to paragraphs 1 and 2, a modification shall be considered to be substantial where the modification introduces conditions which, had they been part of the initial procurement procedure, would have allowed for the admission of other candidates than those initially selected or for the acceptance of a tender other than that originally accepted or would have attracted additional participants in the procurement procedure." In my view, an attempt to somehow "objectify" conditions included in this provision should be made. As one of the potential options, it could require the potential contractor to demonstrate that the modification made affected it in some way, for example that the subject matter of the contract has changed and the contractor is carrying out a business activity that is covered by the modified subject matter of the contract or has already participated in other public procurement procedures of this type. In other words, it could be demonstrated that the interest of a given contractor in participating in the public procurement procedure would be more concrete and real. It does not necessarily mean that it would have to be required to prove that a given economic operator would actually participate in that new award procedure. However, it is submitted that the mere existence of such a possibility should not be sufficient in that respect.[34] Otherwise, each time there could be a potential economic operator claiming that if the operator had known about the change at the stage of the procurement procedure, the operator would have participated in the procedure or would have submitted a more favourable bid. The occurrence of such a situation would be incompatible with the principle of legal certainty, which is one of the general principles of European Union law, including EU public procurement law,[35] and which must be respected by contracting authorities. As a result, the contracting authority cannot consider

provision further specifies that, 'in any event', a modification is to be considered to be substantial, inter alia, where [...]."

[33] For discussion see Bogdanowicz (fn 4) 113–114.

[34] See, to that effect, judgment of 5 September 2019, *Lombardi* (C-333/18), para. 29 and judgment of 2 September 2021, *Sisal* (C-721/19 and C-722/19), para. 63.

[35] S. de Mars, 'General Principles in EU Public Procurement Law' in Katja S. Ziegler, Robert Jennings, Päivi J. Neuvonen, Violeta Moreno-Lax (eds), *Research Handbook on General Principles in EU Law. Constructing Legal Orders in Europe* (Edward Elgar Publishing 2023) 462–479.

a given modification as substantial just because it cannot be ruled out that another economic operator would have participated in the public procurement procedure or another bid would have been submitted.

In any case, a premise that "the modification introduces conditions which, had they been part of the initial procurement procedure [...] would have attracted additional participants in the procurement procedure" should be removed. This expression is far too broad and indefinite.

Pursuant to Article 72(4)(c), "a modification shall be considered to be substantial where [...] [it] extends the scope of the contract or framework agreement considerably." There is a lot of ambiguity in this provision. First of all, is there a considerable extension of the scope of the contract which at the same time does not fulfil the condition referred to in Article 72(4)(a)? Second, why shall a modification not be considered to be substantial where it *reduces* the scope of the contract or framework agreement considerably?[36] Finally, one should consider whether it is correct that one general clause (*considerably*) interprets another (*substantial*)?

One could also consider whether conditions set forth in Article 72(4)(b) and Article 72(4)(c) are not in fact the exemplifications of the condition specified in Article 72(4)(a). In fact, the modification of the economic balance in favour of the economic operator or the considerable extension or reduction of the scope of the contract, had they been part of the initial procurement procedure, could have allowed for the admission of other candidates than those initially selected or for the acceptance of a tender other than that originally accepted.

All this could be revised with a reform of Public Procurement Directives. Article 72(4)(a) could read as follows:

> the modification introduces conditions which, had they been part of the initial procurement procedure, would have allowed for the admission of other candidates than those initially selected or for the acceptance of a tender other than that originally accepted, which can be demonstrated by appropriate means, including but not limited to the situations where the modification changes the economic balance of the contract or the framework agreement in favour of the contractor or where the modification alters the scope of the contract or framework agreement considerably.

2.4 Replacement of the Economic Operator

Article 72(1)(d) defines three situations where contracts and framework agreements may be modified without a new procurement procedure: first, where the

[36] In particular that the Court has already held that a modification involving a significant reduction in the scope of a contract might be substantial. See judgment of 7 September 2016, *Finn Frogne* (C-549/14), EU:C:2016:634, para 28.

replacement of the economic operator is provided for by a review clause or an option; second, when it occurs following restructuring and third, in connection with the contracting authority assuming the main contractor's obligations towards its subcontractors. At least two of these three situations should be reviewed on the occasion of the reform of Public Procurement Directives.

2.4.1 Replacement through a review clause

The literal wording of Article 72(1)(d)(i) suggests that a given economic operator may be changed through a review clause, as a result of which a contract shall be performed by a new entity that does not satisfy the originally established criteria for qualitative selection of contractors. This is because, contrary to Article 72(1)(d)(ii), the provision in question does not require from the new economic operator the fulfilment of the criteria for qualitative selection initially established. The reasons for such difference seem to be completely unclear. One may even argue that the change of economic operator through a review clause, whereby a contract would be fully performed by a contractor that does not meet the initial criteria for qualitative selection, may be considered as a manifestation of unequal and discriminatory treatment of economic operators who participated in a public procurement procedure, met the initial criteria for qualifying, but were not selected. Such a possibility should be excluded.

2.4.2 Replacement following restructuring

Pursuant to Article 72(1)(d)(ii), contracts and framework agreements may be modified without a new procurement procedure where a new contractor replaces the one to which the contracting authority had initially awarded the contract as a consequence of "universal or partial succession into the position of the initial contractor, following corporate restructuring, including takeover, merger, acquisition or insolvency, of another economic operator that fulfils the criteria for qualitative selection initially established". Although Directive 2014/24/EU does not define the notion of "restructuring", it enumerates four cases thereof: takeover, merger, acquisition and insolvency. It should be noted that under national law such cases can evolve into further forms. As a result, a merger can occur, for example, through "merger by acquisition" or "merger by formation of a new company".[37] In any case, the restructuring should lead to a universal or partial succession into the initial economic operator's position. This is where the problems with this provision begin. Neither "universal" nor "partial" succession has been defined in Article 72(1)(d)(ii). In both cases,

[37] See Directive (EU) 2017/1132 of the European Parliament and of the Council of 14 June 2017 relating to certain aspects of company law. OJ L 169, 46–127.

however, this is succession under a general title, based on a single legal event. This distinguishes universal (or partial) succession from singular succession, that is, a succession under a special title, involving the acquisition of an individually designated right or rights. Contrary to that, Article 72(1)(d)(ii) seems to recognise singular succession as a basis for the replacement of an economic operator (i.e., in case of "insolvency" or "acquisition"). At least under Polish law, neither the former nor the latter leads to universal or partial succession into the initial economic operator's position. Although a functional interpretation of Article 72(1)(d)(ii) could be taken in order to explain this contradiction,[38] it seems that the wording of the provision in question should be just clarified. On this occasion, it could also be clarified, with reference to the whole of Article 72(1)(d), that the new contractor shall not fall under any exclusion ground and must satisfy the conditions for participation in the procurement procedure as at the date of making the modification, not as at the date of selection of the original contract (date of receipt of tenders).

3. CONCLUSIONS

In order to ensure the proper functioning of the public procurement market in the European Union and achieve broader common goals such as open competition, it is important that the law is not breached either at the stage of awarding a contract or after such a contract has already been concluded. To this end, the rules on contract modifications introduced into EU law in 2014 should, in my view, be revisited. In doing so, I believe, however, that no revolution is necessary. Instead, EU lawmakers should rather focus on some specific changes thereto.

---

[38] Bogdanowicz (fn 4) 103–104.

18. To terminate or not to terminate

Ezgi Uysal

REFORM PROPOSALS

- The provision on termination (Art. 73) is to be amended to establish an obligation on contracting authorities to terminate a public contract or modification thereof in case of grounds listed, unless objective reasons require the continuation of the contract. Objective reasons justifying non-termination of the contract are to be stipulated in the Recital.
- The provision to incorporate termination of contracts awarded without prior publication of a contract notice, without this being permissible, instead of requiring a CJEU judgment establishing serious infringements.
- The provision to be extended to the prospective need for termination to comply with the rules on contract modifications.
- The provision to be extended to cover other instances where a contract is awarded to a tender/tenderer that does not comply with the requirements, conditions and criteria published.

1. INTRODUCTION

Representing 14% of the Union's GDP, public procurement is a key driver of economic activity in the single market.[1] Though the 2014 revision aimed to align public spending with the Union's horizontal objectives while ensuring the efficient use of public funds,[2] it fell short of delivering its ambitions.[3] In

[1] Enrico Letta, 'Much More Than a Market' (April 2024) 3, 44 <https://www.consilium.europa.eu/media/ny3j24sm/much-more-than-a-market-report-by-enrico-letta.pdf> accessed December 2024.

[2] Recital 2, Directive 2014/24/EU of the European Parliament and of the Council of 26 February 2014 on public procurement and repealing Directive 2004/18/EC [2014] OJ L 94/65.

[3] European Court of Auditors, 'Public Procurement in the EU – Less Competition for Contracts Awarded for Works, Goods and Services in the 10

response, the Commission was urged to review the current framework and explore potential revisions.[4] The need for revision has also been acknowledged by the new Commission, which undertook that the revision will aim at, amongst other things, simplification and modernisation.[5]

The assessment of the current legal framework offers a significant opportunity to critically assess the strengths and limitations of the current Public Procurement Directives, specifically for provisions introduced in the 2014 revision. One such provision is Article 73 of Directive 2014/24/EU titled "termination of contracts", which has left more questions unanswered than resolved.[6] This chapter, first, provides an examination of the termination grounds stipulated in the provision to decipher the regulatory choices made during the legislative process. Then, it addresses the key ambiguity in the area, namely, whether there exists an obligation to terminate, as well as the need for a termination period, focusing on the points highlighted in the literature. Finally, it proposes reforms aiming to ensure the necessary balance between conflicting objectives, taking broader goals into account.

2. TERMINATION IN CONTEXT: CHERRY-PICKING GROUNDS

In certain member states, national laws made it challenging to terminate public contracts, creating a need for a mechanism that would allow contracting authorities to bring contracts awarded in breach of public procurement rules to an end. While, to an extent, the 2007 amendment to the Remedies Directive addressed the consequences of severe infringements of EU public procurement law on the fate of contracts, its objective was not to establish remedies for the

Years up to 2021' 28/2023 (Court of Auditors Special Report) 47.

4 Council of the European Union, 'Council Conclusions on the European Court of Auditors' Special Report No. 28/2023 – Improve a Fair and Effective Competition for EU public procurement contracts awarded for works, goods, and services' (C/2024/3521).

5 Ursula von der Leyen, 'Political Guidelines for the Next European Commission 2024–2029' <https://commission.europa.eu/document/download/e6cd4328-673c-4e7a-8683-f63ffb2cf648_en?filename=Political%20Guidelines%202024-2029_EN.pdf> accessed December 2024, 11–12; European Commission, 'Communication from the Commission to the European Parliament, the European Council, the Council, the European Economic and Social Committee and the Committee of the Regions: A Competitiveness Compass for the EU' COM(2025) 30 final.

6 See also on termination, Articles 44 and 90 of Directive 2014/23 and Directive 2014/25, respectively.

benefit of contracting authorities.[7] To bridge this gap, Article 73 of Directive 2014/24/EU requires contracting authorities to be empowered to terminate contracts as a self-help measure at least in case of certain breaches of public procurement and under the conditions to be determined by national laws.

The provision outlines three circumstances under which public contracts affected by breaches of EU public procurement law may be subject to termination. These include: (a) a substantial modification that would have necessitated a new public procurement procedure, (b) a situation where the contractor should have been excluded based on mandatory exclusion grounds, and (c) a situation where the contractor should not have been awarded the contract due to a serious infringement of obligations arising from the Treaties and Directive 2014/24/EU declared by the Court of Justice of the EU (CJEU) in infringement proceedings. In the majority of member states, the provision is copy-pasted into national law.[8] The following section evaluates these grounds based on their chronological development.

2.1 Serious Infringement Established by the CJEU (Article 73(c))

The possibility of termination of public contracts due to serious infringement declared by the CJEU reflects the CJEU case law concerning Germany's strict adherence to *pacta sunt servanda* in cases where contracts were awarded in breach of EU public procurement law. In the infringement proceedings brought against Germany regarding the award of two contracts without prior publication – terms of which were 30 years – the fate of contracts concluded in breach of EU public procurement law has been put under scrutiny.[9] Germany argued that concluded contracts are protected by Community law.[10] However, the Court held that the infringements persisted as long as the performance of these

---

[7] Case C-28/23 *NFŠ a.s. v Slovenská republika konajúca prostredníctvom Ministerstva školstva, vedy, výskumu a športu Slovenskej republiky and Ministerstvo školstva, vedy, výskumu a športu Slovenskej republiky* [2024] ECLI:EU:C:2024:893 para 71.

[8] Steen Treumer and Mario Comba, 'Trends in the Implementation of Directive 2014/24: Minimalism and Narrow Interpretations' in Steen Treumer and Mario Comba (eds), *Modernising Public Procurement: The Approaches of Member States* (Edward Elgar Publishing 2018) 325.

[9] Joined Cases C-20/01 and 28/01 *Commission of the European Communities v Federal Republic of Germany* [2003] ECLI:EU:C:2003:220, similarly Case C-126/03 *Commission of the European Communities v Federal Republic of Germany* [2004] ECLI:EU:C:2004:728.

[10] Ibid., para 24.

contracts continued.[11] Though member states are given the option to "preserve the effects" of contracts concluded in breach of EU public procurement law under the then-applicable Remedies Directive, the CJEU decided that the contracting authority's conduct cannot be deemed to be in compliance with Union law.[12] As a result, the Court found that Germany failed to fulfil its obligations by failing to invite tenders and publish a notice in one contract and by wrongly applying a negotiated procedure without prior publication in the other.[13]

Under German law, it was not possible for the said contract(s) to be set aside or annulled.[14] This inability to terminate the contracts concluded in breach of EU public procurement law indicated a gap in legal protection.[15] In the subsequent ruling aiming to clarify the obligation arising from the initial judgment, the Commission argued that since the contracts had not been "rescinded", Germany did not comply with the initial judgment.[16] Advocate General Trstenjak supported this view by arguing that the infringement established by the Court must be corrected by "bringing the contract to an end".[17] The Court held that because the contract was not "terminated", the failure to fulfil obligations continued.[18]

---

[11] Ibid., para 36.

[12] Ibid., para 39.

[13] Ibid., para 68.

[14] Marian Niestedt, 'Penalties Despite Compliance? A Note on Case C-503/04 *Commission v. Germany*' (2005) 6 Public Procurement Law Review 164, 170. The strict reliance on *pacta sunt servanda* and legal certainty was not specific to Germany but was also the case in some other member states, for instance Belgium; see Steven Van Garsse, Simon Verhoeven and Alexander Verschave, 'Substantial Modifications of Public Contracts and Their Consequences: European and Belgian Procurement Law Perspectives' (2021) 16 EPPPL 284, 285. Whereas in jurisdictions where the public nature of public contracts was more prominent, such as France, Italy and Spain, as noted by Halonen, *pacta sunt servanda* was never as strong; see Kirsi-Maria Halonen, 'Fundamentals of Contract Modifications in EU Procurement Law' in Dacian Dragos and others (eds), *Contract Changes: The Dark Side of EU Procurement Law* (Edward Elgar Publishing 2023) 19.

[15] Steen Treumer, 'The Discretionary Powers of Contracting Entities – Towards a Flexible Approach in the Recent Case Law of the European Court of Justice' (2006) 3 Public Procurement Law Review 71, 81.

[16] Case C-503/04 *Commission of the European Communities v Federal Republic of Germany* [2007] ECLI:EU:C:2007:432 para 25.

[17] Opinion of AG Trstenjak delivered on Case C-503/04 *Commission of the European Communities v Federal Republic of Germany* [2007] ECLI:EU:C:2007:190 para 76.

[18] Case C-503/04 *Commission of the European Communities v Federal Republic of Germany* para 29. Though admitting that the infringement continues

In sum, the Court found that contracting authorities are required to bring contractual relationships to an end when the infringement is as severe as those established by the CJEU. Member states cannot be deemed compliant if contracts concluded in breach of EU public procurement law continue to produce effects for extended periods – such as the 30-year terms in question. The current provision now precludes an argument that public contracts found to be breaching EU public procurement law cannot be terminated under national law.[19] While it could be argued that it is puzzling why only this specific ground mandates a judgment,[20] the provision simply adheres to the facts of the case law.

2.2 Substantial Modification That Would Have Required a New Public Procurement Procedure (Article 73(a))

Pursuant to Article 72, unless they fall under the exceptions, substantial modifications to public contracts are not permissible and require a new public procurement procedure. Subsequently, Article 73(a) provides that in the case of a modification that would have required a new public procurement procedure, the contracting authority should be able to terminate the contract. However, this provision raises questions in terms of coherence with other grounds and the interplay with the rules on modifications.

First, an illegal direct award is the most serious breach in EU public procurement law.[21] The reason why contract modifications are regulated is that non-permissible contract modifications are *de facto* illegal direct awards. Yet, it is

as long as the contracts preserve their effect, unlike the Commission's arguments, the Court did not expressly establish that the contracts should be "rescinded" or "terminated". Additionally, in different language versions of the judgment, different terms are used interchangeably without paying much attention to the consequences of different concepts.

[19] Kirsi-Maria Halonen, 'Article 73 Termination of Contracts' in Roberto Caranta and Albert Sanchez-Graells (eds), *European Public Procurement Commentary on Directive 2014/24/EU* (Edward Elgar Publishing 2021) 806.

[20] Mari Ann Simovart, 'The Power of Termination under Art. 73(a) of Directive 2014/24/EU: The Challenges of Balancing Implementation' (2018) 6 Public Procurement Law Review 279, 280.

[21] Case C-26/03 *Stadt Halle and RPL Lochau* [2005] ECLI:EU:C:2005:5 para 37; Recital 13 of Directive 2007/66/EC of the European Parliament and of the Council of 11 December 2007 amending Council Directives 89/665/EEC and 92/13/EEC with regard to improving the effectiveness of review procedures concerning the award of public contracts [2007] OJ L 335/31.

unclear why this specific case of illegal direct award is explicitly addressed,[22] especially considering that all illegal direct awards may lead to the rights and obligations under the contract no longer being enforced and performed under the Remedies Directive. One plausible explanation for regulating termination in case of a non-permissible contract modification could be that private enforcement pursuant to the Remedies Directive is challenging for modifications due to a lack of transparency in contract performance, giving rise to the need for a mechanism for contracting authorities to rectify the illegality.

Another issue concerns the part of the contract to be terminated in case of a non-permissible modification. The literal wording implies that the contract that has been subject to modification, that is, the initial contract, is to be terminated without making a distinction as to whether the change can be separated from the initial contract. In the case of discharge and replacement of a contractual obligation or the change of contractual partner, as the initial legal relationship is extinguished, the change is not separable from the initial contract; whereas in the case of addition of a new obligation, it is separable as the initial obligation is not discharged with the change.[23] Therefore, it should be assessed, even in the latter case, whether the termination of the whole contract is needed.

In this context, Olivera argues that partial termination should be possible.[24] Wangelow, however, suggests that due to difficulties in interoperability, termination of the whole contract is the more efficient solution, though allowing both options would be the flexible choice.[25] Halonen suggests that if the amended contract replaces the initial contract, the whole contract should be terminated; however, if the change is separable, the principle of proportionality calls for only the additional part to be terminated, which is yet to be confirmed by

---

[22] Sue Arrowsmith, *The Law of Public and Utilities Procurement Regulation in the EU and UK* (Sweet & Maxwell 2014) 604.

[23] In this context, though different types of novation (privative novation and cumulative novation) can be used with reference to the legal regime of the initial contract in case of replacement or addition of new contractual obligations; see V Janecek and J Brodec, 'How Does the Substantial Modification of a Public Contract Affect Its Legal Regime?' (2015) 24 Public Procurement Law Review 90, 97. The current author refrains from using the term novation as the concept is not harmonised under the EU public procurement law.

[24] Rafael Dominguez Olivera, 'Modification of Public Contracts: Transposition and Interpretation of the New EU Directives' (2015) 10 EPPPL 35, 48.

[25] Vincent P Wangelow, 'EU Public Procurement Law: Amendments of Public Works Contracts After the Award Due to Additional Works and Unforeseeable Circumstances' (2020) 15 EPPPL 107, 122 also referring to Kirsi-Maria Halonen, 'Termination of a Public Contract – Lifting the Veil on Art. 73 of 2014/24 Directive' (2017) 5 Public Procurement Law Review 187, 196.

the CJEU.[26] Similarly, Van Garsse, Verhoeven and Verschave argue that the scope of termination depends on whether a contract is replaced or the change is added as an addendum.[27] Bogdanowicz suggests that, depending on the circumstances, termination should concern the non-permissible modification or the entire contract.[28] Approaches in member states lack uniformity.[29]

A less-explored issue is that while Article 72(5) entails that, at least in the case of non-separable modifications, the original contract should be brought to an end for it to be retendered, Article 73 regulates termination due to non-permissible modification only after a modification is realised, as indicated by the phrase "would have required" rather than "required". On the one side, the underlying rationale is that, depending on the parameters of substantiality under Article 72(4), (non-)permissibility of a modification can only be assessed *ex post* making termination conditional upon the contracting authority changing its mind regarding the legality of modification after it has taken place – with or without challenges from extra-contractual parties.[30] On the other side, the fate of the contract and the conduct required of a contracting authority when it decides that the original contract cannot be executed unless it is modified remain unsettled. In case of a modification that does not require a new public procurement procedure, the new contract may automatically extinguish the original contract without the need for termination.[31] However, the current provision implies that in case of a potential modification that would require a new public procurement procedure, the contracting authority should carry out what would be a non-permissible modification to be able to terminate the contract and re-tender. Interestingly, in the French transposition, the relevant rule

---

[26] Halonen, 'Termination of a Public Contract – Lifting the Veil on Art. 73 of 2014/24 Directive' (n 25) 195; Halonen, 'Article 73 Termination of Contracts' (n 19) 804; Halonen, 'Fundamentals of Contract Modifications in EU Procurement Law' (n 14) 28.

[27] Van Garsse, Verhoeven and Verschave (n 14) 286.

[28] Piotr Bogdanowicz, *Contract Modifications in EU Procurement Law* (Edward Elgar Publishing 2021) 160–161.

[29] See contributions in Dacian Dragos and others (eds), *Contract Changes: The Dark Side of EU Procurement Law* (Edward Elgar Publishing 2023).

[30] This change of mind could be due to internal differentiation between the contracting authority and the individual responsible for contract management, see Maria Edith Lindholm Gausdal, Ole Hansen and Vibe Garf Ulfbeck, 'The Duty of Loyalty in the Contract Performance Stage: Contractual Adjustments Inside and Outside the Realm of Article 72 of the 2014 Public Procurement Directive' in Marta Andhov, Michal Kania and Sylvie Cécile Cavaleri (eds), *Public Procurement and Contract Law: Exploring Overlaps, Defining Boundaries* (Hart Publishing forthcoming).

[31] This may be considered novation, see V Janecek and J Brodec (n 23) 98.

provides that the contract can be terminated if it cannot be continued without modification, which was criticised for going beyond Article 73.[32]

2.3 Failure to Apply Mandatory Exclusion Grounds (Article 73(b))

The possibility of termination when the contractor should have been excluded under mandatory exclusion grounds is particularly perplexing since it does not reflect CJEU case law. Considering that this ground was not present in the initial proposal[33] and, to this author's knowledge, there is still no CJEU case law, understanding its rationale is challenging. There are two possible reasons why this ground was included, which are assessed as follows.

The first is that termination where there existed a duty on the contracting authority to exclude an economic operator ensures equal treatment.[34] However, had this been the reason why, then a similar termination ground would have been provided for a contracting authority's duty to reject a tender that does not comply with requirements, conditions and criteria, as well as duty to exclude an economic operator that does not meet the selection criteria, as both duties also arise from the general principles outlined in Article 56 of Directive 2014/24/EU.[35]

Another potential explanation for termination in case of a contracting authority's duty to exclude could be that mandatory exclusion grounds, such as child labour or terrorist financing, are so severe that a contracting authority must not be associated with an economic operator implicated in such activities and, if associated, terminate the relationship. However, had this been the reason, then a similar ground for termination would have been provided as well in case such grounds arise during contract performance.

---

32 François Lichère and Valentin Lamy, 'Contract Changes in France' in Dacian Dragos and others (eds), *Contract Changes: The Dark Side of EU Procurement Law* (Edward Elgar Publishing 2023) 149. A similar provision can also be found in Spain, which requires the termination of "contracts that need a non-permissible modification"; see Patricia Valcárcel Fernández, 'Contract Changes in the Spanish System on Public Procurement' in Dacian Dragos and others (eds), *Contract Changes: The Dark Side of EU Procurement Law* (Edward Elgar Publishing 2023) 231.

33 European Commission, Proposal for a Directive of the European Parliament and of the Council on Public Procurement COM(2011) 896 final.

34 Halonen, 'Article 73 Termination of Contracts' (n 19) 804.

35 The potential for termination in case of non-compliance with conditions and criteria was foreseen by Treumer after *Commission v. Germany*. See Steen Treumer, 'Towards an Obligation to Terminate Contracts Concluded in Breach of the E.C. Procurement Rules – the End of the Status of Concluded Public Contracts as Sacred Cows' (2007) 6 Public Procurement Law Review 371, 378.

3. THE FATE OF A PUBLIC CONTRACT IN CASE OF INFRINGEMENT OF EU PUBLIC PROCUREMENT LAW – TO TERMINATE OR NOT TO TERMINATE

The fate of a public contract after its conclusion can be influenced by various factors: national contract law rules may deem a contract void or voidable in cases such as illegality or fraud. For the breaches listed in the Remedies Directive, the remedy of ineffectiveness, if declared by the review body, requires the effects of the contract to cease. Nevertheless, Directive 2014/24/EU does not precisely regulate the fate of contracts awarded in breach of EU public procurement law. Though the CJEU recently established that Directive 2014/24/EU "neither requires nor precludes [...] a plea of absolute nullity *ex tunc* based on an infringement of public procurement rules",[36] whether it mandates termination in case of infringement of public procurement rules specified in Article 73 is another question.[37]

Article 73 merely prescribes that member states ensure that contracting authorities *can* terminate contracts, but the exact obligation placed on contracting authorities remains unclear. Nevertheless, as further clarified with Recital 112, the underlying rationale is the premise that contracting authorities may encounter circumstances in which public contracts *should* be prematurely terminated to comply with Union law; hence, national laws should provide for such a mechanism. However, the circumstances that *require* contracting authorities to terminate concluded contracts are unclear.

The question of whether there is a duty to terminate public contracts concluded in breach of public procurement rules has been a subject of debate, with several authors offering separate but parallel perspectives. Following the infringement proceedings brought against Germany discussed prior, but before the regulation of termination, Treumer suggested that "no breach *per se* leads to the obligation to terminate."[38] In determining whether there is a duty, the elements to be taken into consideration are: (i) the severity of the breach, (ii) the impact of the continuation of the contract on the internal market, (iii) how much of the contract has been performed and (iv) public interest and the

---

[36] Case C-28/23 *NFŠ* (n 7) para 79.

[37] Though a preliminary question has been referred to the CJEU, both the AG and the Court deemed the question inadmissible; see Case C-683/22 *Adusbef – Associazione difesa utenti servizi bancari e finanziari v Presidency of the Council of Ministers and Others* [2024] ECLI:EU:C:2024:936.

[38] Steen Treumer, 'Enforcement of the EU Public Procurement Rules: The State of Law and Current Issues' in Steen Treumer and François Lichère (eds), *Enforcement of the EU Public Procurement Rules* (DJØF Publishing 2011) 25.

interest of the contractor.[39] It was deemed inconsequential if the breach was established by a court or simply acknowledged by the contracting authority.[40]

Halonen suggests that termination pursuant to Article 73(b) should be an obligation rather than a possibility; nevertheless, termination would be practically challenging once the performance starts.[41] She further argues that where the serious infringement of EU public procurement law is established by the courts but the remedy of ineffectiveness was not enforced, the contracting authority may be under an obligation to terminate the contract.[42] A conclusion akin to this can be found in the Italian case law concerning disputes on the fate of public contracts when the contract award is annulled by the court, but the fate of the contract was not addressed. While it is accepted that the annulment of the award decisions does not automatically invalidate the contract nor impose an absolute obligation to terminate, the contracting authority cannot be deemed in compliance with *res judicata* in case it remains inactive.[43] Therefore, when an award decision is annulled judicially, the contracting authority must assess, considering the public interest, whether to continue or terminate the contract.[44] Departing from other Nordic countries, the Danish Public Procurement Act provides for a similar duty to terminate in case the award decision has been annulled by a judgment or by the Complaints Board; in such a case, any decision to continue the contract shall be publicised.[45] Unless particularities apply, in case of annulment of the contract award, contracting authorities should terminate the contract.[46]

An analogous point has also been noted in *CROSS* by the Advocate General, who stated that "the judgment annulling the award of a public contract should,

---

39 Treumer, 'Towards an Obligation to Terminate Contracts Concluded in Breach of the E.C. Procurement Rules – the End of the Status of Concluded Public Contracts as Sacred Cows' (n 35) 378–384.

40 Treumer, 'Enforcement of the EU Public Procurement Rules: The State of Law and Current Issues' (n 38) 26.

41 Halonen, 'Article 73 Termination of Contracts' (n 19) 804–805.

42 Halonen 'Termination of a Public Contract – Lifting the Veil on Art. 73 of 2014/24 Directive' (n 25) 190.

43 Council of State, Section IV, 5 May 2016, n. 1798; Council of State, Section V, 2 August 2019, n. 5500; Council of State, Section V, 22 November 2019, n. 7976; Council of State, Section V, 29 April 2020, n. 2731; Council of State, Section V, 14 July 2022, n. 6014.

44 Council of State, Section V, 22 November 2019, n. 7976; Council of State, Section V, 29 April 2020, n. 2731.

45 Danish Public Procurement Act Section 185(2).

46 Carina Risvig Hamer, 'Remedies for breaches of the public procurement rules in Denmark – Is the Danish enforcement system effective?' (2020) 1 Upphandlingsrättslig Tidskrift 1, 12.

as a rule, prevent the contract from producing its effects.'[47] Although this remark concerned ineffectiveness, if ineffectiveness is not declared – either because it was not requested or the review body was not made aware of the conclusion of the contract – termination by the contracting authority becomes a necessary self-help measure to prevent the contract from producing effects. Unless exceptions apply, it may be submitted that the contracting authority cannot be deemed compliant with the annulment decision as long as it continues the contract. In contrast, in the absence of a court decision establishing a breach, contracting authorities might be hesitant to terminate their contracts due to the risk of wrongful termination.[48]

Specifically concerning termination in case of non-permissible modification and referring to grounds suggested by Treumer, Simovart adds that the flexibility and proportionality call for the contracting authority to factor in the current market situation and overriding interest in the continuance of the performance.[49] Additionally, legal certainty and legitimate expectation should be taken into consideration.[50] These grounds are also supported by Bogdanowicz, who argues that overriding reasons of general interest – precluding ineffectiveness – may also influence the decision to terminate.[51] This is because the contracting authority's termination in case of breach of public procurement rules and the remedy of ineffectiveness share a similar purpose, that is, "reinstatement of the state of legality by eliminating unlawful decisions".[52] This point is also raised by Advocate General Bot in *Wall*, where it is stated with reference to termination in case of non-permissible modification that the remedy of ineffectiveness may be of guidance.[53] The argument can also be extended to the

---

47 Case C-303/22 *CROSS Zlín* [2024] ECLI:EU:C:2024:60 para 78.

48 Halonen, 'Termination of a Public Contract – Lifting the Veil on Art. 73 of 2014/24 Directive' (n 25) 197; Halonen, 'Fundamentals of Contract Modifications in EU Procurement Law' (n 14) 29. Halonen also notes that contracting parties may be willing to terminate in order to use termination of the contract as a shield to eradicate the consequences of *ex tunc* ineffectiveness. Nevertheless, neither Article 73 nor the Remedies Directive precludes a contract terminated by the contracting authority from being rendered ineffective *ex tunc* by the review body.

49 Simovart (n 20) 283–286.

50 Ibid.

51 Piotr Bogdanowicz, Contract Modifications in EU Procurement Law (n 28) 161.

52 Ibid.

53 Opinion of AG Bot C-91/08 *Wall AG v La ville de Francfort-sur-le-Main and Frankfurter Entsorgungs- und Service (FES) GmbH* [2009] ECLI:EU:C:2009:659 para 136.

six-month time limit for the declaration of ineffectiveness for reasons of legal certainty.[54]

Nevertheless, it is important to note that the application of exceptions and the time limit of ineffectiveness to termination has been specifically suggested in the context of termination for non-permissible modification, which is predictable, given that non-permissible contract modifications are *de facto* illegal direct awards and, therefore, could be subject to the remedy of ineffectiveness. For breaches foreseen under Article 73(b) and (c), there is no specific fate assigned to the contract under EU law, leaving open the question of whether the exceptions and time limit of ineffectiveness can be extended to a potential duty to terminate.

Taking these points into account, as Treumer has already pointed out, even before the 2014 revision, no breach automatically gives rise to a duty to terminate. There is no absolute duty to terminate under Article 73; rather, the grounds listed may require termination depending on the circumstances. Although it was established in *Commission v. Germany* that EU law requires contracts awarded directly to be brought to an end when such infringement is established by the CJEU, it remains unclear to what extent the long duration of the contracts was the decisive factor giving rise to an obligation.

In answering when there exists a duty to terminate, the only convincing answer under the current framework is that a duty to terminate exists insofar as there is an obligation to hold a new public procurement procedure. For example, in *Commission v. Germany*, there was an obligation on the contracting authority to re-open the contracts for competition due to their long term; hence, an obligation to bring contracts to an end. However, if a contract tainted by one of the breaches, as listed in Article 73, has already been performed, there would not even be a possibility of termination, let alone an obligation. For any circumstance that falls between these two opposite ends of the spectrum, the duty to terminate and re-tender needs to be assessed on a case-by-case basis by taking the circumstances surrounding the contract into account, such as the severity of the breach and the proportionality of termination, overriding reasons of public interest in the continuation of the performance, legal certainty and legitimate expectation, the term of the contract and how much of it is performed, the impact of the continuation of the contract in the market and the potential of a different contractor. The contracting authority's obligation under Article 73 should be to assess the appropriateness of termination in case of the grounds listed.

---

54 Piotr Bogdanowicz, Contract Modifications in EU Procurement Law (n 28) 161 referring to Simovart (n 20) 279.

A related but separate question is whether Article 73 precludes a termination period, requiring termination to be with immediate effect. Undoubtedly, termination with immediate effect may jeopardise the security of supplies.[55] Considering that, on average, a public procurement procedure up to contract award takes 96.4 days,[56] termination with immediate effect leads to approximately 100 days of disruption until a new contract is concluded. While a solution might be the use of negotiated procedures without prior publication,[57] another is the continuation of the existing contracts in line with the principle of proportionality until new contracts are awarded.[58] To the extent a different solution is not adopted under the national law, the same limitations that determine whether there exists a duty to terminate may also be taken into account in the determination of whether termination should be with immediate effect or with a period.

4. REIMAGINING TERMINATION WITH BROADER GOALS

The Court of Auditors emphasised a decline in competition for public contracts over the past decade.[59] In response, the Council highlighted that competition, as well as strategic aspects, depends heavily on how contracts are designed and managed.[60] Though the assessment in the Court of Auditors' report focused on parameters of "no call for bids", "single bidding" and "publication rate", the failure to terminate a contract and hold a new public procurement procedure where circumstances that require it arise may also undermine competition, as such decisions potentially deprive other economic operators of the opportunity to bid, similar to that of illegal direct awards. On the one side, termination of a concluded contract may be "the most suitable penalty for ensuring the effectiveness of Community law and the protection of individual rights".[61] On the other side, ending an existing public contract can cause "considerable upset and financial losses", affecting not only the contracting parties but also

55 Halonen, 'Termination of a Public Contract – Lifting the Veil on Art. 73 of 2014/24 Directive' (n 25) 194.

56 European Court of Auditors (n 3) 26.

57 Albert Sánchez Graells, Public Procurement and the EU Competition Rules (2nd edition, Hart Publishing 2015); 436–437; Halonen, 'Article 73 Termination of Contracts' (n 19) 807.

58 Halonen, 'Article 73 Termination of Contracts' (n 19) 807.

59 European Court of Auditors (n 3).

60 Council of the European Union (n 4) 4.

61 Opinion of AG Bot C-91/08 *Wall* (n 53) specifically for termination in case of modification.

the public.[62] Finding the balance between these conflicting concerns is not a simple task.

In order to eliminate the current challenges, the successor of Article 73 may clarify that there exists a duty to terminate a contract or modification thereof in case of grounds listed, unless justified with objective reasons. The suggested provision, though not establishing an absolute duty to terminate, requires contracting authorities to carry out a case-by-case assessment of objective circumstances that impact the appropriateness of termination. In this assessment, the severity of the breach and the proportionality of termination, overriding reasons of public interest in the continuation of the performance, legal certainty and legitimate expectation, the term of the contract and how much of it is performed, the impact of the continuation of the contract in the market, and the potential of a different contractor can be provided in the Recital as points to be considered.

Currently, the grounds listed are neither systematic nor consistent. Although Article 73(c) seeks to codify CJEU case law, it needlessly links termination to a CJEU ruling. Instead, without prejudice to the potential of a voluntary ex-ante transparency notice pursuant to the Remedies Directive, the infringement proceedings initiated against Germany could be incorporated to require the termination of contracts awarded without prior publication of a contract notice, without this being permissible. Regarding Article 73(a), the current provision only covers the contracting authority's false positive assessments of the permissibility of a modification after a contract has already been modified. Instead, its successor can also incorporate termination in case a contract cannot be performed unless modified, allowing for a new public procurement procedure without necessitating contracting authorities to first illegally modify a contract to be able to terminate it. In case of changes that are separable, the new provision could incorporate the potential of the termination only of the modification. To ensure uniformity, termination under Article 73(b) may be extended to cover instances in which the contract is awarded to a tender that does not comply with the requirements, conditions and criteria published and to a tenderer that should have been excluded due to exclusion grounds or failure to meet selection criteria.

The proposed revision of Article 73 offers the necessary balance between the effectiveness of Union law and legal certainty. The suggested drafting introduces a duty that is not absolute, offering the necessary certainty as to whether there is a duty to terminate while maintaining flexibility. By requiring them to assess the objective reasons, the suggested provision allows contracting

---

62 Case C-166/14 *MedEval - Qualitäts-, Leistungs- und Struktur-Evaluierung im Gesundheitswesen GmbH* [2015] ECLI:EU:C:2015:779 para 40.

authorities, which already exercise discretion in deciding to buy or not to buy, what to buy, and whom to buy from, within the limits of Directive 2014/24/EU, to determine also when not to terminate. By enabling contracting authorities to manage these issues, the revised drafting aims to answer the questions left unanswered under Article 73.

5. CONCLUSION

Article 73 provides three grounds where public contracts can be terminated. While it is questionable why Article 73(c) unnecessarily conditions termination on the existence of a judgment, it is also questionable why only non-permissible contract modifications are made subject to termination under Article 73(a), as opposed to all illegal direct awards. Additionally, not only does the wording of Article 73(a) challenge the potential for partial termination in the case of separable modifications, but it also disregards termination in cases where a public contract cannot be performed without modification. Article 73(b) lacks a consistent rationale. While Directive 2014/24 acknowledges the potential of circumstances requiring termination, it is not evident to what extent Article 73 entails such a duty or encompasses a termination period.

To address these shortcomings, the successor of Article 73 could entail a case-by-case assessment of the duty to terminate a contract or its modification, calling for termination unless justified by objective reasons. Beyond serious infringements declared by the CJEU, the successor could provide termination in case of contracts awarded without prior publication of a contract notice, without this being permissible. In addition to termination in case of a misidentification of the permissibility of a contract modification, the revised provision could also include termination due to a potential non-permissible modification if a contract cannot be performed without modification. Besides termination for failure to apply mandatory exclusion grounds, the rewritten provision could be extended to cover the award of the contract to a tender/tenderer that does not fulfil the advertised requirements, conditions and criteria.

Index

Advocate General (AG) 187, 193–4, 202, 255, 269
AI-driven semantic analysis 126
Anti-Coercion Instrument 167
artificial intelligence (AI) 126, 219, 226, 229

blockchain 226, 229
body governed by public law 31, 34, 38

Classic Directive 15, 192
advantage of 24–5
Article 18 192
contracting authority choice 15
direct economic benefits 19
acquisition 20
pecuniary interest 19
final reflections 25
functional approach 22–4
scope of application 14–15
competitive cooperation 54
competition law perspective 61–3
legislative framework 55
access conditions 59
economic operators 57–8
possibility of 58
principle of equality 59–61
level of 54
public interest objectives 68
public procurement law 63–5, 67–8
structural proposals 65
sustainability objectives 65–6
third-country bidders 67
contract modifications 254
economic operator 263–5
lack of transparency of 258–60
modification of directives 253–5
overall nature of 255–8
proper functioning of 265
substantial modification 260–61
contracting authorities 27
associations of 28–9
automatically qualifies 30
legal personality 29
clarification of 31–2
cumulative conditions 31
majority funding 34–5
management supervision 37
definition of 27–8
legal certainty 38
Court of Justice of the European Union (CJEU) 8, 12, 27–8, 32, 40, 162, 192–3, 241–2, 253–4, 268
COVID-19 pandemic 3, 9, 153, 234, 237, 243–4, 249
crisis procurement 234
defines 239–43
EU initiatives 234
geographical impact of 243
procurement process 244–8
regulatory blind spots 238–9
regulatory framework 239
regulatory instruments 249
temporal element 248
territorial dimension of 250–51
Critical Medicines Act 167

Data Analysis Methodology 104
digital transformation 122
collaborative transformation 132–3
cross-border cooperation 128
entire procurement cycle 129–32
E-procurement platforms 124–7
procurement market 120–24
Directive 2014/24/EU 1, 137
Article 12 41, 52; *see also* institutionalised exemption
Article 12(4) 42
Article 18(2) 171, 189
Article 57 70

future reforms of 7
Political Guidelines of 5
reform process of 4–5
Directive 2014/25/EU 148
Dynamic Purchasing Systems (DPS) 18, 23, 107, 115, 119, 128, 205, 248–9

Early Contractor Involvement (ECI) 140
Electronic Single Procurement Document (ESPD) 70
environmental considerations 170–71
controversial provisions 171
externality costs 174
labels/eco-labels 172
mandatory horizontal clause 171
GPP requirements 175
competition law sustainability 184–5
contract performance conditions 180–81
diligence requirements 178–80
LCC methodology 181–2
monetary calculations 183
procedural requirements 175–8
and public procurement 171
EU public procurement law *see* Classic Directive
core principle of 192
award criteria 196–8
legal impact of 192–5
mandatory character of 195–6
performance conditions 198–9
reserved contracts 199–202
Current European Legislation 189
of dedicated legislation 190
external dimension of 150–54
FSR *see* Foreign Subsidies Regulation (FSR)
international law 166–8
interpretative transformation 162–6
IPI represents 158–62
resilience contribution 156–8
social leverage 187–9
European Commission (EC) 124, 216, 218–19
European Court of Auditors (ECA) 2, 104
European Single Procurement Document (ESPD) 210–11
European Union (EU) 1
innovation partnerships procedure 224
contract modification 229–30
economic operators 226–7
grounds of use 224–6
intellectual property 227–9
innovation-driven competitiveness goals 217–21
preference regime, innovation 231–2
public procurement framework 232
technical demands of innovation 221–3

Foreign Subsidies Regulation (FSR) 5, 14, 78, 153–4, 220
Framework Agreements (FAs) 18, 23, 104, 114–16, 119, 128
anti-competitive effects of 104–6
consequent process of 113–14
contractualization of 106–9
ECA Report 105
improvement proposals 116–17

General Agreement on Tariffs and Trade (GATT) 151
General Agreement on Trade in Services (GATS) 151
Government Procurement Agreement (GPA) 13
Green Public Procurement (GPP) 170

institutionalised exemption 40
activities criterion 51–2
enforcement deficit of 52
horizontal and reversed awards 42–3
joint control 43
private capital participation 44
public–public cooperation 39–40
scope of 46–7
Internal Market Emergency and Resilience Act (IMERA) 236–7
International Procurement Instrument 5, 14

La Cascina case 72
legal consequences 103
Life-Cycle Costing (LCC) 173

Member States 163, 171, 175, 188–9, 191–2, 218–19

most economically advantageous tender (MEAT) 87, 173

Net-Zero Industry Act (NZIA) 89, 153
non-institutionalised exemption *see* institutionalised exemption

Public Procurement Directives 6, 65, 87, 121, 168, 176, 267; *see also* Directive 2014/24/EU
public procurement system 70, 134–5
  at European level 70–71
  classic sectors 135
  discretionary exclusion grounds 77–8
  European legislator 148–9
  mandatory exclusion grounds 72–3
  reform proposals 79
    approved economic operators 79–80
    removing self-cleaning 81–3
  scope of application 146–8
  sectoral legislations 78
  special procedures 135–7
    exceptional uses of 142–4
    innovation partnership 144–6
    use of negotiated procedures 137–42

Remedies Directive 271, 274
research and development (R&D) 220

small and medium-sized enterprises (SMEs) 3, 136, 180, 203–4
  characteristics of start-ups 203–7
  direct participation of 207
    administrative formalities 210–11
    definition of lots 208–10
    reserving contracts of 211–12
  public procurement 215–16
  subcontracting 212–14
Small Business Act (2008) 204
Socially Responsible Public Procurement 190
supplementary rules 84
  context 86
    bigger picture 89
    bureaucratic burdens 94
    fundamental principle of 90–94
    political impulses 86–9
  contracting authorities 102
  equivalent provisions 95
    Article 56(3) 97
    flexible and precise rules 96–7
    principle of proportionality 99–101
  legal framework 85
  potential advantages of 84

Tenders Electronic Daily (TED) 104, 125
termination grounds 267
  broader goals 278–80
  cherry-picking grounds 267–8
    infringements 268–70
    mandatory exclusion 273
    substantial modifications 272–3
  examination of 266
  fate of public contract 274–8
  misidentification of permissibility 280

World Trade Organisation (WTO) 151